Praise for *Of Fear and Strangers*

"Riveting. . . . [George Makari] weaves together a fascinating if powerfully disturbing series of examples of stranger hatred (and exploitation) alongside the internal dissent such encounters have always prompted. . . . Throughout his analysis, Makari brings an impressive range of reading to bear, wearing his learning lightly and interspersing fascinating capsule biographies of transformational figures like Raphael Lemkin, Carl Schmitt and Theodor Adorno with literary commentary on Aldous Huxley, Richard Wright and James Baldwin. . . . All the material is enthralling."
　　　　—Thomas Chatterton Williams, *New York Times Book Review*

"Rejecting the common explanation that suspicion of strangers is hard-wired, Makari traces it instead to often violent encounters. . . . One needn't share the thesis to be engrossed in this lively romp through psychiatry, biology, literature, and history."
　　　　—Stephen L. Carter, Bloomberg's 15 Best Nonfiction Books of 2021

"A wonderfully erudite and elegantly written book. . . . [A] poignant and pointed lesson for today."　　　　—David Corn, *Mother Jones*

"[A] diverse and scholarly history of xenophobia."　　　　—*Nature*

"[An] illuminating, significant historical study. . . . A timely and thorough investigation of a cultural plague."
　　　　—*Kirkus Reviews*, starred review

"This important study by psychiatrist and historian Makari does not pull its punches."　　　　—Martin Chilton, *Independent*

"What George Makari has brilliantly done in this first systematic history of xenophobia is to show what is truly important. . . . Unique in its historical grasp. . . . [P]erhaps in reading George Makari's important and accessible account we can begin to examine our own anxieties and mitigate them."　　　　—Sander Gilman, *American Imago*

"Highly recommend."   —Joyce Carol Oates

"With elegance and passionate conviction, George Makari deconstructs one of the ugliest problems of our time. . . . With penetrating insight, he reveals the history of a grave weakness that is one of the wildest threats against coherent democracy and human kindness. . . . *Of Fear and Strangers* is at once a work of dispassionate reporting and brave moral righteousness."

> —Andrew Solomon, author of *Far from the Tree*

"With astonishing range and lucid erudition, George Makari has again given us an intellectual history that illustrates how little we know about the ideas that animate and rule our world. . . . Breathtaking with its learnedness, dazzling as an easy-to-read narrative of complex ideas and knotty concepts. . . . In an epoch where nations often appear cleaved into equally disdainful mobs, Makari makes an airtight case that an enhanced understanding of the concept 'xenophobia' can serve as a skeleton key that will help unlock many of the psychic terrors currently haunting our cognitive processes and social worlds."

> —Anthony Walton, author of *Mississippi: An American Journey*

"Drawing on philosophy, psychology, sociology, and other disciplines, George Makari's beautiful writing delivers a strikingly original history. . . . A sheer delight to read, this book is a gift for all."

> —Zia Haider Rahman, author of *In the Light of What We Know*

OF FEAR

— AND —

STRANGERS

A History of Xenophobia

GEORGE MAKARI

W. W. NORTON & COMPANY
Celebrating a Century of Independent Publishing

Excerpt from *Sphere: The Form of Motion* by A. R. Ammons. Copyright © 1974 by
A. R. Ammons. Used by permission of W. W. Norton & Company, Inc.

For information about permission to reproduce selections from this book, write to
Permissions, W. W. Norton & Company, Inc., 500 Fifth Avenue, New York, NY 10110

For information about special discounts for bulk purchases, please contact
W. W. Norton Special Sales at specialsales@wwnorton.com or 800-233-4830

Manufacturing by Lakeside Book Company
Book design by Patrice Sheridan
Production manager: Julia Druskin

Library of Congress Cataloging-in-Publication Data

Names: Makari, George, author.
Title: Of fear and strangers : a history of xenophobia / George Makari.
Description: First edition. | New York, NY : W. W. Norton & Company, [2021] |
Includes bibliographical references and index.
Identifiers: LCCN 2021013694 | ISBN 9780393652000 (hardcover) |
ISBN 9780393652017 (epub)
Subjects: LCSH: Xenophobia—History. | Ethnic relations—History. |
Emigration and immigration—Social aspects—History. | Discrimination—History. |
Nationalism—History.
Classification: LCC GN496 .M35 2021 | DDC 305.8009—dc23
LC record available at https://lccn.loc.gov/2021013694

ISBN 978-1-324-05044-5 pbk.

W. W. Norton & Company, Inc., 500 Fifth Avenue, New York, N.Y. 10110
www.wwnorton.com

W. W. Norton & Company Ltd., 15 Carlisle Street, London W1D 3BS

1 2 3 4 5 6 7 8 9 0

FOR ARABELLA

CONTENTS

IT MAY SEEM LAUGHABLE, but for the longest time I didn't realize how much this story entwined with my own. I don't think of myself
as assimilated, because I suppose I am. I have never uttered, "I am the
child of immigrants." Even writing those words is jarring. It reeks of need
and feels false, for I rarely see myself that way anymore. Foreigners' kid?
After such an admission, well-oiled reflexes urge me to rattle off a list
of my hometown allegiances and virtues. My parents, like many immigrants, became experts at such, often mortifying, flag-waving. And yet
long after becoming American citizens, they persisted in the unspoken
knowledge that all those fancy degrees and citations could, poof, like a
broken spell, turn into swirling taunts and mockery, Harvard undone by
a funny accent.

All that was far from my mind when I traveled to London in late
May of 2016. I had come to promote my new book. Unbeknownst to
me, the country was about to vote on leaving the European Union. I was
clueless. Nigel Farage? Never heard of him. In a sweater shop near the
British Museum, the clerk talked excitedly about protecting Britain from
an impending invasion of Turks. Weird, I thought. Something else, however, was much on my mind; I was scheduled to meet with my literary
agent who surely would ask about my next project. Fully spent from the
last marathon, I had no plan, no ideas, nothing. Sarah asked. A cheerful
assistant eagerly readied to take notes. I babbled, mumbling something
about the "other mind" problem, how we mistakenly imagine each other.
I might have mentioned cyborgs. It was embarrassing. I returned to New
York, and soon thereafter the United Kingdom voted to leave the European Union. A few months later, the United States elected a new presi-

dent, Donald Trump. All at once, a word came to many minds. It was a terrible, somewhat bewildering word, and so many sought to understand it at that same moment that an online dictionary dubbed it the "word of the year." *Xenophobia*. It sounded vaguely "other mind-y" and psychiatric. A psychiatrist myself, I decided to look into it.

The beginning of the story, I assumed, would be as old as humankind. Ever since our first ancestors emerged on the eastern plains of Africa, humans have been on the move. A migratory species, Homo sapiens would settle in one place, then, due to fear, enemies, drought, famine, pestilence, or some wild hope over the horizon, move on. While craving home, a stable and predictable resting place swaddled in memory and meaning, we have always been compelled to go. From Adam and Eve's expulsion to the defeated warriors of Troy or the lost Hopi tribes far from their mesas, our myths speak of those who voyage forth from a blessed place, unsure of their next resting place. Once dusty layers of forgetting are swept away, who does not descend from such a journey? Whether it was last week in a dinghy or centuries ago alongside a regal army, whether bound in chains or draped in silk, haven't we all at some point settled as wide-eyed aliens in a swarming, foreign place?

Once these wanderers docked or crossed over those hills, they eventually stumbled upon others who had preceded them. Stranger and stranger came face-to-face. Those who were already established usually had the upper hand. Still, they wondered if these foreigners had come in malice. Will they wrest from us what is ours? Will we become strangers in our own land? Walls were constructed for such fears; barriers of less visible sorts, too.

Such uneasy encounters must be as ancient as our species. And so, when colleagues discovered I was working on a history of xenophobia, they were befuddled. How could I write a history of fears that seemed intrinsic to all time? It seemed Quixotic, Borgesian, like writing a universal chronicle of laughter. Our earliest written records indicate that in many civilizations, strangers were broadly conceived of as objects of fear and mistrust. Some have gone so far as to speculate that, for primal man, all strangers were de facto enemies. In a number of languages, the words for stranger and enemy are the same. Xenophobia, then, one might conclude, is an everlasting trouble, bred deep in the human heart. As such, any history of this behavior would need to gather up all the spilled blood and cracked skulls that lay in the earth, an infinite task without beginning or end.

Of Fear and Strangers is not that. It does not seek to record all those mistreated, enslaved, or slaughtered in ways we might today call xenophobic. Rather, it is an account of another history that lay hidden in this word. Who, I began to wonder, first deemed such reactions "phobic"— that is, irrational and mistaken? How and where was there an awakening of conscience by which some proclaimed it unreasonable to mistreat strangers? How did those voices create an ethic by which such behavior was gradually deemed worthy of censure? And how did varied concepts emerge to account for such dangerous attitudes?

In 2016 when I typed "x-e-n . . ." into my search engine, nothing popped up that might help with those questions. There was a definition— the fear and hatred of strangers—but, unlike anti-Semitism or racism or homophobia, xenophobia seemed to have no history. Take a look. All you will find are passing, vague references to Greek antiquity, not much else. This erasure led some to conclude that the notion itself was empty, little more than an accusation wrapped around thin air. For policy makers, the word seemed to be an abstract synonym for specific forms of discrimination, each better defined by the target of their hatred, be it based on race, religion, ethnicity, gender, sexuality, or class. Since each of these scourges possessed profound histories, there would be no benefit in adding an abstraction like xenophobia to the sorry list.

This dismissal, I have come to believe, is mistaken. Firstly, xenophobia is categorically different. In speaking of anti-Semitism or Islamophobia or homophobia, we name the maligned group, while those who do the discriminating remain otherwise undefined, unknown in and of themselves. "Xenophobia" corrects that imbalance and directs our attention to the source of the trouble, thereby opening up a critical line of inquiry. For, as a century of thinkers from Josiah Royce to James Baldwin have noted, our language has too often unwittingly implied that the nature of the trouble lay within the defining qualities of the "problem group." What if America's social strife, Royce asked in 1908, was better defined not by reference to a "black peril" or a "yellow peril" but rather by the presence of a "white peril"? What was it with *them*?

Of Fear and Strangers tells of a series of attempts to isolate, define, investigate, and answer that question. Our story commences with a burst of invention and the term's shocking rise, followed by a radical reorientation, and an expansion that gave the word its post-1945 ethical and political connotations. As we shall see, xenophobia emerged in French and English, tied to formative Western debates over nationalism, globalization, race, and immigration. As such, *Of Fear and Strangers* is rooted in those locales and does not propose to be a global history. It is not my intention to suggest that such forms of discrimination, much less the ethical and political responses to them, took place only in Europe and America. However, I must leave it to others to examine those histories.

In the next section, I turn to the increasingly frantic efforts to find and defuse the causes of this menace. Responding to a series of defining calamities—in particular, the nationalistic slaughters of World War I, the Belgian genocide in the Congo, then especially the Nazi Holocaust—concerted efforts emerged to find the specific source of what was now broadly considered an irrational fear and hatred. Thinkers developed new terms and concepts to comprehend these phobias of minorities, foreigners, and newcomers, tools like the "stereotype," "projection," the "Other," and more. I then propose a tentative, overarching model of xenophobia assembled from these works.

Of Fear and Strangers concludes with a consideration of the "new xenophobia" that suddenly seemed to confront us. Global technological and economic integration, the 2008 economic crash, the European migrant crisis from the Middle East and North Africa, and immigration from Central America to the United States: all these have placed Western advocates of globalization on the defensive. Blood-stained rhetoric has targeted Turks, Arabs, Jews, Africans, Blacks, Mexicans, and Muslims, to name a few. With Trump and his white nationalist allies, Brexit, and the rise of an emboldened far right in places like Hungary, Poland, Germany, Switzerland, France, Italy, and Sweden, we can no longer ignore the fact that xenophobia, that tribal curse, has returned.

AS A PSYCHIATRIST and a historian, I usually work behind a screen. However, in this case, that seemed impossible, even deceitful. How could

I write a history of immigrants, sectarian conflicts, borders, and failing empires without openly considering how these matters have shaped me? Consider, for example, my namesake.

Born in a Lebanese fishing village in 1877, my grandfather, George Jacob Makari, was placed on an ocean liner with an uncle, aunt, and cousin. He had no say in the matter, for he was only eight. His parents had given him up in despair over his prospects as a Greek Orthodox Christian living under the increasingly intolerant, flailing Ottomans. After mind-boggling days on an infinite sea, he arrived at the port of New York and was asked questions in a language he did not comprehend. Officials renamed him George Jacob, a new identity for the New World. His little troupe then made their way to relatives in Austin, Texas. For a while, the boy was a street peddler; toughs chased and tried to torment him. Much later, he told his son heroic tales of cleverly outwitting these brutes. A few years later, his younger brother, Mike Jacob "McCarie"— alien phonetics at work here—arrived. By 1909, the two founded Jacob Brothers, a store that sold Turkish and Persian rugs. They hung a huge sign and lived upstairs. Five years later, in search of more inventory, George booked his first passage back to his birthplace.

My grandfather's timing was awful. Just as this thirty-seven-year-old with a penchant for Wild West tales landed in a homeland he could barely remember, a world war commenced. Turkish killing sprees against Christian minorities kicked off, ocean travel became unsafe, and in a twist befitting this biblical setting, locusts descended. Allied blockades ensued, Christians were considered internal enemies, and whatever little food existed was confiscated for Ottoman soldiers. Mass starvation followed. Moaning, skeletal figures around Mount Lebanon picked through garbage for orange peels and old bones. Children gobbled up weeds. Some 200,000, a third of the population, died under their barbaric masters, victims of a crime that at that time had no name. Stranded in this whirlwind, my grandfather stepped in to help his family: he took back his last name, married, and never left again.

Born in the same seaside village, my parents came to consciousness after the Ottoman Empire lingered only as a foul memory. As part of the secret Sykes-Picot Agreement that split the region between France, Britain, Italy, and prerevolutionary Russia, their home was now a French

M. Jacob Turkish & Persian Rugs, circa 1920, Austin, Texas

protectorate. Lebanon was a multireligious confederation composed of Sunnis, Druze and Shia Muslims, Sephardic Jews, Armenian refugees, and a mix of old Eastern Christians including Syrian and Greek Catholics, Chaldeans, Eastern and Syrian Orthodox, Melkites, and Maronites. By the time this colony wriggled free of France and declared itself independent on November 22, 1943, it was a nation teeming with heretics.

Though the Western imperial powers had let go, they had not gone. Their competition for hearts and minds drew a line right down the center of my family. My mother, Wadad Tamer, attended Les Soeurs de Nazareth, where the French nuns rechristened her Odette. She began her school day with a hearty rendition of "La Marseillaise." Her private diary, her prayers, eventually her dreams came forth in a language her parents did not comprehend. A hundred yards down the road, my father was ushered into another universe. Enrolled in British and American schools, his name morphed from Jacob to Jack. By the time he stepped onto the campus of the American University of Beirut, he was possessed by his father's yarns about Texan outlaws and was known to recite poems about the Brooklyn Bridge, a marvel he had never seen. His father's death in a car accident in 1938 made the youth dream of that other home he had heard so much about. In 1945, as a young physician, he was awarded a scholarship to study tropical disease in London, then another to Harvard, which commenced his career in American medicine. In 1955, my parents married and formally moved to the United States. They said goodbye to their homeland made up of minorities so as to settle in another, supposedly tolerant and pluralistic place whose ideology was—users be warned—a dream.

Primed to be pawns in a game played out by old Europe, my forebearers discovered that fate had other plans for them. A great tide had swept them up, spun them about in a swarm of shifting identities and disappearing empires, then tossed them onto this shore. Dazed, they landed with a thud on a half-acre lot in New Jersey. Cross-eyed and confused, my sisters and I were raised as unwitting carriers of British, French, Byzantine, and Lebanese quirks, sayings, slang, habits, and customs. We were Greek Orthodox—that is, Christian Arabs—which made us to many a self-nullifying paradox. At home, we spoke a mélange of English, French, and Levantine Arabic. However, outside the doors of our split-level home, Grace, Doris, and I seized our advantage. We had no accents, American first names, and we existed in the then vast middle class. We could make our pasts vanish.

It seemed like the perfect place to blend in. Everyone, save for the decimated indigenous peoples, had come off some boat. Still, my parents remained out of place. Kibbe and za'atar only served to remind them of how far they were from the sensual whorl of that place where they opened their eyes, the one that became their first world, perhaps the only one to be so taken into the body that it could evoke all the safety and ease of that word "home." Every new day pushed them further from the sounds, smells, and sights that in the beginning ordered their days. I came to realize that they had never truly left those environs where they first blinked reality into being. Do any of us? Instead, the days came with a low grinding loss of who they once were. They talked incessantly of their imminent return. At parties filled with baseball and business chitchat, my father would whisper, "*una ghareeb ma hal'alum*": "I am a stranger among these people." I thought I would become one, too.

It didn't work out that way. Early on, I was forced to choose. As a young boy, my mother advised me to turn the other cheek if bothered on the playground, but after a few experiments, I determined this was awful advice. I learned to fight back when bullies mocked my mother's accent. Meanwhile, into my flickering brain came *The Dating Game, The Rifleman*, Newark riots, Mrs. Walsh reading *Charlotte's Web*, Mark Twain, Thomas Alva Edison, Sly and the Family Stone, CBS News body counts, Nixon, the classical heroism of Muhammad Ali, Apollo 11, miniskirts, Farrah Fawcett, barefoot hippies by the duck pond, the Camaro, and Clyde and the Knicks. Most of all, I fell in love with that magical, universal solvent called rock and roll. I affected all kinds of swagger, let my hair grow, wore my Landlubbers low, refused to go to church, and read as if my life depended on it. My parents watched, bemused, at times bewildered. I was deciding whose side I was on. Painfully for all of us, it was not theirs.

I devoted myself to *E pluribus unum* and harbored a guilt charged by more intimate uncertainties. Of course, I noted the disdain: the Harvard professor who dismissed my father, saying a "little Arab" could never do such big things, or the all-Arabs-are-terrorists logic so rife during A. M. Rosenthal's stewardship of the *New York Times*. It wasn't racism; that term was reserved for the brutal struggle that African Americans fought. And while I was technically Semitic, my trouble was not what anyone meant by anti-Semitism. Whatever. I wanted to get away from my family's strangeness. If that might be called assimilation, it could also be called a small act of self-annihilation.

When confronted with an application or official document, I would hesitate. I would have gladly checked "late-twentieth-century American," but no such luck. When "Other" was an option, I happily dove into it.

Often, it was not available. Since I was not Black, Hispanic, or Jewish, a confusing array of skin color, language group, and religion, I must be . . . that odd American category, white?

When I left for college, I eagerly shed these tensions. Frozen in time, I can still see my parents on that cobblestone street on College Hill in Providence, waving goodbye as if from across an ocean. In a burst, I began to write, formed deep friendships, played in a rock band, and fell in love. Then, during senior year, my bigger-than-life mentor, the African American poet Michael S. Harper, in one of his terrifying office hours, stared at me with his wide dead-eye and, clutching a swath of my empty, late-twentieth-century American poems, declared like some sphinx, "Makari, where is your history?" I whispered that I really didn't know what he meant, but of course I did.

———

WE LANDED IN Beirut in 1974, a year before the shooting started. I was thirteen. Staggering from the Pan Am flight onto the tarmac, we were greeted by waves of heat. We waited in line, presented our passports, gathered our bags, then piled into an old burgundy Mercedes. Night had fallen, so it was easier to breathe. Our taxi rattled up a pitch-black road lit by a string of feeble orange lights. Under them, my parents' faces shone with anticipation; they loved these long summers, their return to their other home. I began to doze when suddenly, as we rounded a turn, our driver stopped. In the distance, balls of fire leapt up toward the heavens. Far ahead, I could make out a row of burning tires and the reddened faces of long-haired *shebab* with keffiyehs. I didn't know who they were, but I was sure we were okay. After all, I thought with all the experience of a child, we didn't *do* anything.

Our driver thought otherwise. He doubled back, turned off his headlights, and snuck down an unlit dirt road. It must have taken us through an olive grove or a farm. I can't be sure. In the eerie silence, no one spoke. Tree branches whipped the sides of the car. Eventually, we emerged behind the checkpoint. The taxi driver flipped his headlights back on, and we zoomed up the *autostrade*. Nothing more was said. That summer, our relatives warned us not to travel to Sidon or Tyre. I vaguely understood that there we might again encounter roadblocks and armed men. We hadn't done anything, but it was becoming clear to me that innocence alone was not enough.

For two months, I played cards with my sisters, listened to one of our three cassettes of seventies pop, and floated about in the still water of our local cove. At night on the veranda, the adults gathered for arak, gossip, politics, and laughter. Some carried holstered pistols. When August came to an end, we stuffed our bags with souvenirs and, without incident, returned to the airport. I kissed my adoring grandmother goodbye, a bit sickened by the premonition that I would never see her again.

I remember how, eight months later, as my father drove me to school, suddenly Lebanon was on WINS 1010 radio—"you give us twenty-two minutes, we give you the world." For the briefest moment, I felt proud; our little country was on the map! That enthusiasm rapidly dissolved. Over the next weeks at seven o'clock, we gathered around the television and took in shaky clips of streets sprayed with gunfire and concrete buildings that collapsed with thunderous groans. Just as I was seeking to disappear into America, my parents watched in stunned horror as their homeland burst into flames. They were like sailors docked on a teeming, dark shore who awoke to discover that the captain had torched their ships. After years of fantasizing a return, there was no going back.

Months passed. One atrocity led to another. Massacres mounted. The combatants divided and multiplied, until a melee erupted. Referees never stepped in; even more shocking to my childhood imagination, it seemed like there *were* no referees. Over the next years, a drumbeat of terrifying dispatches disrupted our days. At night lying in bed, contemplating the latest outrage, I entertained the thought we all had but never shared. What would have happened, I wondered, if my parents hadn't left? What would have happened to a teenage hothead like me?

Lebanon was once seemingly a tolerant, pluralistic confederation that sheltered many outsiders. War commenced between two parties—Lebanon's Maronites and the exiled Palestine Liberation Organization. It transformed into a battle between Christians and Muslims, then divided into a confusing Rubik's cube of combatants. Religious sects formed militias. Nationalists took up arms for a pan-Arabic state and were rivaled by Socialists and Communists. Syria invaded to save one side, then, when it was convenient, switched sides. Israel invaded to dismantle the PLO, and in the process radicalized the Shia, who with Iranian aid formed Hezbollah. America sent troops, then left after a terrorist attack on their barracks killed 241 Marines. Along the way, journalists, peacemakers, and prime ministers were assassinated, villages were torched, and the survivors huddled in bomb shelters. From one nation, an endless number of tribes had taken to killing and kidnapping each other in a manner so incessant, it became a metaphor. "Beirut" was now a warning: this is what happens when neighbors transform into strangers, strangers turn into enemies, and a society dissolves in a bath of fear and hatred.

To me, it was bizarre. All these bewildering sects were far more alike than different. All were Levantines who spoke the same dialect; all loved the same punning humor, devoured the same cuisine, abided by strict rules of hospitality, and approached any purchase as a three-act play: bargain, stage a walkout, then settle. They were quick with proverbs and went agog when Fairuz sang. And yet, subtle distinctions in their identities now meant life or death.

I remember the metallic ringing that woke us in the middle of the night, and how we gathered to pray as all the televised cruelty became real. Tante Evelyn lived on the wrong side of the Green Line, that popup border that suddenly cut through Beirut. Since this aged widow was Greek Orthodox, since her apartment was here not there, by that sick logic my aunt was pinned down by militiamen and smothered to death. My parents began to receive letters that described streaks across the sky, the *pop-pop-pop* of nightly artillery, and bombs dropping in a whistling arc of destruction. Two of my favorite cousins slipped away during a nighttime mortar attack; they boarded a boat to Cyprus with dollars sewed into their jeans and made their way across the oceans to our house in New Jersey. A phosphorescent missile incinerated another aunt's home as she dashed into the street. In the letters we received, there was a refrain, a recurrent dismay. Increasingly, these notes from our family spoke of the pained recognition that their beloved land had transformed into a biblical place, one it was thought impossible for the living to know. Again and again, they spoke of their home as Hell.

After 100,000 were dead and nearly a third of the country displaced, suddenly it was over, though after fifteen years of carnage, who dared trust that? A general amnesty was proclaimed. Enemies, as if waking from a delirium, emerged and resumed life together. What had happened? Was there a name for this? The Lebanese civil war had the hallmarks of other social collapses, but *why*? How did a thriving, tolerant nation blow apart? Once the killing started, I could see that a vicious cycle drew many into its vortex. As tragedy sank its teeth into their flesh, once reasonable and peaceful citizens devoted themselves to violence and vengeance. This metamorphosis haunted me, the way good-enough folks could turn into stone-cold killers, and the way that very transformation too often has held the bloody rags of history in its hands.

Three weeks before peace was declared in Lebanon, I was married on a brilliant, sunny day in New York. From that rooftop in SoHo, my future glimmered before me. However, frozen in time, there was another, a dark-haired fifteen-year-old dropped into a warren of Beirut's backstreets, half-crazed with grief, obsessed by the animals who had done this to him, to his family, to his clan. In my imagination, I have sunk into this counter-factual existence, my alternate fate, the one I was saved from by chance. It is merely a fantasy, but fantasies can direct a life. I have devoted myself to psychiatry, where all day long I strive to settle internal and external con-flicts, work more than one patient has referred to as peace negotiations. When I am doing my job well, I am the referee who jumps in.

And so, in the fall of 2016, as I turned my interest toward a cryptic Greek word, my teacher's haunting question forcefully returned. *Where is your history?* Xenophobia is a word filled with sea-tossed exiles, dreams of welcome, and the flashing specter of violence. Within its wide expanses, there lies my immigrant namesake in Texas; my bewildered parents so often lost in New Jersey; a groggy, high school freshman who sat up straight as news on the radio inaugurated a decade of civil war, and finally the descendant of all those others, a psychiatrist who, hearing shrill and swelling cries of division, needed to remember, needed to understand.

PART I

THE ORIGINS OF
XENOPHOBIA

But I should like to ask our stranger here, if agreeable to him, what people in his country thought about these matters, and what names they used.

—PLATO, *The Sophist*

CHAPTER 1

In Search of *Xénos*

THE ARRIVAL OF a stranger creates mystery. *Who is it? Why is he here? What does he want?* These simple inquiries tap into some of the greatest quandaries of existence. From time immemorial, strangers have brought forth questions of identity and meaning, self and community, power, knowledge, and belief. Confronted with new arrivals, we search for clues somewhere between the light of the world and our clouded imaginations. Should these newcomers be from another land, should they speak in a strange tongue, should they look and act in unintelligible ways, the discomfort may increase. For these enigmatic beings pose a challenge; they disrupt our mind's invisible reliance on sameness and analogy. Their presence challenges our expectations.

Strangers, foreigners, and aliens provoke anxiety. They remind us that, outside the islands where we have made sense of ourselves, there exists an unimaginable array of others. A globe nearly 25,000 miles around now holds nine million species and, among them, nearly eight billion human beings. Each of these men and women possess histories, habits, norms, and specificities that can only stagger us with their complexity. To get on with each day, we narrow our sights, universalize our local verities, and extrapolate from scant experience. Strangers destabilize those illusions.

The result of such a disruption may be not just confusion and anxiety but also its flip side, aggression. Scared human beings are capable of terrible things, and in spasms throughout history, strangers have scared us terribly. Only later, often much later, may we discover these victims had little to do with the fear that possessed us.

Are such reactions, then, simply "natural"? Biologists have documented how fear and aggression toward outsiders can be observed throughout the animal kingdom. Anthropologists have found it among many human tribes. Developmental psychologists make it intrinsic to normal childhood; infants under the age of two, for a short while, suffer from "stranger anxiety" and burst into tears when an unknown person approaches. Evidence such as this seems to point to the same conclusion: fear of strangers is a highly conserved, biologically driven reaction that has long conferred an important evolutionary advantage. Fighting off foreigners worked. Tens of thousands of years ago, we may imagine, when one motley band of cave-dwelling hominoids encountered another, they showered stones on the intruders without pausing to ask if they were friend or foe. Those that leapt at outsiders survived and passed down that same predilection to their offspring. Soon enough, such reactions became "hardwired." Sociobiologists like Melvin Konner have suggested that what others call xenophobia is simply that. By such an accounting, xenophobia would be a misnomer, for there can be nothing irrational or phobic about struggling for survival.

There are obvious problems with this logic. If evolutionary psychologists can easily conjure up Neanderthals celebrating after driving off a band of wild marauders, they struggle to make sense of a critical, contrary reality. The restraint of such aggressive behavior also clearly conferred great survival advantages. Only in that way could smaller bands merge and, over time, create complex, safe societies based on interpersonal cooperation. The evolutionary biologist Stephen Jay Gould pressed this point: wouldn't natural selection favor those who figured out when it was necessary to fight and when it was not? Bands that avoided unnecessary conflicts, unlike those isolated tribes that hid deep in the jungle, had the capacity to build diverse, powerful groups, a fact Charles Darwin himself recognized. As Jared Diamond pointed out, a crucial cultural adaptation occurred—he dared to date it at 7500 years ago—when bands and tribes learned "for the first time in history, how to encounter strangers regularly without killing them." By managing conflict with outsiders, small tribes merged into larger populations, capable of food surpluses that allowed for stratification and technological progress. In such complex societies, individuals might compete and look out for number one, but they also buzzed about like worker bees. If we are hardwired to fight, we are also hardwired to, well . . . flirt. Humans meet strangers, form couples, families, larger tribes, and new nations. In these emerging structures, xenophobia is hardly an advantage. In fact, it is perhaps the most destabilizing kind of disaster.

Our contemporary predilection to biologize complex social phenomena has proven premature, empty, or ideological before. In this case, I concluded, it had again. If a modicum of anxiety before strangers is adaptive and commonplace, xenophobia is not. Nor can this set of perceptions and actions be reduced to genetic dispositions without losing the very thing itself. While the capacity for acceptance and for fearful rejection rest in our makeup, these inborn capabilities do not explain why unreasonable fear and hatred rise up in him not her, here not there, and then not now.

———

WORDS LIKE XENOPHOBIA are relics from forgotten times. What dramas led to the term "xenophobia" being born? What was the ecosystem of meaning that gave it birth? When did humans adapt and erect dams that sought to restrain excessive fear of strangers, seeing it as dangerous, wrong, even a touch mad?

Ancient Greece seemed to be the answer. In one history of racism, the author asserted that the term was "invented by ancient Greeks to describe a reflexive feeling of hostility toward the stranger or Other." It made sense. Two Greek roots had been united, probably during that fertile period when the Western world was said to originate. If undue hatred of outsiders trailed humanity like a deepening stain, perhaps awareness of this force emerged during the great awakening that took place some four centuries before Christ. Did the same blossoming that gave us Socrates, Plato, the Sophists, Hippocrates, Euclid, and the Stoics alert us to this danger?

Descended from the proto-Indo-European "ghos-ti," the ancient Greek word *xénos*—I discovered—was Janus-faced. *Xénos* meant foreigner or stranger, but it was also a relational word, more like guest. To be a *xénos* was to imply that a host existed, and that both parties would be guided by the social codes of *xenia*. These rules of hospitality dictated that the *xénos* would be cared for by his host, who, in return, would be praised. In this way, a potentially fraught encounter was choreographed, routinized, and safeguarded. Gift exchanges, laudatory poems, and solemn pronouncements heralded the implementation of this code. Similar performances were used to cement alliances between neighboring cities.

This ancient code can be traced back to the earliest Greek written records. In the eighth century BC Homeric epic, *The Iliad*, a breach of *xenia* started the Trojan War, when Paris, a guest, abducted Helen from his host's home. The ethical logic of *xenia* also ran throughout *The Odyssey*, where the exiled Odysseus struggled to return to Ithaca, often without shelter, often in need. Approaching the land of the one-eyed Cyclopes, he worried:

> What *are* they—violent, savage, lawless?
> or friendly to [*xénoi*] strangers, god-fearing men?

The civilized were known by their kindness towards strangers, and after the Cyclops Polyphemus devoured six of his sailors, Odysseus discovered that this monster was uninterested in such protocols. So too, were those cruel hosts, Calypso and Circe. Then after finding his way back to Ithaca, Odysseus stumbled upon another breach. A group of *xénoi* had taken up residence in his home and flagrantly pressed his wife to remarry. Odysseus took his revenge upon these poorly behaved guests.

Rules of Greek hospitality were not just social etiquette. They were of such consequence that the rules came from the gods. Zeus himself was the protector of travelers. "We must consider the laws of intercourse with strangers," Plato mused, "to be matters of the most holy kind . . . for a stranger being destitute of companions and kindred, is an object of greater pity both to men and gods." *Philoxenia* was coined to refer to those who took pains to be friendly to strangers. This term filtered into the Bible, where in Hebrews it was written: "Let brotherly love [*philoxenia*] continue. . . ." From there, a short path led to the Book of Matthew, where Jesus said: "Thou shalt love thy neighbor as thyself."

Revealingly, the author of Hebrews anchored his exhortation to *philoxenia* with a dire warning: "Be not forgetful to entertain strangers for thereby some have entertained angels, unawares." To abide by the rules of *philoxenia* was not just morally just, it also acted as a hedge against the possibility that the outcasts at one's door were divinities, known to sometimes sally forth incognito among mortals. In *The Odyssey*, Homer wrote: "The gods, like wandering strangers, take on every sort of shape and visit the cities." For Plato, this was a superstition that terrified children and was a prime example of why poets should be banned from the republic. Yet even Plato, in *The Sophist*, has Socrates ask the "Eleatic Stranger" if he was not some god.

The Cyclopes defied the rules of xenia

Myths of encounters with divinities continued in Roman times. Ovid wrote of how Zeus and Hermes, arriving ragged and friendless, were coldly turned away by many and not offered a bed. An elderly couple named Baucis and Philemon took pity on these *xénoi*; they fed them and gave them shelter. The gods then revealed themselves and showered the couple with gifts. They also granted the couple's wish to never suffer the other's loss; therefore it was determined that when the moment came, they would die simultaneously.

Even if not exactly descended from the heavens, homeless strangers also could be exiled or incognito dignitaries. Such was the surprise awaiting the denizens of Colonus who lifted their noses up at a scruffy, blind beggar, King Oedipus. Royals of this sort also tended to have a long memory for mistreatment. Odysseus took vengeance upon those who refused him refuge during his arduous journey. As the traveler and geographer Pausanias once wrote, the "Wrath of the God of Strangers is inexorable."

Alongside the moral and humanitarian implications, these taboos and rituals regulating the treatment of strangers were functional. Movement on land or by ship was treacherous. If turned away without drink or shelter, a traveler might easily perish. Conversely, taking an unknown being into one's home posed obvious risks. How could one know he was not a scoundrel like Paris? The code of *xenia* helped establish a scripted dance that reassured both parties. The host opened his house and pantry; the stranger showered him with extravagant tributes. As the Theban poet Pindar sang of his host: "I am a guest [*xénos*]. Keeping away dark blame and bringing genuine glory, like streams of water, to a man who is near and dear, I will praise him."

In a number of ancient texts, I came upon *philoxenos* or *xenophilia*, and was sure it was but a matter of time before I came upon their opposites, *phoboxenos* or *xenophobia*. After all, like "*philos*," "*phobos*" was common in compound words. Then as now, it meant fear or dread. In the plays of Aeschylus, Euripides, and Sophocles, strangers regularly appeared and provoked "*phobos*." I scoured everything that I could find. I turned to ancient Greek lexicons. I consulted scholarly tomes. I spoke to experts. Nothing.

It was befuddling. The Greeks were hardly blind to the host's fears or the gratuitous cruelties that could befall a stranger. After all, *xenodaites* referred to those who, like the Cyclopes, eagerly devoured their guests. *Xenoktónos* named those creeps who took in unsuspecting guests so as to murder them. Xenophobia? Nowhere.

The word's absence surprised me for another reason. As contemporary scholars have shown, the ancient Greeks often behaved in ways that we would call xenophobic. Aristotle originated an infamous tradition in which outsiders were deemed subhuman, hence naturally intended for enslavement. In his *Politics*, he cited Euripides, who wrote: "it is proper for Greeks to rule non-Greeks." The one whom early modern Western thinkers simply called "The Philosopher" then extended this, so "that non-Greek and slave are in nature the same." Foreigners, Aristotle argued, were like bodies without souls, animals that required masters, and women who needed to be led about by men. In "the great order of things," it was natural for foreigners to be subdued, enchained, and put to work by their male Greek overlords. No one, it seems, called Aristotle xenophobic. Not in Athens.

Perhaps these soulless half-humans did not qualify as *xénos*, but rather were lumped together in a different category. *Barbaroi* for the Greeks of antiquity were at first merely those who spoke an inscrutable language. Scholars have contended that originally no negative judgment was implied. That changed, some scholars say, after the shocking invasion by Persia that was repulsed by the Greeks at Marathon. Over the next decades of war, barbarians became specifically the Persians, now seen as inferior, foreign enemies. Military leaders like Alexander the Great found this term useful to rouse men to war. And so, while such strangers/enemies were foreign-tongued barbarians from far-off, *xénoi* were more likely to be Hellenes traveling from another city-state. In the *Republic*, Plato distinguished rules of battle with barbarians—where brutality and slavery were allowed—from "factional" conflicts between Greeks, where no such cruelty was sanctioned. Tellingly, *xénoi*, for Plato, seemed to refer to traveling merchants, honored philosophers, or civic dignitaries. Not a particularly menacing group.

In the end, despite finding rampant bias against "barbaric strangers," despite learning of the strict etiquette offered to *xénoi,* my search had come up empty. I never found the compound term I was in search of, though I did find traces of the idea. Sprinkled in the Greek Bible, a number of Hebrew words for sojourner, alien, or foreigner are at times rendered as "*xénos.*" In the Book of Exodus, the Jews were told: "You shall not oppress a stranger for you know the feeling of the stranger having yourself been strangers in the land of Egypt." Saint Matthew depicted Judgment Day as one when the Son of Man damned those who did not feed and give drink to a *xénos*. Most memorably, Saint Paul took a stand against the way foreigners became enemies. Once Saul of Tarsus, this convert won Corinth over to his new faith, but after returning home, he learned that his success was short-lived. The new Christians had already divided into camps and turned on each other. In his first letter to the Corinthians, Paul challenged the rationale for labeling foreigners as barbarians: "There are, it may be, so many kinds of voices in the world," he wrote, "and none of them is without signification. Therefore, if I know not the meaning of the

The Greeks fought off the Persian "barbarians" at Marathon

voice, I shall be unto him that speaketh a barbarian, and he that speaketh *shall be* a barbarian unto me."

In the end, however, "xenophobia" simply was not to be found in the surviving texts of antiquity. With so much literature lost, it is impossible to know whether "*xénos*" and "*phobos*" were ever linked by some lost scribe. However, one thing was clear: those who assumed that our xenophobia descended from ancient Greece were simply wrong. While wrapped in a toga and looking as ancient as the Acropolis, this word did not spring forth there or then.

———

I WENT TO MY SHELVES and pulled down the *Compact Oxford English Dictionary*. Made from a million index cards and lives of scholarly hard labor, this has been called the greatest dictionary ever compiled. It is the first stop for students eager to discover the history of English words. Originally twenty volumes, my copy had shrunk all that into tiny, micrographic print, crammed into a fourteen-pound behemoth. I pulled out my magnifying glass and began to hunt. Squinting hard, I found my prey on page 2533, between Xenon and Xenophontean, and there lay another clue. The first use of "xenophobia" in English, it said, was from a British magazine in 1909. Italicized and misspelled, "*xenophoby*" reeked of a quaint bygone era, like "*Ye Olde Sweet Shoppe*." The actual quote was vague, so I decided to pull up the original article. A few paragraphs in and it all fell into place. The origin story seemed obvious.

On March 13, 1909, an Italian correspondent, the esteemed archaeologist and cartographer of ancient Rome, Rodolfo Lanciani, excitedly made an announcement in the back pages of the liberal London weekly *The Athenaeum*. A stunning find had been unearthed underground in Rome. Nearly every inch of Rome had ancient ruins and wonderful stories underfoot. What, I wondered, could be so special? Lanciani assured his reader that his news was startling, and as one read on, it seemed true. For what had been unearthed upset beliefs about the very identity of Western civilization.

The origins of the "West" and the "East" as geographic markers can be dated to the third century AD, when Diocletian split the Roman Empire in two, dividing the domains on the opposite shores of the Mediterranean. By the nineteenth century, these boundaries had solidified into broader identities and organizing ideologies. As every schoolchild knew, Western civilization commenced in ancient Greece, was transplanted to Rome, then unfurled in Europe and America. It was populated by heroes like Aristotle and Socrates, then Caesar, Augustus, Seneca, Virgil, and Cicero. In this hallowed time, humans were said to have overcome their animal emotionality (never mind old Nero and Caligula) and established the foundations for European civilization.

This history of the West was not always so easy to separate from the East, especially around the easily traversed Mediterranean basin. Dusty fields like archaeology, philology, and classics were enlisted to make sure West and East did not become confused. For this laudatory account of history was valuable: it helped justify Western colonial expansion as a benevolent effort to bestow civilization on the East. Scholars prepared Western antiquity for its starring role by scrubbing it of foreign influences, an effort that was especially vigorous among nineteenth-century German scholars, who hoped to transform the ancient Greeks into descendants of northern Aryans. In this and other ways, ancient stones and weird glyphs moved to the political front lines, for who we were back then meant a great deal about what we felt entitled to do right now.

Shocking, long-buried remnants now challenged all that, Lanciani reported. A wealthy American art collector and diplomat, George Wurts, had bought an estate on the second-highest hill in Rome, the Janiculum. This mythic place was supposedly founded by Janus, the two-faced god. In 1906, while laying foundations for a gardener's house, workers stumbled upon Greek and Latin marbles. Wurts became excited when the stones indicated his property stood on the spot that Cicero called the "Grove of the Furies." Workers continued to dig. Nearby, they pulled up tablets with strange Eastern inscriptions.

A French expert, Paul Frédéric Gauckler, was brought in to assess the finding. Despite his lack of formal training, Gauckler had become a star in the archaeology world. After studying history and geography at the École Normale Supérieure in Paris, the asthmatic young man departed for a warmer climate. In 1890, he chose the French protectorate of Tunisia, once home to Carthage, Rome's great Phoenician rival. Through pluck and talent, Gauckler became an expert on both Carthage and Rome, and was rewarded by being appointed as a curator of antiquities in the protectorate. As a correspondent for the Academy of Inscriptions and Literature, Gauckler's work in the Orient found its way into the French press. His meteoric rise, however, came to an end when, in 1905, he abruptly resigned and left Tunisia, perhaps run out of town due to rumors of his homosexuality. Happily for George Wurts, the talented Gauckler resettled in Italy, welcomed as a member of the French Academy of Rome, where his expertise on Western and Eastern antiquity made him a perfect choice for this dig.

After examining the site, Gauckler made a startling prediction. Underfoot, he announced, a sanctuary and temple to Syrian gods existed. Though jarring, this had some logic to it. In their vast empire, the Romans modified the Greek notion of barbarian, making it less a matter of birth and more a cultural condition that could be altered. Conquered provincials, foreign elites, and even slaves could become Roman citizens. Many august Roman citizens assimilated, despite being born in North Africa, Syria, and Turkey. However, Gauckler's prediction was not about those who had adopted Roman ways; shockingly, he now claimed that Semitic gods were venerated on sacred Roman ground.

His hypothesis drew an "especially severe" rebuke from a German scholar, Christian Hülsen. An expert on Roman topology, Hülsen scoffed at the idea that a temple to Syrian gods could possibly have been allowed, not in the outskirts but in the Grove of the Furies. Immigrants and former slaves in such a sacred spot? Never. French and German professionals

Paul Gauckler in his Tunis apartment

faced off, but in the end, this was not an abstract debate. "Here clearly was a problem," wrote the Harvard professor George Chase, "which only the spade could decide." And so it did.

In April of 1908, beneath a fountain opening, Gauckler's crew pried up a stone and beheld a ruined Syrian temple. "A Semitic Discovery in Rome!" one journal cried. "A Temple to the Oriental Gods," another proclaimed. The *Classical Weekly* reported that Paul Gauckler had shaken "the foundations of the archaeological and scientific world, and the Italian government." Yes, the Italian government.

Lanciani informed his readers that at the center of the Roman Empire, an immigrant colony with its Eastern "superstitions" once thrived. Worshipers of Mithras and Isis were in this sanctuary, not on the margins of the capital. The unavoidable implication was this: there was a time when some powerful Romans worshiped Eastern Syrian gods. Someone high up went over to the other side. Even more distressingly, perhaps the sides were never so clear.

As the dig went deeper, more upset lay in store. Gauckler and his workers uncovered a secret chamber with a human skull and an even spookier find. Inside a triangular altar, they came upon a small, mummified statuette of Mithras, wrapped in a snake, with five cracked chicken eggs deposited between the coils of the serpent's tail. Readers of *The Athenaeum* must have felt a familiar thrill, for this tale read like then-popular adventure stories. Our intrepid explorer had entered the "dark, unexplored East" and, while peering into its mysteries, had come face-to-face with horrid sacrifices and savagery. The only difference was that the savage land sat at the epicenter of Western Christianity. And it was not fiction.

During the second century AD and afterward, a Syrian cult was a part of Rome, was Roman. Was "Oriental superstition" and "Eastern savagery" part of the origins of Western civilization? How did this square with the rational mastery of animal desires? In 1911, the Italian government shut down such questions by closing the site. In a tragic finale, a few years later, Gauckler drank poison and ended his life.

By the time of this discovery, Europeans had long since swept out into the world carrying ennobling accounts of their identity. Ancient Greece, Rome, the West, Christianity, and Enlightenment modernity: these were their stories and they packed them in their bags as they went forth into foreign lands. That patrimony granted them reason, law, and cultural superiority; it justified conquest. However, as the dig at the Janiculum in Rome demonstrated, the difference between West and East could become murky. And the discomfort such impurity created could be acute. Lanciani's tale bespoke of a shock regarding Eastern infiltration into Western origins. His report from the underworld evoked that discomfort, for in this buried temple to Mithras were strangers so comfortably ensconced inside the origins of the West that they may not have been strangers at all.

As his report in *The Athenaeum* drew to a close, Lanciani shared his distress over the politicized reception of this discovery. It was easy for me to anticipate where this was going. For British liberals, suspicious of Rudyard Kipling's injunction—"East is East, and West is West"—the entire thrust of this tale seemed to require a comment on bigotry. Obviously, this dignified Italian scholar would now scold those whose *xenophoby* forced them to deny the presence of a Semitic temple in the heart of Rome.

Having set the stage, Lanciani delivered his summation:

> These, then are the discoveries which have absorbed the interest of professional people for the last three weeks. They appear even more remarkable if we consider them, not as a gift of chance, but as the outcome of a plan most carefully studied, and carried into execution inch by inch, by one who knew what lay concealed underground. I say this because the gentle breeze of chauvinism is already blowing in the direction of the Janiculum: but let there be no misunderstanding on this point. Those whose sense of justice and fair play, is not impaired by prejudice or "*xenophoby*" know to whom the honor is due for this new and exciting chapter in the history of Roman excavation.

I read it again. And again. Finally it seeped in. This was not at all about the East and the West. Lanciani "inaugurated" this term to chide those whose professional rivalry and national prejudice pressed them to diminish poor Gauckler. While France had been busy touting their countryman's discovery, experts from Germany, Italy, and elsewhere had discounted this discoverer due to "*xenophoby*."

I was crestfallen. Had Lanciani's recriminations been any more oblique, my own biases would have hurtled me toward the conclusion I already held. It was a useful warning. While studying a reflective bias against strangers and strangeness, I would need to manage my own preconceptions, my own assumptions about what was strange and what was not. In this vertiginous and uncanny tale of a Semitic shrine buried in Rome, the quick read for a twenty-first-century reader, or at least for this one, was obvious and wrong. If the whole story pulsed with an anti-Semitic subtext, the only acknowledged *"xenophoby"* focused not on that at all. No, *xenophoby*, that terrible allegation, had issued forth in 1909 to condemn a petty and frivolous competition for national accolades. It referred to the rejection of a French scholar by competitive Germans and Italians. That was my first real clue, and I followed it.

CHAPTER 2

Avant la lettre, or The Black Legend

WORDS ARE TOOLS. They do things. What was Rodolfo Lanciani trying to do when he obliquely wrote of *xenophoby*? What problems did this word name and perhaps even help solve? I began to dig around in earnest, searching archives, newspapers, and databases, and quickly discovered that, much like the assumptions regarding Greek antiquity, the *OED* had it wrong. "Xenophobia" originated three decades before Lanciani's essay, but his meaning, the *xénos* as rival nation, was right on the mark. This neologism first applied to a new, wild kind of patriotic fervor, before it changed shape and took on meaning in the contested geopolitical ideologies of West and East, the never-addressed subtext of Lanciani's essay.

Before diving into that, however, we need to step back. For if around 1880 there was a moment of xenophobia's birth, there was a much longer period of gestation, a slow, less-visible process by which the ancient, antithetical assumption that strangers *were* enemies began to break down. Paradigm shifts, the historian of science Thomas Kuhn argued, do not take place until so many exceptions accrue that they can no longer be explained away. It would require another book to fully explore the many anomalies and slow conceptual cracks that gradually wore away at this presumption. Instead, let us pick up these fissures as they began to widen during the beginning of Western modernity, a period of nation building and expansion abroad, in which the problem of domestic minorities and foreign aliens became increasingly critical. The prehistory of that moral and political peril called xenophobia may be grasped by zooming in on the creation of the very first modern Western empire, for there the dynamics of host and stranger played out *in extremis*.

The sun never set on the kingdom of Spain. That polity consolidated in 1492 when the rulers of Castile and Aragon linked arms to end Iberian Muslim rule. Before that, for the prior seven centuries, the Moors had overseen a relatively tolerant society in which Christians and Jews were allowed to retain their religious identities. Non-Muslim subjects were not equals; for example, they were required to pay higher taxes. However, they could retain their beliefs and coexist. Centuries of intermingling gradually blurred the lines between groups. Muslim musicians and jugglers performed at Christian festivals; Jews and Christians took up the Arabic tongue. During droughts, plagues, and calamities, all three faiths joined forces so as to cover their celestial bases. In Cordoba, Seville, and Granada,

Christian Castilian emissaries ask the Muslim Almohad king to join their alliance

denizens practiced what one scholar has called "toleration without a theory of toleration."

When Ferdinand and Isabella conquered the Moors' last stronghold in Granada, that changed. Devout Catholic monarchs now presided over hundreds of thousands of Muslims, Jews, and intermixed populations, all of whom were accustomed to religious freedom. At the same time, the conquerors faced challenges from a host of feudal lords. Regions like Asturias, having never succumbed to Muslim rule, saw no reason why they should now cede their autonomy. Catalans, Basques, and others showed a similar reluctance. And so, as the King and Queen raised their red-and-orange-striped flag over the majestic Alhambra, Spain was a nation only in name.

These rulers confronted a central problem of political life: how to unite disparate clans and tribes into a nation, a group with a common past, when in fact such a past did not quite exist. How could they incentivize the many to become one? The Crown quickly trotted out moves from the Roman and feudal playbook; they bribed local lords and sought to curry favor. However, forging one Spain remained dizzyingly difficult due to the many hybrid identities that had emerged under Moorish rule. Numerous Christians and some Jews, during those centuries, had converted to Islam. Would they return to their older faiths? Mozarabs were Christians who, under Muslim rule, retained their faith but adopted Arabic as their mother tongue. Would they now speak Spanish? As for the hundreds of thousands of Mudejares, those vanquished Moors, what place for them existed in what was once their homeland?

Out of a mix of piety and cunning purpose, Isabella and Ferdinand found a solution: by simple edict, they would make the least demographically Christian nation in all of Europe into the purest. Catholicism became the rallying cry of the kingdom; the one Holy, Catholic, and Apostolic Church would unite many into one. Becoming Spain now meant rooting out enemies of the faith and uniting their otherwise disparate subjects through fear. Their method was not novel; the ancient historian Sallust noted that, as long as the Romans were frightened of a common enemy—in their case, the Carthaginians—they remained united in purpose. Victory and the end of hostilities preceded disaster, as Rome descended into internal disputes and eventually civil war.

In pursuit of a purely Catholic Spain, the King and Queen relentlessly prodded, provoked, and made symbols of the Moors and the Jews, now that nation's common enemies. These outsiders faced banishment or forced conversions, yet even those who took Christ into their hearts would be forever suspected of having done so just to save their skins. Muslim converts to Christianity, the Moriscos, remained uneasily in Spain for a century before, in 1609, having been suspected of being a potential secret column for the Turks, all 300,000 were expelled. That act of ethnic cleansing found its way into Miguel de Cervantes's *Don Quixote*, where Sancho Panza encountered an old friend, that dear Morisco Ricote, hidden among German pilgrims. He was sneaking back home to retrieve the gold he had buried before he fled. Later, Sancho happened upon Ricote's daughter, who had transformed herself into a pious Catholic. Cervantes played this for comedy, but the anxiety was real. As the girl loudly recited her Hail Marys, who knew what lurked in her heart?

Worries regarding fake converts reached a fever pitch with Spain's Jews. Even in more tolerant times, Iberian Jews had been periodically targeted by mobs and flash frenzies. During those episodes, many Jews converted, becoming the so-called New Christians or "*conversos*." Then, on March 31, 1492, Ferdinand and Isabella issued an Edict of Expulsion: they demanded that all 250,000 Jews immediately depart from Spain. As for the New Christians, they remained but under a cloud of suspicion: how could anyone tell a real *converso* from a fraud?

Enter the Inquisition. Established in the Vatican during the thirteenth century, the Tribunal of the Holy Office of the Inquisition in Spain was invoked by Ferdinand and Isabella in 1478. While other Inquisitions sought out heretics like the Cathars in southern France, the Spaniards focused on the strangers among them, those false converts. Confessions were extracted through gruesome methods such as placing the victim on metallic impaling devices, waterboarding, hanging them by the wrists, placing their heads in a vice, or pulling them apart with the rack. Muslim or Jewish witnesses would be called to testify on the hidden practices of their supposedly "Christian" neighbors, and in the process old scores could be settled. At least 15,000 victims were murdered for their supposed lack of sincerity toward their savior, Jesus Christ.

The centripetal force created by the search for these strangers-within grew, as subversives and subterranean heretics were said to lurk everywhere. And yet, so few visible differences between Iberian Muslims, Jews, and Christians remained after centuries of interbreeding. How might one *truly* discern those who served in a secret network of infidels, those traitors who—it was said—had wormed their way into the courts, the army, and even the church? Fearmongers suggested that New Christians—like Ricote's daughter—were poised to destroy the nation's institutions from within. This was therefore a matter of survival.

Since matters of faith could be lied about, the Inquisitors began to focus on *limpieza de sangre*, the genealogical purity of one's Christian ancestors. The nation's subjects would now be those with pure blood, with clear Christian ancestry. With this new mission, the Inquisition turned its sights from tricky *conversos* to those Spaniards who were openly Jewish and Muslim. As a tool for nation building, this never-ending witch hunt was both effective and deeply corrosive. It spun wildly and knew few limits. Only the foolish or the very powerful dared to question the excesses of the Inquisition. Well-placed clerics like the Jesuit Juan de Mariana, or that ambivalent Inquisitor, Luis de Páramo, might raise questions, but others who challenged this institution might easily find themselves accused.

By the time Queen Isabella and King Ferdinand died, their strategies of dividing the populace by faith and then bloodlines had transformed Spain. Under their rule, rigid Catholic beliefs created a perpetual process of uniting "us" in our fear of "them." Once dazzlingly pluralistic and diverse, Iberia consolidated and became the most inflexible of Catholic countries, one that advertised its purity of ancestry, a claim so absurd as to constantly require vigorous justification. Rooting out the hidden heretics and traitors became symbolic, hence always required, eternal, unreal. For centuries, the bureaucratized institution of such cleansing, the Inquisition, shouldered its unending mission. It would not cease until 1826. For its bonfires were not meant to kill merely a few, scattered heretics, but rather the ghostly spirit of a Semitic and Moorish past.

If the Iberian Moors practiced toleration *avant la lettre*, it could be said that the Spanish nation that followed it provided an example of the opposite. Out of a shared hostility to heretical beliefs, Spain bound itself together. Subjects were to be zealots in the pursuit these national goals. Shared hatred of aliens and enemies pulled a diverse people together. A religiously and ethnically mixed nation embarked on a quest to deny its past and purify its future. If these tasks were partly fantastic and thereby infinite, so much the better, for then the bonds of the nation would never loosen.

————

AS THE SPANISH NATION consolidated around blood and Cross, their desire to rid themselves of strangers ran into a cosmic-sized irony. For just as Ferdinand and Isabella declared victory over the Saracens and expelled the Jews, their fantasy of Catholic homogeneity encountered millions of would-be subjects who were so different as to be almost from a dream. That year, the Spanish-funded, navigational wizard from Genoa, Christopher Columbus, stumbled upon islands thick with heathens. Reports filtered back across the Atlantic of dark-skinned beings whose world had been unmapped, unknown, unspoken of even in prophecy. If attacks on religious heretics at home led to the torture, exile, and murder of thousands, Spain's attempts to create the first modern global empire in the New World unleashed mass murder of a different order.

To be fair, no European nation was prepared to take in the nearly unfathomable differences confronted in the New World. For wide-eyed Spanish and Portuguese sailors, tossed between wonder and fear, it seemed as if they *had* fallen off the edge of the earth. They had set sail for a known destination. And though these were not the Indies, though these were not Indians, the newcomers named them thus anyway, alerting all who could see to the trouble ahead. The discoverers defined this land and these people in a way that signaled the hegemony of their own illusions.

In sources from antiquity or the Bible, in maps that marked Asia, Europe, and Africa, there was no mention of these creatures. Were they even human? Gonzalo Fernández de Oviedo wrote:

> They have no heads . . . not like other people. They are so thick-skulled that Christians hold as a basic principle never to hit them on the head in battle so as to avoid breaking their swords. As their skull is thick so is their intelligence bestial and ill-disposed. . . .

Perhaps this was Atlantis, or maybe Arcadia. A few of Hernán Cortés's conquistadors, upon spotting the painted beings awaiting them on the coast, scoured their inner map of humanity and concluded these must be wandering Jews. A Dominican scholar, Diego Durán, dedicated himself to showing that these natives were one of the lost tribes of Israel. Columbus first believed that he had stumbled upon a kind of Eden; the natives, he wrote, "are the best people in the world and the most peaceable." They were the naked children of Paradise, the unfallen. When some rose up against him, he swiftly changed his tune. The inhabitants, he declared, were ugly, bloodthirsty, scheming savages, as well as sodomites, demon-worshippers, and cannibals.

Still, hearing of so many lost souls, all to be won over for Christ, Ferdinand and Isabella sank to their knees and wept. A sacred evangelical mission commenced, but it was quickly overwhelmed by a more mundane one. Tapping the New World's gold and silver, the homeland became the wealthiest power in the Western world. To make this empire run, however, required a great deal of labor. Here, the counsel of Aristotle would prove useful. Since these barbarians were subhumans, many cited the Greek sage, arguing they could be justly enslaved. Columbus so advised Queen Isabella. However, the Queen preferred not to empower the conquistadors by allowing them to amass small armies of chattel. Instead, she declared that these brown people were her vassals. Legal subjects of Spain, they were not owned by the conquistadors, but nonetheless were compelled to do whatever work their masters demanded.

This did not end the debate, nor did it put a stop to de facto slavery. Driven by the need for bodies to work fields and mines, the colonists continued to press their view that these indigenous inhabitants were intended by Nature and God for servile domination. Enforced labor killed legions. Epidemics of smallpox and other diseases—we know now—did much of the rest. Millions perished.

After Hernán Cortés's razing of the Aztec kingdom and Francisco Pizarro's devastation of the Inca empire, qualms began to be voiced about these missions. Were these "just wars" countenanced by the Church? In the university town of Salamanca, the finer points of justice were discussed by legal experts like Francisco de Vitoria. Disturbed by the violence in New Spain, but openly in search of legal grounds by which to protect the empire's revenue stream, Vitoria equivocated and danced between possibilities. On another subject, he cited Saint Thomas, who wrote, "It is evil, but not so evil that it can never be good." That might have stood as his motto.

However, even Vitoria was forced to go beyond routine justifications. He did not resort to theological claims or Aristotle, but he sought laws that gave these foreigners some standing. Travelers and traders, he reasoned, had a universal right to freely move about in another country. If they were impeded or restricted from movement or from proselytizing by their hosts, he argued, the newcomers justly could take up arms. This principle, Vitoria well knew, worked for the growing bands of Spanish conquistadors, but it raised questions about power asymmetries that might apply as hosts confronted strangers. Typically, one assumed the strangers were weaker, in need perhaps of shelter or aid. However, what if they were an invading army? One of Vitoria's students sarcastically asked if it would be unjust for the hosts to impede the march of Alexander the Great and his fellow "travelers." The Spanish had come to the Americas not as strangers in need of a bed, but as invaders. Should their hosts be morally obliged to entertain them? This question would dog debates over xenophobia.

Meanwhile, the natives of Mesoamerica and the Caribbean continued to die at appalling rates. Finally, the stark conflict between Christian brotherly love and these brutalities became too much. Standing before such decimation, a few priests began to search for the hole in their own morality that allowed for the dehumanization and annihilation of the "barbarians," "heathens," and "vassals." On the island of Hispaniola, some Dominican friars decided they had had enough. On a warm morning in 1511, Father Antonio de Montesinos rose to deliver his Sunday sermon. In the pews, along with the local elite, was Governor Diego Columbus, the eldest son of the man who had named this island after Spain. Montesinos began thundering like an Old Testament prophet. You are sinners, he told them, with no better chance of reaching Paradise than a Moor. For you have grievously waged war on innocents. Did these Indians not have souls? Did they not deserve brotherly love? Then why did the Spanish treat them as cruelly as they did? By what right? The congregation filed out in shock.

That day, an agitated Governor Columbus demanded to meet with Montesinos. He summarily instructed this traitorous, impudent priest to recant on the very next Sunday. A week later, as Columbus and his fellow settlers settled into their seats, they found to their dismay that Montesinos had doubled down on his condemnations. Neither he nor his brothers would give sacraments to anyone who did not immediately free their vassals, he declared. Some in attendance were horrified. Others, like a young landowner named Las Casas, were not moved. The Indians were dying in droves because God wanted them to, he had heard others say, and God would soon wipe them off the face of the earth due to their sinful ways.

———

BARTOLOMÉ DE LAS CASAS was born to the sea. Raised in the great port city of Seville, he was one of the excited locals in the swollen crowd that gathered as Columbus returned from his earth-shattering voyage. The boy watched in awe as sailors paraded by with seven natives, green parrots, fine gold, and masks of stone and fishbone. Swept up by these sights, his father Pedro signed up to accompany Columbus on his next voyage. When Pedro returned, he brought his son a gift, a young black slave. None of this stirred the boy's conscience. To the contrary, he wanted in.

In 1502, the eighteen-year-old boarded a vessel with his father and crossed over to Santo Domingo. A year later, he possessed a parcel of land with subjugated vassals to work it. He became acquainted with men in high places like Cortés and was there in the pews when Father Montesinos delivered his blistering denunciation. He didn't care. "Greed increased every day, and every day Indians perished in greater number and the clergyman Bartolomé de Las Casas," he later wrote of himself, "went about his concerns like the others. . . ."

At some later date, perhaps after witnessing a massacre of Taino Indians in Cuba, Las Casas became uneasy. He recalled Montesinos's warning and, after some indecision, freed his vassals and returned home. After a long period of crisis, he finally took his orders as a Dominican priest. From that point on, a tonsured Father Bartolomé de Las Casas, haunted by what he had seen, made it his calling to let all know of the crimes the

Spanish nation had committed. He risked the hot irons of the Inquisition to publicly denounce barbarous outrages, justified in the name of the
Crown and Christ.

To make this point, Las Casas was relentless. He harnessed the power
of the word, describing in vivid, unforgettable detail atrocities and acts
of butchery. A reform-minded Dominican, Las Casas adapted familiar
language of vice and corruption to make sense of these nearly unimaginable scenes. Analogies of rot and venom flowed freely from his pen. Still,
the massacres in the New World beggared his capacities. There were no
words that captured the easy demonization of other human beings, or the
wiping out of whole tribes. He struggled to communicate the scope of
these tragedies, the fields of the dead, this Gomorrah of sin. "Who will
believe this?" he wrote. "I myself an eyewitness writing this, I can hardly
believe it."

As later commentators would note, he freely exaggerated and then,
perhaps out of frustration, latched on to a symbolic reversal, one that
would force his self-righteous readers to freeze in their tracks. God and
goodness dwelled among these natives of the Americas. Kind and Jesus-
like, they were worthy of full assimilation into the Spanish nation.
However, the so-called Christians—who, according to Las Casas,
included criminals whose sentences had been dismissed in exchange
for service in the New World—were diabolical savages. "I left Christ in
the Indies," he wrote, "not once but a thousand times beaten, afflicted,
insulted and crucified by those Spaniards who destroy and ravage the
Indians."

As for "just wars," Las Casas could barely contain his disgust.
Since the days of Pope Innocent, the Vatican had forbidden military
actions based solely on political or religious differences. There was,
however, one loophole. A just war could be waged in self-defense or
to combat the biblical sins of idolatry or sodomy. Thus began the
odd habit throughout the history of Catholic warfare, of highlighting
the enemy's supposed sexual proclivities. After his ascension in 1516,
Charles V in Spain added a critical proviso: only those captured from
a "just" war could be enslaved. For a war to be just, a 1513 document
known as the *Requerimiento* had to be recited, in which the natives
were offered the chance to immediately submit to both the Pope and

the King of Spain. When the natives did not promptly agree, a just war commenced.

Las Casas didn't know whether to laugh or cry at the absurdity of this public reading, proclaimed in a language foreign to the listeners, made by a gang of "cruel, pitiless, and bloodthirsty tyrants." At times, these robbers, in the dead of night, leagues away from a sleeping village, dutifully read the *Requerimiento* before commencing their pillage. Even if the locals had heard and understood this proclamation, was there a nation on earth, he asked, who would not act as the Indians did when ordered to

Illustration from Las Casas's A Short Account of the Destruction of the Indies, *1552*

summarily relinquish their king and God? Las Casas dismissed Aristotle and the Pope, so as to ask his reader to look inward and consider whether the natives' actions were different from anyone else's. The ones fighting a "just" war, he bravely concluded, were the Indians who acted in defense of their families and their lands.

Over the course of two decades, Las Casas furiously attacked the assumption that these New World strangers were Spain's enemies. They were more moral than his own tribe. And over the years, his advocacy only grew more militant. Guiltily, he also repented for an earlier sin; he had supported bringing in African slaves to the Spanish colonies, in the hopes that they would save the weakened, decimated Indians. In retrospect, he recognized that this was a despicable act of complicity, an ignorant utterance, and perhaps unforgivable in the eyes of God. In penance, he redoubled his attacks on the brutal regime his nation had instituted abroad.

Somehow, Las Casas was allowed to keep up this crusade. Scholars have suggested that the King did not mind challenges that kept his restless, far-off colonists on their back foot. Furthermore, the Dominican had won favor in high places. In 1537, when Pope Paul III declared that the Indians were fully rational beings, some discerned Father Las Casas's fingerprints on the decree. In 1550, the priest also took part in an epochal debate staged before King Philip at Valladolid. There he took on, among others, Juan Ginés de Sepúlveda, a distinguished lawyer who, despite never having traveled to the New World, confidently rolled out Aristotle's notion of natural slavery. While there was no official victor, only Las Casas's arguments were printed in the official proceedings.

In 1552, Las Casas cemented his legacy with the publication of *A Short Account of the Destruction of the Indies*. "Everything that has happened," it began, "since the marvelous discovery of the Americas . . . has been so extraordinary, that the whole story remains quite incredible to anyone who has not experienced it first-hand." As the reader readied for exotic delights, he quickly discovered that what was nearly impossible to convey were Spanish "massacres," "atrocities," and "horrific excesses," which annihilated "whole kingdoms." Las Casas hammered this home: our nation has been the enemy of righteousness. We met the "simplest," kindest people, and what did our countrymen do? "They hacked them to pieces," he wrote, "slicing open their bellies with their swords . . . they grabbed suckling infants by the feet and, ripping them from their mother's breasts, dashed them headlong into the rocks. Others, laughing and joking all the while, threw them over their shoulders into a river. . . ." If that was not grisly enough, he went on to describe how the Spaniards hanged and burned thirteen victims at a time, in honor of Jesus and his apostles, taking sadistic pleasure in binding them in a griddle of wood, so as to "grill them over a slow fire." When images and language seemed to fail him, Las Casas grasped at numbers. After forty years of Spanish occupation, he estimated that twelve million natives had perished. Of three million pre-Columbian natives on Hispaniola alone, Las Casas reported, two hundred remained.

All this slaughter had been lost on the moral imagination of the West, the Dominican concluded, due to a confusion of identities. Spanish Christians were supposed to possess virtue, reason, and civilization; the indigenous strangers were enemies of all that was right and good. In truth, we were "ravening wolves" who devoured these lambs. The Spanish colonist was "like someone out of his mind and gone crazy. His mind is not his own, it is enveloped in clouds. . . ." "Such a type," he continued, "is hardhearted, merciless, does not have faith, does not love peace, lacks love. . . ." Pointing to Saint Paul, he protested that these beings were also merely "strange in ways of speaking." They were God's children, while the subjects of the king were savages.

A Short Account of the Destruction of the Indies infuriated the conquistadors. Gentle, kind Indians? Cortés scoffed in widely published letters that emphasized the Aztec practice of human sacrifice. Bernal Díaz, one of Cortés's men, described Montezuma's priests striding by him in a trance, their hair wild and stiff, caked in human blood. These natives smiled, he reported, but were ever ready to snatch out your heart. Juan Ginés de Sepúlveda went further: he argued that Spanish domination was just, for the conquerors were saving natives from homegrown tyranny and the sacrificial altar.

These rebuttals may have forced Las Casas to rethink his initial idealization of the natives and strive for a more complex, less Manichean position. What if we looked past tribal or national labels? What if we judged all inhabitants in the New World equally? What if only one standard applied? The Aztecs revered their God; they were devout, law-abiding men and women whose sacrifices showed that they passionately worshipped the divine. Such devotion made them more religious than most Spaniards, whose hunger for lucre drove them to heinous acts. As for human sacrifice, Las Casas did not hesitate to condemn it as a monstrosity. Still, this rite paled in comparison to the extermination of whole peoples.

With that, the Dominican's moral journey landed him in a startling place. Who was "barbarous" and who was "civilized" seemed to depend not on sharing the same God, tribe, nation, or heritage but simply on one's actions. *The same moral principles could be applied to everyone.* This breathtaking conclusion went against the powerful dividing practices that had long unified Spain. Everyone should be judged by the same principles; therefore, strangers were not necessarily the enemies of righteousness. We, the Christians, may be. Las Casas thus began to consider a moral system that applied to devotees of any religion. All this from a Dominican who never wavered in his own conviction that there was one true God, that Jesus Christ was his son, and that in that final hour, He would judge all.

Las Casas had no single word for the blood-crazed degradation that his kinsmen had perpetrated upon these New World strangers. Instead, he deployed hundreds of words strung together into a scream. Readers found it hard to look away from the lurid, stunning set pieces he created; they broke the heart of even the stoniest reader. He used the Christian language of universal souls and mortal sins against the Spanish, and brought to life a monster, the Great Goddess of Greed. Gold, silver, and self-interest led to the desire for more, more, and more again. Material lust drove his nation to treat these innocent strangers like devils and, despite a bloodbath, nary a soul protested.

———

"A MIRROR DOES NOT develop because an historical pageant passes in front of it," wrote the novelist E. M. Forster. "It only develops when it gets a fresh coat of quicksilver—in other words, when it acquires new sensitiveness. . . ." Bartolomé de Las Casas applied a layer of reflecting paint onto the ideologies that made violence against strangers legitimate. He questioned the assumption that the foreigners were to be feared and hated, and declared that by labeling these strangers as subhuman, his own people had granted themselves license to do whatever served their own interest. By undermining the assumed righteousness of his own tribe, he opened up the dizzying possibility that ethics should not be distorted by tribal identity. Thus Las Casas became a central figure in an emerging modern ethic that, over time, would see such justifications as xenophobic.

Las Casas broke through a *cordon sanitaire* of prejudices that defended Imperial Spain from examining its self-defining practices in the New World. He forced his readers to reflect on a national identity so rigidly tied to a fantasy of blood and purity that it sanctified crimes against others. After flipping the equation and declaring the New World inhabitants to be good and his own tribe to be evil, he moved past that. Applying an impartial moral calculus, Father Las Casas concluded simply, ye shall know them by their acts. By that criteria, those who ritually sacrificed and ate humans were still more virtuous than his brothers and sisters who had laid waste to whole nations.

Publication of *A Short Account of the Destruction of the Indies* led to Las Casas falling out of favor at home. Around Europe, however, newly created printing presses rushed out his revelations, accompanied by gruesome illustrations. Thus began what became known as the "Black Legend," a condensation of Spanish history into hooded inquisitors and bloodthirsty conquistadors. For some two centuries thereafter, it stood as a stark warning of bigotry run amuck. Rivals like the French, the British, the Dutch, and the Germans used the Black Legend to distinguish themselves from their southern rivals. Protestants took Spain to be the prime example of Catholic zealotry. When the English sent Sir Walter Raleigh out to create a colony in the New World, each of his men received a copy of Las Casas's book, which was intended to convey to the sailors and all they met that the English were *not* the Spanish.

The problem, however, was hardly restricted to Spain. Las Casas's message filtered out into a Europe torn by its own wars of religion. In 1619, the new Holy Roman Emperor rescinded laws protecting religious freedom and decreed that the realm would be Catholic alone. Bohemia revolted, as did many other Central European Protestant nations. These battles were then joined by Sweden, France, Belgium, Spain, and England. During thirty years of war, death prospered. In 1648, all the inter-Christian killing finally ceased with the Treaty of Westphalia.

The philosopher Georg W. F. Hegel proposed that history moves in pendulum swings, as thesis is met by antithesis. Over the next decades, these dark chapters of the persecution of minorities at home and slaughters abroad can be seen as engendering such a reaction. After reading critics of the Spanish empire, the Frenchman Michel de Montaigne, in a famed essay on cannibals, summoned Saint Paul and wrote, "each man calls barbarians whatever is not his own practice." Beyond such sheer relativism, a politics and ethics was needed that did not descend so easily into rank prejudice. In search of that framework, early modern thinkers turned to two related principles: radical egalitarianism and toleration.

A central architect of these views was the doctor, political operative, and philosopher John Locke. Raised as a Calvinist, Locke was nonetheless distressed by the "I heard it from God" insurrectionists he encountered during Oliver Cromwell's reign. He struggled to find a rational basis by which the state would make way for differing faiths, while outlawing dangerous sects. God and natural law had created all human beings as equals, he believed, but could he justify this? The doctor and philosopher spent the next twenty years doing precisely that, and in the process inaugurated the Western notion of a natural, fallible, brain-based mind.

Understanding, for Locke, commenced at the same starting place for all humans. The mind began as a blank slate, then built up an associative web of knowledge from sensory inputs and memory. That meant human understanding was always partial and contingent, never more. Since absolute truths were unknowable, the state had no right to limit the liberty of others. Strange, even repugnant beliefs, as Locke wrote in his famous letters on toleration, needed to be accepted, as long as they did not threaten others or the state.

In 1688, the Glorious Revolution enshrined Locke's credos and solidified a place in the public square for strange faiths that differed from the official Anglican Church. Religious groups, even those commanded by "fanatical enthusiasts," were allowed to pursue their beliefs. Quakers, Lutherans, Calvinists, Diggers, Levelers, and more would not be defined as outsiders or enemies. Even if these religions might seem to be "false," even if the followers might resemble the Devil's spawn, diverse religious minorities would be politically accepted. Liberal toleration demanded that in contradistinction to the Spanish Inquisition, nations accommodate an array of dissidents who were, in their minds, capacities for knowledge, and essences, nothing more or less than equal.

In the seventeenth and eighteenth centuries, as the secularizing Enlightenment gathered momentum, radical egalitarian tracts and disputations on toleration flourished. When in need of a powerful example of error, they often employed the Black Legend. François-Marie Arouet, famed as Voltaire, turned to Las Casas to help his readers grasp the nature of intolerance. The cries over Aztec human sacrifice were a smokescreen, he concluded, much hyped to cover up the greater crimes of the Spanish Catholics. Baron de Montesquieu also used the Spanish Conquest to make his point: he depicted Cortés as a hypocrite who spoke of freedom and justice while committing barbarities, and he pressed forward a daring position. Differences between the French and the Aztecs were not intrinsic. What one man or woman believed simply came, following Locke's psychology, from local inputs. Humans were equal; only in their cultures did they differ.

In 1770, many of these Enlightenment strands came together in the first Western history of colonialization. Published anonymously in Amsterdam, the book became one of the most avidly read works of the time. *A Philosophical and Political History of the Settlements and Trade of the Europeans in the East and West Indies*, despite its heft, ran through fifty French, fifty-four English, twenty-nine German, fifteen Russian, and eleven Italian editions. Readers gobbled up accounts of far-off members of their species who lived so differently that it was hardly imaginable.

The author was Abbé Raynal, though he was no priest. Educated by Jesuits, Guillaume Thomas Raynal left the church to become a journalist and editor in prerevolutionary Paris. The immense success of his anonymously published six-volume magnum opus must have thrilled him, until his identity was leaked. As sales skyrocketed, the Catholic Church banned his book, which guaranteed continued success on the black market and Raynal's exile. Somehow his clandestine collaborator, the brilliant polymath Denis Diderot, remained undiscovered.

The discoveries and conquests of the Dutch, English, and French each warranted one section in this work. The Spanish required three, and within them the authors were scathing. The conquest of the New World

Guillaume Thomas Raynal

demonstrated the mad extremism of *both* the Catholics and the Aztecs. Religion was a universal source of zealotry, a prescription for seeing others as fallen and demonic. To pound home this point, Raynal and Diderot turned to their hero, Bartolomé de Las Casas, who:

> summoned his nation to the tribunal of the whole universe, and made the two hemispheres shudder with horror. O Las Casas! Thou were greater by thy humanity, than all thy countrymen by their conquests. Should it happen in future ages, that these unfortunate regions which they have invaded be peopled again, and that a system of laws, manners and liberty should be established among them, the first statue that they would erect would be thine. We would see thee interposing between the American and the Spaniard, and presenting thy breast to the dagger of one, in order to save the other.

Natural law established human equality and freedom from tyranny, these *philosophes* believed, and as Western nations spread out to foreign lands, this meant that toleration must be exercised, even with very strange strangers. Only in that way could one transcend subjective prejudice, think and judge and act free of one's biases. Raynal and Diderot called for a new dawn, in which these secular morals would hold back prejudice and make space for an array of foreigners, all of whom in their essence were equivalent.

Raynal and Diderot were not just utopian dreamers; they were among a chorus of radical prophets. Only six years after their book appeared, a revolution took place and the American Declaration of Independence enshrined these same beliefs. Thomas Jefferson returned from France, took out a quill, and wrote: "We hold these truths to be sacred and undeniable, that all men were created equal." It was a good start. He passed his draft on to Benjamin Franklin, who crossed out "sacred and undeniable" and inserted "self-evident," an irreligious phrase that took its authority from what was natural. And so, the ringing first words of this document insisted that a rejection of universal equality was bigoted, deluded, and false.

A secular ideal was being born in which a tolerant nation-state, predicated on universal human equality, might resist the easy demonization of inner and outer strangers. In the beginning, though, the only ones to be tolerated in fact were odd, weird, or deviant white freemen. Yet, even if the American founders wished it to be so, their hymns to liberty, equality, and toleration could not be so easily confined. These uplifting proclamations would be taken up in revolutionary France's 1789 Declaration of the Rights of Man and of the Citizen. They would inspire the first successful revolt by enslaved peoples, who in 1791 rose up in Saint-Domingue. In 1787, the Society for Effecting the Abolition of the Slave Trade was founded in Great Britain, and in 1794, the French outlawed slavery. Throughout Europe, Enlightenment reformers began to call for the civil emancipation of Jews.

Over the next century, promises of equality and toleration would rise, recede, and need to be renewed. For the powerful forces that led to the demonizing and degradation of strangers did not disappear. In the coming contest of ideas, however, there were new tools by which one could fight. "Zealots" and "fanatics" practiced "intolerance," and in so doing, like Cortés and the Inquisitors, they committed crimes. To be intolerant was no longer just an idle accusation; it pointed back to horrifying histories of persecution and murder. A tradition now linked the poet of

Hebrews and Saint Paul's Letters to the Corinthians to Father Las Casas, Michel de Montaigne, John Locke, Denis Diderot, Abbé Raynal, abolitionists, and more. As partisan quarrels and conflicts repeatedly ignited, some would take a stand, placing themselves among Las Casas's progeny, as they demanded that Westerners consider an expanded moral community, one that did not stop at national or religious borders and therefore did not restage the tragedies of the past.

————

BEFORE THE TERM "xenophobia" made its first appearance in the 1880s, what had been learned from the first modern European empire and its trials? The first lesson was that the dehumanization of strangers thrived on ignorance. Barbarism, following Saint Paul, might be due to the inability to comprehend each other. When Columbus approached "India," the ocher-painted, pierced figures before him were unfathomable. This stoked fantasies and fears. However, when linguistic barriers fell and customs were decoded, a commonality could emerge. The shipwrecked Spaniard Cabeza de Vaca, having lived in the wilds with different American tribes, came to view these natives as not essentially different from his own people. They could be violent and gentle, greedy and generous, duplicitous, cruel, sensual, and warm.

However, for those who believed reason and knowledge would one day make the world sing together in harmony, there was a second problem. In Spain, the Moriscos and Jews were very well known to their fellow countrymen; they were friends, trading partners, lovers, and relatives. Urged on by the divisive strategies of their leaders, Catholics nonetheless began to consider Habib and Saul as dangerous Moors and Jews. Intimate knowledge and human contact was hardly the problem. Driven by the mandates of their monarchs, citizens came to be defined as internal strangers and enemies. The staying power of the Inquisition proved that within groups, leaders could endlessly stoke uncertainty about one's safety and status, and thereby encourage scapegoating. The robed hunters of difference compelled many to secure their place among a symbolic "us" by turning on "them."

Liberal toleration worked to unite heterogenous members of a political community around the acceptance of differences that did not threaten the state. If enshrined, toleration could act as a dam against the sins of tribalism. However, there was a third problem. Somewhere in the darkest corner of humanity, a force lurked that yearned to dominate others. For Las Casas, beneath the absurdity of the *Requerimiento* stood the heathen Great Goddess of Greed. Lust for lucre hid, but it bullied logic and coolly plotted out its crimes. Legal contests in Salamanca might weave around fine points, but the conclusion was predetermined: we need free Indian labor because we want silver and gold.

This same dark force marred the founding of the United States of America. While the writing of the Constitution declared that each citizen had an unalienable right to life, liberty, and the pursuit of happiness, this stirring call contained a nearly fatal contradiction. Advocates of equality and liberty—heroic figures like George Washington, James Madison, and Jefferson himself—perched between self-interest and their own moral imaginations, choose the former. In this newly born nation committed to universal equality, other self-evident truths existed: they included seven hundred thousand enslaved African Americans, uncounted thousands of dispossessed Native Americans, and fully disenfranchised women.

During the writing of the Constitution, the question of how to declare war on inequality while perpetuating it nearly derailed the entire process. With evident disgust, abolitionists could not prevail on the others to outlaw slavery. Heated debates ensued over whether shackled Blacks were people or property. Were they to be represented or taxed? This debate ended in sick absurdity, when James Madison's three-fifths compromise counted enslaved Blacks as that fraction. Then despite rancorous debates, the whole matter of slavery was hushed up and simply left out of the Constitution. A representative from Pennsylvania, John Dickinson, wrote: "The omitting the *Word* will be regarded as an Endeavor to conceal a principle of which we are ashamed."

The forces that led to the Black Legend of Spain had hardly died. Ignorance, tribal bigotry, and lust for power continued to trouble the sleep of egalitarians and those committed to toleration. However, for late nineteenth-century thinkers distressed by such questions, Las Casas's universal moral ruler, Locke's liberalism, Raynal's rich history of misdeeds, and the French and American revolutions, all acted as coats of quicksilver that enhanced the mirrors by which individuals and nations might examine themselves. In these ways, they might reflect upon their successes and inevitable failures, for despite all these efforts, the armies of division had hardly been vanquished. Instead, they had merely changed their names.

CHAPTER 3

The First Xenophobes

THE MOST INFLUENTIAL physician to ever preside over Western medicine observed that a man bitten by a rabid dog developed a raving form of madness. During the second century of the Roman Empire, Claudius Galenus wrote that "hydrophobia" was heralded by a frothing at the mouth and a bizarre aversion to water. So the "phobias" in medicine began, and as Galenic medicine reigned, there they remained. Around 1800, however, that limited notion of pathological fear changed gradually then all at once.

Soon after the French Revolution, an entirely new class of phobic troubles appeared. During the Jacobin Terror, Philippe Pinel, the French founder of "mental medicine," noted that some of his traumatized patients suffered from a nervous state akin to canine madness. It too was marked by a foaming fear, but his patients' troubles were preceded not by a dog bite, but rather by a sudden, violent emotion. Alienists began to follow the influential Dr. Pinel and refer to these patients, with their agitation, shortness of breath, and tight throats, as cases of "nervous hydrophobia."

That was the first crack. After 1850, as more nervous specialists left the hospitals and opened outpatient offices, they happened upon many outwardly normal citizens who secretly suffered from what was called, among other things, anxiety, *Angst*, obsessions, morbid fears, and deliriums of doubt. In 1871, phobia would be added to that list, when the German alienist Carl Westphal wrote of a gentleman who came to him with an overwhelming terror of open spaces. The doctor suggested that this state was best named by combining the Greek word *phobos* with the prefix *agora*, the place of public assembly in ancient Athens. And so "agoraphobia" was born. Eight years later, another physician published a case report of an otherwise healthy fellow who became giddy and confused in narrow spaces. Grabbing a Latin prefix, the doctor dubbed this "claustrophobia."

All of a sudden, a swarm of phobias seemed to menace the populace. Doctors reported cases of zoophobia, hematophobia, toxophobia, syphilophobia, monophobia, and phobophobia, the fear of being frightened. Demonophobia may have seemed silly to some, but what of theophobia, the fear of death? Anxieties revolving around contamination joined social phobia, gynophobia, and, lastly, pantaphobia, a terror of everything. In this gathering of great frights, the neo-Grecian compound term "xenophobia" made its debut. *Roget's Thesaurus* listed "xenophobia" as a synonym for "repugnance" and cross-referenced it with "hydrophobia" and "canine madness." Its cause—a violent shock or some strange inheritance—never was clear. Still, the term found its way into Thomas Stedman's influential medical dictionary, defined as the "morbid dread of meeting strangers." A quarter of a century later, Richard Hutchings's psychiatric dictionary still listed xenophobia among its list of seventy-nine phobias.

Xenophobia, like most of Hutchings's seventy-nine morbid fears, would have no future in medical discourse. By 1900, skeptics had begun to roll their eyes at this naming furor. Either phobias were a new plague, some said, or the physicians themselves were worked up into some frenzy. When a patient presented with a new dread, someone grabbed hold of a fancy prefix, added "phobia," and presto, a malady was born. Some synthesizers, including Sigmund Freud, suggested these maladies were mostly symptoms of a very few underlying illnesses. Another commentator dryly noted that the number of human phobias seemed limited only by the Greek dictionary. He was being kind. There were also lots of choices from Latin.

As xenophobia splashed then sank into medical obscurity, it simultaneously bobbed up within political discourse. Around 1880, anonymous journalists in the British and French press began to describe an extreme trouble called xenophobia or *xénophobie*. From London and

Paris, this expression spread, carried forth during the heyday of newspaper publishing.

During the last years of the nineteenth century, readership skyrocketed as hundreds of dailies and weeklies sprang up, thanks to increased literacy, decreased censorship, technical advances in printing, and telegraphic lines that ran under oceans. Centralized press agencies like Reuters emerged as nodal points for gathering and dispersing stories from abroad. During this fertile age for print journalism, *xénos* was linked to *phobos*, in a manner that might seem to be associated with medicine and science, but in reality had little relation to them. Instead, it made sense of a new kind of political antipathy, not so much the religious zealotry of earlier times, but a malady called "nationalism."

After the American and French revolutions, as well as the Napoleonic wars, many nineteenth-century Western nations gradually altered their makeup. Once feudal European states secularized and adopted more republican values, by which sovereignty was vested in the people. Weakened traditional elites and religious authorities, once wielding the crown and cross, could no longer as effectively use such time-honored methods to ensure social order. Into this vacuum, nationalism emerged with different self-defining strategies intended to cement the commitment of the citizenry.

A state is a bounded geographic and political entity, but a nation may be little more than a shared group of ideas. While these might seem parochial, overvalued, or arbitrary, a firm commitment to them was lauded by that seminal, Counter-Enlightenment thinker, Johann Gottfried von Herder. Against the universal principles carried forth by Napoleon's invading armies into Germanic lands, against abstractions like liberty, fraternity, and equality, this friend of Goethe sought to protect, preserve, and invest pride in one's own nation and its mother tongue. A brilliant, wide-ranging thinker whose work on linguistics and anthropology would be seminal, Herder took a stand for the local cultures that he believed were menaced by French edicts. He defended the Germanic adaptations and solutions that made up their culture. Thus for Herder, national identity was founded not on natural law, philosophy, or ethics, but rather on history. It took shape from common customs and beliefs, and a body of defining stories. National unity and pride were supported by public monuments, the hoopla of rousing anthems, flags, festivals, shrines to the dead, and commemorative holidays. All this boosted the nation as the focus of individual loyalty and sacrifice, in places where the princes and priests were in hiding, and the populace was said to be king.

If patriotism and pride of place were sound results of these efforts, nationalism also found its way into the dark political arts. By undercutting the universality of Enlightenment principles, nationalism could be used to justify oppression, inequality, and division, and it had the power to unleash conflict based on hyped-up differences with other nations. That was a chronic problem, but also an advantage, since national enemies made even a quarrelsome, divided community sacrifice their young, pay their taxes, and remain closely united. Such rivals were best if irredeemable, thus available to be invoked at any time. Newly constructed national identities were especially likely to stabilize themselves by pitting a "unique" national character, *just the way we are and always have been*, against those of a rival. Minor discrepancies could be made immutable, essential. Ancient massacres and battles could be cultivated, taught to the young, and repeated in days of remembrance. Old wounds could be pried open and never allowed to heal.

Such nationalist strategies proved to be potent, so much so that they risked spiraling out of control. Alarmed, commentators began to discuss the risk of stoking these embers. Take, for example, the burning hatred that existed between the British and the French. At war on and off for five hundred years, these nations during the nineteenth century were said to be ill. Londoners worried that France harbored many "Anglophobiacs" or "Anglophobists." On other side of the Channel, French journalists commented on their readers' ravenous appetite for anything that fed their "Anglophobia." They wondered if the British public had equally succumbed to "Francophobes."

Patriotic zealotry began to be referred to as a "phobia." Given its position as the most dominant power on the globe, Great Britain was said to be the most popular target for such a wild animus. In 1793, Thomas Jefferson told James Madison that he worried his fellow former colonists harbored an irrational "Anglophobia." Others concurred and noted that a near "delusional" Anglophobia had swept through the United States.

Educated readers in London were bemused by the "illogical animosities" of the Germans, said to be nothing more than their Anglophobia. Fretting about such trouble was so common that it became ripe for humor. In 1845, *Littell's Living Age* announced that Englishmen suddenly were in fashion in Paris; Anglophobia mercifully had been replaced by "Anglo-indifference, if not Anglomania."

These phobias called attention to the demands that European nationalism placed on its members. And by 1870, the field of national phobias had grown more crowded. Heated rivalries led journalists, scholars, and diplomats to routinely claim that fair-minded, rational political dialogue had been supplanted by "Francophobia," "Germanophobia," and "Russophobia," not to mention "Austrophobia," "Sinophobia," and "Turkophobia." In addition, there was a phobia for that supposed nation of wanderers, a "Judeophobia" or "Hebrewphobia."

As discussions of national prejudices mounted, an even more menacing distemper stepped forward. Some nations were so deeply hostile to rivals that they targeted *all* other nations. "Xenophobia" described such an overheated hatred. Extreme but mercifully rare, "xenophobia" was the most vicious form of ultranationalism. An early, revealing use of this anonymously coined term occurred in 1880 during a visit to London by the ardent Frenchman, Ernest Renan.

Born in 1823, Renan was a diligent, provincial boy who seemed headed for the priesthood. He excelled in his seminary studies and developed a passion for the Hebrew language, which he told his mother "holds the greatest charm for me." A sensitive young man, he could feel the spirit course through him as he translated Solomon's Song of Songs. He expanded his study to other Semitic languages at the Collège de France and became deeply immersed in philology. This, however, led to a profound crisis. Renan was dismayed to find that mistranslations of Hebrew guided certain matters of Catholic faith. Stung and shocked, the sincere youth forever renounced the Church. As a friend wryly observed, he "gambled his life on a comma."

Renan turned his considerable energies to the Near East, Semitic languages, and the history of religion. In 1855, his *General History of the Semitic Languages* led him to offer a conclusion not just about these languages but about the "races" that created them. With evident pride, he proclaimed: "I am then the first to recognize that the Semitic race, compared to the Indo-European race, actually represents an inferior combination of human nature." For that achievement, he would also be dubbed the first "anti-Semite."

Five years later, the French government sent Renan on an archaeological expedition to Lebanon, a trip he undertook with his wife and his sister Henriette. The pilgrimage was life-altering. Inspired by the sights and smells of the Holy Land, Renan began to write a popular history of Jesus Christ. The project, though, was tinged with tragedy, for the originator of this idea, his sister, succumbed to malaria in the seaside town of Amchit. After returning to France, Renan published his biography of Christ, that "incomparable man." *Man*? His *Life of Jesus* was swiftly denounced by the Church, and following that well-worn path, it became a bestseller.

After France's humiliating loss to the Prussians in 1871 and the chaotic rise and fall of the Paris Commune, the once liberal Renan became a

Ernest Renan

devout nationalist, an authoritarian, and an advocate of foreign conquest. France must become a colonial power, he declared, or it would descend into civil war. It must spread *la richesse* of being French. This was the Ernest Renan who arrived in London to deliver the Hibbert Lectures a decade later. By then, the traditional enemy of the English, the French, had established an empire that was growing at a staggering rate, and Ernest Renan was rightly considered a zealous nationalist.

Despite all that, Renan's lectures in London were mobbed. To win the crowd over, he used flattery, telling them that England had established the one dogma that "our society" should always hold: "Liberty, respect for the mind." He then launched into his history of Christianity, singing the praises of the Savior who rose above Judaism—a religion far too "primitive" to ever become global. He piled contempt onto Rome and the Pope. And then he departed, bathed in British adulation. The *Daily News*, stunned by Renan's popularity on British soil, called it a "xenomania." This stance, they added in what may have been a dig at the French, was always preferable to "xenophobia, which is of necessity and always unintelligent."

A few years later, the *Saturday Review*, a London weekly, scolded those afflicted by an unthinking fear of and hatred for foreign nations. Discussing the many, shifting alliances in the Balkan states, an author was dismissed as both a rabid "Turcophobe" and "Austrophobe," but even this bigot, the reviewer declared, was more tolerant than the Bulgarians. That nation harbored a distaste for all kinds; it suffered from "xenophobia."

Xenophobia, for some, seemed to be nationalism gone utterly mad. Or was it the foundation beneath all the specific national biases? The French Baron d'Estournelles de Constant, a future Noble Peace Prize winner, believed it was the latter. He wrote: "before being Germanophobe," the warmongers "were Anglophobe and Russophobe," that is, always "xenophobe or demophobe."

Such irrational loathing was not unlike those described by the medical men, only this time the illness struck whole nations. If the nation offered a powerful framework for identity—I am English, I am French, I am German—if it puffed itself up with ceremonies and song, it also might whip up fright and dislike for foreign nations, perhaps *all* other nations. The French sociologist Gaston Richard wrote: "It is only for the

TABLE 1: **NATIONAL PHOBIAS**

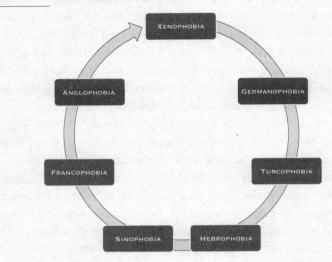

rhetoricians that modern patriotism, that attachment to national territory, resembles that of the Greek or Jewish zealot, a patriotism which, like the nationalism of our amiable contemporaries, was less altruism than xenophobia, the sacred hatred of the Impures."

One of the most influential thinkers to contemplate such risks was none other than the same Ernest Renan. In 1882 at the Sorbonne, he delivered a widely circulated lecture entitled "What is a Nation?" While some equated the nation with one's bloodline and race, Renan—despite his own bigotry—rejected this as absurd. What race made up France? Celtic, Iberic, and Germanic, and more. No, the most noble nations were of mixed heritage and "mixed blood." Purity of religion, ethnicity, and language defined no nation. Large, successful nations glued together multitudes. Diverse populations—Goths, Normands, Franks, Lombards, Catalans, and others—were fused into one, the French.

Across the Atlantic, the African American orator extraordinaire, Frederick Douglass, had made a similar case for a "composite nation," one whose citizenry included Chinese immigrants, with "the negro, mulatto and Latin races," offering all full citizenship and benefiting as a result. However, in such a composite, what was the glue that held everyone together? If states had geographic borders, what boundaries defined a nation? Nations, Renan

declared, were not racial or hereditary, but man-made. A national community bonded over a set of remembrances, but perhaps more importantly,
shared amnesias. Everyone would thereby inhabit the same memory-scape.
They could recount the glorious and heroic legacy of their forebearers, and
stare blankly ahead, when mention was made of episodes better left forgotten. Nations were forged by willful acts of communal imagination. Resting
on such a foundation, nationalism fostered common goals for the future
and encouraged anger and mourning for well-selected grievances and traumas. Of these two forces, Renan admitted, "griefs are of more value than
triumphs, for they impose duties and require a common effort."

Omelettes, as the proverb goes, can only be made by cracking eggs.
For Renan, making a nation required a violent relation to one's past. Continuities must be broken, failures erased, and false connections inserted so
as to serve the nation, this dreamed-up creation. Citizens were emboldened by accounts that claimed "so-called" victims of their nation's actions
never existed or deserved what they got. For Renan, that also meant that
shifting the boundaries of memory could be political dynamite. Prior
members of the nation might suddenly seem like outsiders. Forgotten
actions might bring to light injustice or illegitimate acts. In a flash, brothers might seem like foreigners, allies like enemies, and supposed enemies
not so at all.

Tottering nations were often characterized by unresolved, competing
narratives that sowed division and failed to resolve questions of identity.
The "Turkish system," Renan argued, which maintained an "absolute distinction" between religious groups, meant they would forever struggle
to unite as one nation. What then might a nation do if it suffered from
such instability? The Frenchman didn't develop this point, but a few years
later, a Parisian journalist in *Le Figaro* pointed to one outcome. Flanked
by the Russian and Austro-Hungarian empires, Romania had recently
liberated itself from Ottoman rule. On the edge of Europe, this newborn
nation was home to Hungarians, Germans, Jews, Russians, and more. As
it sought unity, it witnessed intense anti-Jewish attacks and seemed to
stoke a broader anger toward surrounding nations. In 1895, this fervor
had ramped up into a "xenophobia," that "exaggeration" of patriotism
that turned a virtue into a vice. The Romanians seemed to hate everybody,
it was said, so as to more clearly and ardently know themselves.

TABLE 2: **XENOPHOBIA, CIRCA 1890**

XENOPHOBIA AS A PSYCHIATRIC ILLNESS	a pathological fear of strangers
XENOPHOBIC NATIONALISM	an irrational political animus toward foreign nations

The first usages of xenophobia never caught on. As a medical diagnosis, xenophobia was a flop, perhaps due to the proliferation of phobias that brought many others into disrepute; years later, the same irrational fear of strangers would resurface as "social phobia." In journalistic and political circles xenophobia receded, for it always carried the whiff of exaggeration. After all, who actually feared and hated *all* other nations? And if drumming up hatred against a targeted enemy was a dangerous form of patriotism, what use was this general hatred, in which the enemy remained unnamed? When Rodolfo Lanciani used this term in 1909 to decry attacks on the Frenchman Gauckler, he was already being a bit precious. His choice was worthy of the italics he provided, and in line with the professor's preference for innuendo and archaism. For by then, his concept of a nationalistic xenophobia was fast receding as another meaning took center stage.

CHAPTER 4

The Boxer Uprising

ON APRIL 14, 1900, the *Exposition Universelle* in Paris threw open its doors to adoring crowds. Sparkling hopes for the new century were heightened by this celebration, which showcased an electrical palace, films from the Lumière brothers, a Ferris wheel, a diesel engine, and other wonders. A staggering fifty million people streamed forth to take in these miracles of the modern world. Among many marvels, visitors toured ethnological villages and human zoos stocked with members of far-off tribes like the Malagasy from Madagascar and the Dahomean from West Africa. A poster for the event depicted Arabs and Asians at the foot of a heavenly, white goddess. Thanks to Western technology and industrial wealth, the entire world was coming together.

Alongside these festive reports, French newspapers also featured a more disturbing story, one of things falling apart. On July 17, 1900, in *Le Constitutionnel*, a venerable paper famed for serializing the fictions of Honoré de Balzac, a short, unsigned dispatch appeared. This report from Shanghai told of a new "xénophobe" movement in northern China. Three days later, Georges Clemenceau's left-wing paper, *La Justice*, picked up the story and that term. Next, it showed up in *L'Univers*. Then, on August 31, one of the most literary papers, *Le Journal*, published a piece by a Chinese "mandarin" who denounced his country's outlaws and their xenophobia. As fall arrived, *La Presse* featured a headline warning of China's xenophobia, and by October, *Le Figaro* and *Le Matin* assumed readers knew

Exposition Universelle, *Paris, 1900*

exactly what was meant when they denounced Chinese "xénophobes."
In less than a year, *xénophobe* and *xénophobie* had become part of the
French vocabulary.

Parisians learned that the trouble with "*les xénophobes*" had commenced in a corner of northern China during the winter of 1899. These
xénophobes were not engaged in specific national rivalries, but rather
were focused on broader divisions, ones that greatly mattered due to the
unprecedented expansion of Western powers abroad. Having watched

their crumbling empire be infiltrated by not only one nation but by Germans, British, French, Russians, and the Japanese, a group of impoverished youth staged an uprising. Thanks to their reliance on martial arts, they came to be known in the West as the "Boxers." While some of their goals remained inchoate, their motto made one explicit. "Support the Qing," it declared, "destroy the foreigners."

The Boxers' revolt against all colonial powers followed decades of furious globalization. Like the sixteenth-century rush to grab land in the New World, during the nineteenth century, a second major wave of Western expansion had been sparked by new technologies. Hordes of European settlers moved into once forbidding places, as travel was increasingly facilitated by machines that powered not just people, but also ideas and products across seas, mountains, and deserts. In a crackle and whir, isolated tribes now communicated, traded, and intermingled. Bands of humans—long segregated and curiously distinguished by their pet notions of God and nature, the sacred and profane, ethics, politics, and individuality—found themselves in astonishing proximity. Much like the meeting of the Spanish and Nahuas people, these long-lost cousins had little knowledge of each other and could not help but consider many of their newfound kin quite strange in their looks, habits, and customs.

Demographics helped push globalization forward. After 1850, prosperity led to increased population densities within industrialized Western countries, and an unprecedented exodus of hundreds of thousands searching for opportunity in other lands. British, French, Germans, and Russians left home, aided by the telegraph, the emergence of a functional worldwide postal service, and the transformative power of steamships and locomotives. While once only the most desperate or foolish would traverse oceans or trek mountain ranges, increasingly such risks might be taken just for fun. Armed with Cook, Baedeker, or Michelin travel guides, fin de siècle pleasure-seekers came to be known as "globe-trotters."

This grand reunion of humanity encouraged some to welcome the dawn of a universal age. As the inhabitants of the technologically advanced nations spread out, dignitaries spoke of the need for universal laws or even a world government. Conventions in Geneva, Paris, Berne, London, and the Hague brought together lawyers, pacifists, and diplomats who pressed for international bodies that would govern warfare, trade, patents, and copyrights. Optimists proposed a "World Federation" or a "United States of the World." Globalists like the German Walther Schücking contemplated a future in which nations and their distinct illness, nationalism, were recognized as failed experiments. Schücking and his allies were citizens of the world, who echoed the words of Terence, that North African slave turned Roman dramatist, who wrote: "I am a man: I consider nothing pertaining to man foreign to myself."

Beneath the grandeur of such proclamations, however, quite another reality lurked. These reunions between long-segregated tribes were not always so brotherly. International interdependence commenced at the end of a long gun. Between 1870 and 1914, Britain, Germany, France, Italy, Portugal, Spain, and Belgium—thanks to industrial strength and sea power, repeating rifles and explosives—conquered weaker lands in a veritable stampede for new markets, cheap resources, and forced labor. This unprecedented conquest spread out over nearly all of Africa, as well as many parts of Asia and South America. At the same time, the Chinese and Ottoman empires were collapsing, offering more opportunity for land grabs.

While Japan, Russia, and the United States were eager to participate in these orgies, this was mostly Europe's party. The European imperial powers rushed to divvy up immense vistas, in what one disgusted observer called "the vilest scramble for loot that ever disfigured the history of human consciousness." For the colonists, this feeding frenzy raised two distinct risks: the lesser one involved trouble from the poorly armed, indigenous peoples. Comforted by a stark asymmetry in power and the belief in their own beneficence, this concern could be assuaged. The graver peril was that competing invaders, in their intoxicated rush, might stumble into war with one another. Pan-European coordination was deemed critical.

In 1885, the Berlin Congo Conference brought together thirteen European powers, as well as the United States. To avoid inadvertent conflict, they sliced up the African continent, giving each imperial power their share. Yet, despite such treaties, what ensued was not a United States of the World, but scattered skirmishes and tangled alliances that foreshadowed another possible outcome of globalization: world war.

The world was shrinking. Armed with breech-loading rifles, stocked up on quinine to prevent malaria, and powered by steam to go upriver,

Europeans strode into once impenetrable domains. These uninvited guests insisted on staying; they created trading companies, which then morphed into plantations. As for the natives, they were not enslaved; the Berlin Congress, like Queen Isabella of Spain before them, outlawed that indignity. Rather, they were "employed" as indentured laborers. Foreign commercial outposts gradually transformed into national protectorates and then colonies, possessions of the home country. In a relatively short period, a smattering of intrepid traders became colonial masters, whose rule was backed by European gunboats and troops.

A thick web of narratives justified these actions. At the Congo conference, the expansion of European culture eastward was celebrated, thanks to what the French called its "civilizing mission." Like the Spanish in the New World, the British Anglo-Saxon, the German Teutonic, the French Catholic, and the Russian pan-Slavic expansionists were encouraged to imagine themselves as philanthropists. These liberators brought a mix of Christianity, science, and justice. They came, it was said, not just for wealth, land, and power, but as peacekeepers, liberators, and educators. In exchange for their property, their culture, and, in essence, their freedom, these savages would be saved from superstition, cannibalism, cruelty, and poverty.

Missionaries, schoolteachers, and functionaries carried the flags of freedom forward. They rubbed up against fortune hunters, ex-criminals, libertines, slave traders, and pirates. So confident were they in their righteousness, the good of their God, the supremacy of their lineage, and the superiority of their culture that the reaction of their hosts begat some confusion. Western travelers noted that in foreign lands, they would be met by accommodation and servile assistance, then suddenly rage and violence. Within the stories the colonists told themselves, it made little sense. And so, when a whirling group of rebels in China announced their mission to attack and destroy foreigners, a rarely used term for irrational fear, plucked from Greek, seemed appropriate.

———

THE DRAMA UNFOLDING in China was especially captivating for the French. After their humiliating defeat in 1871, they had followed

Ernest Renan's prescription for avoiding civil unrest at home by vigorously embracing overseas expansion. Renan had little patience for those with ethical qualms about such enterprises. "The conquest of a country of racial inferiors by a superior race, established there to govern them," he declared, "has nothing shocking about it." In 1879, the author of *Les Misérables*, Victor Hugo, also lustily urged on his compatriots. "God," he proclaimed at a public ceremony, "has offered Africa to Europe. Take it!" The crowd broke into hearty applause.

The Third Republic embraced this strategy, and its imperium grew at breakneck speed. By 1895, colonial inhabitants living under French rule had multiplied from five million to fifty million. By 1913, France controlled thirteen million kilometers of foreign land. Soon France was second only to Great Britain in overseas holdings. In 1889, an *École coloniale* was established to train functionaries in anthropology, colonial sociology, and mass psychology. To serve their sudden empire, French newspapers fed readers a steady diet of events from China, the Ottoman Empire, regions of Africa, South America, the Baltic states, Japan, Russia, and India. Seemingly minor events—the arrival of a diplomat, a colonel being sent home on unnamed charges, or tension in the Upper Nile—were newsworthy. When an uprising took place in an obscure, northern region of China, dozens of French newspapers grabbed on to the story.

Discord in China was itself no shock. In 1873, an anonymous Catholic French missionary had delivered a prophetic warning. He applauded Pope Pius IX's aggressive effort to expand missionary work in China, but mentioned the possible reaction, a "*xénophobie*" in the Far East. Japan and China, the unnamed priest advised, remained deeply unwelcoming to foreigners. A French proconsul similarly wrote of the risk of such anti-stranger reactions in "Oriental" countries that had been "hermetically sealed" for centuries.

These descriptions could not be waved away as simple Western bias. In fact, the Japanese had a long history of hostility toward "*Yabanjin*" or barbarians. These foreigners included the northern people of Hokkaido as well as all Westerners. When the Portuguese landed on Japan's shores in 1542, they were described by the amused inhabitants as "long-nosed goblins." In the following years, Western missionaries settled on Japanese soil, winning over some local lords and building a community of approximately 300,000 Christians. Ultimately, this led to a fierce reaction and an edict of expulsion against the Christians in 1587. From then on, the Japanese shoguns kept a lock on entry into their country, restricting foreign trade to one port, Nagasaki, and one nation of traders, the Dutch. Japan remained quite closed until American gunboats, captained by Commodore Matthew Perry, forcibly demanded entry in 1853. Even after the 1868 Meiji Restoration, a program of modernization that made the Japanese more open to the West, their political elite remained deeply suspicious of foreigners, especially as they noted what was happening across the sea in China.

For while the French proconsul and missionary had a point about Japan, the notion of a "hermetically sealed" China was absurd. True, China with its Great Wall embodied such insularity; once, it too allowed sea traffic through only one port, Canton. However, after the Second Opium War ended in a crushing defeat, the great Qing dynasty had been falling apart. As victors, the British, French, and Russians made their way into the country, where freedom of religion and opium use now had been conceded. Peace came only when Tianjin was opened as a port, British ships were given the right to haul indentured Chinese to the Americas, land was surrendered to Russia, and more. Over the next decades, this weakened empire under the rule of the Dowager Empress Cixi had been increasingly infiltrated by Western missionaries and traders. Chinese loyalists bitterly noted that their desire for autonomy had been grossly violated, as this once regal empire lost control of its own borders.

Then, in 1897, a match was lit. In the Shandong Province, two German Catholic missionaries, Richard Henle and Franz Nies, were murdered. The killing was carried out by the Big Swords, a secret society. The crime provided Kaiser Wilhelm with a long-awaited pretext for invasion. German troops took control of land inhabited by 60,000 Chinese. Observing how easily the Kaiser had waltzed in, other foreign armies deployed their forces into the tottering nation. By 1900, Russia had taken Manchuria, only to have it snatched away by Japan. Great Britain spread out their holdings in Hong Kong and grabbed for Tibet. France fattened its Indochinese empire. Portugal grabbed Macao.

Meanwhile, in northwest Shandong, a drought had made many destitute and raised fears of starvation. A group of young men merged the

EN CHINE
Le gâteau des Rois et... des Empereurs

Imperial powers divvying up the "cake" of China, 1898

traditions of mass possession from the Spirit Boxers with the invulner-
ability rituals and beliefs of the Big Sword Society. Using spells, swallowed
charms, deep breathing, and martial arts, they came to believe themselves invulnerable to swords and bullets. These "*Yihequan*," or "Boxers
United in Righteousness," adopted the slogan "Support the Qing, destroy
the foreigners."

The Boxers began as a loose cluster of thugs who indulged in loot-
ing and thievery. At first, they tormented those *conversos*, the Chinese
Christians, and the rare Western missionary. As the attacks continued,
the government found itself in a bind, torn between European powers
who demanded that the safety of their nationals be ensured and a restless,
angry populace. Advisers to the Dowager Empress were split. Meanwhile,
a catastrophic flood of the Yellow River created a mass of new refugees
and more destitute converts who joined the Boxers. Insurgents now suddenly massed throughout north China; their desire to attack foreigners,

however, remained mostly unfulfilled, since few lived among them. None-theless, these peasants rose up against these symbols of all they had lost to Westerners.

As the Boxers became popular heroes, their call filtered into cities like Tianjin and Beijing, where many foreign nationals did reside. On December 31, 1899, a British missionary was murdered, followed by a group of four French and Belgian engineers. As the identities of the victims made clear, the Boxers were not Anglophobic, Francophobic, or Germanopho-bic. Their country was occupied by many powers and they had declared war on all of them. Seemingly overnight, thousands of Boxers swarmed the streets, eager to burn down Western churches and chase down immi-grants. In the rioting, nearly two hundred non-Chinese were murdered.

In France, the Boxer Uprising continued to share the front page with the glories of the Paris *Exposition*. All across the country, newspaper read-ers learned of dazzling inventions like the Palace of Electricity in one col-umn, and a savage, primitive reaction in another. Xenophobia, they were told, targeted no individual, no maligned group, not settlers or colonists or invaders, but *any* foreigner. A group of possessed, half-mad Chinese rebels would attack anyone who was not Chinese.

After two of their missionaries were killed, German political com-

The Boxers, China, circa 1901

mentators warned of the emergence of what they called a "*Fremden-feindschaft*," "stranger-as-enemy relationship," in China. That term never translated into other tongues. Instead, the French *xénophobie* shot forth into English, Spanish, Italian, Portuguese, and more. Almost immediately, Western readers drank in stories about xenophobic "propaganda," "Mandarin" xenophobia, "secret xenophobic societies," and the power of "xenophobes" to stir up bloodlust in the masses. Xenophobia no longer applied to some rare medical illness or a broad rivalry between Western nations; it now served as an explanation of the fearsome trouble Western globalists might encounter in the East, where an irrational, violent hatred of all outsiders might take hold as exemplified by the spirit-worshipping, rampaging Boxers.

———

AFTER THE PRIOR, failed usages, here was the moment when xenophobia took hold. "*Xénos*" now referred to Western foreigners, immigrants, strangers, and travelers. "*Phobos*" seemed at first glance to be a misnomer; were the Boxers motivated by fear or rage? Xenocide, the desire to kill strangers, might have made more sense, given the circumstances. Instead, some scribbler during a long, hot July in Paris, latched onto this neo-Grecian compound and made it famous. Newspaper dispatches, like the first one published on July 17, 1900, in *Le Constitutionnel*, were routinely unsigned. Someone must have sent basic information from Shanghai, I imagined, that was relayed to the French newspapers, probably through one of the news services. Whoever received that report, and in the process revived "xenophobia" in this new context, would surely be lost to history, I assumed. Discovering the author's identity would be like finding a proverbial needle in the haystack.

A note to needles: your time in the haystack may be up. Thanks to online search engines, I discovered a letter buried in a newspaper archive. Written to the editor of the *Globe*, one of London's leading newspapers, it was published on June 4, 1915, years after the events in China. The author, an obscure fellow, quickly established himself as a pedant, the kind of fellow who took pleasure in correcting another's grammar or offering explanations no one requested. His letter chastised the editors for their misguided usages of "Boche." This derogatory French term for Germans had emerged after the war of 1870, and the letter writer carefully explained that it stemmed from "Teutobochus," Latin for "Kaiser of the Teutsch." This same etymological matter so deeply distressed this gentleman that he whipped off a second letter of protest, this time to the *Sheffield Daily Telegraph*. However, in his note to the *Globe*, he ended with this aside:

> The process by which some words come into general use is rather obscure. During the days of the Boxers' Rebellion, I launched the word "Xénophobe." It caught on in the French Press, and is now to be found in some dictionaries!

The letter was signed, "Yours faithfully, Jean de Saintours, The College of Preceptors, W.C."

I was flabbergasted. Without this bit of boasting, who would have known? But who was this? Not surprisingly, Jean de Saintours turned out to be a man who loved to play around with language, including his own name. After piecing together his *noms de plume*—Jean P. A. Martin de Saintours, Jean P. A. Martin, and J. Martin-de Saint-Ours—I discovered that he descended from a dwindling noble line with its roots in the Périgord region. In 1883, this young scion was listed as French deputy consul to the United States. Under that title in the city of Lyon, Saintours hosted a conference on the need to teach French in the colonies. When the proceedings were published, the editors noted that his proposals happily coincided with the formation of the French Alliance for the Propagation of Our Language in the Colonies and Among Foreigners. And so, this patriot played a small role in boosting what became one of the most successful institutions of cultural expansionism. This alliance now promotes French culture in 850 centers in 137 countries.

Afterward, Saintours left the consulate and began to teach at an educational society in the Rhône. By 1906, this language buff held a post at the London College of Preceptors, which trained and granted diplomas to secondary school teachers. During the intervening years, he developed a formal expertise in stenography, at the time a lively semiotic science, quite useful when deployed in tandem with that new marvel, the tele-

Jean Martin de Saintours

phone. Foreign dispatches would be called in telephonically; the words would be swiftly coded by stenographers, who acted as go-betweens between the far-flung dispatchers and local editors. Our man took out ads in French newspapers offering his services to journalists who wished to employ transatlantic telegraphic or telephonic means to send or access news from London. By 1893, operating under the name Jean Martin, he was appointed senior telephone stenographer for Reuters in London. In this capacity, he gathered information, wrote reports, and disseminated them to news outlets.

Jean Martin de Saintours claimed he coined the French term "*xéno-phobe*" and then disseminated it. But could one be sure? Just as news of the Boxer revolt broke, I found an ad for his services that placed him at 32 rue du Rocher near the Gare Saint-Lazare in Paris. The right place at the right time. The notion that he would have taken the liberty to coin a new term also was not difficult to believe. In scattered writings, Martin was a bit of a troublemaker who reveled in puns and neologisms like British "red-tapeism." He jumped into kooky debates, like the ones stimulated by the Simplified Speling Sosieti, a British group that argued English would become the world's *lingua franca* if phonetic spelling was adopted. A partisan of French, Martin mocked the idea that English would dominate only if "utility, post, and pint" were spelled "yutiliti, poest and pient."

Unless he chose to lie about a matter that no one cared about, Jean Martin de Saintours received a report from Shanghai, wrote it up, and in the process labeled the Boxers as "xenophobes." Then he sent this label out over the expansive network of Reuters' outlets. Of course, Saintours was incorrect about being the first to use the term, but that could have been an honest mistake, since those other usages were obscure. And then there was another detail. Fifteen years after the fact, when Jean Martin de Saintours took credit for this invention, the term "xenophobia" had become so widely dispersed that its moment of inception had been erased from history. No subsequent author, to my knowledge, ever memorialized the fact that, during the Boxer Uprising, this term took root then and there. That fact seemed to be lost, forgotten by all except Jean Martin de Saintours, xenophobia's self-proclaimed inventor, and now me.

CHAPTER 5

Colonial Panic

AS NEWS OF THE Boxer Uprising spread, *xénophobie* leapt from French into other Western languages and sped out over an international network. It was as if cognoscenti around the world awoke from some confusion, and all at the same time fastened on a clarifying word that spelled out something they had vaguely suspected but never named. For the logic that drove the Boxers could be applied elsewhere. In the metropoles of Britain, France, Italy, Spain, Belgium, and America, and in their far-off outposts in Morocco, Mexico, Romania, Argentina, Brazil, and India, this dire warning sallied forth. Fear of xenophobia sprang up far and wide, as if the seed had been sprinkled from on high. Soon everyone from multilingual British diplomats to readers of glossy American magazines to French infantrymen were aware of a new kind of beastly hatred for foreigners.

The Boxers themselves would not survive. The major imperial powers, all of whom had a foothold in China, made sure of that. This rebellion temporarily accomplished what those rival powers could not manage on their own. Eight nations—ones that soon enough would wage war on each other—joined together to crush these insurgents and topple the Chinese government, which had belatedly allied itself with the uprising. This defeat unleashed a new, even more unrestrained search for earthly spoils. German, Russian, British, French, American, and Japanese forces demanded exorbitant reparations and grabbed what they could. The Chinese were left devastated.

The Boxers slipped away as quickly as they had once emerged. Still, the memory of this rebellion persisted. The Boxers' spirit practices, spells, and belief in magic protections made it unambiguously clear that they operated in a realm beyond reason. They promoted a violent hatred of all those from other lands and made no effort to distinguish the beneficent from the rapacious ones. Their motto said as much. They were unabashedly xenophobic.

Could this happen again? For readers in the metropoles, accounts of whirling Chinese zealots entered a well-tended garden of explanation. Such Oriental wildness was well known, anticipated, and quite familiar thanks to rivers of ink from the pens of writers who focused on the colonies. By 1900, Western writing about these exotic outposts had become somewhat of an obsession, compelling everyone from literary masters to Grub Street hacks. It was a regular staple of dailies and weeklies, as well as novels and travel narratives. One could choose from breathless magazine articles and forgettable memoirs to the French stylistic master Gustave Flaubert on Tunisia, or the wildly popular Englishman H. Rider Haggard, whose romances such as *King Solomon's Mines* transported readers deep into the wild. In the burgeoning literature on the colonies, however, the master of such depictions was the Indian-born Englishman Rudyard Kipling.

By the time Kipling was writing, Great Britain had amassed the largest global holdings in the world. By 1900, one quarter of the world's inhabitants lived under the Union Jack. Signs of dominance were everywhere. At the International Meridian Conference in 1884, the baseline slice that ran perpendicular to the equator was placed not through Jerusalem or Rome but through the Royal Observatory in Greenwich. Time was also calibrated at that same observatory; it was Greenwich Mean Time. Space and time were centered in England, a fitting homage to what was by far the greatest power on earth.

Kipling was raised in the cross fire of white supremacy and empire. His highly cultured, British parents were colonists who settled in Bombay; their son grew up surrounded by art and privilege, while also being immersed in Hindi, Sikh, and Muslim Indian culture. As a young writer, not surprisingly, he became fascinated by "Eurasians," those who lived in "the Borderline" "where the last drop of White blood ends and the full tide of Black begins." Despite that, or perhaps because of it, Kipling became an ardent spokesman for white purity. The young Kipling wrote of India's masses: "Faces of dogs, swine, weasels and goats, all the more hideous for being set in human bodies . . . all giving the on-looker the impression of wild beasts held back from murder and violence, and chafing against restraint." The locals were half-humans, unable to govern themselves and prone to irrational violence against strangers. In 1888, one of his narrators advised:

> A man should, whatever happens, keep to his own caste, race and breed. Let the White go to the White, and Black go to the Black. Then whatever trouble falls is in the ordinary course of things—neither sudden, alien, nor unexpected.

For Kipling and a host of lesser writers, an army of assumptions, clichés, and pseudo-objective facts supported the belief that White trouble was of one sort, while rabid tribalism and mass bloodlusts existed only on the Black side of the line. Xenophobia now named one such Black trouble. It was the force that swept seemingly peaceful towns and tribes up into its hateful swirl, making the good go bad and the bad go wild.

Xenophobia, that one word, now made sense of a central scene often staged in adventure narratives. Our intrepid voyagers headed downriver, into the forest, over the sands or endless waves, and then suddenly they came face-to-face with natives. Not infrequently during such dramatic encounters, these exotic beings hopped up and down, made terrifying noises, and seemed to be preparing to massacre the peace-loving foreigners. In *She*, Haggard's tale of well-tailored Cambridge men exploring Africa, the Brits are surrounded by cannibals, who tell them that strangers are traditionally "put to death without mercy. . . ." "'It is hospitality turned upside down,' I answered feebly," says the narrator. "'In our country we entertain a stranger and give him food to eat. Here ye eat him and are entertained.'"

Part of the appeal of these scenes was the knowledge that the Western heroes would never be eaten. Haggard's Cambridge chaps possessed firearms and scientific know-how, while the natives were riddled with comical delusions. Reason and technological prowess made the outcome certain, even a cause for merriment. If the reader was afforded a delicious shudder when it seemed possible the lads might be tossed in a pot and boiled, that subsided when the natives turned out to be good fellows who understood the value of being civilized. If they refused, they would be subdued.

All of that was fine until this staple of the Western imagination confronted realities, like the Chinese Boxers. The Boxers were not so easily put down; it took an international army to do the job. Some back home began to wonder if they had been fed a feast of lies. In Guy de Maupassant's extraordinary novel *Bel-Ami*, a French soldier just back from Algeria launched his journalistic career in Paris by fabricating gauzy, romantic dramas of life with the Moors. It was made-up nonsense, the reader learned, bearing no resemblance to his boring time overseas. Maupassant duly warned his readers that much of what they knew about their exotic colonies was no different: it simply reflected what they wanted to believe. Other realities lurked behind these myths.

Xenophobia, as it was conceptualized, preserved those lies. It made the Boxer Uprising a matter of primitive unreason and intolerance. However, if the event was distressing in itself, the Boxers were even more menacing as a simile. Who else might be *like* them? For colonizers and their supporters at home, a word now existed that lifted the curtain on all that could go wrong when we installed ourselves as their civilizers, reformers, and masters. Still, what caused these troubles? Why were the Chinese Boxers xenophobic? If the sixteenth-century Spaniards deployed religious categories of sin to explain such violence, twentieth-century xenophobia offered a medical, scientific answer. It was a phobia, but not one that took hold after a violent trauma, à la Pinel. Rather, this reaction was due to these savages' race.

Racial science had emerged alongside of, and in competition with, radical eighteenth-century arguments for human equality. During the late eighteenth century, as Quakers, abolitionists, French revolutionaries, and Americans like Jefferson and Franklin declared it "self-evident" that all men were created equal, these theories demurred. Inaugurated by eighteenth-century naturalists like the French Comte de Buffon and the German Johann Friedrich Blumenbach, racial science became widely established by the middle of the nineteenth century. It sought to distinguish those who were, thanks to their nature, healthier, smarter, and more advanced than others. Based on rudimentary notions of genealogy and crude biology, dualities were drawn up—civilized/barbaric, progressive/regressive, and evolution/degeneration—that sorted and classified humans into a racial hierarchy.

As Western empires expanded across the globe, these ideas regarding race were put to use. If the sign by the front door preached radical equality, new "natural" hierarchies slipped in the back. By 1900, seemingly egalitarian nations used typographies of race to organize politics, law, medicine, social policy, biology, and the human sciences. Science, that great engine of progress and arbiter of secular reality, seemed to have demonstrated that all humans were *not* created equally. The self-aggrandizement in this "science" was immense; theorizers of race, somehow inevitably, stood atop the racial pyramids they themselves built.

And so, racial explanations rushed in to account for xenophobia. Primitive races, it was said, were instinctively fearful of outsiders and perceived all strangers as enemies. In 1870, the anthropologist Sir John Lubbock wrote: "amongst the very lowest races every other man—amongst those slightly more advanced, every man of a different tribe, is regarded as naturally, and almost necessarily hostile." Xenophobia was soon said to be ingrained in Africans, Asians, and other non-Western races. They simply could *not* be tolerant; it was not possible for those on their rung of the evolutionary ladder. Primitive races easily succumbed to emotions such as fear, much like children and women. With such races, hope for peaceful coexistence, much less assimilation into Western societies, was dim. Xenophobia was a biological problem. It stemmed not from economic domination, cultural destruction, or military provocation, but from a primitive racial mindset. Why do they hate us? Here was an answer to the colonists' plaintive question: because, dear traveler, they were made that way.

If this were true, it became critical to discover exactly *which* races were xenophobic. In 1902 the French diplomat Roger Turpaud offered his diagnosis in a book meant to advise future French consuls to the Levant. While xenophobia was inherent to the Japanese and the Chinese, he was emphatic: Arabs definitely were not xenophobic. French travelers would encounter a civilization in the Near East that was mostly closed to them, so the "annexation" of lands might prove difficult. Arabs, however, with their rich customs of hospitality, would not attack strangers. It was not in their racial makeup.

Five years later, in the Arab nation of Morocco, what was widely described as a feverish outbreak of xenophobia shook the land. Like China, that country had been tugged at and fought over by too many imperial masters; German, French, British, Spanish, and other colonizers claimed parts as their own. In 1907, Mulai Hafid, the rebel brother of the king, exploited what one Western commentator called a "wave of xenophobia" to mobilize tribes. Roger Turpaud notwithstanding, the *London Evening Standard* reminded its readers of the "inherent xenophobia of the Moors."

The number of "xenophobic races" began to grow. Along with the Chinese, "a mutinous and wild people," and the insular Japanese, racially based xenophobia began to be detected in colonies, anywhere really when it simplified and explained away revolts. After picking up on Chinese *"xenofobia"* from London telegraph services in 1900, Italian journalists soon pondered the "irreducible" xenophobia of those whom they would colonize, the Ethiopians. Spanish papers that had carried tales of Chinese xenophobia soon labeled the violence across the Strait of Gibraltar in Morocco with the same term. Reports of xenophobia popped up in pro-Western newspapers published in Brazil, Argentina, India, and Mexico. Wide-eyed colonists now were left to wonder when and where this crazed hatred would hit. Rival imperial powers began to worry that a latent xenophobia in some races would be weaponized and stirred up against them. Was the French press intentionally inciting xenophobia in Beirut? Were Germans spreading rumors to provoke xenophobia among the inhabitants of Tangiers?

A decade after its invention, xenophobia had become a powerful biopolitical tool tied to science and race: it defined who was a primitive Easterner or Oriental, and who was a civilized Occidental Westerner. As applied by Western journalists, diplomats, experts, and observers, xenophobia was linked to a kind of primitivity that afflicted only the colonized, non-Europeans. Outbreaks of rebellion did not need to occasion soul-searching: these were not contests between competing moral, economic, or political entities. In this up-is-down world, the primitive hosts were mistreating the civilized immigrants—that is, the Western missionaries, traders, and colonists. In response, there could be no rebuttal. Xenophobia had become a magic cloak that made the colonizers' use of overwhelming force invisible.

If racial xenophobia, *prima facia*, served to exonerate the European settlers, it also resulted in sheer terror. For if the colonists' actions had nothing to do with these outbreaks, it meant they had no control. Kindness, currying favor, and offering opportunities for mutual advancement no longer provided any reassurance. Racial xenophobia meant whole tribes might smile and kowtow, but thanks to their primitive nature, they would eagerly slice a stranger's throat. If this was in their makeup, there was no way around it. Trading posts and settler colonies, where intercourse with the locals was based on something less than brute force, would need to consider whether, with *these* people, the only safe path forward was to become their prison-keepers, their occupiers.

Writing about mounting tension in British-held Egypt, an American-owned paper, the *Mexican Herald*, in 1906 bluntly laid out the problem:

> It has been recognized by all—by Britain's foes and friends alike—that English rule in the land of the Pharaohs had been productive of many and varied benefits to the common people of Egypt, that the humble are protected in their rights, and safeguarded in their possessions, shielded from the exactions of petty officials and enjoy the blessing of even-handed justice to a degree which they had never known at the mercy of their native rulers.

Thus, the writer concluded, one could only be bewildered and mystified when these same beneficiaries expressed "anti-foreign" sentiment. Only in passing did he consider whether the humiliation of the sultan in a dispute over the Sinai may have led to this "menacing spirit of fanaticism and xenophobia. . . ."

Such an aside, that odd detail glimpsed from the corner of the eye, was not uncommon in these accounts. In 1900, the French National Society of Political Economy queried an expert on Chinese xenophobia, who insisted that the Chinese race had a "general intolerance" for strangers. Still, he could not help but add that the missionaries and German troops occupying Kiao-Tchéou stoked the spirit of hostility. A London newspaper covering the xenophobic uprising in Morocco added, parenthetically, that the French had few excuses "for remaining in occupation of a Moorish territory." These observations were of anomalies, stray details that had no place in a framework that declared race to be determinative.

Meanwhile, attempts to predict which races were xenophobic continued to fail spectacularly. In *Everybody's Magazine*, the American journalist Eugene Lyle Jr., later the screenwriter of Hollywood's *The Gaucho*, informed his readers that, in Mexico, "the hateful European term of Xenophobia does not exist." Uncle Sam was met in Mexico with "a hearty welcome." The Mexican people embraced foreign economic activity and considered Americans an inspiration. Xenophobia? Not a chance. Seven years later, *The Nation*'s readers were informed that Mexico had yielded to "waves of xenophobia," uprisings that culminated in the peasant revolution led by Emiliano Zapata.

Sleepwalking, Western readers repeated their mantras: we bring freedom, justice, God, reason, progress, material wealth, all great aids. They greet us in China, Ethiopia, Morocco, Mexico, and Brazil with "xenophobic delirium." Xenophobia, as one Frenchman argued in 1907, was the distorted patriotism of the racially primitive: these natives were always ready "to exterminate, but never to welcome or assimilate."

Unlike Father Las Casas's call for a morality based on behavior, racial xenophobia firmly established Westerners as civilized and tolerant, and the others as not. At times, this made for dizzying narratives in which the moral weight of actions became confused. For example, in 1907, the *New York Times* covered an outbreak of violence in Morocco. In response to the murder of thirteen colonists by rebels in Casablanca, the French navy moved a gunboat into range and showered the city with artillery. Between two and seven thousand men, women, and children died in the attack. "Thus far," the *Times* reported, "it has not seemed that there was any organized anti-crusade about the 'xenophobia,' or hatred of foreigners, which instigated the massacre of Casablanca." The phrasing might make a follower of Las Casas's ethics hesitate for just a moment and wonder, which xenophobes? Which massacre? The Moroccans who butchered thirteen French colonists, or the French who slaughtered thousands of Moroccans?

For the *Times* reporter, there was little ambiguity. Xenophobia was intrinsic to the Moroccans. The French were not xenophobes; it was not in their racial makeup. They had come as immigrants to Morocco, carrying ideals of liberty, equality, and brotherhood, while it was well known how Arabs could be toward strangers. In this encounter between racial primitives and the heirs to the Declaration of the Rights of Man, the outcome was determined in advance. If the massive reprisal created some passing disturbance in the moral certainty of the *Times* readership, we will never know.

The world's peoples were coming together. As powerful Western nations spread out across the globe, a racial theory of xenophobia carried with it a dangerous invitation; it licensed limitless violence against the inhabitants encountered, for it would always be their own fault. Magnified, repeated, and dramatized, this shibboleth readied the colonists for confrontation. Xenophobia, journalists proposed, offered clarity and sense to the Boxer revolt in China, the "Egyptian Situation," those feverish, desert rebels in Morocco, and Zapata's peasant rebellion. In the process, more common human motives vanished, as did the grounds for mutual understanding or rational negotiation. In a phrase that would be repeated by militarists over the next century, it was said that the only language *these people* understood was force.

Between 1900 and 1914, xenophobia rapidly spread across Europe, for it helped Western expansionists justify themselves as they fell into conflict with their hosts abroad. We came to you as innocent foreigners. You attacked us. We brought civilization and progress. You were irrational and intolerant. Thus the concept of xenophobia went to work for expanding Western empires. Explanations based on race obscured other motives, including whether it was really unjust to deny welcome to those strangers who, like Alexander the Great, approached with an army.

However, there was an inherent instability in this explanation. When the British bureaucrat, French consul, German missionary, or American businessman landed in India or Congo or Mexico, could they not but note that these natives were *their* strangers, and that their presence could be deeply frightening? Did anyone notice that the Western panic over Eastern and Oriental xenophobia might be driven by motives that were themselves xenophobic?

CHAPTER 6

Commence the Unraveling

AS FEAR OF xenophobia spread throughout the colonies, a vanguard of Western writers ripped at the language and one-way logic that made the xenophobes always only *them*. Beginning around 1900, their voices, though few, began to create sparks of conflict and moral outrage where once there had been popular agreement and self-justification. In a decade, these seeds of challenge were fed by a stream of shocking revelations that developed into a dangerous challenge to colonial ideology.

One of these dissidents was the iconic Russian writer Leo Tolstoy. After creating a pair of nearly unsurpassed literary masterpieces, *Anna Karenina* and *War and Peace*, the famed count chose to devote his remaining days to a religious and ethical quest. During this period, Tolstoy, like Leibniz, Voltaire, Emerson, and others, came to revere the beauty and wisdom of Chinese philosophy. Thus he could only scoff at the ignorant bigotry that claimed such a magnificent civilization was "barbaric." "When a man is unable to understand a thing, he ridicules it," Tolstoy wrote, echoing Saint Paul.

A decade later, when the Boxer Uprising erupted, Tolstoy dared to side with his nation's enemies. Russian troops had committed atrocities in China, including the forcible drowning of five thousand civilians who lived on the banks of the Amur River. The count was horrified. Already a committed anti-imperialist and pacifist, he rained contempt on his own Czar Nicholas. When he heard that the German Kaiser had ordered his troops to take no prisoners, Tolstoy asked how that did not land him in a lunatic asylum? Addressing the Chinese directly, he wrote:

> "Armed people, calling themselves Christians, are now committing the greatest crimes among you. These people are not Christians but a gang of the most terrible, shameless criminals, who have never ceased to plunder, torture, corrupt and destroy, bodily as well as spiritually. . . ."

On the other side of the globe, another writer satirized the know-nothings who demeaned Chinese culture and blamed an occupied people for "irrational" acts of violence. After 1898, Mark Twain, the immortal creator of *The Adventures of Huckleberry Finn*, had grown disgusted by his nation's desire to annex the Philippines. He joined the American Anti-Imperialist League. Two years later, he took up his pen after being sickened by reports that a Reverend Ament of the American Board of Foreign Missions had returned from China, having successfully demanded exorbitant reparations for the Boxers' outrages. "To the Person Sitting in Darkness" appeared in the *North American Review*. In it, Twain quoted the reverend to devastating effect. Twain railed against "a blasphemy so hideous and so colossal . . ." Oh, so these Asians were simply ignoramuses awaiting the "Blessing" of Western civilization, he sneered. What a gift! They would be required to purchase it with "blood and tears and land and liberty." Invisible in their humanity, obscured in darkness, an entire people had been defined by bigotry and sanctimony, and in the end would be left "swimming" in their own blood.

As the rationales for Western civilizing missions cracked, more critics came forth. None did so with more devastating effect than the novelist Józef Teodor Konrad Korzeniowski. Born in the Ukraine, the boy grew up inspired by his father, a fierce Polish patriot and poet, eventually imprisoned by the Russians and forced into exile. After his mother died when Józef was seven, his father sought to homeschool his son but then perished five years later. Orphaned, and deemed by relatives to be an unpromising student, Korzeniowski decided to take to the seas. At the age of sixteen, he made his way to Marseille and joined the merchant marine. After voyages to Africa and South America, he worked his way up from crew member to captain. By then, he had learned English, and at the age of thirty-seven, he published his first novel. The 1895 tale set in Borneo was called *Almayer's Folly*, and it would be the beginning of his new life as the writer Joseph Conrad.

Conrad's reputation for exotic tales grew, but he was still frequently broke and depressed. A resident of Great Britain, he never shook the feeling of being an exile. Though he loved his new country, he never felt accepted in British circles. Even after he achieved celebrity and literary acclaim, he remained embarrassed of his accent and referred to himself as a "homo duplex." Near the end of his life, he wearily refused the honor of knighthood.

This outsider had much to tell his readers about strangers, but it was not what they expected. A 1901 short story, "Amy Foster," featured a shipwrecked foreigner who washed up on Albion's shores. The British natives duly stoned, beat, and ridiculed him, Western xenophobes at work. Nonetheless, this immigrant won gradual acceptance and assimilated. He even married Amy, a local girl. One day, however, he grew ill. Burning with fever, a bit delirious, he lapsed into his native tongue to beg for water. Amy became terrified and interpreted his impassioned gibberish as a mortal threat. She ran off, leaving her husband to die.

Stranger fear and terror emanated not just from far-off "primitives," but also from the self-proclaimed civilizers of the globe. By the time "Amy Foster" was published, Conrad had already published a serialized adventure tale that explored how deeply rooted such Western xenophobia might be. It appeared in an 1899 special double issue of *Blackwood's Edinburgh Magazine*, one of the swelling number of periodicals that fed the populace's appetite for news from the corners of their unimaginable empire. Conrad's account commenced in a typical manner. Our narrator, having recently returned from Africa, had a tale to tell. From this well-worn opening, readers had every reason to expect thrilling savagery and charming sketches, much like the accounts from Jamaica and the Ottoman lands that graced other pages of that same issue of *Blackwood's*.

The Heart of Darkness proved to be different. Docked on the Thames, a man named Charles Marlow, having just returned from an unmapped part of Africa, narrated his quest to find Mr. Kurtz. Kurtz was a cultured functionary who had carried the banner of progress to an ivory trading station, up the Congo River. While on his civilizing mission, something had gone wrong. Kurtz, it was said, had become consumed by hatred. Before

Blackwood's *Special February 1899 issue*

disappearing, he had scribbled "exterminate all the brutes" in the margins of his otherwise tightly reasoned pamphlet on uplifting the natives. Mad with power, this once dignified man—Marlow would discover—had transformed himself, despite his evolved race, into a murderous savage.

Back in London, a traumatized Marlow could not tolerate the lying niceties that now surrounded him. "The conquest of the earth," he bitterly declared, "which mostly means the taking it away from those who have a different complexion or slightly flatter noses than ourselves, is not a pretty thing when you look into it much. What redeems it," he continued, "is the idea only . . . something you can set up, and bow down before."

At first, Marlow hoped that by finding Kurtz, he would discover that idea. After all, Kurtz possessed a "universal European genius"; he was a talented poet, musician, and artist, and thus not dissimilar from the brilliant European explorers who populated colonial adventure stories. Here, however, this pure product of Western civilization had gone crazy. Up the Congo, he embraced sadism, greed, and the rule of the whip. He had discovered powerful demons inside himself, inside the colonial project.

With *The Heart of Darkness*, Conrad took the exotic travel story and gutted it. He forced readers to consider whether they, like Kurtz, implicitly supported savagery. What idols, what ideas, had they set up to justify themselves? Would they too be left in the end, like Kurtz, staring into infinity, muttering, "the horror, the horror"?

Conrad masterfully described Marlow's transformation. Traveling upriver, our guide's attempts at understanding kept getting upended. For example, when their boat—in that inevitable scene—was confronted and attacked by natives, Marlow concluded that something mythic had transpired. "Prehistoric man was cursing us, praying to us, welcoming us— who could tell?" Marlow and his mates assumed the natives were simply xenophobes, closed-off primitives who welcomed strangers with a flock of arrows. Then the meaning of that assault grew murky. "What we alluded to as an attack," he decided upon reflection, "was really an attempt at repulse. The action was very far from being aggressive—it was not even defensive, in the usual sense: it was undertaken under the stress of desperation and in its essence was purely protective."

Tossed off as an aside, the implications of this reversal were seismic. Marlow acknowledged common human motives in the Congolese; they were not inscrutable and prehistoric, but rather were no different from anybody else. Armed men from the ivory mining company had overrun their villages, so they tried to fight back. Conrad, however, refused to leave it there. In a final twist, Marlow discovered *that* interpretation also was wrong. The natives had been ordered to attack Marlow's boat by his blood-crazed countryman, Kurtz. A xenophobic attack by savages dissolved like a mirage, and in its place there emerged violence by a mad Westerner out to defend his evil domain.

The instability of perception—the sense of certainties unraveling in the Congo heat—were heightened by the fact that Marlow, like Conrad himself, was hardly free of colonial ideology. Marlow fell into and out of that reassuring social order as he sought to apprehend what was transpiring before his eyes. In the end, his sense of himself, his nation, reality itself, never would be stable again. His hero, like his civilization, stood guilty of mass murder.

Broken, bobbing up and down on the Thames, Marlow remained on the margins, unsure about how to reenter British society. To do so, like the hero in *Bel-Ami*, he would need to live within the lies demanded by his countrymen. He would be forced to provide them with censored and prettified fabrications that justified the flow of riches to their vast empire. Marlow handed in Kurtz's report after ripping out the annotation "Exterminate all the brutes!" He then paid a courtesy call to Kurtz's fiancée, who begged this messenger to relate her "intended's" final words. Instead of that haunting repetition—"the horror, the horror"—Marlow miserably muttered that, of course, it was her name.

If early twentieth-century English readers had encountered such an assault on their sensibilities, never had it been delivered with the masterful artistry of Joseph Conrad. Like Las Casas's short report from the Indies, *The Heart of Darkness* took a genre most often intended to reassure readers and twisted it to expose the crushing psychic and moral tolls of domination. We have become the new conquistadors, Conrad informed his readers; greed and power have turned us into Kurtzian monsters. And not just some of us. Conrad intentionally made his villain a man of French and English parentage, endowed him with a German-sounding name, and had him followed around by an adoring Russian sidekick. All of colonial Europe was riddled with this disease. All thrived on lies that confused race with virtue, sadism with love, civilization with domination, and their hatred of us with our hatred of them.

Marlow returned to London, but his future was undone. His very categories of identity had collapsed. In the Congo, there once stood before him a mystery: different-colored kin. They existed on the other side of a chasm created by Western boats and guns as well as fortified ideas about race and nature. Marlow himself never surmounted the belief that the Africans were intrinsically inferior. As the Nigerian writer Chinua Achebe pointed out, there is a good deal of easy, unironic racism in Joseph Conrad's tale. The reader waits in vain for an African to articulate a view that might challenge Marlow's assumptions. It never happens. The few words that the residents of the Congo speak sound like a minstrel performance. In one critical moment, Marlow irritably reported that the manager's "boy put his insolent black head in the doorway and said in a tone of scathing contempt—'Mistah Kurtz—he dead.'" Insolent, indeed.

Retitled and published in book form, *Heart of Darkness* decimated the heroic, imperial adventure story; it upended a symbolic order that dictated that the Africans were savages, and the European colonists were the righteous bearers of liberty and light. The genre that encouraged lads like the young Conrad himself to dream of one day winning glory by striking out like Dr. Livingstone, now seemed riddled by paranoia and soaked in piss and blood. Before Marlow departed for the Congo, a doctor for "the Company" obliquely mentioned that he had been developing a theory regarding the mental alterations that occurred in the colonies. Conrad never elaborated, but he did not need to. By the time Marlow returned home, his mind, his vision of himself, his morals, and his ideals were in shambles. Earlier, in a "flash of inspiration," Marlow seemed to understand what was happening to him. He told Kurtz what he believed was also now his own fate: " 'You will be lost,' I said—'utterly lost.' "

———

A YEAR AFTER *Heart of Darkness* appeared in book form, the author received a fan letter. Roger Casement admired Conrad's novella and he wrote to remind the author of a fortnight in June of 1890, when the two men lodged together. They had met in the seaport of Matadi, at the mouth of the Congo River, in the "Congo Free State." This was the personal possession of King Leopold of Belgium, who in 1885 had presented this massive region to himself as a gift. It was not Belgian, but his private dominion. Both Conrad and Casement had been indirectly under the employ of King Leopold; the former on a river steamboat called *Roi des Belges*, while the latter had been hired by a Belgian group trying to build a railway between Matadi and Kinshasa. Both were there, then, because of ivory, rubber, and money. A decade later, Casement sought out Conrad. Like the fictional Marlow, Roger Casement had seen too much. He needed his old acquaintance's help.

Casement was born in Dublin to Anglo-Irish parents in 1864. Like Conrad, his childhood was brutal. His mother died when he was nine, his father four years later. Young Roger turned to the charity of relatives but only completed a modest amount of schooling. At sixteen, he went to work for a Liverpool shipping company. Then, in 1884, he traveled to the

Congo to work for the International Association for the Exploration and Civilization of Central Africa, a philanthropic-sounding group that was a front for King Leopold. After surveying land along the Congo River for railroad construction, Casement became the British consul in Congo just as rumors began to swirl. A year before his appointment in 1890, the African American writer George Washington Williams sounded the warning. Over the next decade, scattered newspapers and magazines carried hints and rumors of terrible things taking place in Leopold's Congo Free State.

Conrad's acclaimed novella breathed more life into these disturbing allegations. Then a series of minor scandals led the Balfour government to half-heartedly establish a Commission of Inquiry on the Congo. Casement was asked to evaluate wild-sounding claims of wrongdoing. After ten weeks of travel, the stunned consul returned to London with a sixty-one-page report. What he witnessed had devastated him. He feared for his life, and swore that if he made it back to London alive, he would do anything to "let my countrymen know what a hell on earth our own white race has made. . . ." Recognizing that his report would meet entrenched resistance, Casement reached out to the acclaimed author of *Heart of Darkness*, reminding him of their days together and asking for support in the upcoming fight.

While his tale won acclaim for exposing the fictions that sustained the empire, Joseph Conrad, unlike Roger Casement, was still a grudging imperialist. He believed that a civilizing mission based on the noble idea of aiding others toward self-rule and liberty was possible. The novelist half-heartedly invited Casement to his home, and to his dismay found that the Irishman seized upon the opportunity. Casement recorded a delightful day spent at Pent Farm; he regaled Conrad with tales from his investigations that vindicated the novelist's worst imaginings. Conrad's wife recalled that their visitor made a powerful impression: handsome, commanding, he possessed a strong moral force. She also noted in passing that he was a "fanatical Irish Protestant."

Casement was eager to start an organization to fight for the rights of the Congo people and asked if Conrad would help. Conrad was not a joiner; he begged off, instead asking a friend, the first-ever Socialist member of Parliament and a Scottish nationalist, Cunninghame Graham, to jump in. Of Casement, whom Conrad recalled from their long, hot days in the Congo, he added: "I have always thought that some particle of Las Casas' soul had found refuge in his indefatigable body . . . I would help him, but it is not in me. I am only a wretched novelist. . . ."

Indeed, Roger Casement became a modern Las Casas. His 1903 report was so explosive that the British government delayed publication and deleted names; even still, when it appeared it caused an international furor. Companies and colonists tried to shout it down, but Casement had listed fields of skulls and skeletons, rows of chopped-off hands, chain gangs, sadism, greed, and, in all but name, slavery. Casement's report inspired Mark Twain to write "King Leopold's Soliloquy." Anatole France, John Galsworthy, Booker T. Washington, and others raised their voices in horror. Demands were made for further investigations.

As the uproar built, Roger Casement traveled to Liverpool to meet

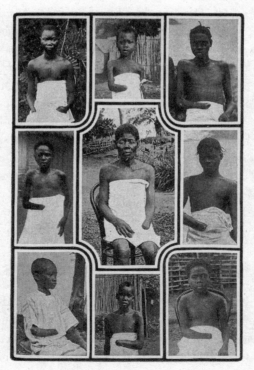

Atrocities from the Congo Free State

with an obscure pamphleteer named Edmund Morel. It was a meeting Morel would not forget. A harsh, wintry wind blew, as the consul almost went into a trance, recounting the unbearable scenes he had witnessed. Then, overwhelmed by emotion, he would mutter, "poor people, poor, poor people." Morel became haunted, too:

> I saw those hunted women clutching their children and flying panic stricken to the bush; the blood flowing from those quivering bodies as the hippopotamus hide whip struck again and again . . . that tortured African world, to the "heart of darkness," as Joseph Conrad described it in his memorable story.

Since Casement was a government representative, he asked this Liverpool firebrand to be the figurehead leader of a Congo Reform Association. Now a rebel with a cause, Morel dove in. He cranked out pamphlets and books like *The Congo Slave State* and *King Leopold's Rule in Africa*. Morel described a "carnival of massacre," and a "diabolic, and unholy so-called civilising power" that casually massacred our "black brothers."

The outrage spread. A Belgian socialist named Emile Vandervelde successfully lobbied for an internal investigation. In 1905, the Belgian government confirmed Casement's accusations and eventually annexed the Congo, taking it away from their king. Much of the world now knew that behind the moralizing clichés and race science, evil of stunning proportions had transpired. Photographs of bodies and children with their hands cut off circulated. Mortality estimates, as with Las Casas, were difficult, since sleeping sickness and other diseases also surely played a role. Recently, one historian estimated that ten million men, women, and children died in what would be called the African Holocaust.

———

IN THE YEARS PRIOR to the Great War, a crucial paradigm of Western globalization began to be destabilized. A righteous ideology of benevolent white rule over hostile, inferior, dark races once structured routine interpretations and explanations, but increasingly it failed to account for a host of horrifying events. Nothing-more-to-see-here denials began to lose their credibility, and were thrown open to accusations of deception, hypocrisy, and the justification of rapacious cruelty.

The tipping point, for many, came with the revelations regarding the Congo Free State. After all, this project had been held up as one of mercy and benevolence. After annexing 900,000 square miles in Central Africa and turning them into labor camps for ivory and rubber, King Leopold had proclaimed: "Our only program, I am anxious to repeat, is the work of moral and material regeneration." After the revelations of Casement and Vandervelde, who could hear such rhetoric in the same manner again?

Roger Casement helped provoke a crisis of conscience regarding imperialism itself. And he was not done. After an article claimed that the British had their own Congo-like plantation in the Peruvian Amazon, he was dispatched to investigate. Again, he broke through the lies of native betterment and brought to light the abuse of Putumayo natives. In 1911, his government honored him for his services by knighting him.

Five years later, they would hang him as a traitor. For, as Conrad's wife noted, this Irish Republican raged against his homeland's occupation. Having taken up the cause with the Irish Home Rulers, Sir Roger traveled abroad to seek support for a planned Easter Uprising. On April 20, 1916, a "Norwegian" steamer named *The Aud* tried to land on the coast of Ireland. The British navy intercepted the ship, and the captain scuttled the boat, but that did not hide the fact that it turned out to be a German vessel, carrying twenty thousand rifles, a million rounds, and three machine guns. A German U-boat soon followed with the Irishman who negotiated the arms shipment, Roger Casement. Promptly captured, he was imprisoned in London's Tower. Allies appealed for clemency, but Conrad, characteristically, declined to participate. It hardly would have mattered. Casement's enemies privately circulated diaries that revealed he was gay. Support faded away, and his fate was sealed. After a summary trial, the man who unmasked the African Holocaust was convicted, stripped of his knighthood, and executed.

Like Marlow, Casement had come home from the colonies utterly changed. Imperialism and white superiority were diabolical hallucinogens. Their wild and primitive xenophobic rejection of us was actually our violent dehumanization of them. Morel put it succinctly: the Congo Free State was actually the Congo Slave State and the "white man's burden" was in fact the "black man's burden."

Soon, another blinding abstraction came under attack. Imperialism was a grandly festooned notion, stuffed with patriotic virtue and nationalist pride. The British imperium was intended to be beneficent, in line with the liberal commitments of the nation. The mission was to subjugate in the name of freedom, and lead these others to independence and self-rule. The task to some seemed holy: in 1843, *Blackwood's* magazine claimed British imperial conquest to be "destined by Almighty God to be the instrument for effecting his sublime, hidden purposes." Institutions like the Royal Colonial Institute and the Imperial Federation League were dedicated to this purpose. In 1897, Queen Victoria's reign was celebrated by a Diamond Jubilee, in which her glorious rule was marked by cheering throngs, bands blaring, and 46,000 troops marching through London. The soldiers in their finest regalia included Maoris, Malays, Canadians, and Sikhs, all loyal subjects of the Queen. Victoria then sent out a telegram to the four corners of the earth, her entire empire, in which she expressed thanks and gave blessings to her people. The imperium was good, kind, and beloved.

By then, however, over a century of racial murder, scandal, and servitude had rotted such pledges to their core. From the pillaging rampages of the East India Company to the heartless viceroy of India, Lord Lytton; from the little dictators dropped into Africa, like General Baden-Powell, General Horatio Kitchener, and Governor Edward Eyre, to brutal consuls like Harry Johnston and corporate rulers like Sir George Goldie's Royal Niger Company as well as Sir William Mackinnon's Imperial British East Africa Company, the crimes were almost too lengthy to list. Casual, even jolly sadism, the eye poked out of a servant for his insolence, the "necessary" torture and summary executions, the piles of brown and black bodies brought down by Gatling guns—all these acts continued to stream forth.

A change was coming, a reversal in the ethical valence of imperialism, of which the historian of the fall of Rome, Edward Gibbon, had warned when he remarked simply that the history of empires was the history of human misery. Marching bands could not drown out the sounds of suffering. Soon a rabble-rouser named John Hobson and his so-called New

Liberals would take stock of all the death and destruction in far-off lands and seek to make imperialism a miserable, dirty word.

Born in Derby, Hobson was often sickly and afflicted with a stammer, but by the time he reached Oxford University, he was known for a sizzling wit and piercing insight. As a young journalist, troubled by his nation's conduct in its colonies, he set out to see for himself. In July of 1899, a New Liberal paper, the *Manchester Guardian*, sent him to South Africa to report on the Boer War. The Boers were descendants of Dutch colonists who demanded freedom from Great Britain. The British in turn sought control over Boer territories, including the gold-laden Transvaal. It was all about money, Hobson concluded, and the masses at home who cheered this on had been fed a pack of lies. Sickened, he first let fly with *The Psychology of Jingoism*, in which he attacked the press for drunkenly promoting an idiotic war that only served industrialists like Cecil Rhodes. Then Hobson took up another matter that he observed in South Africa. He had been shocked by the casual inhumanity with which both sides, the British and the Boers, treated the Bantu, Zulu, and Matabele people.

In 1902, Hobson's manifesto, *Imperialism: A Study*, took this honorific term and hurled it into the mire. First, he coolly listed Great Britain's foreign holdings, which by his count included 13,142,708 square miles and 366,793,919 people in Europe, Asia, Africa, and Australia. The unpleasant requirements necessary to establish and control such an imperium were hidden by a twisted game. The British people had been duped by psychological acts of deception and linguistic ploys. Underneath all the games was one real and true thing: raw economics. Industrialists faced underconsumption at home and the need for new markets abroad. This central, driving motive was obscured by the supposed inferiority of a suspiciously vast array of other human beings. Hobson attacked the crude application of racial theories and Herbert Spencer's "survival of the fittest" theories of Social Darwinism to dress up what were straightforward conquests. He mocked the puffed-up nationalism that accompanied these ludicrous rationalizations. When Lord Rosebery announced that the British Empire was "the greatest secular agency for good the world has ever seen," Hobson asked, did not the entire continent of Europe double over in mirth? Similarly, when Victor Hugo told the French that it was their responsibility to civilize the rest of the planet, didn't the British, Germans,

Russians, and Italians roll their eyes? Why, Hobson pressed, was the superiority of each imperium obvious *only* within its own borders?

Such self-deception was no laughing matter. An epidemic of willful blindness had destroyed the imperialists' ethical vision. Whole nations had convinced themselves that greed was generosity, servitude care, and power charity. Sincere priests, educators, doctors, and scientists could thus become corrupted. Imperial control hid behind those schools, clinics, and churches, that irrigation project with its clearly beneficial, cleaner water. The British consul at Canton, Hobson noted, inadvertently lifted this veil, blurting out that the Christian missionaries in China were to "cooperate with our Consuls in the exploitation of the country." "For completeness of analysis," Hobson acidly noted, this sentence "leaves nothing to be desired."

Decades before George Orwell militated against the political corruption of language, Hobson drew attention to the corrosive power of "masked words." What were those mystifying, bloodless terms like "rectification of the frontier" meant to do, if not deceive? Imperialism would be morally impossible without the "lie that does not know itself to be a lie." In a globalizing world, where many in imperialist lands were asked to provide their consent for events far from any direct experience, such words and phrases possessed the power of dreams. "The mind of the nation" became habituated to deception that rendered it "incapable of self-criticism." This constituted the "gravest peril of Imperialism." Hobson's friend, the New Liberal leader Leonard Hobhouse, agreed and wrote: "If men say equality, they mean oppression."

Nurtured on such a diet of delusion, the colonizer and his supporters back home assumed that the colonized should be deeply grateful; rebellions were irrational, animal reactions—that is, primitive xenophobia. However, the lies could not stop the body counts from rising. Soon the editor W. T. Stead rallied to the cause. Exposés by Emily Hobhouse showed that the "refuge" camps for Boers and Africans were in fact brutal concentration camps for women and children that led to 28,000 deaths, mostly by starvation. Adolf Hitler would take note of this British strategy, and Lloyd George would charge the government with employing strategies of extermination.

Following fervent anti-imperialists like Leo Tolstoy, Mark Twain,

Roger Casement, Edmund Morel, and John Hobson, a growing chorus attacked the legitimizing narratives of colonialism. While conservatives held firm, liberal parties, once loyal to expansionist agendas, began to divide on this issue. Socialists cried out against worker exploitation abroad. In the process, the notion that xenophobia was a primitive reaction by non-Westerners was undercut. This term, it began to seem, was deceitful, part of the propaganda that made the abuse of foreigners their own fault. Such a perversion was corrosive and ultimately deformed one's inner world, thanks to what Hobson called a necessarily "unconscious" psychic division into "watertight compartments." Without this psychic split, Western violence against far-off strangers would be morally unbearable.

As imperialism began to take on this dark meaning, the original xenophobes from the Orient found defenders. "The pretended xenophobia of the Chinese, of which Westerners speak," a sinologist named Alexandre Ular wrote, "only exists in reality in proportion as the Western refuses to treat the Chinese as a civilized man." "Chinese xenophobia," he continued:

> is in direct ratio with the civilizing claims of the Westerns. On the other hand, it doesn't exist where a European lives alone among the Chinese without claiming to impose upon them their morals and ideas of the Christian invaders. . . .

Some went further. Was this panic about xenophobic uprisings in far-off places a manifestation of Western xenophobia? Was this the pot calling the kettle black? In *The Nation*, a journalist upended two pillars at once when he coined the phrase "xenophobic Imperialism." It was the union of two concepts that, as in a bad marriage, seemed to highlight the worst in each.

———

WHEN OUTBREAKS OF stranger fear and violence occurred in the colonies, a closed circle of interpretation neatly accounted for these distressing events. The Westerners had arrived on a civilizing mission. They had been met by a feral tribe, racially endowed with an irrational fear and hatred of strangers. After 1900, this logic traveled from China to other outposts, until it fell into doubt. Critics like Tolstoy, Twain, Conrad, and Casement exposed this as a self-satisfied delusion. The story of the Congo Free State told of a dramatically different kind of cause and effect: these were militarized invasions which had been met with legitimate resistance. The tension between these contrasting frameworks could be great. Scientific theories of race tilted the balance of interpretation one way, but that "proof" kept being undercut by a disquieting realization. In the capitals of the Western world, xenophobia of the sort ascribed to the inferior primitives seemed to consume the supposedly civilized folks next door.

CHAPTER 7

Immigrant Boomerang

THE INVADERS, inevitably perhaps, began to fear invasion. As their imperium fell into question, foreigners began streaming into the colonizers' homelands. The same technical innovations that made for the highest rates of overseas immigration during the late nineteenth century made it feasible for the denizens of the Ganges or the Nile to make their way to the Thames and the Seine. The frenzy of imperial conquest coincided with this backflow of dark strangers. They had come with no armies, often as impoverished refugees, who walked long distances, then boarded trains, and streamed into the ports of the Western world. Once proudly liberal and tolerant nations began to be convulsed by a rash of fear, violence, and protest against these new immigrants.

European powers had swaggered into far-off lands, carrying progress as a promise and servitude as a threat. Having transported so many of their own subjects, in reality or imaginatively, into the bush, the desert, and the jungle, and having coexisted in sweaty proximity with so-called savages, they forged tight psychic links between their own identities and those half-humans they sought to rule. Thus, when in London and Paris these colonized immigrants appeared in the market or street, they generated alarm. Had these people come with revenge in their hearts? Would they remain a foreign outpost inside the nation? Could they be assimilated? If the challenge of maintaining one's identity abroad was in not "going native," an inverse threat now surfaced. Would these strangers seek to alter our homes, to alter us?

In the world's foremost empire, the heirs of the Magna Carta and the Glorious Revolution began to read in publications like *The Athenaeum*, *The Nation*, and the *New Statesman* reports of "xenophobia" by Westerners at home. The nation itself had been convulsed by the presence of "aliens," a masked term that referred to East European Jews. Jews had a long, turbulent history in Great Britain. After being expelled from England in 1290, they were allowed to return and achieved something close to equality by the middle of the Victorian era; the rise of Prime Minister Benjamin Disraeli, a Jew who converted to Anglicanism, marked a golden age, but also presaged a reaction as intense anti-Semitism followed in his wake. That hatred and bias worsened as refugees began to arrive from Russia.

Supporters of the Romanovs had formed ultranationalist groups that terrorized Jews, who were often referred to as a "foreign nation." After the assassination of Czar Alexander II in 1881, a rash of pogroms broke out in Russia. These were often festive, community-building affairs in which the hosts drank, feasted, and gazed on in amusement as Jews were tortured. Ludicrous fantasies of Jewish world domination, most infamously in the 1903 *Protocols of the Elders of Zion*, encouraged vigilante violence. With no protection from the state, Russian Jews took what they could and left en masse, heading for seemingly tolerant havens like Great Britain and France.

Before 1880, Jews had made up only 0.4 percent of Britain's population. The Russian terror resulted in the arrival of some 200,000 exiles, many of whom clustered in the East End of London. While this group of impoverished refugees hardly posed a threat to the greatest power on earth, their arrival provoked an outcry. Right-wing newspapers fulminated and waged a campaign, claiming again and again that there was an "Alien Immigrant Problem." In 1901, the British Brothers' League formed, a movement that mobilized working-class anger by portraying these arrivals as cheap, foreign labor. A Royal Commission was convened to look into this "problem," and in 1903, its leading commissioner, Conservative Party member Major William Evans-Gordon, shared what he had learned after a fact-finding mission to Eastern Europe. In *The Alien Immigrant*, he protested—perhaps too much—that prejudice held no sway over

him. Prior immigrants—Catholic
or Calvinist—intermarried and
became English. Here was the
rub: the Hebrews would not.
Just take a stroll along the East
End, he suggested. It had become
"a foreign colony." The world's
most dominant colonizers had
been colonized. The invaders, he
warned, had been invaded.

Prime Minister Balfour
agreed that the Jews could not
assimilate, and so, Parliament
passed restrictive legislation. The

> **A GREAT**
> **PUBLIC DEMONSTRATION**
> Under the auspices of
> THE BRITISH BROTHERS' LEAGUE,
> in favour of restricting the further immigration o
> DESTITUTE FOREIGNERS
> into this Country, will be held at
> **THE PEOPLE'S PALACE,**
> MILE END, E., on
> **TUESDAY, JAN. 14TH, 1902.**
> The Chair will be taken at Eight p.m. sharp, by
> **MAJOR EVANS-GORDON, M.P.,**
> who will be supported by Members of Parliament,
> County and Borough Councillors, Members of
> Boards of Guardians of all shades of politics, and
> Ministers of Religion of all Denominations.

British Brothers' League protest against
alien immigrants, 1902

Aliens Act 1905 created new administrative structures for immigration
registration and control. It was relatively ineffective but was rightly perceived by some as a breach in values, an indirect attack on Jews, and
the harbinger of worse things to come. This prediction was borne out
in 1914, with the passage of the more draconian Aliens Restriction Act.
Incensed, Alfred Zimmern, an internationalist who later helped found
the League of Nations, penned a jeremiad. Born to German-Jewish parents in Surrey, Zimmern attended Oxford and converted to Christianity;
he uneasily began his essay by denying that his ancestry had anything to
do with his outrage. He protested, also perhaps too much, that he was
not writing as one connected to the Jewish community. Yet this was one
of the most "immoral and hypocritical" pieces of legislation in memory,
due to its being "purely and plainly anti-Semitic" as well as crudely anti-
immigrant. Other liberals jumped in, denouncing the act as a hysterical
furor and sheer intolerance. Critics pointed out that the inflated numbers
of aliens the commission counted were puffed up on purpose. The numbers neglected the fact that most of these Russian Jewish migrants left;
they were "trans-migrants" on their way to the United States, and when
subtracted from the final tally, those added to the British population were
minuscule. Data like that reinforced the conclusion that this was not an
act of statecraft but simply xenophobic bias.

Alongside the liberals, a louder political community joined the fray. Revolutionary socialism had risen rapidly in Europe. For a decade after Karl Marx's *Das Kapital* was published in 1867, there were but a few socialist agitators on street corners. However, by the first decade of the twentieth century, Labor and Socialist political parties had become commonplace. Once legal restrictions against them were lifted in 1890, the German Social Democratic Party shot forth and became a force. By 1900, French politics featured a number of Socialist and Workers parties, and in Great Britain, the British Labour Party had gathered enough support to compete with the Liberal Party.

For the followers of Marx, a different framework helped justify their support of immigrants. Socialists dreamed not of toleration and individual liberty, but rather of classless equality that crossed racial and ethnic lines. They had been sensitized to the ideological workings of nationalism, as well as the racial and ethnic scapegoating that masked economic exploitation. Early on in Britain, the cause of foreigners and Jews was taken up by parties like William Morris's Socialist League. Joseph Finn, a one-time member of the Socialist League and a Jewish trade unionist living in the East End, argued in his 1895 pamphlet, *A Voice from the Aliens*, that such ideas about strangers only served to mask economic manipulation. Different immigrants and minorities around Europe were being targeted by the ruling class, precisely to divert attention. "Everywhere," Finn wrote, "he is the scapegoat for others' sins." In reality, the suffering of the worker had nothing to do with these strangers. And so, when few were willing to do so, the British Labour Party stood up for Russian Jews and campaigned for mistreated Chinese workers.

However, the allegiance of the left with the cause of Jews in England came at a price. In the fevered minds of many liberals and conservatives, Karl Marx and his radical followers were Eastern European Jews, and these Jewish radicals were linked most distressingly with Anarchists. These long-bearded disrupters of the status quo seized Europe's attention thanks to a string of dramatic terrorist bombings in Spain, France, and Britain. They included the 1894 plot to detonate the Greenwich Royal Observatory, fictionalized by Joseph Conrad in *The Secret Agent*. For wobbly liberals in Great Britain, clamping down on "radical agitators" became a plausible way to support anti-immigrant measures without being openly anti-Semitic.

Across the English Channel, the world's second-greatest colonial power also began to feel menaced by *les étrangers*, their word for strangers as well as foreigners. Along with the United States and Great Britain, France had become a favored destination for late-nineteenth-century immigrants. Initially, most newcomers arrived from Belgium, but when a wave arrived from Italy, so did trouble. On June 17, 1881, in the port city of Marseille, victorious French troops returned home after wresting control of Tunisia away from Italy. As festivities spilled out into the streets, someone claimed that derisive whistles had emanated from the Italian Club. A mob formed and commenced a "bear hunt." Hundreds of French patriots went on a rampage against Italian immigrants; three died and more than twenty were gravely injured.

In Paris, the right-wing Paul Leroy-Beaulieu of the Collège de France defended the rioters. Between 1882 and 1889, some fifty-eight "bear hunts" took place. Meanwhile, nationalists like Leroy-Beaulieu commenced a campaign to make immigration itself a problem, a social ill that required remedies. His allies demanded that the government track all foreigners inside their borders. On October 2, 1888, a law doing so was fixed by decree. Henceforth, immigrants in France would be legally mandated to register with the police.

Anti-foreign Frenchmen soon turned their eager eyes toward the Jews. "Anti-Semitism" had a long history in France, having first been so named in 1860 by an Austrian who sought to account for Ernest Renan's writings on Semitic peoples. As in Great Britain, the actual number of French Jews was tiny, only 60,000. Still, rage was periodically directed at them, most explosively during the 1894 trial of a Jewish French colonel accused of handing secrets to the Germans. Alfred Dreyfus's trial for treason was a circus, and featured venomous accusations spit forth from newspapers like Edouard Drumont's *La Libre Parole*. A long-standing hater of Jews in France, Drumont had five years earlier founded a militant group, the National Antisemitic League of France.

The Dreyfus affair fractured a France torn between right-wing nationalists like Drumont and liberal or leftist internationalists. After being convicted in 1896, Dreyfus's innocence began to become more apparent and evidence of a cover-up emerged. An international outcry ensued, and the famed novelist Emile Zola penned his 1898 essay, "J'Accuse . . . !" It pointed a finger directly at government officials who refused to acknowledge new, exonerating facts. For his efforts, Zola was prosecuted and convicted of libel. He fled France. Nonetheless, the "Dreyfusards" had been mobilized.

Among them was Georges Clemenceau. The future prime minister was, at the time, the publisher of *L'Aurore*, the leftist newspaper that splashed Zola's accusations onto its front page. However, Clemenceau was not new to such advocacy. In 1885, he denounced colonialism in the Chamber of Deputies and heaped scorn on racial rationales for oppression, reminding his countrymen that the Germans justified their victory

Emile Zola's 1898 letter, "J'Accuse . . . !"

over the French in these same "scientific" terms. Once he realized that Colonel Dreyfus had been wrongly convicted due to anti-Jewish bias, he spent the next eight years fighting for a full exoneration. In 1902, as the tide of public opinion turned, Clemenceau would be swept into office, thanks to his moral clarity and courage. In 1905, a coalition of pro-Dreyfusards headed by René Waldeck-Rousseau took over the French government.

Still, the terms of the debate over *étrangers* was harsh. If in Britain, even the British Brothers' League tried to keep a fig leaf over their bias and deny the accusation that they had succumbed to anti-Jewish prejudice, little such effort was required in France. A radicalized group of officials and military men had learned hard lessons in the colonies and brought them home. Legions of administrators filtered back to their homelands having grown used to exerting total control over the population. Jurists in the colonies found the "Declaration of the Rights of Man" to be totally irrelevant. Soldiers, having broken taboos of violence against women and children, having imbibed the logic of incommensurate reprisals and collective punishment, looked at these foreigners and minorities in *La Patrie* through jaundiced eyes. Colonel Dreyfus's lawyer, in his appeal, referred to the way that the brutal treatment of the colonized abroad had contributed to the rapid descent of liberal values at home. Foreign adventures, he implied, justified intolerance and helped to cause this anti-Semitic travesty of justice.

Others were unmoved, for an amoral logic of dehumanizing control had won them over. A former French naval officer in China and Japan named Léopold de Saussure was one. In 1899, the brother of the famed linguist published his doomsday work, *Psychology of French Colonization in Its Relations with Indigenous Societies*. If the French did not awaken from their Enlightenment slumber, he warned, their empire would crash. The soul of foreign races was fundamentally different. Integration was suicidal. Seven years later, Georges Leygues, the French minister of the colonies, warned of the same danger. Then, in 1910, after returning from Indochina, the French ambassador Jules Harmand joined this chorus. In his *Domination and Colonization*, Harmand mocked the silly evangelists who spoke of inalienable human rights. Humanitarianism was a "strange illness born of false idealism." General Paul Azan similarly sought to disabuse his compatriots of their fluffy beliefs. Immigrants from the colonies and other lands—including that Asiatic group, the Jews—could not be afforded the same rights as Frenchmen.

The struggle over minorities and immigrants remained a rallying cry for both sides of France's political divide. Liberals with an international focus heaped scorn on the right wing; their proposed legal restrictions, one student of international law wrote, were simply "xenophobic." In 1902, the Frenchman Gaston Richard asserted that xenophobia was easily found in Paris. French Socialists themselves were initially torn: if impoverished foreign workers flooded the market, some worried about the effect on wages. Hadn't Karl Marx himself warned that a "reserve army" of workers could undercut the local proletariat? Despite this concern, during their 1910 Copenhagen Congress, after much discussion, the Socialists of Europe reaffirmed their support of all immigrants as equal brothers of the global proletariat.

As the two largest Western empires struggled with minorities and immigration at home, it became clear that xenophobia described groups like the British Brothers' League and the National Antisemitic League of France. Meanwhile, the port of destination for most of the world's immigrants, the United States, had already been convulsed by reactionary forces. In the case of this young nation, immigration had in fact changed its ethnic composition. In 1860, the legal citizens of the country—read "white"—were 60 percent British and 35 percent German, but by 1914, after twenty million new arrivals in merely two decades, the melting pot contained descendants who were 11 percent British and 20 percent German, 30 percent Italian and Hispanic, and 34 percent Slavic. Xenophobic vit-

Anti-Chinese rally, United States, 1892

riol became focused especially on the Chinese, the so-called Yellow Peril. Anti-Chinese laws were enacted, especially in California, where legislation was so petty as to target the ponytails favored by Chinese men. Some argued that Asians were not of the same species, not Homo sapiens, and if allowed to intermarry, they would lead to an infertile hybrid. This conviction somehow coexisted with the claim that the Chinese were unusually fertile and reproduced at dangerous levels. In 1882, thanks to growing nativism, the Chinese Exclusion Act was passed. It halted any immigration from that country, the first American law to specifically target one ethnic group. Naturalization was also forbidden. The law, which would come to be seen as the epitome of xenophobia, was not repealed for six decades.

During the same period, the long-normalized violence that targeted African Americans continued. They had been subject to the largest forced migration ever recorded, some twelve million Africans brought in chains to the Americas. Their presence had powered economic growth, and made them objects of their owners' moral depravity.

Meanwhile, the bigotry that Blacks encountered, even in Northern states, began to be openly decried by abolitionists. "Black-phobia," Frederick Douglass wrote in 1850, "was our national epidemic." Douglass parodied those suffering from "Colorphobia" and "Negropho-

Address given by an Imperial Wizard on "Klan Day" at the Texas State Fair, Dallas, 1923

bia," drawing on analogies to cholera and hydrophobia. This illness, Douglass noted, confronted him as he walked the streets of New York and Rochester. It had ruined minds, making the afflicted shriek and recoil from phantasms of differing complexion. "Ridicule and indignation," he advised, were the best weapons against such madness, until of course, slavery was abolished and equality prevailed.

After the great liberation came, with the end of the Civil War, "Red Shirt" bands in southern states morphed into the Ku Klux Klan, hooded symbols of anti-Black terror. Lynching became their weapon of choice. These ritual murders, like Russian pogroms, were often ghastly carnivals accompanied by food vendors, postcards, and prizes, which might be mementos cut from the dangling body. In 1892, 241 lynchings were recorded. Two-thirds of the victims were Black Americans; most of the rest were Italians and Chinese. Outrage abroad led to the federal government paying reparations to China and Italy.

As for African Americans, these forced exiles and perpetual strangers in their own land had no government to demand reparations for them. However, activists did rally. In 1898, a group called the National Afro-American Council formed to protest terrorist violence. The journalist Ida B. Wells mocked a civilization that would give schoolchildren a holiday to watch their elders incinerate a neighbor and distribute his ears, fingers, and toes as souvenirs, all because he was accused of misspeaking to a woman of another skin color. In 1909, Wells, W. E. B. Du Bois, and others like Henry Moskowitz, Moorfield Storey, and Mary White Ovington, formed the National Association for the Advancement of Colored People. Ten years later, they sat at the center of three hundred branches, and from that base they began to raise legal challenges to racist laws. Their 1917 anti-lynching campaign featured a New York City protest attended by 10,000 people.

The tribulations of minorities and immigrants in Great Britain, France, and the United States, the supposed standard-bearers for liberalism, toleration, and individual rights, exposed the fact that xenophobia was hardly confined to "primitive" non-Westerners, but thrived in these Western democratic lands. In 1908, writing on the "race question," the Harvard philosopher Josiah Royce dared to wonder out loud: "Is it a 'yellow peril,' or 'black peril,' or perhaps, after all, is it not some form of

TABLE 3: XENOPHOBIA, CIRCA 1920

RACIAL XENOPHOBIA	Xenophobia occurs when a Western emigrant is met by a reflexive hostility and fear based on the Easterner's primitive race.
XENOPHOBIC IMPERIALISM	Xenophobia occurs when biased Western imperialists invade lands that they see filled with primitive Oriental and Eastern hosts.
ANTI-IMMIGRANT XENOPHOBIA	Xenophobia manifests as a form of intolerance. It occurs when residents in Western nations attack "foreign" minorities as well as immigrants, often refugees or denizens from that nation's colonies.

'white peril,' which threatens the future of humanity in this day of great struggles and complex issues?" Xenophobia shot to prominence as a way of comprehending the revolts of the Boxers and other colonized peoples, but it boomeranged and struck back in the metropoles. As one French critic of anti-immigration laws wrote in 1908, the same "xenophobia" diagnosed abroad had swept through the halls of justice in Paris. Lest any reader be confused by its shifting meanings, he asserted that xenophobia was an aversion to strangers that only existed in unadvanced civilizations . . . such as his own.

In 1923, the *New York Times* opined:

Xenophobia is a disease more dangerous to a free people than a physical plague. If a political Pasteur could tell the world how to isolate and destroy the germ which shows itself in the indiscriminate hatred of other nationals or other races, in self-conceit and intolerance, he would bring to mankind a blessing of which it is greatly in need at the present hour.

Inaugurated as a rare medical disorder and a prejudice between rival nations, popularized during imperial expansion as an explanation for rebellious "inferior" races, xenophobia now took root in this new context. It flipped from being a convenient accusation by Westerners against foreigners to the failure of the ethic of toleration among those Westerners themselves. In this manner, the term would be pressed into service to make sense of British and French anti-Semites, French haters of Italians, the Ku Klux Klan, anti-Chinese Americans, and others who, while championing equality for themselves, seemed all too eager to deny it to others.

The fears raised by globalization were no longer a one-way street. They could not be limited to the colonized in far-off posts. As for the deeper source of this hostility, if it was not racial, no one seemed to know. One thing was clear: this was not a straightforward problem. Xenophobes routinely declared that foreigners—whether of Jewish, Chinese, Arab, or African descent—would never be able to assimilate, would always remain as an untrustworthy, foreign body. At the same time, many frantically warned that these aliens were rapidly stealing their way into the nation's bloodstream, silently mixing so much that they would annihilate the nation from within. Which was it? Being irrational, it was both. As a lawyer from the Maghreb ordered an aperitif in Paris or a student from Gujarat strolled through Kensington in derby and cuffs, there was an uncanny reversal. We came to your home to take possession of your past and control your future, and now you have come to our home to do the same to us. The invaders began to feel invaded. No walls could protect them.

CHAPTER 8

The Road to Genocide

THE TERRIBLE CORRUPTION of Western imperialism was not that it was simply a land grab based on voraciousness and power. Worse, it mingled some of the greatest Enlightenment ideals—human equality, liberty, acceptance, and dignity, a commitment to science and reason, the rule of law, and the rights of citizens—with the worst excesses of injustice, lies, oppression, and predatory brutality. The two became so entwined that they could no longer be easily teased apart. Imperialist expansion brought life-saving medicine and increased literacy, Locke and Voltaire, hospitals and universities, electricity and roads. Many benefited from the arrival of foreigners committed to these humanitarian efforts. However, the prices exacted—through indentured servitude and the ideologies of intrinsic inferiority—were heavy. They were made the more so by being denied, unacknowledged, and hence unchecked.

As followers of Tolstoy, Twain, and Casement, as well as Arthur Zimmern, Emile Zola, Ida B. Wells, and others advocated for equality for aliens abroad, and immigrants and foreigners at home, an imposing barrier still stood in their path: racial science. Across Europe and America, for more than half a century, scientific researchers had mapped genealogies, measured cephalic indexes, categorized facial characters, and timed atavistic twitches. Criminal and insane racial types were schematized, their shapes and bumps and colors photographed, quantified, and recorded. Seemingly objective studies determined that humans possessed unalterable differences and that primitive races were, by their mental natures, xenophobic. They spurned newcomers because to do so was in their nature.

But that was not all. Comprehending racial differences was said to be a matter of life or death. The mixing of races—much like the breeding of a horse and a donkey—would lead to extinction. Eugenics—pioneered in 1883 by Darwin's half-cousin, Francis Galton—looked to avoid such a fate and improve the human stock. His followers would eliminate an array of medical and social ills by recognizing who was born feeble or bad and, based on this "science," would restrict breeding. Galton's American acquaintance, Charles Davenport, spearheaded a campaign to deploy this progressive science in the New World. The melting pot was, of course, the eugenicist's nightmare. Open immigration posed a grave risk, Davenport believed, for it led to the amorous intermixing of unsuitable races. Throughout the Western world, politicians, physicians, and scientists dedicated to social policy and public hygiene sought to clean up their own genetic pool and prevent the ruin caused by miscegenation. Progressives and conservatives here agreed; normally inviolate moral standards dissolved in the face of science. Cocksure pronouncements about race justified discrimination, not to mention the isolation, sterilization, and even elimination of the biologically cursed. Western xenophobia in this context was misnamed, it was not a phobia or a prejudice. It was science.

Such claims helped to justify xenophobic laws on immigration and miscegenation. Jules Ferry, twice prime minister of France, argued that the superior French race had a responsibility to establish dominant colonies among its inferiors. From there, such thinking grew more extreme. Consider the founder of "anthroposociology," Georges Vacher de Lapouge. Based on his research, the Frenchman declared that the end of history would come when the superior, long-headed Aryans triumphed over the inferior, round-headed, darker races. It was inevitable, merely a matter of heads. Lapouge, surely a long-head himself, proposed that progress might be facilitated if one long-headed male impregnated 200,000 females of the long-head variety each year through artificial insemination. Mass breeding of this sort would speed up the victory of the fine-skulled.

In Germany, the supposed superiority of the Aryan race mingled and mated with Social Darwinism, in which survival was due only to the fit-test. Inspired by this mix of beliefs, Dr. Carl Peters founded the Society for German Colonization and pushed a reluctant Bismarck into found-ing African outposts. Race segregation and domination, he believed, went hand in hand. Such was also the belief of General Lothar von Trotha. After gaining experience putting down the Boxer Uprising, this race war-rior dedicated himself to the defeat of the dark tribes. Brought in to quell a revolt in Africa, the general embarked on the goal of not just defeating but annihilating all the Hereros, women and children not excepted. He too was fond of that murderous cliché: this was a race of "terrorists," who only understood the "language of violence." His troops killed 80 percent of the Herero population in what many consider the twentieth century's first genocide. For von Trotha, this was no war crime; he had only hurried nature along on its inevitable path.

With such doctrines, ethical niceties could be dismissed. Fired-up nationalists and anti-immigrant bigots justified their bias as self-preservation. Revanchist monarchists and aristocrats now could lift their glasses and make a toast; science recognized the import of their superior lineages. Progressives also embraced eugenics as part of the path toward a better future. In France, Britain, America, Germany, and elsewhere, theories of degenerative heredity explained mental illness, intelligence, crime, and sexual differences. Evolution had its winners and losers. If the long-heads kept winning, it wasn't their fault.

So, while from 1880 to 1914, among liberals and socialists, xenopho-bia had come into focus as a serious moral and political problem, in this other cognitive universe no such trouble existed. Discriminating against immigrants or minorities was not based on the ancient notion that the "stranger is my enemy"; this was not a phobia, tribalism, or emotional partiality. It was predicated on cold, hard facts.

Until it wasn't. Some peered into the scientific basis of these theories and grew suspicious. A new term debuted that flipped the original mean-ing of racial science on its head. "Racial science," some argued, was a dressed-up form of prejudice called first, in French, "*le racisme.*" Was that so? For the problem of xenophobia to be more broadly accepted, racial science and its hierarchies would need to make way for ethical claims based on human equality. That shift would take decades, but it took a leap forward at a massive gathering in 1911, when a scientist from Columbia University declared, with mounds of data, graphs, and tables, something stunning. Discrimination by race could *not* be justified by science, he argued, because there was no such thing as race.

———

OVER FOUR DAYS IN the summer of 1911, diplomats, intellectuals, scientists, and students gathered in London to participate in the First Universal Races Congress. They had come from across the globe to explore the sources of "inter-racial conflict." Sponsored by lists of dignitaries, the congress was attended by over two thousand people who gathered at the Imperial Institute of the University of London.

The congress was the brainchild of an American educator, Felix Adler. Adler was the son of a prominent German rabbi who had immigrated to New York City so as to lead Temple Emanu-El, a prominent Reform temple. Felix was meant to follow in his father's footsteps. He would dedicate his life to preaching, in fact, but of a different sort. After studying Kantian philosophy in Heidelberg, Adler returned home and, in 1873, delivered his first sermon at his father's temple. He would never be invited to do so again.

In "Judaism of the Future," the rabbi's son horrified the congregation by calling for a secular religion for all. Felix called for a nondenominational, moral community, one that welcomed Gentiles, Jews, and all believers, including nonbelievers. Shunned by the temple, Adler did not give up. At the tender age of twenty-six, he founded the Society for Ethical Culture and began to deliver popular lectures that argued for a focus on righteousness, shorn of theism or sectarianism. Echoing Las Casas, he urged his followers to judge others by "deed not creed." Do not be shamed by accusations of atheism, he counseled his listeners, and do not be frozen by the do-nothings who "loll by the wayside, rehearsing an ancient liturgy." Ethical Culture would be a "religion of duty."

As an apostle of this vision, Adler was indefatigable. Three decades later, a number of Ethical Culture societies existed in the United States and Great Britain. There was even an International Union of Ethical Societies, and it was at one of their meetings, in 1906, that Adler and his colleagues conceived of an ambitious conference on race and global conflict. Their idea struck a nerve. The Universal Races Congress was sponsored by twenty-eight different official government representatives, as well as representatives of fifty nations. In comparison, four years earlier, a conference on "Nationalities and Subject Races," held in England, focused on only eight nations. Adler's congress dwarfed that.

The organizers were determined to make this not another gathering where Western scholars pontificated about "subject" races. "Each people should speak for itself," the founders proclaimed, "and it is for this reason that every paper referring to an Oriental people will be found written by an eminent person belonging to it." In itself, one reviewer would exclaim, this was "a new departure in the history of the world."

In the summer of 1911, lecturers from Japan, China, India, Persia, West and South Africa, and Egypt trekked to London to share their experiences and ideas with scholars and diplomats from Britain, France, Germany, Russia, and the United States. In attendance were prominent intellectuals such as John Dewey, H. G. Wells, John Hobson, Emile Durkheim, Ernst Haeckel, and Georg Simmel. Anthropologists, sociologists, biologists, lawyers, pacifists, socialists, globalists, and other activists also came to consider the sources of interracial conflict. All the foreigners in their traditional robes and exotic finery made for an astonishing sight, one American breathlessly reported, as did the "freaks," by which he meant those Western "men with long hair and the women with short hair."

In pre-circulated papers, the organizers articulated their mission:

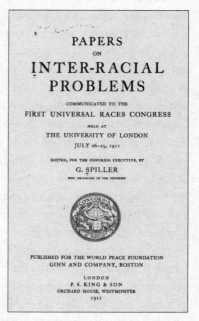

Report on the Universal Races Congress, 1911

The object of the Congress is "to discuss, in the light of science and the modern conscience, the general relations subsisting between the peoples of the West and those of the East, between so-called white and so-called coloured peoples, with a view to encouraging between them a fuller understanding, the most friendly feelings, and a heartier co-operation."

The tip-off was that qualifier, "so-called." For while many came to discuss race, others asked if the very idea was a mistake. The organizers' preferred answer to this radical question could be deduced from a pre-circulated questionnaire. Was it legitimate to infer mental differences from physical ones? the participants were asked. Were racial characters permanent and unmodifiable? These and other queries seemed reverse-engineered, for one of Adler's close colleagues, Franz Boas, would unveil data at the congress that answered both questions in the negative.

Boas would be recognized as the anthropologist most responsible for challenging science's attachment to race and fostering a shift by which racial science dissolved into racism. Like Felix Adler, he was a German Jew who had left behind his nation and his religion. Born in 1858, the son of assimilated parents who ran an import-export store, Boas studied physics and geography during his university years, where he also encountered the anti-Semitic Union of German Students and fought them off with more than his fair share of duels. After receiving his doctorate, he took to the seas to explore far-off lands, in his case the Arctic. His hope, as he wrote to his parents, was to produce a "fairly major geographical work" while doing work on psychophysics, which he expected would win him a university job. After weeks blinded by fog and frozen in ice, Boas's expedition arrived at Baffin Island, a German outpost among the Inuit people. Among crashing ice and massive fjords, the young man began collecting Inuit words and scribbling notes on their customs. For a year, he observed and photographed these Arctic dwellers, before returning home with a new passion.

On his second expedition, Boas explored British Columbia, then returned via New York and never left. He united with his American fiancée, whom he had met on vacation, and got a job working as an editor at *Science* magazine. By then, he had come to see culture, not biology, as determinative of morality. In 1889, Boas secured a job at Clark University and, seven years later, he was made both a curator at the American

Franz Boas among the Inuit, circa 1884

Museum of Natural History and a lecturer in the fledgling discipline of anthropology at Columbia University.

Boas reached out to Felix Adler and invited him to one of his lectures. On March 30, 1899, Adler sent a warm reply to "Doctor Boas," apologizing for having a prior commitment but suggesting he would try and steal away, since the subject "interests me immensely." The two men soon became allies; Adler was proud to have Boas on the "Committee" of the Ethical Culture school, and a decade later, Boas could count Adler as a supporter for a 1906 *Festschrift* in his honor. For by then, as Adler built his Ethical Culture network, the prodigious Boas had made landmark contributions to linguistics, folklore, and ethnology. However, like Felix Adler, Franz Boas was deeply concerned over sectarian strife, bias, and anti-Semitism. An opponent of racial hierarchies and Social Darwinism, Boas shifted some of his wide-ranging research to examine theories of race. Those two questions that were distributed to the entire congress were ones that Boas had come prepared to answer in his presentation.

"Instability of Human Types" held masses of quantified data that showed how supposedly permanent racial characteristics could be altered by environmental influences. Immigrants to the United States, after a while, found their children's cephalic index, a supposedly critical scientific distinguisher of race, mushroomed to American size. The longer an immigrant mother had been in the United States, the more her son's cranium equaled that of his neighbors. If cephalic index was one of the most scientific markers of race, and if mental differences among races were implied from those measurements, then that was all wrong.

Boas's science buttressed the suspicion shared by others in the Ethical Culture circle. Speaking before the group, Harvard's Josiah Royce dismissed racial science as all bias and egoism. And at the congress, Boas's views found an eager audience. The opening speaker, Brajendranath Seal of India, already had argued that racial types were fluid and dynamic. The editor of the congress's papers, Gustav Spiller, declared that the races displayed no difference in intellect or morality. All that stood between cavemen and those who wielded electricity, he declared, was their respective cultures. The difference between these thinkers and Franz Boas was that he presented reams of data, thereby meeting the science of race on its own ground.

Baron d'Estournelles de Constant wrapped up the proceedings by declaring that racial claims of superiority or inferiority were dangerous illusions. To hammer home that message, congress planners took the extraordinary step of arranging for the publication of Jean Finot's *The Death-Agony of the "Science" of Race*. A Jewish Pole who had immigrated to France, Finot considered scientific claims for race to be utterly ridiculous. "The term race," he wrote, "is but a product of our mental gymnastics." Races existed "as fictions of our brains."

If the congress planners were hoping for unanimity, however, they would be disappointed. A star of the congress, the co-secretary of the American delegation, W. E. B. Du Bois, worked within the parameters of race, arguing that the reality of the "Negro" and white races did not need to be questioned to reject false hierarchies. The president of the Royal Anthropological Institute, John Gray, insisted that racial hierarchies had been validated. However, the most ardent defender of racial differences came from Germany. A Berlin professor, Felix von Luschan, extolled the merits of racial science and warned of the dangers that attended mixing with "coarser or less refined elements." "We are all more or less disposed to dislike and despise a mixture of Europeans with the greater part of the foreign races," Luschan opined. "The brotherhood of man is a good thing," he conceded, but it paled before "the struggle for life." Racial and national antagonisms were natural. As for race war, the German cheerily concluded, it was nothing to dread.

While Luschan struck a discordant note, the Universal Races Congress seemed to be a remarkable success. One reviewer noted that the idea of race was now a question mark. In *Science* magazine, a Cambridge anthropologist reported that colleagues at the congress now acknowledged there was no pure race, while others concluded race was "chimerical." Felix Adler returned home having established a worldwide community dedicated to undoing racial prejudice, upholding ideals of human commonality, and reinforcing ethical claims against xenophobic biases. The participants spoke of a new chapter in world relations and planned their next gathering four years hence in Paris, the City of Light.

They would never meet again.

———

DESPITE THE CHALLENGES of Franz Boas and a growing cadre of like-minded humanists, and scholars, in the decades that followed the congress, it would be Felix von Luschan's view of strangers that drove history. The outbreak of World War I quickly silenced globalists, anti-imperialists, pacifists, and liberals who formerly had denounced nationalistic and racial xenophobia. In New York, Franz Boas dared to challenge anti-German jingoism, only to be accused of being a traitor and nearly fired from his university post. In a 1915 essay published in *The Atlantic*, W. E. B. Du Bois argued that the Great War, this "terrible overturning of civilization," was rooted in European racism and colonial rivalries in Africa. Pressured to desist, he too agreed to censor himself during the war effort. Internationalists and pacifists were worn down by waves of propaganda and the mournful sight of their nation's boys coming home dead. Idealists like Great Britain's L. T. Hobhouse soon lined up behind their flag, as the killing exceeded the worst expectations.

The Great War ended a wave of globalization that had helped define the second half of the nineteenth century. During this period, Europe's population skyrocketed from 188 million to 458 million people; fifty million or so had participated in a migration. "By 1914," a demographer recently noted, "there was hardly a village or town anywhere on the globe whose prices were not influenced by distant foreign markets, whose infrastructure was not financed by foreign capital, whose engineering, manufacturing, and even business skills were not imported from abroad, or whose labor markets were not influenced by the absence of those who had emigrated or by the presence of strangers who had immigrated."

At the same time, the warring parties of this global conflict were egged on by mass media, which made the other side into monsters. Fought for four brutal years among self-anointed "civilized" nations of the West, the conflict inaugurated total warfare, interminable trench battles, sudden death by submarine or nerve gas, and over thirty-five million buried, a number so staggering as to freeze the imagination. The 1918 peace brokered at Versailles led not to a full resolution, but rather to years of bitterness and tension. Striding forth like a colossus, American president Woodrow Wilson, whose late entry helped tip the balance of the war, arrived in Paris in 1918 having already presented his Fourteen Points for peace to the United States Congress. Among his points was one that garnered much attention: he demanded a "free, open-minded and absolutely impartial" adjudication of all colonial claims, through negotiations in which the colonized peoples should have an equal say in their fate. H. G. Wells later recalled that the American was treated like a messiah; his message would excite the hopes of Indians, Koreans, Egyptians, and other colonized and stateless peoples.

The last of Wilson's fourteen points was his call for a League of

Nations. This recommendation was granted, though, in a humiliating rebuke to their own president, Congress rejected the plan. The United States never joined the League of Nations, which was immediately charged with numerous tasks, including both settling masses of stateless immigrants and protecting the world's minorities. The Minorities Section took complaints and sought to negotiate with the accused nation-states. Ironically, the nation that most often petitioned the Minorities Section of the League of Nations for relief in its first years was Germany. In the wake of their defeat, they had six million ethnic compatriots who resided in non-Germanic, eastern nations. Meanwhile, the problem of unwanted refugees wandering about Europe became acute. As the huge multilingual Russian, Ottoman, and Austro-Hungarian empires crumbled, more than one exodus commenced. The Russian revolution sent more than one million "White Russians" into flight; Turkish atrocities against Armenian Christians, Assyrians, and Chaldeans led to their desperate departures. Millions of exiles lined up at Europe's borders in search of asylum, and as they sought help, doors began to slam shut. Debates over whether it was possible to assimilate strangers—many of another race—now became a matter of life or death. The League of Nations issued so-called Nansen passports to the stateless, the first being hundreds of thousands of Russians living abroad, stripped of their national identity by the newly formed Soviet Union. After a mighty effort to resettle half a million prisoners of war, the League's meager resources ran out.

In 1927, the League of Nations tried to again step in, this time by creating a universal standard for the treatment of immigrants. The presence of displaced foreigners, officials noted, raised complex juridical, demographic, economic, social, and cultural questions. Xenophobia, it was noted, could be stoked in such circumstances, based on trumped-up ethnic and national rivalries, as well as claims of biologic difference, which the league bluntly labeled "racism." A third category of bias was created for Russians, targeted for their political beliefs. Still, in the end, not one practical proposition was adopted.

The problem of exiles in search of asylum grew as European countries passed laws that allowed them to strip whomever they deemed "undesirable" of citizenship. Vladimir Lenin's Soviet Union inaugurated this denaturalization process; it spread to Benito Mussolini's Italy, Raymond

Poincaré's France, and Adolf Hitler's Germany. By simple decree, nations denied minorities their passports and their identity. Overnight, an "undesirable" was no longer Soviet, German, or French, but a man or woman of no country.

While dignitaries at the League of Nations decried the xenophobia at the core of restrictive immigration policies, the very extremity of these laws created a vicious cycle. As the quantity of deportees and displaced persons skyrocketed, their presence at another border en masse seemed to be a burden, even a threat. Fervent nationalists deemed restrictions ever more necessary. In 1926, the French newspaper *Le Matin* ran a front-page article that complained of refugees who taxed French hospitality, hospitals, and prisons. Such perceptions prompted calls for more expulsions and tighter borders, which kept this noose tightening.

Internationalists who dragged themselves out from their bunkers after 1918 tried to douse the fiery beliefs that still lingered after all this senseless slaughter. "Xenophobia is rampant in Europe," a Dutchman warned in the *New York Times*. "Xenophobia is an ugly word," another wrote in 1924, "and it represents something that is still uglier. Almost all countries from time to time develop a dislike of the foreigner which may even amount to hatred. France is no exception. . . ." In Great Britain, one of the leaders of the Labour Party believed that the war had destroyed the "spirit of tolerance." Now it was too easy to stir up a panic against strangers. "We do not have the Black Hundreds or the pogroms in England," he wrote. "In their place is the Xenophobia."

Early on, the great Black American sociologist W. E. B. Du Bois predicted that the central problem of the twentieth century would be "the problem of the color-line." As the century progressed, this prophecy could be expanded to include the religious line, the ethnic line, and the ideological line. Xenophobia was a violent form of zealotry, one of the greatest evils of the times. In an ever-more interconnected world, if strangers were enemies, the state of war would be permanent.

A gathering storm seemed to presage such a fate. In 1935, a call went out for the international community to address "world-wide xenophobia" targeting many different outcasts. A year later, an immigration expert for the League of Nations declared that Europe seemed to be in a "general panic" against foreigners. In 1939, another noted that the globe was now subject to "wave after wave of xenophobia." Jean Martin de Saintours' accusation could now be heard in English, French, Portuguese, Spanish, Italian, and German. Anyone keeping tabs would learn of Fascist and Soviet xenophobia; anti-Semitic and American xenophobia; Italian, French, Norwegian, Arab, Japanese, and Chinese xenophobia. There was political xenophobia, religious, administrative, and trade unionist xenophobia, examples of anti-capitalist, anti-Western, and "reactionary" xenophobia here, and anti-Communist and nationalist xenophobia there. It seemed the world was crazily dividing up and attacking itself like cancerous cells. But what caused this? The old racist answers were useless, for if there was any wild hopping up and down, any chanting around a ritual murder, the incantations were less likely to be in Swahili than in German.

EVEN BEFORE Germany's abject defeat in 1918, racial theories and anti-Semitism were especially rampant in that country as well as in the Austro-Hungarian empire. After World War I, these believers in their own inherent Aryan superiority watched in horror as they lost their colonies, saw their currency destroyed, and found themselves occupied by Belgians and Frenchmen. Even worse, they awoke to discover they had been "colonized" by Slavs and Poles, all degraded inferiors. For a nation that had become the third-largest colonizer in the world, this was a humiliating reversal.

Germany's path from fledgling nation to global power had been rapid. In 1871, the Imperial German state emerged from a rough patchwork of duchies, grand duchies, kingdoms, and principalities, filled with different dialects and local allegiances. The Reich was beset by endless internal rivalries. Chancellor Bismarck focused on national unification and followed the ancient strategy of rousting up and demonizing enemies within. He pitted the nation against Catholics, Jews, Poles, and revolutionary Socialists. Bismarck deftly isolated the liberal opposition by ranting against minorities, then cleaved them in two by taking up colonial expansion. A Greater Germany in the East awaited the nation, he declared. They would colonize Polish lands and create financial incentives for Germans to move in.

In pursuit of these objectives, liberal ideals of toleration, pluralism, and peaceful coexistence faded. Racial biology had chosen winners and losers, and it was the duty of the Aryans to win. To do this, they must stay pure. "The first commandment," one writer opined, "is: 'No racial mixing with aliens.'" Colonization needed to be accompanied by vigorous campaigns against Magyarization, Russification, Slavification, and Judification. Like the Spanish centuries earlier, this young mongrel nation made purity a rallying cry.

After eastern expansion, the Germans took up overseas conquests. And, like France, the lessons learned abroad filtered home. Bans on mixed marriages in Africa and Asia meant that the children of such unions held no right to citizenship. Nationalists demanded the very same treatment for mixed races born in Germany. In 1913, Socialists fought off these anti-miscegenation laws. However, such claims had won legitimacy and some traction. When they returned in 1935, the infamous Nuremberg Laws passed, forbidding the intermarriage of Jews and Aryans.

Deluged with positive news like the acquisition of Slavic lands, thanks to the Brest-Litovsk "peace" pressed on the reeling Soviets in March of 1918, Germany's sudden defeat that November stunned the populace. Peace meant that their nation was divested of Eastern European and overseas holdings; ethnic Germans made up the largest minorities in what were once vassal states. This inscrutable collapse led to wild rumors of an internal "fifth column"; the saboteurs were said to be Slavs, Poles, and Jews. Founded in 1920, the National Socialists were bolstered by a fantastical condensation of the Jew as both Bolshevik and greedy money lender, inferior Easterner as well as corrupting Western modernist, weak and diseased as well as omnipotent and manipulative. Jews became *the* problem. Resolving the "Jewish question" seemed to be *the* mission: it offered Germans clarity of purpose and the possibility of redemption.

"Old style" German liberals had been deeply weakened by the war. Toleration was said to be a misguided notion, both by those in favor of Soviet Communism and by right-wing intellectuals like the influential Carl Schmitt, a political theorist whose ideas were worked out during the peaceful interwar years, but were built for the next battle.

Descended from the contested French-speaking Lorraine region, Schmitt's family were small-town German Catholics existing in a Protestant land. The son of a railroad worker, Schmitt showed promise in school and won a scholarship to attend a gymnasium and then a university in Berlin. Tossed into this cosmopolitan city, the provincial youth felt alone. "I was an obscure young man of modest descent," he wrote. "Neither the ruling strata nor the opposition included me." He left the capital for Munich, where he continued his studies and threw himself into the intoxicating café nightlife. There, this floating man met and married a bohemian con artist, a faux countess who soon absconded with, of all things, his books. Attempts to annul this humiliating hookup failed, a fact that would later get Schmitt excommunicated when he remarried. Meanwhile, he took his state exams in Strasbourg, where he hoped to get a university job, a prospect that vanished when, in 1918, the region was reannexed by the French. He hung on, thanks to a string of teaching jobs, and wrote books on the politics of romanticism and the nature of dictatorship. Influenced by Thomas Hobbes and Max Weber, Schmitt sought to legitimate such mighty sovereigns. Their authority, he believed, must include the power to call for exceptions to the law, as might be required in emergencies. It was a line of thought that soon would find an eager audience.

In 1927, Schmitt developed his "concept of the political," an ambitious attempt to undo more than two centuries of liberal theory. Politics powerfully molded identities, he argued, and national identities were based on an oppositional dynamic of friend versus alien foe. Strangers were by *definition* enemies; there was nothing ethically improper with such a "*Fremdenfeindschaft.*" And what even constituted a stranger? It was "simply the Other, the Alien." It was the one who provoked the feeling of being "existentially" different. Therefore, strangers threatened to negate one's own existence. They needed to be fought off. In the same way that aesthetics distinguished the beautiful from the ugly, the political realm precisely sorted out friends from foreign foes. Pushing back against strangers, for Schmitt, was the foundation of political life.

The political was neither good nor bad, in his view, it was absolute. The stranger-enemy relationship simply *was*. States helped their inhabitants recognize those enemies, but the enemies required little more rational justification than that. The intensity of hostility toward the alien was quite natural and sufficient in itself. None of this was contingent on grievances or perceived crimes. For Schmitt, it was an existential relation and could be applied to all of history. Politics was war, humans were tribal beasts, and homogenous groups were founded on hatred of strangers. In a globalizing world, that meant each state confronted many foes and forever must be ready for combat.

While relying on the Hobbesian view of the state of nature as war, Schmitt was also reinvigorating a particular nineteenth-century German line of attack on Enlightenment universalism. The importation of British and French Enlightenment ideals into German lands was met with resistance by Romantics as well as thinkers like Herder, who helped prompt a Counter-Enlightenment tradition. For Herder, ideals of universal reason and equality were destructive, for they seemed to demand the wiping out of communities based on local customs, beliefs, and historical traditions. Despite a prominence among anti-Enlightenment thinkers, Herder's claims were always overstated. Universalist philosophies were intended to

Carl Schmitt, Nazi political theorist

establish a normative rational consensus around public matters, not take away one's lederhosen or pilsner. The Counter-Enlightenment argument tended to confuse the demand for equality with one for individual sameness; it conflated the protection of basic, legal rights with the crushing of human possibilities. In the face of his nation's humiliation to the French, British, and Americans, Schmitt's return to this Counter-Enlightenment thought can be seen as partaking of the same resentments that Herder voiced as Napoleon's troops swept through his countryside.

In 1933, after debuting his "concept of the political," Schmitt joined the Nazi Party and soon became one of its most eminent political thinkers. In that role, he legitimated the Führer's emergency decrees and, like the theoretician of the total state, Ernst Forsthoff, gave Hitler transcendental authority. He took up racial notions of German identity and called for the burning of Jewish books. The Jew was the Alien and political life was instinctually driven to oppose him. The very idea of xenophobia, for Schmitt, would have been laughable, a misbegotten bit of post-Enlightenment claptrap. Each state was constituted by its strangers; the Nazi Party had successfully located those of the Germans.

Germany had once incessantly petitioned the Minorities Section of the League of Nations regarding the unfair treatment of their people in eastern lands; now it became the leading exponent of an ideology that extolled the virtues of treating minorities like serfs, or finding ways to dispossess and eliminate them. For a short while, exactly what that meant was unstated. However, by 1936, the very terms of the discussion in German-speaking lands had become deeply distorted. Universities, an eminent Swiss professor of international studies noted, had been infected by this "fanatical epoch," which taught and practiced "xenophobia" and elevated such intolerance to what he sarcastically called a "moral principle." For those under the Nazi spell, questions regarding why hosts might hate strangers dissolved. Followers of Carl Schmitt might ask a German citizen: why don't you hate Slavs and Jews?

Adolf Hitler enacted Schmitt's theories. An Aryan supremacist and ultranationalist, Hitler's hatred ran deep and wide. He took up plans for the Jews, those internal stranger-enemies, and for Eastern Europe with its white "negroes." As his armies gobbled up Czechoslovakia, Poland, and Ukraine, the Führer made no pretenses; this was bare-fisted colonialism.

There would be no civilizing mission, no schools or hospitals, only the whip. Hitler sent troops and settlers out east to Germanize those lands and transform their former inhabitants into slaves, exiles, or corpses. His dream? A homogenous Aryan empire, rid of Slavs and Jews, Communists, gypsies, and the hereditarily unfit.

Alarmed observers like the German philosopher Hannah Arendt and the French thinker Simone Weil could not but note that Nazi answers for dealing with masses of racial inferiors had been auditioned long ago in the colonies. "Hitlerism," Weil wrote in 1943, "consists of the application by Germany to the continent of Europe, and more generally countries of the white race, the methods of colonial conquest and domination." Universal standards of justice inside the fatherland followed the course laid out in the colonies: they first became relative, then meaningless. Foreigners like the colonized Polynesians, whose children were taught that their ancestors were blond, blue-eyed Gauls, had been "deracinated," forcefully shorn of their history, their culture, and hence their moral and spiritual weight. After that, the rest was easy.

The relation between colonialism abroad and dictatorship at home was not just theoretical: it was personal. General von Trotha had become a military hero in Germany thanks to the war against the Boxers and then his genocidal suppression in southwest Africa. Italy's Fascist leader, Benito Mussolini, initiated a brutal war of colonial conquest in Ethiopia. Spain's Falangist Francisco Franco engaged in the reconquest of Morocco, aided by his ally, Philippe Pétain of France, the hero of Verdun who later turned into a Nazi apologist. Dictatorial lessons for managing populations now came home.

Civilians also had been prepared for the logic and necessity of extreme measures against aliens. For example, in 1885, long before Hitler's rise, a widely esteemed Sorbonne historian and fervent advocate of French colonization abroad, Alfred Rambaud, helped pave the way for others when he wrote:

> So what is the situation of the Jews? They are like an Asiatic colony established in France. They are among us as if in a foreign land. Triply foreign. They are neither French, nor Christian, nor even European.

Triply foreign. Not our nation, not our religion, not even our civilization. After being elected to the French Academy, Rambaud peacefully passed away. However, his words would not be forgotten. A half century later, when Parisians entered the new Institute for the Study of Jewish Questions, housed in commandeered quarters on 21 rue La Boétie, they were greeted by this same passage, immortalized on a large placard. The institute, founded in 1941 thanks to the Gestapo, reminded visitors that, for years, Frenchmen had seen the need to exterminate this foreign colony in their midst.

During that same year of 1941, the Nazi empire began its fateful overreach. As Hitler's tanks rolled through more of Eastern Europe, the dream of an ethnically pure realm seemed increasingly improbable. Facing millions of vanquished strangers, the Reich's administrators and military leaders began to strategize. Poles and Ukrainians were savages to be used for brute labor. Eventually, pure-blooded Aryans would take over from them, but for now their muscle was needed. Jews, however, posed a lethal threat from within. They would need to be ferreted out, deported, placed in camps, then eliminated. A program commenced for the "natural enemies" of German political life. In 1942, the network of Nazi concentration camps and ghettoes, filled with POWs and "undesirables," was joined by extermination camps, exclusively meant to gas the Jews, the disabled, and others. In the end, Carl Schmitt's natural enemies died in extreme numbers. Seventeen million European prisoners were murdered, including six million of those "triple foreigners," the Jews.

While the Nazis devoted resources to mass murder, their empire—which stretched from Finland to North Africa, from Crimea to the Netherlands—wobbled. By 1943, flashes of revolt occurred among occupied populations. At home, Germans faced food shortages and rolling defeats on the battlefield. Still, for some of their leadership, ridding Europe of the Jews remained a crazed priority. In the final months of the war, as utter devastation and collapse approached, a drunken Heinrich Himmler stared out at the smoldering wreckage. At least the Jewish question had been solved, he declared, and that was "something awesome."

The culture that had given the world Kant, Beethoven, and Goethe had been overcome by an evil commitment to annihilate millions of strangers.

The Nazi program of eliminative anti-Semitism killed six million European Jews

If the Black Legend of Spain and Leopold's Congo Free State once served as cautionary parables for mass murder, this twentieth-century infamy would now eclipse them. The nearly unimaginable crimes of the German National Socialists were Carl Schmitt's politics gone insane. The facts alone beggared description. So grotesque were the crimes, so immense, that to categorize them seemed tepid, a dishonor to the dead. Was this xenophobia? That term—with its nonspecific object, its depersonalizing of the victims, its broad range from minor prejudice to ethnic cleansing— seemed to fail to do these events justice. The Nazis' crimes seemed to have broken the back of language itself. "Xenophobia," snorted Alvin Johnson, the director of New York's New School for Social Research, in 1945, "what a word, to cover next to nothing."

———

AS THE BLACK SMOKE from concentration camps and the mushroom clouds over Hiroshima and Nagasaki dispersed, a dazed process of accounting began. After 1870, globalization had taken off and had culminated in deep economic, cultural, and political interconnections, as well as two world conflagrations. The second killed over one hundred million human beings. If one wrote out the simple names of the dead, they would fill 750,000 pages; if each was given a short obituary, honoring their children and parents, those pages would make a mountain. How might any word communicate such loss?

Before the gates of Auschwitz were thrown open for all to see, *Fortune* magazine considered anti-Semitism "the classic example of that dislike and fear of strangers which the Greeks knew as xenophobia, and which appears as a familiar phenomenon among primitive peoples and peoples reverting to primitivism." After 1945, that simply would not do. This was not some mere act of bias against strangers. Massacre? Slaughter? Atrocity? Four years earlier in a radio address to the British people, Winston Churchill exclaimed: "We are in the presence of a crime without a name."

"New conceptions require new terms," a scholarly jurist named Raphael Lemkin wrote as if in response in 1944. Born in 1900 on a tenant farm in Russian Belarus, Lemkin was a Polish-speaking Jew. His family were tenant farmers, inhabiting a contested borderland that in his lifetime bounced from Germany to Russia to Poland. Despite that broader unrest, Lemkin fondly recalled a childhood filled with roosters at dawn, horse riding, potato farming, mushroom hunting, and the sheer delight of tending to farm animals. At the same time, he noticed the way his parents' overlords mistreated them. Then, as a schoolboy, an odd moment stuck in his head: a man named Beilus had been accused of killing a child for Jewish Easter. When Lemkin arrived at school the next day, his teachers referred to him as "Beilus."

"As soon as I could read, I started to devour books on the persecution of religious, racial, and other minority groups," he recalled. His dark fascination pointed him toward, among others, the Christians in Nero's Rome. Why, he asked his mother, didn't the persecuted followers of Christ call the police? Her answer could not have been reassuring.

During World War I, as German troops raced toward them, the Lem-

Raphael Lemkin

kins fled into the forest and foraged to survive. Just before that onslaught, Raphael's mother, a painter and linguist who had tutored her three sons, hurriedly buried their precious items, including the family's books. Once the troops moved on, the family emerged to dig up their things. They resumed their lives without Raphael's brother, Samuel, who had perished of starvation.

Raphael devoted himself to linguistics at the University of Lvov before switching to law, already filled with the hope that international restraints could be created to protect minorities. While working as a prosecutor in the Ukraine and then in Poland, he studied the devastation of hundreds of thousands of Armenians, Assyrians, and other Christians under Ottoman rule, attempts, he determined, that were not just to win a war. These were acts meant to destroy an entire people and their culture. Shockingly, he discovered a bitter truth. War crimes applied only to victims from other nations. The Turks went unpunished for crimes that took place with their nationals on their own sovereign turf. The killers got away with it.

Eloquent, erudite, and passionate, Lemkin rose through the ranks in cosmopolitan Warsaw, and became an advocate for the "law of nations" in which states might be held accountable to a global body for such atrocities. He advocated for "crimes against humanity" with the League of Nations; then, in 1933, as the Germans were storming out of that body, Lemkin delivered a proposal at a Madrid conference on international penal codes. In addition to matters like piracy, slavery, and counterfeiting, he called for the explicit criminalization of the extermination of ethnic, national, or religious collectives by "barbarism," defined as the destruction of a people, and "vandalism," the destruction of their culture. His proposal went nowhere, and with Adolf Hitler in office, this outspoken Jewish prosecutor was soon fired. Lemkin nonetheless continued to pore over histories of group massacres and the building menace in Germany, even as the object of his study crept up behind him. Reading *Mein Kampf* and Hitler's public declarations, he began to understand the full intent of Nazi anti-Semitism: it was another attempt to wipe out an entire people and their culture, this time his own.

Six days after the Nazi invasion of Poland, on September 6, 1939, Raphael Lemkin hurried to the Warsaw train station, carrying little more than his shaving kit and a coat. Along the way, houses were "burning like candles." After squirming to get on a packed train, he seemed to be on his way to safety when Luftwaffe planes struck, hurtling the railcar off its track. Scrambling to safety, Lemkin began his long trek through the woods; he hid in barns, ate wild plants and rotten potatoes, and, with a small band, made his way toward the border. After months of walking, near starvation, saved by the kindness of random hosts, he made his way from Lithuania and Latvia to Sweden, where diplomatic connections got him out of Europe.

Having found a safe harbor at Duke University in North Carolina, Lemkin immediately sought to call attention to the mass atrocities that he had studied and then been nearly swept up by. Published in 1944, *Axis Rule of Occupied Europe* hardly seemed like a *cri de coeur*. Rather, it was a technical, dry analysis of laws and decrees that Germany, Italy, and their allies had imposed on occupied peoples. It drilled down into the ways that minorities were stripped of their rights, dehumanized, and brutalized. For this process, there simply was no single word. Bland concepts like "Germanization" revealed nothing of the stunning crimes being committed. "Denationalization" did not "connote the destruction of the biological structure," as Lemkin put it. "New conceptions require new terms," he concluded, and so Raphael Lemkin proposed the combining of *genos*, the Greek for "race or tribe," with *cide*, for killing.

"Genocide" was more than barbarism or mass murder. It represented an intent to annihilate a human identity, a collective, whether it was a national, racial, or religious group. It commenced with the destruction of "the national pattern of the oppressed group," and ended with the imposition of the oppressor's "pattern." To prevent genocide, Lemkin argued, there must be a radical shift in morality, so that even victors in battle considered such behavior beyond imagination. International law must codify such morality and override claims of national sovereignty. In this appeal, Lemkin placed himself in a lineage that prominently featured Bartolomé de Las Casas near its beginnings. Together, these moralists formed a chain, an "awakening of humanitarian feelings."

Skeptics scoffed. What would a word do to stop such slaughters? Nevertheless, Lemkin worked tirelessly to do more than get his word adopted by dictionaries; he traveled to Nuremberg to petition those writing up charges at the Nazi war crimes trials to use this term. In October of 1945, the Nuremberg indictments accused all twenty-four defendants of systematic genocide.

During his return to Europe, Raphael reunited with his brother only to learn that his parents, aunts, uncles, and cousins—49 members of his extended family in all—had been murdered. His determination became fevered. He stalked legislators, diplomats, and dignitaries, and after much behind-the-scenes lobbying, on December 9, 1948, the newly created United Nations passed the Genocide Convention. This human rights treaty was not just a reaction to the recent war, the document declared, but also the sacking of Carthage and Jerusalem, the routing of the French Albigensians, the victims of Christian and Islamic holy wars, and the Spanish Conquest. Genocide was an international crime against humanity, and it had just led to the death of six million European Jews. Lemkin's word became part of international law, naming a form of extreme identity-based violence, framing it ethically and politically, and linking it to some of the worst atrocities in history.

Lemkin's relief, however, was short-lived. As he pushed for ratification of the UN proposal, he found resistance coming from his new homeland. The United States refused to accept the Genocide Convention; some senators worried the rules might be retroactively applied to their own treatment of Native Americans or African Americans. This embarrassment, perhaps a tacit confession, lasted for half a century. During those years, Lemkin's law did not put an end to genocide, but neither did it prove empty. It helped spread a new consciousness of ways that the politics of division could devolve into a depraved desire to kill off an entire people.

WORDS ARE NOT just part of lexical maps or pragmatic tools. They may be incantations, invitations to imagine and remember. By 1945, xenophobia had become all of those. It started out as a name for psychological illness and extreme nationalism, then moved to notions of racial and cultural primitivity, before it settled as an animus against immigrants and minorities. After Auschwitz, xenophobia now also possessed a sickening, nightmarish resonance. Its very mention could unleash searing images of pencil-thin bodies in striped work clothes. It carried the stench of flesh turned into smoke, crushing images of children behind barbed wire, histories of immense sadism and cruelty. In the postwar years, the definition of xenophobia stabilized; it became part of that broader discourse deployed to stir the dead and warn the living.

Among other incantations, xenophobia still retained its difference. It pointed away from the "Jewish question," directly at the perpetrators. What was the source of their malicious desires? In the postwar era that cause, that *need* to be xenophobic desperately required explanation. Where did such inhumane hate come from? Why here not there, now and not then? Those questions were articulated by the American sociologist Nathan Reich. If anti-Jewish vitriol in Germany came from a "deep-seated, irrationally motivated state of xenophobia," he asked, why "may [it] remain latent and relatively innocuous in periods of well-being and social tranquility but can, under the guise of any rational façade, easily assume forms of active discrimination and hostility in times of strain and stress?"

Five years after the Axis powers were defeated, international migration had rebounded. Once again, ships filled with immigrants who disembarked in foreign lands. Airplanes, highway systems, automobiles, telephones, film, radio, and television ushered in ever more interchange between strangers. There was a foreigner at the gas station, on the playground, in the baker's shop, and by the schoolroom. Globalization threw more tribes together. So it was fair to ask: when and where would it start again? Xenophobia lurked in the cracks of history. Invisible for a while, it periodically rushed forth and loosed decimation, only to then disappear. Despite its countless victims, the nature of this beast remained elusive. It was clear only that, if the past was any guide, it would surely strike again.

To make matters worse, if xenophobia recurred, it would be accompanied by an additional terror. In a desperate race with the Germans, the United States had pulled together some of its best scientific minds for the Manhattan Project. On August 6, 1945, their achievement, the first atomic bomb, was dropped on Hiroshima. It unleashed a mushroom inferno, the greatest explosion in history. Soon thereafter, a second nuclear fireball consumed Nagasaki and led to the Japanese surrender. In two swift strokes, some 200,000 Japanese lives had vanished, and the Atomic Age had commenced.

After the joy of Allied victory, a slow, rising panic ensued. "What if" scenarios were articulated by the very physicists who had ushered in this new age. Given the genocide that had just occurred in Europe, the idea that a hateful despot might gain access to these weapons was unthinkable. In 1947, atomic scientists created the Doomsday Clock to measure how close we had inched toward the end of life on Earth. What would need to change to stop this countdown? What stood between all of us and apocalypse? A great many survivors concluded that what was required was another Manhattan Project, but one of a very different sort.

PART II

INSIDE THE
XENOPHOBIC MIND

These were the modes of a people, small in number, beset by dangers and in terror. They dared not think. If frightened . . . they shook and committed horrid atrocities in the name of their creed, the cost of emptiness.

—WILLIAM CARLOS WILLIAMS, *In the American Grain*

That invisibility to which I refer occurs because of a peculiar disposition of the eyes of those with whom I come into contact. A matter of the construction of their inner eyes. . . .

—RALPH ELLISON, *Invisible Man*

CHAPTER 9

Little Albert and the Wages of Fear

THE BIRTH AND early life of that political and moral peril called xenophobia commenced in the shadows. Coined simultaneously by an unknown doctor as well as anonymous enemies of ultranationalism and then reminted for colonial use by Jean Martin de Saintours, this term spread far and wide, floating about among foreign journalists and diplomats, imperialists, racists, liberals, and socialists, its meaning stabilized at times by one author and one context, only to be flipped around and reconceptualized by the next. After the Nazi Holocaust, the word's implications became more set. However, xenophobia had not yet found its theoretician, someone who could answer the critical question: why? No one had yet established what lay under the iceberg's tip. No one provided explanations that might make sense of this trouble's origins and menacing power.

In 1936 a League of Nations expert noted that the seemingly political problem of xenophobia was "in reality essentially psychologic." Intense hostility toward strangers had no single pattern, he wrote, but must be explained by a deeper understanding of the inner workings of those who were carried away by such hatred. By then, this claim was not novel. Philosophers, psychologists, sociologists, behavioral physiologists, psychiatrists, and psychoanalysts had already begun to promote differing psychic and behavioral explanations for stranger hatred. After Auschwitz, these experts—unlike the forgotten consuls and journalists who first deployed the term—became revered figures, even celebrities, who increasingly were seen as crucial to the survival of humankind. The man who unleashed the atomic bomb, President Harry Truman, addressed the American Psychiatric Association in 1948, and rather stunningly declared that world peace lay in his audience's hands. Such desperate hyperbole said much about the fear and the burden, the mystery too, that made experts of the psyche move to the foreground.

By then careful students could have recognized that xenophobia was three-headed, like the hound that guarded the gates of the underworld. This Cerberus was made up of knotty questions regarding human identity, its relation to emotions like fear and aggression, and, lastly, the nature of groups. If postwar thinkers were hoping to slay this monster, each of those heads needed to be lopped off, dissected, and better understood. Otherwise, in a continually globalizing world armed with nuclear weaponry, the same intolerance that haunted prior periods of history might make for mass murder on a scale never before seen.

These three interrelated questions were rarely taken up together; mostly, they were divided from each other. Different intellectual communities focused on what was most amenable to their methods. Some asked who was this *xénos*, this stranger? What made him or her different? What linked me to you, but not her? Others zoomed in on the misperception of threat that seemed to lead to either a phobic retreat or a violent reaction. What made the normal regulation of emotion, which routinely managed everyday dangers and forms of novelty, go berserk? Lastly, some noted that from the Chinese Boxers to the British Brothers' League, from the KKK to the Hitler Youth, xenophobia took up residence in many at once. It possessed certain qualities that emerged only in groups.

During the second half of the twentieth century, varied experts went to work on what seemed to be a catastrophe waiting to happen. Their efforts led to a series of powerful, if never fully integrated, models, defined by new terms, new explanatory concepts, some empirical research, and a slew of therapeutic applications. All this in an effort to make good on the promise, "Never Again."

WHAT MAKES A man phobic of strangers? In the 1880s, when xeno-phobia first appeared in a clinic, the doctors who observed this fear had little to offer by way of explanation. For most of them, heredity provided a one-stop solution. To explain phobias, models of inheritance could be deployed, including Herbert Spencer's model of Social Darwinism, in which human life was geared for the survival of the fittest; the French biologist Jean Baptiste Lamarck's view that learned experiences could be inherited; and Ernst Haeckel's contention that the life of the individual recapitulated the life of the species. Mix and match these speculative theo-ries and almost anything could be given a supposed reality, a biological cause, and an essence that required no further explanation.

Degeneration theory was such an intoxicating mix. It explained numerous problems—psychiatric, neurologic, rheumatic, addictive, and others—as the result of an unspecified hereditary decay. Family trees would be marked by this damage, which could even be tied to thinly veiled Christian sins like boozing and whoring. Through Lamarckian mechanisms, the punishment for these venal excesses, it was said, would be visited on the children. Evolution thus went into reverse. In Dreyfusard France, degeneration and its ills were found—surprise!—among "foreign races" like the Jews.

Alongside degenerative heredity, another proposed cause of morbid fear was trauma. A prophet of that peril was the American neurologist Dr. George Beard. Having cured himself of lethargy through self-administered electrical shocks, Beard proposed that many urban dwellers were short-circuiting. In the whirring metropolis with its ceaseless competition, the strain was much too much. Humans had only so much nervous force, and as one's batteries ran down, the capacity for emotional self-regulation diminished. "Neurasthenia" ensued, marked by unceasing fatigue, jittery states, and odd fears. Beard's 1881 book, *American Nervousness*, was taken up by the popular press. Early self-help books followed with titles like *Don't Worry (Worry: The Disease of the Age)* and *Why Worry?*

However, as the new century arrived, degeneration theory and neuras-thenia both began to lose scientific support. If phobias were due to degen-eration, one Harvard doctor quipped, we all must be degenerates. A third suspect now stepped forward: was there some disruption in childhood development? In this search for phobias stemming from the playground, the American psychologist G. Stanley Hall played a pivotal role.

After graduating from Williams College, Hall considered the priesthood but then went to Harvard to study with William James. There he received the first American doctorate in psychology, before traveling to Germany to train in their state-of-the-art labs. Upon his return, Hall became a professor at Johns Hopkins and promptly turned his sights toward morbid fears. Fear was the expectation of pain, he reasoned, and it led humans to consider "whether to fly or fight," his anticipation of the famous "fight or flight" reaction, demonstrated by the landmark physiological research of Walter B. Cannon a dozen years later. Acutely frightened individuals faced a stark choice: escape or lunge into defensive violence. Phobics were *not* just people who shied away from their fears; they were also those who leapt irrationally into battle.

G. Stanley Hall

Armed with this basic understanding, Hall sought to map out the fears of childhood. Unlike his meticulous, lab-based German colleagues, his method was simple, sloppy, and, like America itself, gargantuan. Hall sent out thousands of questionnaires across the nation to youngsters of all ages. Recipients sent back a landslide of replies to his rather vague queries. By 1897, Hall had collected more than seventeen hundred reports from infants to young adults. He reported on 6456 kinds of fear. Reptiles and thunder were the most common source of terror, but coming in third, acknowledged by over a quarter of his respondents, was a fear of strangers.

If Hall's data could be trusted, stranger fear was extremely common among American youth. But who were these bogeymen?

> Children's fears of persons are often at first directed to black, lame, ugly, or especially deformed people, to gypsies, rag men, Chinamen, police-men, coal men, tramps, tinkers, doctors, teachers, peddlers, and often extend to almost all strangers.

Hall hurried on from this list, never bothering to ask why the foremost stranger was "black"? What made the "lame" or "rag men" or "China-men" frightening? Instead, he offered a deeper explanation. Once upon a time, humankind believed "all strangers were dangerous." Now such fear existed only in sparsely populated areas, where the stranger incited unnec-essary trepidation and awe. Such worry was atavistic, irrational, part of a lost world. "Serpents are no longer among our most fatal foes," Dr. Hall wrote, and "strangers are not usually dangerous." The transformation of strangers from enemies to others we simply do not know was not unlike the conquering of a superstition. As children became adolescents, they mostly made this transition; the older adolescent didn't dash away from a Chinese boy. Knowledge and maturity tempered such reactions.

Hall's conclusions aligned with the beliefs of American progressives, who placed their faith in reason and education. However, he yearned for a deeper revelation. An unsure theoretician whose piles of data never added up to very much, Hall one day awoke from his discontent to an epiphany. Embracing Lamarck and Haeckel, he concluded that phobias were inher-ited. Great-granddad's dog bite was long forgotten, but little Billy, three generations later, on his first sight of a mutt, would recoil as if he had been mauled. Ancient traumas led children to instinctively distrust strangers. Once bitten, many generations shy.

In 1904, Hall compiled his masses of data and published *Adolescence: Its Psychology and Its Relations to Physiology, Anthropology, Sociology, Sex, Crime, Religion, and Education*. It was a fourteen-hundred-page tome that had the effect, by sheer heft, of making that stage of life an object of study. Near the end of his encyclopedic work, Hall confessed a desire to broaden his purview to include the "nearly one third of the human race" that lived in "136 colonies and dependencies" under "a few civilized nations." How did this relate to adolescence? Thanks to Social Darwinism, eugenics, and ethnic psychology, Hall soon made that clear.

Natives across the globe were "adolescents of adult size." Virtuous, confiding, and affectionate, they—like children in Hall's survey—saw strangers as enemies. Diversities that Westerners accepted, they found intolerable. Education could lift up these childish minds, but in the same way that obstinate children refused to grow up, some primitives rejected civilizing. If so, an unavoidable fate awaited them. Like the "great auk" or the "Southern buffalo," these groups would be driven to death. Never before, Hall marveled, had so many "lower races" been plucked like "weeds in the human garden." He listed these killed-off tribes—Beothuks, Aztecs, Tasmanians, Huichols, Maori, Burra, and Adelaide . . . he innocently went on and on. When the Nazis prepared their Final Solution, the ground had been prepared by progressive do-gooders like G. Stanley Hall. All that was left was to define the Jews as recalcitrant children.

———

G. STANLEY HALL WAS a transitional figure who explained morbid anxiety states by both childhood development and nineteenth-century evolutionary models. The next generation of American psychologists stepped free of hereditarian explanations and embraced environmental models. The most prominent theory in the first decades of twentieth-century America was behaviorism. It narrowed psychology's focus to external stimuli and their observable reactions alone. In this way, behaviorists rid themselves of the need for inferences about what was going on inside that black box called the mind. If the price was high—essentially a psychology without a psyche—so too was the potential profit, for unlike other psychologies, everything behaviorists concerned themselves with was observable and comported with the rules of empirical science.

Without saying as much, behaviorism actually banked on an older psychology called associationism, a theory that commenced with Thomas Hobbes and John Locke. The mind/brain operated like a loom, weaving together perceptions, feelings, and thoughts. Phobias, it followed, might be due to an aroused sense of fear linked to the wrong perception. Morbid fear of strangers might be the result of such a mis-association. Or so it was said. There was never much proof until a stunning series of experiments were reported from Moscow. In these seminal 1890s studies, the Russian physiologist Ivan Pavlov demonstrated exactly how, in dogs, mis-associations created physiological responses. Reactions once considered "inborn instincts," like the natural fear of strangers, now seemed to be clearly the result of learned connections.

Life for Pavlov's dogs was bewildering. The Russian scientist and his army of coworkers trained their canines to link the sound of a buzzer with a forthcoming meal. When they heard the buzz, they eventually began to secrete saliva in anticipation. After a while, even with no food in sight, the buzzer alone would create a "psychic secretion." The buzzer—mistranslated from Russian and passed down to non-Russians as a "bell"—led to a gush of spittle. The association of a buzzing sound with the (now absent) food activated a reaction in the animal's glands. Pavlov labeled this a "conditional reflex." Again, thanks to a mistranslation, it entered English as a "conditioned reflex," and there it would remain.

Pavlov and his dogs became celebrities. Scientists from around the world came to examine them and they left astonished. The Russian had demonstrated that supposedly automatic reactions—not just hunger but also fear and hostility—could be *created* and not only for truly terrifying stimuli, but also for innocuous objects. How many of the supposedly inborn "instincts" or "inherited illnesses" were actually conditioned reflexes? Was this the source of stranger phobias? Pavlov pushed forward, eager to unlock those secrets. He was awarded the Nobel Prize and received the full backing of the Soviet Union, after they realized that his psychology meshed with Marxism. However, despite his immense ambition, Pavlov did not dare to take the obvious, if morally dubious, next step. In 1920, an American named John Watson did just that. He applied Pavlovian methods not to a dog but to a child.

Born in South Carolina, Watson was an unruly, bright, and cocky boy. When his father ran off, he experienced both stark poverty and strict Baptist discipline. He hated both and was in a hurry to get away and make his fortune. After a lackluster college career, he demonstrated his self-promotional skills by talking his way into graduate school at the University of Chicago. Psychology there was being severed from philosophy, and Watson took up this new scientific crusade. Graduating with his doctorate in 1903, the debonair instructor stayed on to teach, and fell in love with a student, Mary Ickes. They secretly married, an act the bride's upstanding brother, a future political powerhouse, Harold Ickes, denounced. Watson, in his view, was a "selfish, conceited cad."

Watson didn't care. He displayed a lack of interest in niceties. In his hope to make psychology more biologic, he gained quick notoriety when *The Nation* lambasted his experiments on rats as vicious. Nonetheless, he was recruited to Johns Hopkins, where he took up rat models to study learning, seeking to extend Pavlov's work. In this effort, Watson was joined by a graduate student, Rosalie Rayner, who soon became his lover. Together, they decided to extend Pavlovian methods. In a foster home, they found a human subject and named him "Little Albert."

In their groundbreaking paper, the psychologists assured readers that Albert was a sturdy fellow. Then they detailed his conditioning. Confronted with a white rat, a rabbit, a dog, and even a monkey, the nine-month-old displayed no alarm. That changed when Watson and Rayner made crashing cymbal-like sounds behind the boy's head whenever the white rat appeared. Albert quickly grew terrified of the rodent. Whenever it approached, whether sonically assaulted or not, Albert shrieked and quivered. Furthermore, his fear generalized so that any animal that approximated a white rat drew forth the same terror. Watson and Rayner announced to the world that they had created an infantile phobia.

Children, they concluded, were equipped with two sources of innate fear: loud sounds and the sensation of falling. Every other fear was acquired from their surroundings. Dr. Watson believed America had created a generation of crybabies and nervous Nellies, riddled with irrational phobias. Aware of the social implications of his work, he also insisted that racial or ethnic "instincts" were created, and aversions between races or ethnicities were conditioned. "I defy anyone," Watson wrote, "to take these infants at birth, study their behavior, and mark off the differences in behavior that will characterize white from black and white or black from yellow."

Little Albert became famous. His case would be endlessly cited as the origin story for American behaviorism. It underwrote innumerable experiments, for it seemed to show that human psychology was sculpted from conditioned cues. But a follow-up study proved to be just as important. In 1920, Watson and Rayner had predicted that conditioned emotions in infancy would "persist and modify personality throughout life." However, a few years later, their Johns Hopkins colleague Mary Cover Jones showed that was not so. A child that she called Peter had been condi-

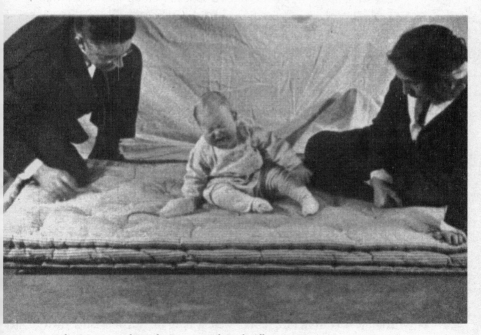

John Watson and Rosalie Rayner with Little Albert, 1920

tioned to have a phobia of rabbits. However, by presenting him with delicious treats alongside the bunny, little Peter gradually shook off his terror. He had been deconditioned. Phobias could be created through classical conditioning, Jones concluded, and eliminated through what she called "habituation." Armed with these twin models of cause and cure, behaviorism was launched as a potential remedy for individuals and societies.

The startling findings from this team at Johns Hopkins seemed to augur more to come. However, soon after Watson and Rayner published their study, their worlds fell apart. Watson's affair with Rayner became public; his love letters to her were entered in court during the divorce proceedings with Mary Ickes, and then printed in Baltimore's newspapers. Johns Hopkins dismissed him, and soon afterward, the founder of American behaviorism resurfaced at the J. Walter Thompson advertising agency, where he spent the next decades seeking to establish conditioned reflexes among consumers, so that they might reach for Maxwell House coffee or Pond's cold cream.

At the same time, Watson remained a popular lecturer and writer, who tirelessly extolled the ameliorative possibilities of behaviorism. Critics in the United States responded to his work ecstatically. In 1925, some said Watson had ushered in "a new epoch in the intellectual history of man." The *New York Herald Tribune* said of his latest work, "Perhaps this is the most important book ever written. One stands for an instant blinded with a great hope." The thrill might have been in the fact that American progressives—not to mention socialists and Marxists—found vindication for their beliefs in Watson's science. This "major intellectual revolution" actually confirmed their agenda. This was not without irony, for liberals needed to look past their commitment to individual freedom in order to accept science that made no room for free will. Many did, dizzied by the prospect of endless social improvement.

John Watson did not shy away from this adulation. The evangelist for behaviorism ramped up his promotional activity; he wrote countless articles for magazines, lectured widely, and even offered a course by mail. All other psychologies were ridiculous, he declared; his alone was science. All the riches and mysteries of the mind, from Plato to Shakespeare, from envy to adoration, from love to war, were stimuli in, reactions out. There were no unknown forces, no mediating mechanisms; it was all right there.

John Watson, like others in the history of science, confused the limits of what was observable with the limits of what was real, but in all the excitement, few noticed.

In the 1920s and 1930s, while its impact in Europe was small, American behaviorism spread into psychology, medicine, pedagogy, literature, and business. Its impact was perhaps greatest on education. Traditional Judeo-Christian ethics had created maladies, Watson believed. These destructive teachings needed to yield to sound behaviorist approaches. Numerous progressive educators agreed. The Child Hygiene and Mental Hygiene movements tried to apply his lab work in the classroom, where teachers might strengthen good impulses and weaken bad ones. A 1924 compendium, *The Child: His Nature and His Needs*, noted that while G. Stanley Hall had discovered "numberless" things that children were afraid of, Watson had proved that these fears were all due to conditioned reflexes.

Behaviorism offered a model by which fear was conditioned and could be easily linked to false, unreal, or mistaken sources. Economic collapses or sudden cultural alterations now could be seen as buzzers that shocked individuals into misdirecting their anxiety toward strangers. For behaviorists, those children in Hall's survey who feared "blacks," the poor, the disabled, and "Chinamen" had been conditioned to do so. These were America's white rats, waved in the faces of the jolted masses. Behavioral psychologists linked up with reformers, who joined in this new faith: change the stimuli, disrupt the conditioned reflexes, and make social ills like xenophobia into ancient history.

———

IF BEHAVIORISM GAVE liberals and social reformers great hope that they could recondition intolerant bigots and dissolve intergroup conflict, there was an equal possibility that the bigots might reeducate them. Behaviorism's emergence in America coincided with the rise of totalitarian states in Europe, especially Pavlov's own Soviet Union. The same psychology that might be used as a cure could provide a how-to guide for *creating* xenophobia. In his 1932 *Brave New World*, Aldous Huxley grasped the risk of such a dystopian world, in which—as he explained to his father—Pavlovian conditioning of children would be undertaken by a dictatorship. Flowers would be associated with shocks and deemed by all to be terrifying. Books would be accompanied by ear-splitting noise and equally dreaded. The state could flip anything it desired from safe to frightening, from loved to hated.

This was not just a fantasy. Arthur Koestler's *Darkness at Noon* described the way the Soviets broke down dissidents. The possibility of what a former American OSS member, Edward Hunter, nicknamed "brain-washing" in totalitarian states would lurk over the next decades. Pavlov, Hunter claimed, personally gave Lenin the keys to the kingdom of human behavior. A psychiatrist warned that Stalin had developed a special "Pavlovian Front" to indoctrinate the unwitting. For Americans, however, there was no need to travel to Moscow or to a dreamed-up dystopia to witness the effects of such negative conditioning. In 1940, a stunning novel explored the way this process unwittingly operated at home. Entitled *Native Son*, the ironic title announced its central theme. An American native grew up in an environment where he was treated as a despised and dangerous alien.

The author was Richard Wright. This grandson of slaves was born in 1908 on the Ruckers' plantation near Natchez, Mississippi, where his father was a sharecropper. Wright's childhood was filled with loss. His father abandoned the family, and his mother was so poor that she had to place her boy in an orphanage. He had little schooling until the age of twelve, but once enrolled, he excelled. Surrounded by racial insults and the specter of white violence in the Deep South, the nineteen-year-old followed the Great Migration to Chicago. There he fell in with a group of local Marxists, and the scales fell from his eyes. Dehumanizing economic forces had destroyed the inner lives of his fellow Americans, Black and white. Wright began to crank out short pieces for leftist periodicals like *New Masses* and soaked up all he could.

Wright had a big idea, which he spelled out in his successful application for a 1939 Guggenheim Fellowship. He wanted to write a novel that told the story of "Negro juvenile delinquency on Chicago's Southside," as created by the "strange and warped conditions" of segregation and racism. Published a year later, *Native Son* was greeted by rave reviews. It sold over 200,000 copies in the first three weeks; *Look* magazine and many others featured Wright. John Houseman and Orson Welles quickly sought the rights for a stage adaptation. However, some were not pleased. James Baldwin, one of Wright's protégés, condemned his mentor for letting sociological aims overwhelm his artistic obligations. This was a "protest" novel, Baldwin complained, in which the reader never came to understand the main character's inner life. His crimes were depicted as mere compulsions. This was true, but it missed the larger point. Bigger Thomas was a man whose inner world had been so mutilated that he had little capacity to experience it or share it with others, including the reader. He had been reduced to fear and conditioned responses; those *were* the elements of his psyche. He did not possess his experiences, they possessed him.

Written in a taut, riveting style, *Native Son* immediately placed readers inside that wide-eyed, phobic world. The first section, entitled "Fear," commenced with a Pavlovian shock. "*Brrrrrrriiiiiiiiiiiiiiiiiiiinng!*" An alarm bell startles Bigger into consciousness. He wakes alongside a brother, sister, and mother, all crammed into a tiny bedroom in the Black Belt of Chicago. A huge rat appears and runs crazily about, desperately biting and attacking them, and as his sister passes out, Bigger kills it.

This opening scene—with all its references to Watson and Pavlov— lays out in miniature what is to come: Bigger is like a child in an evil psychologist's lab. The entire Thomas family subsists in a world where constant threats from white predators and poverty keep them on edge. They have only two alternatives: fight or flight. The path taken by Bigger's religious mother and his fainting sister symbolize two of those paths— capitulation and a retreat into phobia. Bigger takes the other path: he will fight. And, like that rat, his mad, violent dash will be doomed, a protracted act of suicide.

Thanks to a childhood of chronic fear, Bigger's capacity for inner freedom, empathy, and ethical choice have been strangled. Wright exposes the way Bigger seeks to compensate for his sense of helplessness by adopting the pose of a bully. When he gets a break, he is too broken to use it. Hired by a liberal white family to be their driver, Bigger finds himself in the bedroom of their well-meaning daughter, the drunk, blacked-out Mary Dalton. Panicked that he will be falsely accused of rape when her blind mother enters the room, Bigger smothers Mary to death. This murder is reflexive: "It was not Mary he was reacting to when he felt that fear and shame. Mary had served to set off emotions, emotions conditioned by many Marys. And now that he had killed Mary he felt a lessening of the tension in his muscles."

When his crime becomes known, Bigger "stared without a thought or an image in his mind. There was just the old feeling, the feeling that he had had all his life; he was black and done wrong; white men were looking at something with which they would soon accuse him. It was the old feeling, hard and constant now, of wanting to grab something and clutch it in his hands and swing it into someone's face." Then, however, making the narrative even more disturbing, Bigger rapes and murders his Black girlfriend, just to cover his trail. He has become what white society always said he was, what it conditioned him to be: a violent monster.

After Bigger's capture, a lynching mob howls outside the courtroom, and he is asked to explain his actions. He can't. But, in conversation with his communist lawyer, Bigger confesses that his life as a Black man in America has meant one thing: constant, unyielding fear. A Mississippi newspaper covering Bigger's trial chimes in with the Southern solution of "conditioning Negroes so that they pay deference to the white person. . . ." "We have found," the editorialist writes, "that the injection of an element of constant fear has aided us greatly in handling the problem." That of course was not fiction. That was life for African Americans, especially in the Jim Crow South.

Reviewers picked up on the behaviorist underpinnings of Wright's masterfully paced tragedy. In the *New York Times*, one critic noted of Bigger that "it is Mr. Wright's purpose to show it as a typical kind of social and racial conditioning." The protagonist does not fully consider his choices; he reacts. In the *New York Herald Tribune*, the reviewer noted that each of Bigger's actions is traced back to "a significant reflex, and all of these, finally, to the social set-up that conditioned it."

For those who might have missed Wright's behaviorism, a heavy-handed introduction, written by the influential editor of the Book-of-the-Month Club Dorothy Canfield Fisher, pulled back the curtain:

How to produce neuroses in sheep and psychopathic upsets in rats has been known to research psychologists so long that accounts of these experiments have filtered out to us, the general public, through books and periodicals. The process seems to be a simple one: the animal is trained to react in certain ways to certain stimuli and then placed in a situation in which these reactions are impossible.

Fisher went on to explain that some rats give up and others madly bash themselves to death. Without missing a beat, she then turned to the American Youth Commission's work on Negro youth. This stolid and patronizing exercise was mercifully cut after the first edition, for Fisher

Richard Wright

seriously understated Richard Wright's artistry, wrongly reducing his masterpiece to a psychosocial experiment. In fact, Wright's extraordinary skill, another critic correctly noted, was what took a cardboard notion—Black America as tormented Little Alberts—and made it pulse and pant.

In 1941, Wright himself weighed in on the controversy in "How Bigger Was Born." He described growing up in Mississippi alongside many pseudo-tough boys who, having been shocked too often, grasped a moment of freedom in violence, before being duly lynched, maimed, imprisoned, or murdered. Bigger's "behavioristic patterns," Wright warned, were not limited to American Blacks. They were the same for many of the poor and maligned around the world.

Native Son remains a deeply unsettling work. It asks the reader to identify either with a brutal killer or with an evil social order. In so doing, it prevents any easy way out. Wright felt his first book, *Uncle Tom's Children*, allowed for sentimental reactions in which readers could take the side of victimized Black heroes without grasping the depth of American racism. *Native Son* allowed for no such easy identifications. The book also understandably made many African Americans deeply uncomfortable, for it suggested that white American terror had made their own people not just fearful but also violent. Worse, it played directly into the myth of the Black rapist.

However, Wright's confidant, Ralph Ellison, noted that *Native Son* served an important purpose. "In the novel," he wrote to Wright, "you sliced deep and opened up the psychic wound," bringing forth raw emotions that "tear" at our insides but "we Negroes refuse to talk of. . . ." *Native Son* shattered the myth of the pastoral, cheery, easygoing African American, those beings often portrayed in Harlem Renaissance works, who emerged from the inferno unscathed. In another impassioned letter, Ellison revealed that Bigger awoke memories of his own lacerating youth, and the way he too tried not to remember and feel. "We are not the numbed," Ellison defiantly declared, "but the seething." In the end, being able to remember the source of that rage and pain led the younger writer to note a kind of "pride which springs from the realization that after all the brutalization, starvation, and suffering, we have begun to embrace the experience and master it." "It makes you want to write and write and write, or murder," confessed the future author of *Invisible Man*.

Nevertheless, the immense success of *Native Son* must have given its author pause. To not tell this story, Wright insisted, would be to allow racism to silence him. But his astronomical sales meant his white countrymen were lapping up this tale of an African American racist. For make no mistake, Bigger *is* a racist. That was the daring gambit that Richard Wright took up. Deformed and traumatized by a white racist society, Bigger is forced to take his place in their bifurcated symbolic order of white hosts and black strangers, good whites and bad Negroes, as if all the shades and colors of the universe had shrunk into two. To survive, he has been forced to construct an identity that fits in that world and to constantly discriminate based on race. To do anything else under Jim Crow would be madness. When Bigger and his friends "play" white, they talk with stiff demeanors about golf and J. P. Morgan. And despite the fact that Mary Dalton treated Bigger with humanity and kindness, "she looked and acted like all other white folks," Bigger believes. When asked to explain his murder, Bigger says, "White folks and black folks are strangers. We don't know what each other is thinking."

It is only in jail, when Jan, Mary's boyfriend, and Mr. Max, Bigger's Marxist lawyer, treat the prisoner with respect, that his own racism melts. "For the first time in his life," Wright wrote, "a white man became a human being to him; and the reality of Jan's humanity came in a stab of remorse: he had killed what this man loved and had hurt him." Through exposure and habituation, behaviorists would have put it, Bigger's conditioned reflexes gave way.

Bigger Thomas's epiphany was also, as James Baldwin did not fail to note, a literary disaster. This beautifully paced novel features a climax that includes a tedious, preachy summation by Mr. Max, who goes on and on in Bigger's defense. It is a telling misstep. How else could Wright trust that his audience would reach these conclusions themselves? "Today, Bigger Thomas and that mob are strangers, yet they hate," Mr. Max explained. "They hate because they fear, and they fear because they feel the deepest feelings in their lives are being assaulted and outraged. And they do not know why; they are powerless pawns in the blind play of social forces."

Ellison, then a fellow traveler writing for the *Daily Worker*, could not help but note the strain at the novel's end. In Mr. Max's speech, Ellison wrote to Wright, "you were struggling to create a new terminology, i.e.

you were trying to state in terms of human values certain ideas, concepts, implicit in Marxist philosophy." Eight days later, Ellison reported that, despite this heavy-handedness, many in their circle still missed the point, which was that Bigger was "more human than those who sent him to his death, for it was they, not he, who fostered the dehumanizing conditions that shaped his personality."

For those who wondered, Richard Wright had not neglected to also describe the toll on the white perpetrators in a racist society. In his 1938 collection of stories, *Uncle Tom's Children*, Wright portrayed how this symbolic order turned them into Pavlovian killers. "Big Boy Leaves Home" would seem to advertise a coming-of-age story. Big Boy, along with three of his buddies, Bobo, Lester, and Buck, go skinny-dipping in a pond. Joshing and roughhousing, the boys tease each other and mess around. However, when they are spied by a white woman, the story plunges into horror. White Southerners also operated out of deeply conditioned fear. Black males, they have been taught, cannot stop themselves from raping white women. In reality, from the time of the first enslaved Africans' arrival on, white masters far more frequently raped enslaved women; somehow, this historical reality had been magically turned into its opposite. Stimulus: naked, Black adolescents splashing in a pond. Conditioned reaction: the white woman shrieks. Danger closes in. The boys scramble out of the water. The woman's husband, Jim Harvey, grabs a gun to "defend" his wife. He blows away Lester and Buck. Big Boy struggles for his life, and in the process Jim Harvey is shot. Later, from a hiding spot, Big Boy witnesses the tar and feathering, the burning, and then the lynching of Bobo. Our hero leaves home and three dead playmates, all washed away in a torrent of conditioned racist fear and hatred.

Jim Harvey and his wife cannot see impish children splashing and joking. They cannot feel anything other than fear and rage. Bigger Thomas cannot recognize how Mary Dalton, in her youthful, awkward ways, strove to treat him as a human being. He too feels conditioned fear and rage. The cymbals crash, the buzzers sound, and three centuries of racist hatred make them all react in a scripted manner. Racial fear and hatred have soaked so deeply into America's social fabric, it seemed, not even children would be spared.

BEHAVIORIST THEORIES on the conditioned fear of strangers opened a Pandora's box. How were these responses created, stoked, and unleashed? At the University of Chicago, an influential group of sociologists sought answers. Their efforts began in 1908 when a wealthy heiress, Helen Culver, donated $50,000 to Professor William Thomas for the study of bias against immigrants and other races. He traveled around Eastern Europe doing fieldwork, before deciding to study the problem in his backyard, with Chicago's community of Polish immigrants. Like most early-twentieth-century sociologists, Thomas hoped to use quantitative methods, but he supplemented these with oral histories, documents, and letters. While flirting with evolutionary points of view, by 1909 Thomas concluded that "the inherited mind of different races is about the same." The differences of intelligence *within* races was greater than *between* them, and much of those distinctions were simply the acquired result of racial prejudice. Environmental forces ruled.

The Chicago school produced work that often meshed neatly with behaviorism and the work of their former colleague, John Watson. Irrationally phobic reactions to foreigners were mistaken, conditioned responses learned in a social milieu. Reactions of fear, disgust, and hatred were wrongly linked to foreigners, but why? Thomas's student Emory Bogardus dedicated himself to that question.

Born to Illinois farmers in 1882, Bogardus attended Northwestern University, where to make ends meet, he worked at a settlement house then a boy's club. After getting to know immigrant laborers and "juvenile delinquents," he grew interested in their plight. He enrolled in the psychology department at the University of Chicago but was taken by the witty and wide-ranging Professor Thomas, who encouraged Bogardus to switch to sociology. After taking a job at the University of Southern California, Bogardus published his method of quantifying stranger anxiety, which he called the "Social Distance Scale." It measured the discomfort Billy experienced when consorting with his brother, then his neighbor, then a stranger in a store, then someone with a different religion, country, or race. A team fanned out and administered this scale to 8000 Americans.

In 1928, Bogardus published *Immigration and Race Attitudes*, which reported on responses to an array of out-groups, including foreign nationals (English, Japanese, Mexican), non-Christian believers (Hindus, Russian Jews, German Jews), and America's historical outsiders ("Negroes," "Mulattos," and "Indians"). He inquired about early formative experiences that might make the subjects associate fear or anger with a stranger. A few could come up with something: a Black neighbor killed my dog, one reported, and I've hated *them* ever since. Chased by a Chinese man in the woods as a young girl, a woman lived in fear of Asians. However, most bigots could muster up no trauma, no personal associations, nothing. Many detested entire ethnicities whose members they had never met. The most hated group in America, Bogardus discovered, highlighted this point. It was not the "Negro" (who came in a respectable second) but the "Turk." Among Turk haters, most confessed that "they had never seen a Turk, much less did they know even one." And yet this animosity ran deep.

Why? Bogardus had a thesis, one that made him credit the flurry of stories—145 in the *New York Times* in 1915 alone—that had focused on the Armenian genocide. Americans read "lurid headlines," Bogardus suggested, and tales about "the exotic life behind the mysterious veil and barred window." It was impossible, one respondent confessed, to divorce the Turk, in general, from their Muslim religion as well as from their killing of Armenians and their nasty habit of despoiling young girls. After watching a movie at age seven, another reported, he concluded that Turks had no morals. Another confessed that his most hated group— Mexicans—had been discovered at school. "I learned that Mexico was a lazy, hot, dirty country," he confessed. He had never set eyes on a Mexican.

Racial and ethnic hatred, in some cases it seemed, could be simply learned. It could be picked up in schools or the papers or the motion pictures. However, if that was true, how did that mesh with behaviorism? Where were the crashing cymbals that made one tremble before the Turks? These were just ideas, and according to Watson, ideas did *nothing*. They didn't even really exist. And yet here were 8000 subjects with a lot of hate that did exist. Bogardus concluded that phobias were formed by both frightening experiences and also by what he delicately called "derivative" experiences. In those cases, consumers of media felt *as if* they had been startled, wounded, or terrorized. They reacted *as if* these had been their own experiences. "The person who relies heavily on second-hand and hear-say racial reports usually gives evidence," he wrote, "of having entered imaginatively into them so often and so thoroughly, that they seem to have become his own personal experiences." Imaginatively? The imagination? Was there any role for that faculty in the world of Little Albert?

In Nella Larsen's novel *Passing*, the unwitting husband of an African American woman, John Bellew, jovially admits that he has never met a "Negro." However, he quickly adds, "'I read in the papers about them. Always robbing and killing people. And,' he adds darkly, 'worse.'" It was as if Little Albert had become a father who taught his children to fear white rats. Was such a heritage equivalent to Pavlovian training? Even Bogardus's phrase "derivative" experience seemed to be forced, or at best mystifying, since traditionally such "derivatives" were not considered experiences but rather ideas, the very element of the mind that John Watson and his ilk dismissed.

Despite these contradictions, Bogardus held the same hope as the behaviorists. "Derivative race antipathy is all-compelling," Bogardus concluded, "until dislodged later by a series of direct personal experiences of an opposite character." Exposure would lead to habituation. Meet the Turk. Know the Turk. No longer fear the Turk. However, Bogardus's sobering data also called that into question. Of the 4290 examples of stranger hate tracked over a ten-year period, only 8.9 percent registered any alteration at all.

Behaviorism created a powerful model for understanding the way intense fear could latch on to a stranger. Yet Emory Bogardus's results showed that, more often than not, a quieter route led to xenophobia. When James Baldwin complained that there was something missing in Richard Wright's portrayal of Bigger Thomas, it was precisely that—an inner life filled with ideas, imagined fantasies, intentions, desires, and beliefs. And it was there, it seemed, that many, perhaps most, of this antipathy resided. If behaviorism explained how some xenophobes were formed by traumatic "fight or flight" reactions linked to a stranger, something more serpentine was at work in many of these cases, where the animus took nourishment from a storehouse of fact and fantasy, symbols, stories, and myths. If one were to understand xenophobia, that cognitive realm would need to be understood. For while less dramatic than Pavlov's conditioned responses, it was ideas, as Joseph Conrad's Marlow knew, that were often worshipped on the way to the slaughter.

CHAPTER 10

The Invention of the Stereotype

BEGINNING IN THE seventeenth century, when John Locke pulled the mind apart from the Christian soul and made it into a natural object, this realm created great opportunities and complex problems. John Watson was hardly the first to insist that no science could enter that dark realm and not get lost. Yet common sense indicated that ideas were critical to human intention and action. Xenophobic bigotry, some suggested, was not external stimuli and reactions alone, but also due to ideas. That the most powerful cognitive theory of such bias would come from an American newspaperman, and be named not after Plato or Locke but a printing process, well, that was impossible to imagine.

Since antiquity, ideas were attached to grand philosophical questions about the mind's capacities to represent reality. However, a particular set of such problems had been forced into the open with globalization. Ideas often simplified and coalesced groups into categories. For example, in the eighteenth century, Western philosophers, doctors, and scientists took up this task of codifying and distinguishing humans into what John Stuart Mill in 1843 called "natural kinds." Unfortunately, these categories often proved anything but natural. A lifetime colonial administrator for the British East India Company, Mill himself sorted by race, temperament, gender, and age—a Herculean effort that, by the advent of the new century, was exposed as little more than prejudice. As critiques of the categories of race and ethnicity emerged, these self-serving typologies began to be seen as a reflection not of the world but rather of the way the prejudiced mind created ideas. Divisions of humanity into order, family, and genus were too often not based just on archaeological and biological verities, but rather fantasies. As racial theory was accused of being racist, nationalist typologies were challenged as xenophobic. Perhaps these efforts simply should be abandoned.

Or maybe not. What if these crude categories were not just errors, but *revelations*? What if they exposed the misguided manners by which the everyday mind came to erroneous notions of others? After the propaganda campaigns of the Great War, where such biased national types were put to murderous use, a journalist took up that question and, in the process, invented the concept of the "stereotype."

Walter Lippmann was not just any journalist. From a startlingly young age, he was an American power broker. Born in 1889 to wealthy German-Jewish parents in New York, this serious man attended Harvard, wrote for the *Crimson*, and studied philosophy and history with George Santayana and William James. After graduating, Lippmann moved to Washington and, as one of the founders of *The New Republic*, quickly became an insider whose ideas seamlessly found their way into the world. Despite his inexperience, he earned a reputation as a political whiz kid who had the ear of up-and-coming politicos before and after they made it, including Herbert Hoover, Woodrow Wilson, and Franklin Roosevelt.

Lippmann became self-conscious of the power his little magazine yielded, though initially, he was hardly squeamish about using all the tools at his disposal. "I just got back from Washington," the twenty-seven-year-old wrote a Harvard friend, the future Supreme Court justice Felix Frankfurter, "with the feeling *The New Republic* must get in the Brandeis fight with the heaviest guns." President Woodrow Wilson had nominated a controversial, outspoken liberal and a Jew, Louis Brandeis, for the Supreme Court. Lippmann put *The New Republic* to work so as to provide support for this nominee, and after a struggle, Brandeis took his place on America's highest court. Confident of the righteousness of his moral vision, Lippmann was not shy about using his megaphone to mold mass opinion.

When war broke out in Europe in 1914, most of America wanted nothing to do with it. Lippmann, however, called for the United States to

Walter Lippmann

enter the fray. When his call was heeded, he left for London and joined
the Inter-Allied Propaganda Board, where among other things he composed leaflets urging Germans and Austrians to give up. By the end of
this experience, having taken in the scope of war propaganda on both
sides, Lippmann became alarmed by the power that the modern media
possessed. He especially was disturbed by how the German, French, and
British outlets whipped up a frenzy of hate, using cartoons and caricatures
of national types. The Kaiser's helmet or the French beret were metony-
mies that defined and reduced complex human beings without a word. As

more sophisticated methods of communication like radio and film spread, Lippmann recognized that opportunities for manipulation would multiply if "derivative experience," like reading a book or seeing a cartoon, was all it took to create hatred and bias. The manipulative use of more immersive media like film could undermine democracy and peaceful coexistence. New technologies had the power to create imaginary worlds, what Lippmann called a "pseudo-environment," which could support deluded ideas about others.

Lippmann struggled to find a conceptual key that would help him articulate his concerns. In 1919, after five years of labor, he penned an article for *The Atlantic* but was not impressed with the results. He sheepishly wrote to another friend, the legal giant Oliver Wendell Holmes, worried that the great man would think poorly of his effort. Something better was forthcoming, he assured Holmes, a book on "how public opinion is made." In 1922, Lippmann made good on his promise. In *Public Opinion*, Lippmann sought to make sense of how mass democracy was dependent on a fickle, at times hysterical, foundation, and in the process he snatched a term from printing and altered its meaning.

"Stereotypes" or "stereoplates" were a variety of metal plates that marked an early-nineteenth-century advance in the printing process; they didn't require the setting of individual type and were used to swiftly make identical imprints. By the middle of the nineteenth century, "stereotype" migrated into general discourse to connote a mechanically repeated phrase or formula. It floated around as a useful metaphor; in medicine, a tic might be referred to as "stereotypical." In *Public Opinion*, Lippmann retooled this term, for it beautifully captured commonly held distortions of ethnic and national kinds, which could be created and then easily reproduced.

Though he seemed unaware of it, Lippmann's stereotype landed squarely in the center of debates roiling academic psychology, for it directly challenged behaviorism. Pavlov and Watson considered perception to be a matter of individual stimuli coming together in associations. There was no place for a stereotype in their then-dominant model. However, Lippmann's theory dovetailed with Gestalt psychology. Between 1914 and 1917, the German Wolfgang Köhler had proposed that perception was not based on meticulously piecing together associations; it was grasped all at once. Humans did not build up impressions piece by piece; they took in whole configurations through inferences, guesses, and biases. Stereotypes fit neatly into the Gestalt framework.

Walter Lippmann didn't dive into those deep waters. Quoting his teacher William James's celebrated description, he agreed that the world was a "great, blooming, buzzing confusion." Innumerable sights and sounds bombarded the perceiver as every moment passed. Overwhelmed by this onslaught, humans developed simplified and flattened signifiers of reality. Gesturing to Plato's famous cave of illusion, Lippmann asserted that the mind was built to distill, generalize, and then exist in a theater of its own making.

However, these shadows of the real world were mostly not idiosyncratic, Lippmann proposed. We are primed to pick up inputs that make sense with the stereotypes laid down for us by our culture. In the flux and flow, we grasp that which already has been marked as meaningful. Faced with the incongruous and undefined, we grab for the common solution, our culture's answer. In this way, stereotypes spread and one mind becomes much like another. When a stranger arrives in town, all that is confusing, threatening, and unreadable becomes tamed, contained, and defined when it is whispered that he is Russian. In a snap, the stranger becomes a known entity, a stereotype.

To drive home his point, Lippmann described an experiment conducted at a psychology congress. At a festive, masked ball, the experts on the psyche were hobnobbing, when suddenly a melee broke out:

> A clown rushed in madly pursued by a negro, revolver in hand. They stopped in the middle of the room fighting; the clown fell, the negro leapt upon him, fired, and then both rushed out of the hall.

Afterward, the stunned experts were asked to describe what had transpired. Secretly, the whole scene had been photographed for veracity's sake. Nearly two-thirds of the respondents got over forty percent of the basic facts wrong. Trained observers described "the stereotype of such a brawl." The visual experience fit into a pre-existing cognitive model, which came to predictable and familiar conclusions. Lippmann did not reveal what those communal distortions had been, but perhaps he assumed his reader's own stereotypes regarding "negroes" would fill in the blanks.

There was a great economy in having a warehouse stocked with such preconceived notions. No extra mental effort was required to get to the bottom of group or individual identities. But how closed was this system? Stereotypes, Lippmann believed, were rigid and not easily corrected; worse, they had the power to pervert the search for truth. The stereotype "stamps itself upon the evidence in the very act of securing the evidence," he wrote. Incongruous or contradictory facts received no hearing. If behaviorists hoped that positive experiences would lessen prejudice, Lippmann's model pointed to a source of resistance. Counterfactuals like a peaceful "negro" or a violent clown were brushed aside. Stereotypes ruled.

"By stereotypes," Lippmann wrote to an excited Dartmouth sociologist, "I mean fixed habits of cognition. . . . It is a pathological term for the kind of cognition which classifies and abstracts falsely. . . ." Negative stereotypes did not require personal trauma or frightening Little Albert–type experiences. These ideas, once established, provided an everyday answer to the problem of sorting different beings with their weird cultures, inscrutable languages, and odd beliefs. Stereotypes provided answers by which other nations, ethnicities, and genders were typecast, so much so that many were ready to fight and even die in the service of the cartoons lodged in their heads.

———

PUBLIC OPINION WAS published during a time when progressive and reactionary forces struggled over America's future. On the one hand, the National Association for the Advancement of Colored People had been founded, and the so-called New Negro demanded equal rights. Suffragettes formed the National Woman's Party and fought for women's rights, and leftists pressed for workers' rights. At the same time, these groups were challenged by religious conservatives, nativists, white supremacists, and supporters of anti-Semitism and European fascism. In 1920, with one constitutional amendment, Americans granted women the right to vote, and with another they sought to impose strict Christian values by the prohibition of alcohol. Affordable cars, paved roads, airplanes, and telephones brought citizens closer together, as Congress began to enact increasingly restrictive immigration laws, which culminated in the rabidly anti-Asian Immigration Act of 1924.

Lippmann was a witness to this push and pull, and his theory of stereotypes was a timely warning. A change in the way information was produced and consumed was approaching, and its impact would be enormous. If stereotypes were gestalts that could be created by simulated and reproduced experiences, then film, sound recording, and photography all carried great risk.

While Lippmann sought to alert his readers to such danger, others found different inspiration in his work. A graduate student in applied psychology named George Gallup began to measure public views. Sigmund Freud's American nephew, Edward Bernays, read *Public Opinion* and then created the first public relations business: a suggestible public who were offered the right stereotypes might be led toward socially beneficial waters and made to drink. And in Germany, a philologist, having just received his doctorate from the University of Heidelberg, became deeply interested in Bernays and American ideas on public relations. His name was Josef Goebbels.

Propagandists could now reach far beyond a row of pews or a Saturday fairground. Visual and audio representations of strangers had already begun to affect the citizenry, and only more of these mediated experiences were to come. The danger that lay ahead was dramatized by D. W. Griffith's blockbuster film, *The Birth of a Nation*. Technically brilliant and morally heinous, this 1915 film, based on the novel *The Clansman*, captivated audiences, who dizzily exited the theater filled with ugly visions of African Americans. The film itself was a justification of Jim Crow laws, and the taking back of the South by white supremacists after the Civil War. President Woodrow Wilson, who instituted Jim Crow rules in the nation's capital, made it the first film ever screened at the White House. The box office receipts were immense, over sixteen million dollars. *The Birth of a Nation*'s success showcased a dangerous new power to manipulate human cognition through "derivative" experience. That the director, a grandiose racist, would dare to follow up his widely criticized film with another entitled *Intolerance*—an epic that made Griffith himself the voice of *toleration*—only heightened concern that the movies held the

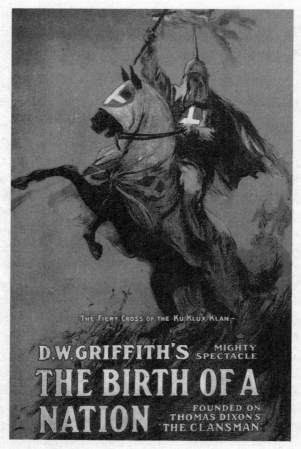

The Birth of a Nation *poster, 1915*

capacity to distort reality and establish delusions that might control the public as never before.

Lippmann's theory of stereotypes emerged as cinema became a worldwide form of entertainment. Unlike opera or theater, movies were more affordable, reached a broader swath of society, and could be shown anywhere, anytime. In Germany, France, the Soviet Union, and Japan, national cinemas stocked up on stereotypes of their rivals. In America, the film industry was particularly obsessed with racial stereotypes. Nearly every great technical advance in Hollywood was accompanied by derogatory images of African Americans. In 1907, the first animated film, *Humorous Phases of a Funny Face*, employed a joke about "coons." The most expensive film yet made, the aforementioned *The Birth of a Nation*, banked on stereotypes of rapacious Black men. Sound came to the movies wrapped in racism: *The Jazz Singer*, a 1927 picture, featured Al Jolson in blackface calling for his "Mammy." *Steamboat Willie*, the first sound-synchronized cartoon, was released a year later by Disney, and it too leaned on caricatures of Blackness.

Racial and ethnic minorities were rarely the main Hollywood characters, but more often were peripheral, intended for a cheap laugh, to evoke an exotic locale, or to spark effects like lust or contempt. Stereotypes, filmmakers understood, provided a whole backstory without any work. Viewers had these narratives preloaded in their heads: Aunt Jemima flipped pancakes, the happy barefoot Black child danced, the maternal maid tended to the white heiress, the watermelon-eating hick slobbered, while nearby the sleepy do-nothing somehow alternated with the sexually violent beast. Americans knew these . . . well, not people, but stereotypes. Little was required to make them come "alive" on the screen.

Animated cartoons made stereotypes even harder to miss. These were stocked with heroes, rascals, brutes, idiots, con men, and sexpots, each revealed with a few strokes of the pen. In "Uncle Tom's Crabbin'," the creators of the 1919 animated cartoon "Felix the Cat" took viewers down South to visit Blacks and their slothful lives. "Merrie Melodies" made a string of comic cartoons like "Jungle Jitters" and "Hittin' the Trail for Hallelujah Land." "Looney Tunes" created a character called "Bosco," ambiguous as a species but clear in "Congo Jazz" and other shorts as a send-up of African Americans. Betty Boop's "Bamboo Isle" used minstrel gags. Foreigners also provided easy laughs. In "Felix the Cat Goes to China," "Japanicky," or "Arabantics," Felix gratified his viewers' biases. The motto for these storytellers might have been "nothing strange not made familiar."

Students of the stereotype began to comb through fiction and journalism, advertising and art, but film seemed to be the leading offender. This attraction was perhaps in part born of the medium. The constraints of silent movies could be daunting; the famed French filmmaker Abel Gance in 1927 argued that film representation was a bare form of hieroglyphics. The expense of moviemaking also meant that every second counted.

Directors were forced to swiftly create recognizable characters. So why not steal powerful symbols from their culture and use what the German critic Walter Benjamin called an unconscious optics? In the early years of cinema, such cheap characterizations were combined with the power of the big screen—with its lighting tricks, close-ups, and slow-motion—to make a dazzling impact. Critics warned that no language had yet emerged to articulate what was happening to viewers as they took in the action.

Synchronized sound should have allowed movies to move beyond some technical limits; that it did not, however, showed that the problems were never merely technical. Filmmakers unwittingly relied on stereotypes because they themselves were equally preoccupied by them. For example, in the 1921 blockbuster *The Sheik*, starring Rudolph Valentino, the heart-throb at one point exclaimed, with a bug-eyed look, "When an Arab sees a woman that he wants he takes her!" And yet Ahmad was a kind kidnapper who abducted Lady Diana to win her heart. The dissonance created by casting the noble Valentino as an evil Arab was resolved in the end, when viewers learned near the finale—phew!—that the sheik was not an Arab at all, but rather a mix of British and Spanish. When his parents died, he had been adopted. The frisson of all this was so delightful that the studio quickly lined up their sequel, *The Son of the Sheik*.

As the lights dimmed in the theater palace, a world of unintelligible complexity, populated by immense differences, was transformed into an entertaining spectacle. Films, one critic declared, were "the most formi-dable engine of mass control the world had seen." Uncritical movie watch-ing, he wrote, was akin to a psychology experiment, in which derogatory and frightening stereotypes were created or reinforced.

Stereotypes performed a homogenizing function. If you got the joke—and the joke was so crude, it was hard not to get it—you were welcomed in as one of *us*. Lippmann himself proposed that tribal identi-ties were nothing more than a set of shared stereotypes. He scoffed at the so-called French soul or Chinese psychology or Bolshevik character. There have been "oceans of loose talk about collective minds, national souls, and race psychology," but these were nothing but minds infiltrated by exactly the same stereotypes. If John Watson's phobics were ready to leap at the first stranger in an alley, Walter Lippmann's were huddled together, cer-tain of their own place in the world thanks to crude typologies of others.

This then was one answer to the sociologist Emory Bogardus's conundrum, the one he faced when he realized that many Americans hated groups they never had a traumatizing experience with or had even encountered. One didn't need to know a Mexican to hate one. One could simply exist in a community in which stereotypes of vicious Mexicans were held. Behaviorist relearning, exposure, and habituation, therefore, would not always work, because a shared stereotype offered its own rewards. Undoing all this would be difficult, even dangerous, for Lippmann warned that challenging someone's stereotypes felt like an assault on their "universe." These beliefs meant that "[w]e feel at home there. We fit in. We are members." This was not just fast thinking in a tumbling, whirring world; it was a protected form of cognition that sorted out friend from foe. As Lippmann stated:

> And since my moral system rests on my accepted version of the facts, he who denies either my moral judgment or my version of the facts, is to me perverse, alien, dangerous. How shall I account for him? The opponent has always to be explained, and the last explanation that we ever look for is that he sees a different set of facts. . . . It is only when we are in the habit of recognizing our opinion as a partial experience seen through our stereotypes that we become truly tolerant of an opponent. Without this habit, we believe in the absolutism of our own vision, and consequently in the treacherous character of all opposition.

———

IN THE *Annals of the American Academy of Political and Social Science*, a reviewer proclaimed that the stereotype was the first great advance in Western political philosophy since John Locke. Research projects were launched, statistics began to be collected, and analyses of the effects of stereotypes were undertaken. Even the proud Nobel laureate Ivan Pavlov waved the white flag. After long rebuffing challenges from Gestalt psychologists, in 1930 the discoverer of the conditioned reflex added a cognitive element to his model, something that mediated between outer stimulus and behavioral response. He called them "dynamic stereotypes."

In 1926, the first American research trials on stereotypes were conducted by Stuart Rice, a professor at the University of Pennsylvania. Rice recruited 258 Dartmouth students and 31 members of a Vermont grange to look at newspaper photos of nine white men—a financier, a prime minister, a Bolshevik, and a bootlegger, among others. Who were these men and what did they do? the researchers asked. The results confirmed the hypothesis that class and ethnic stereotypes led to gross errors. In 1926, the journal *Social Forces* explored the way stereotypes rationalized the subjugation of the Negro. Experimenters asked one hundred Princeton students to rank ten ethnic groups based on their preference and group characteristics, amply demonstrating racial prejudice based on stereotypes. Pedagogues asked how stereotypes infiltrated a child's mind. Kimball Young, the freethinking grandson of Mormon founder Brigham Young, focused on how a child, oppressed by parental dos and don'ts, became angry and impulsive and then, when a negative stereotype appeared, latched on to it. In this way, he was stirred into "violent emotional attitudes and stereotypes toward the Negro or the Oriental or the immigrant."

Some resisted this rush to apply stereotypes to America's social problems. Their position had been previewed by the president of Princeton University, John Grier Hibben, in his 1911 essay "A Defence of Prejudice." If all thinking relied on prejudice, then surely it alone could not be the cause of pogroms and lynchings. Stereotypes, then, would be merely thinking shortcuts, bound to include errors in generalization. Big deal. Humans did it all the time.

There was something to this rejoinder. For the theory of the stereotype did not address a critical element, the emotion, that is the "*phobos*" in xenophobia. To integrate that element, sociologists turned to Georg Simmel.

Simmel was a rebel, and he suffered for it. Born in 1858 to Jewish chocolatiers, who died and left him with a sizable inheritance, this Berliner embraced a life of scholarship. His advancement in the German academy, however, was stymied by anti-Semitism, which dogged him despite his parents' conversion to Protestantism. Repeated rejection from superiors and colleagues, however, had a liberating effect. Simmel grew hard and fostered an aggressive, even theatrical nonconformity, as demonstrated in his untethered lecturing style and his free-wheeling prose. He chose to bite the hand that should have fed him, and refused to seek the favor of those who held the keys to his advancement. As German sociology turned away from philosophical models to quantitative methods, he remained defiantly out of step.

Around 1900, Simmel began to look more closely at his own marginalization and to take it as a subject of inquiry. What resulted was a sparkling kind of sociology as autobiography. Simmel assumed that raw experience was unself-conscious, akin to being afloat in infinite, unified space. Under stress, the pacific unity of self and world came undone. Forms emerged that divided consciousness from the external world. For example, in a sun-drenched Italian city, a walker strolled on the boulevard. Suddenly, amid the half-blinding glare, she was jolted out of her reveries by a passerby walking too close, cursing and muttering. Quickly she took hold over this frightening situation; it was a "madman." That cognitive form immediately regulated her beliefs and actions. However, was that fellow actually mentally ill or just distracted, or drunk, or perhaps speaking Urdu? Simmel's "fragmentary form," like Lippmann's stereotype, provided a swift answer. Forms came to our rescue, but they then could create problems as they locked in.

Simmel took pains to explore different "forms," from the "leader" and the "miser" to the "prostitute" and the "stranger." The last one remained closest to his heart. For Simmel, despite friendships with celebrities like Max Weber and Rainer Maria Rilke, remained on the periphery of his society. His unconventional writings had begun to slip into obscurity when an American student seized on this stranger's work and revived it.

Robert Park was an unlikely conduit for fancy European philosophizing. Born in Harveyville, Pennsylvania, and raised in Minnesota, he was such a lousy student that his father, a grocer, initially refused to throw away money on college. The boy ran away and enrolled himself. After receiving his undergraduate degree, Park became a journalist and editor who wrote stories on the underclass, covering everything from their stoicism and courage to gambling rings and opium addiction. At the ripe age of thirty-five, he decided to go back to school. He studied philosophy at Harvard with Josiah Royce and William James before traveling

to Berlin to pursue his doctorate. Park took several courses with Georg
Simmel, before he completed a thesis in Heidelberg on problems of mass
psychology.

As a former journalist, Park was well aware of the way in which the
masses could be manipulated. While in Europe, he was shaken to learn of
King Leopold's genocide in the Congo. After returning home, he secured
a position at Harvard, became the secretary of his local Congo Reform
Association branch, and began to plot a trip to South Africa. Park reached
out for advice to Booker T. Washington at the Tuskegee Institute and
visited with him, only to realize that the situation with the "Negro" in
the American South was not that different than in South Africa. When
Washington offered him the opportunity to stay at Tuskegee, Park leapt at
the chance. After seven years of field research, Park joined W. I. Thomas
and others, to make the University of Chicago a powerhouse for the study
of sociology.

One of the department's founders, Albion Small, had translated Simmel and introduced him to readers of the *American Journal of Sociology*.
Robert Park went further, merging Lippmann's concept of the stereotype
with Simmel's notion of forms:

> [E]very society had its own universe of discourse, and that is what Wal-
> ter Lippmann means when he says that the public thinks only in ste-
> reotypes. There is, in fact, no other way in which the public can think.
> Where there is substantial agreement as to the categories, as there is
> bound to be in every stable society, there the status of every individual
> is defined by the class in which, by tradition or general consensus, he
> happens to find himself. The individual who is in no class at all is a
> pariah and an outlaw.

Stable stereotypes were ubiquitous, nearly invisible, and were the basis
of social knowledge. However, as Simmel showed, turmoil fostered the
need for new forms. With conflict, new winners and losers would emerge
as would new stereotypes. The "Southern Negro," after being freed from
slavery, for example, was a "stranger." Was he coming for our jobs, our
women, our children, our identities? Was he coming for revenge? Fear
incited the manufacturing of a new stereotype. This form would contain

and manage those intense emotions. Social anxieties, according to Park, were codified and managed through emergent stereotypes, even as they divided up communities.

This especially applied to strangers. The stranger, according to Simmel, was the wanderer who came and then stayed. As such, he existed both within that collective's prevailing beliefs and a bit beyond their reach. His point of view was privileged, for he could lucidly observe community assumptions and proclivities up close; however, thanks to his outsider status, he was free from demands to conform to those rules, rituals, and illusions. This was the stranger's advantage: he could know what the insiders knew, but also what they had been compelled to ignore. He lived inside the law, but he was an outlaw.

In return for all that, Simmel argued, the stranger was treated with a double dose of suspicion and anger. For those whose individuality was constantly oppressed by the demands of the collective, the stranger's freedom was enraging. His capacity for critical distance—the freedom to see when the emperor had no clothes—also made him a threat. For all this, he was stereotyped not just as odd, but also as irrational and a danger. This was the way that the "*xénos*" engendered a phobia. And the classic example of such an envied and dangerous stranger, Simmel suggested, was the European Jew.

Park expanded on this brilliant analysis. Worldwide immigration had deposited strangers in every port and polity. It had created a new kind of "marginal man." This foreigner settled on society's periphery, then, after the shock of arrival wore off, he would find himself in conflict. The marginal man would struggle to integrate two distinct sets of stereotypes from his old and new cultures. Global intermixing of this sort fostered the emergence of a "new type of personality," the "cultural hybrid," and it was precisely there, Park believed, that hope for the future resided. A new global civilization was quietly being born "in the mind of the marginal man."

Of course, the old world resisted. In cultures where no integration was tolerated, the marginal man would need to hide. If hybridity brought with it a brew of bigotry, exclusion, and even violence, this creative mixing would be disrupted. In more open cultures, like in the welcoming lands of Latin America or Hawaii, Park argued, strangers married locals and their progeny openly forged new identities. In places where the old stereotypes strictly held, the stranger remained perpetually outside, a foreign body. Such a cultural refusal of passage was exemplified by the fate of European Jews and American Blacks.

With globalization, marginal men were omnipresent, as was the inner and outer conflict they might engender. W. E. B. Du Bois described this as "double consciousness," where self-consciousness as an American and as a Black person were "two warring ideals in one dark body." T. E. Lawrence also wrote of a battle waged between British stereotypes of the "Semitic mind" and Arab stereotypes of the British. "Sometimes," he wrote, "these selves would converse in the void, and then madness was very near, as I believe it would be near the man who could see things through the veils at once of two systems, two educations, and two environments."

DESPITE ITS easy integration with Köhler's Gestalt psychology, the idea of the "stereotype" did not catch on in Europe, but over the next decades in the United States, journalists and critics used this notion to critique stock characters in plays and movies. Stereotypes were also said to be the cause of failures in international diplomacy and the unreliability of court witnesses. Most centrally, however, cartoonish depictions of African Americans, Jews, immigrants, and ethnic types were seen as socially toxic, in part responsible for race bias and class tensions, and rife in newspapers, magazines, cartoons, literature, cinema, theater, and marketing campaigns. Demeaning stereotypes were so common for Madison Avenue advertisers and mass journalism that they seemed essential to those domains. Aunt Jemima sold syrup and the *Saturday Evening Post* shamelessly trafficked in cartoons of dangerous immigrants. Meanwhile, Hollywood continued to sleepwalk. In 1930, the Hays Code forbade film depictions of interracial love, and nine years later, the largest-grossing film of all time, *Gone With the Wind*, was released. Based on a novel by Margaret Mitchell, an early devotee of Thomas Dixon's novels of the South like *The Clansman*, *Gone With the Wind* originally included an explicit reference to the Ku Klux Klan riding to rescue Scarlet O'Hara. Through the intervention of the producer, that was deleted, and criticisms of the blatant stereotypes in the blockbuster movie were drowned out by wild applause.

However, a self-consciousness about stereotypes began to creep into American culture. The Harlem Renaissance commenced with a rejection of degraded and debased stereotypes. The dean of that cultural outpouring, Alain Locke, denounced Southern Reconstruction literature for its "stereotypes by which the Negro is still popularly known." Locke helped foster notions of the cultured and refined "New Negro." George Schuyler called out depictions of Aunt Jemima and Uncle Tom as a "composite stereotype." Theater pieces now dismissed blackface and minstrel caricatures. Instead, Langston Hughes, Zora Neale Hurston, James Weldon Johnson, Claude McKay, and Countee Cullen shot to prominence by revealing a depth of character and complex subjectivity obscured by these crude forms.

At the same time, American immigrants began to find publishers for their own stories, ones that, by their depictions of complex individuality, often negated stereotypes. Fiction here took up its moral function, as readers encountered a stranger and, in a coming together on the page, became their intimates. Abraham Cahan's *The Rise of David Levinsky* chronicled the travails of Jewish immigrants; Irish Americans found their struggles depicted in James T. Farrell's *Studs Lonigan* trilogy. Stories of Norwegians in the Dakotas, Syrians in Brooklyn, Chinese on the West Coast, and Bohemians in Nebraska added to this mix. Often, these narratives featured bewildered foreigners who wrestled to make sense of the New World, alongside hosts who struggled with preconceptions about these aliens.

This same process of awakening and recognition was more difficult in film, for as the German playwright Bertolt Brecht noted, the inner life of characters in the movies took a back seat to actions and visual effects. In Europe, governments had already grasped the power of this new art form for not undercutting, but rather promoting, useful stereotypes. During World War I, the once sleepy German moviemaking industry grew tenfold; Vladimir Lenin pronounced film to be the most important art for the revolution; and Benito Mussolini handed the film industry to his brother, who was tasked with creating bombastic nationalistic epics. As

World War II commenced, the American Office of War Information also looked to Hollywood. However, their task was different.

Facing a zealously anti-Semitic and racist enemy, the military recognized that these same fissures in American society posed a threat to the war effort. Their job was made trickier by Executive Order 9066, signed by Franklin Delano Roosevelt on February 19, 1942, which rounded up 112,000 Japanese, including 79,000 United States citizens, and placed them in internment camps. Though this order was upheld in the Supreme Court, Justice Frank Murphy noted "a melancholy resemblance to the treatment accorded the Jewish race in Germany." Then there was the 1941 threat of a massive Negro March on Washington protesting Jim Crow discrimination, a spectacle quelled only after a horrified Roosevelt agreed to use an executive order to ban racial discrimination in defense industries. In 1942, former Republican presidential candidate Wendell Willkie delivered an address to the NAACP in which he called on moviemakers to take this opportunity to drop their African American stereotypes. A year later, before the Hollywood Writers' Congress, the soon-to-be-blacklisted screenwriter Dalton Trumbo pointed out that the "most gigantic milestones of our appeal to public patronage have been the anti-Negro pictures, *The Birth of a Nation* and *Gone With the Wind*." This homegrown legacy of race hatred muddied the moral waters and hurt the war effort against Hitler.

To remedy this, the Office of War Information enlisted the director Frank Capra, a hitmaker responsible for *Mr. Smith Goes to Washington*. Capra's first effort in a series called *Why We Fight* was a fifty-minute documentary called *Prelude to War*, which laid out the rise of race hatred in Germany, Italy, and Japan. Capra called on the authority of Moses, Mohammed, Confucius, and Christ, and claimed them all as foundations of American equality.

If, as Renan argued, it was in the very nature of nations to forget their own debacles, their enemies tended not to play by the same rules. Capra knew that America's foes would seek to sow division by forcing American racism to the fore. To combat such German propaganda, Capra produced *The Negro Soldier*, in which he countered negative stereotypes and wove a heroic tale of African American patriots, from Crispus Attucks forward. African Americans were exhorted to enlist in the fight against

Hitler, the monster who called them "half-monkeys." Other films, like *The House I Live In*, starring Frank Sinatra, confronted American anti-Semites and reminded theater audiences that "the home of the free" was for all immigrants. While the United States positioned itself as the antithesis of German and Japanese racism, its propagandists sought to purify their nation of its past by pivoting against these dehumanizing stereotypes and promoting the "self-evident" truths enshrined in the Declaration of Independence.

These war efforts made a splash, but none matched the reception of a slim pamphlet called *The Races of Mankind*. The leaflet was written by two former students of Franz Boas, the anthropologists Ruth Benedict and Gene Weltfish. Professor Boas, after his takedown of racial science in London, had turned his studies toward the laws that governed cooperative societies. In the process, he helped move his field toward cultural anthropology. Much earlier, in 1871, Edward Tylor had argued that cultures came in three successive stages: primitive, barbaric, and civilized. Cultures therefore could evolve. Boas studied tribes who, by custom and myth, considered all strangers to be enemies, then changed:

> We can trace the gradual broadening of the feeling of fellowship during the advance of civilization. The feeling of fellowship in the horde expands to the feeling of unity of the tribe, to the recognition of bonds established by a neighborhood of habitat, and further on to the feeling of fellowship among members of nations. This seems to be the limit of the ethical concept of fellowship of man which we have reached at the present time.

The Trobriand Islanders, who believed white men were ghosts, and the Germans who persecuted Jews for world domination were no different for Boas; both were culturally devolved. If human hordes first saw all strangers as enemies, once social units grew in size and diversity and began to act cooperatively, economic complexity and interdependence led to decreased hostility. Nonetheless, a primal abhorrence to strange hordes did not dissolve. It remained in what Boas called the "so-called race-instincts." These hatreds—white against Black, Christian against Jew—were not really instincts but rather the mobilization of emotion so as to reinforce social cohesion. Whites hated Blacks so as to feel whiter. Cultural myths, repeated over and over—what Lippmann would call stereotypes—served the same function. If a tribe of islanders shared a myth that whites were from another planet, their bonds grew closer.

For over four decades, American anthropology was under the sway of Franz Boas and his wide network of anthropologists, luminaries who included African American Zora Neale Hurston and Native Americans Ella Deloria and William Jones, as well as Margaret Mead, Edward Sapir, and Ruth Benedict. For them, understanding the way that in-groups reviled outsiders, Boas concluded, was to be a central and critical task:

> Most important of all, if we understand that the feeling of opposition to the stranger, which accompanies the feeling of solidarity of the nation, is the survival of the primitive feeling of specific differences, we are brought clearly face to face with those forces that will ultimately abolish warfare. . . .

And so it made sense that, during the war effort, two of Boas's former students would be tapped to produce a seemingly rote bit of propaganda for schools, churches, and military personnel, targeting the destructive power of stereotyping strangers. "The World is Shrinking," or so began *The Races of Mankind*. Thirty-five nations had formed one giant alliance against evil, thus proving that the planet was one great neighborhood. Eugenics and biological racism were lies. Yes, there were three different races—"white," "yellow," and "black"—but, no, they had no significant physical or mental differences. Inborn, national, or ethnic minds or characters were all just myths—that is, stereotypes.

This booklet was meant to unite Americans together in common cause, to be the anti-Nazis. Instead, it initially provoked outrage. For while ploddingly demonstrating the environmental influence on intelligence, the authors included a graph which showed that Northern Negroes scored substantially higher on IQ tests than Southern whites. Seeing this, Andrew May, a Kentucky congressman, blew his top. He denounced the whole effort and insisted that the United Service Organizations halt distribution. However, the ensuing brouhaha thrust the brochure into dinnertable conversations across the nation. Soon 750,000 people had spent a

The Races of Mankind, *1943*

dime to take a look for themselves. *The Races of Mankind* was ultimately sent out to all soldiers through the Army Morale division. After that, it spawned a traveling exhibit, "Meet Your Relatives," a musical, and even a film, "We Are All Brothers—What Do You Know About Race?"

In 1946, an animated cartoon inspired by the booklet was funded by the United Auto Workers. Cowritten by Ring Lardner Jr., *The Brotherhood of Man* was a charming short. It told of a tubby, white suburbanite who woke from a dream in which exotic foreigners were camped in his yard. When he rubbed his eyes and looked outside, he found his dream had come true. Camped out on his front lawn were an African, a Chinese, a Mexican, an Arab, and others. Delighted by his new neighbors, this welcoming American strolls past an igloo, a windmill, a tepee, and a pagoda. He is thrilled for, as the voice-over informs us, our future depends on brotherhood. Suddenly a green silhouette appears: "We can't get along with those people," it says; they are "too different." Swiftly, each foreigner succumbs to the same mistrust. They all begin to thump each other. Why?

a calm voice asks from above. "Because we are all so different," the quarrelers cry in unison. Really? the omniscient narrator replies, before pitching into a lecture on the wrongheaded racial stereotypes that led them down this dangerous road. Under different skin colors and rounder or pointier noses, human brains, blood, and physical capacities differed as much *within* racial groups as *between* them.

As World War II raged on, the War Department produced perhaps its most powerful attack yet on stereotypes and the way they stoked xenophobia. *Don't Be a Sucker* opens with a series of con jobs—a fake wrestling match, a card-game hustle—before cutting to a commuter on his way home. Climbing down from the train, this dapper, young man pauses before a soapbox orator. This red-faced fellow has called for an America for "American Americans," a country without "Negroes, alien foreigners, Catholics, and . . . Freemasons." The sucker has been nodding eagerly in agreement, until this agitator denounces the Freemasons. "What?" he mumbles. "Why, I am a Freemason!" The commuter then falls into conversation with a German refugee, a former professor who had lectured on the myths of race until Nazi soldiers hauled him off. America, the refugee reminds Joe Normal, is made up of many ethnicities, many colors, many religions, all free. That dies, he warns, when demagogues use stereotypes to divide us.

In the war against Nazism, American film—without much sense of irony—both cautioned against stereotyping and banked on it. For Hollywood was cranking out melodramas that relied heavily on stereotypes of our enemies. In *The North Star*, *Bataan*, *Winged Victory*, *The Purple Heart*, *The Fighting Seabees*, *Objective Burma*, and *Betrayal from the East*, Germans and Japanese were often depicted as animals. However, in a testament to the growing force of those who morally opposed all stereotyping, some dared to make this point.

The most courageous voice to rise from this clamor was James Agee. Raised in the Episcopal Church, Agee lost his God but not his acute sense of the fallen ways of mankind. After attending Harvard, this poet turned to journalism, and in 1936 he was commissioned to travel with the photographer Walker Evans to document the lives of impoverished Southern tenant farmers. Tormented by his self-serving desire to use their stories, troubled by his failure to grasp another in full, acutely aware of his Harvard heritage and privilege, Agee shared his agonies in his 1941 masterpiece, *Let Us Now Praise Famous Men*. He and Evans were "quite monstrously alien human beings, in the employment of still others still more alien. . . ." Of one of his mostly forgotten subjects, he wrote: "It is that he *exists*, in actual being, as you do and as I do, and as no character of the imagination can possibly exist. His great weight, mystery, and dignity are in this fact."

Agee was not without his blind spots; this film buff somehow defended the artistry of D. W. Griffith. As a wartime film reviewer for *The Nation*, though, he also brought an exquisite sensitivity to the responsibilities and risks of representing others. An avowed patriot and anti-Fascist, he often approved of war movies since they brought the cost of war closer to home. However, he began to sicken before screenings of films like *This Land Is Mine*, *The Moon Is Down*, and *Hangmen Also Die*. In *The Fighting Seabees*,

Let Us Now Praise Famous Men *by James Agee. Photograph by Walker Evans*

the Japanese were depicted as "subhuman." *The People's Avenger* was simply barbaric and could never be forgiven for jovial remarks about dragging a "frantically abject German soldier" to his doom. Another film elicited roars that Agee called "cheerfully bestial." "When you can make such a picture or watch it with untroubled approval," he concluded, "some crucially important moral nerve has, I believe, gone dead in you."

Stereotypes numbed, and this diminishment of human feeling could lead to the killing floor. War was driven by national and racial stereotypes that dehumanized strangers and made their destruction necessary. After 1945, many used Walter Lippmann's concept to decry caricatures of African Americans as violent, Jews as stingy, Irish as drunks, and Mexicans as lazy. Stereotypes ranged from the relatively innocuous to the homicidal. What's more, even after the great victory over the Axis powers, they remained a terrible problem. After the war, a leader of American academic psychology, Harvard's Gordon Allport, threw himself into research on prejudice. Biases were sustained by "stereotypes," he argued, those "exaggerated beliefs associated with a category," whose function is "to justify (rationalize) our conduct in relation to that category." Based on extensive field research, Allport estimated that nearly 80 percent of his countrymen led mental lives driven by stereotypes. If that was so, and if stereotypes killed off one's moral nerves, America was a land filled with the walking dead.

CHAPTER 11

Projection and the Negative of Love

AS AMERICANS PURSUED behaviorism and cognitive stereotypes in the hopes of solving the riddle of xenophobia, Europeans followed alternative strategies. After all, there was much room to differ. Behaviorism featured actions without actors, while psychologies of the stereotype were models of thought shorn of thinkers. In Europe, those absences seemed glaring and would be taken up.

In Western and Central Europe, models of the mind emerged that focused on the concept of "projection." Projection was an old idea and, at first blush, rather simple. We stare out at complex, ambiguous realities and unwittingly discover feelings, ideas, attributes, and identities *out there* that actually emanate from our own minds. The pre-Socratic philosopher Xenophanes of Colophon may have been the first Westerner to recognize this human proclivity. An exiled itinerant, he noticed that when Homer or Hesiod described the gods, they bore a great resemblance to the authors themselves. Since then, many—from Plato to the post-Kantian idealists— have observed how we clothe the outer world in our own predilections, how we falsely and unwittingly generalize from our own condition.

The original theory of projection did not account for xenophobia, but rather its opposite. By willfully seeing ourselves in others, we flatten out differences and turn those who may be quite distinct into beings no different from ourselves. Numerous thinkers saw romantic love, the national family, and other collectives as derived from Xenophanic projection. "Sympathy," as deployed by eighteenth-century thinkers from Adam Smith to Jean-Jacques Rousseau, and the nineteenth-century German idea of "empathy," that process of feeling one's way into another, both held at their core the kind of projection that can be boiled down to this: "I am like you."

Projection could quickly degenerate into a self-centered, complacent stance. If we all relied on projection to know the world around us, perhaps reality might be concocted, close to a dream. This worry found its way into debates on the philosophical problem of other minds. How do we know anyone else has a mind? We can't see it, touch it, or confirm its presence. The less spooky version of the question veers from whether we are surrounded by zombies who have no minds at all to the more modest problem of how we truly know anything that goes on inside another's head. In 1865, John Stuart Mill acknowledged that the only stream of consciousness we could know was our own, but he refused the skeptic's conclusion that we had no evidence of "our fellow creatures" and were "alone in the universe." Between my sensory inputs and my behavior, Mill argued, I directly know of a third element, my mental experiences. I am right to infer that other humans have an *analogous* inner experience. And so the only way to know another's mind, in fact, was through projection.

Mill's solution was attacked. Weren't his conclusions unverifiable, mere analogies, and unjustified generalizations based on a single case, that is, his own? In addition, didn't similar effects in nature commonly have a multiplicity of causes? So why were his mental processes necessarily those of another? In the 1920s, philosophers, particularly those centered at Cambridge University, took up this head-scratching conundrum. The refined, at times esoteric, philosophical debates engaged by Ludwig Wittgenstein, Bertrand Russell, Gilbert Ryle, and others paralleled a rising tide of social and political challenges in a global community, in which confident claims about knowing the mind of "primitives" and foreigners began to be challenged. If Wittgenstein asked whether his itch *really* was the same as your itch, his red the exact replica of your red, an administrator at the East India Company, like John Stuart Mill, could be forced to consider whether what he claimed to know about a Bengalese farmer's mind was all a projection.

By the time Wittgenstein took up this problem, the notion of projection as delusion had been employed by psychiatrists and neurologists, none more influential than Sigmund Freud. The son of Galician Jews who immigrated to Vienna, Freud attended university and medical school in Vienna, where he joined a generation committed to scientific knowledge, secular ethics, and liberal politics. They lived in the center of Emperor Franz Joseph's struggling empire, a sprawling multiethnic entity, so polyglot that its parliament was a Babel of languages. Amid vast ethnic and linguistic differences, a unifying force was widespread anti-Semitism. As they had in Spain long before, Jews became a symbolic enemy that united many who might otherwise have been quite foreign to each other.

Deeply influenced by the thought of his time, Sigmund Freud also was boldly, at times radically, innovative. He rebelled against theories of degenerative heredity, that mark of Cain that magically explained an array of illnesses and often stigmatized the Jews. Instead, Freud began to consider the role of psychological forces alone in mental health and illness. Toward that end, he assumed that the mind—like other biological entities—existed in a dynamic balance. Disruptive ideas and affects needed to be regulated or neutralized. But how? If external threats like a lion were managed by the "fight or flight" response, what to do when the threats came from within?

Around 1895, Freud came to conclude that the mind must possess some sort of self-regulating, defensive system. Defenses allowed the psyche to manipulate or even dispel disruptive ideas from consciousness, and thereby regain the repose that came with not knowing or not feeling one's own distress. One primal defense was projection. Writing to his colleague, the physician Wilhelm Fliess, he declared: "Whenever an internal change occurs, we have the choice of assuming either an internal or an external cause." In choosing to locate the cause outside of ourselves, we take advantage of "the mechanism of projection for purposes of defense."

While inaugurating projection as a defense, Freud powerfully altered the term's original meaning and engendered an ambiguity that would long befuddle readers. Sometimes in his vast writings, he used projection in the older manner: his first notions of transference, for example, take off from Xenophanes. The Viennese physician spoke of inner "stereotypes"—in the printing press sense—prototypes of qualities and relations with significant others that, once imprinted on a child, were replicated. In this manner, bosses, lovers, and doctors unconsciously became our parents. Sibling competition took shape on a factory line, and a new boyfriend somehow seemed to do the same mortifying things as one's father. Thus old dramas magically kept being restaged. From this one could neither run nor hide. What was shall always be. Sameness ruled.

However, simultaneously, Freud developed a totally contrary, quite original theory of defensive projection, which involved two steps. The first was repression, the internal capacity to make some intolerable thought or feeling or memory unconscious. Then, in paranoia for example, unconscious ideas or affects were projected onto another. If Xenophanes's conception erased external difference, this did exactly the reverse. It constructed a "not Me," from all I shudder at and reject in myself. The equation could be boiled down to this: *you are what I am not.* You are what I loathe (in myself). Freudian projection artificially created interpersonal difference. Peace was restored internally, while war was declared on a concocted enemy. A perfect and sanitized Me had become conflict-free by dumping its shameful and guilt-ridden contents onto some unwitting Not-Me.

What was expelled here was precisely what must not be my own. Inner strife was thereby resolved by creating conflict with an eerily familiar foe. The stalker, the permanent enemy, and the threatening foreigner were laden with all that was repelled from the self. And so these tense encounters strangely resembled reunions; they were misted with an uncanny sense of return. Never has the motto "Hold one's enemies close" been more to the point. Through this kind of projection, our enemies possessed parts of our own inner lives. Thus the con man denounced his accountant as a secret schemer; the philandering spouse became obsessed by oddly dubious evidence of his partner's infidelity; and the brutally quieted and intimidated child, ashamed of his own helplessness, brutally intimidated the class weakling.

The problem with projection was not only did it impact reality testing, it also mandated warfare that was unending. No compromise or rational peace could be worked out when the enemy was psychically so required. Defensive projection allowed for an internal peace only as long as the battle with the enemy was engaged. If the dreaded ones were defeated, new enemies would be required to contain what otherwise felt unbearable.

Xenophanes's projection glibly assumed commonality, while Freudian projection made for an equally unreal relation. If knowing others was constantly a matter of imagining and inferring, projective theories now embraced two polar kinds of distortion, the first a presumption of sameness that falsely papered over individual difference, and the second a fantasized disjuncture that created hostile division.

For Freud, defensive projection first made sense of severe cases of paranoia. Hallucinated devils and tormenting voices escaped from the diseased mind and occupied the air. However, he increasingly began to see that the same mechanism was involved in the phobias. As troubling feelings disappeared from within, a localized terror took their place. The patient now was frightened of a mouse or crossing an empty square. Rid of the intolerable anxiety that stemmed from their own urges, feelings, and ideas, the sufferer became consumed by the scary embodiment of those urges. There was no shock or buzzer here. For Freud, the trauma was simply the oppressive demand to be civilized. "Life, as we find it, is too hard for us; it brings us too many pains," he would write in his masterful dystopian essay, *Civilization and Its Discontents*.

After Freud, the thinker who expanded psychoanalytic models of projection most was Melanie Klein. Klein was an original who had the courage of her convictions and then some. Born in Vienna in 1882, she married and moved to Budapest in 1910, where the young mother became depressed and went into analysis with Sándor Ferenczi. He encouraged her to work with children, and after she met Freud at the psychoanalytic congress of 1918, she was inspired to make child analysis her calling. Observing fearful children, she noted that they were fretful whether their teachers were bullies or lovely and kind. Was this projection, even at such a tender age? A terror-ridden, obsessional six-year-old named Erna concocted imaginary games in which Klein would undergo "fantastic tortures and humiliations." The girl lustily partook of "rages which were vented on objects in my room, such as cushions, etc.; dirtying and destroying of playthings, smearing paper with water, plasticine, pencils and so forth." All this was a source of great mirth, but once her wild games ceased, fears and phobias came roaring back. Freudian projection, Klein concluded, played a central role not only in paranoiacs but also in children—that is, in all of us.

During the late nineteenth century, psychologists had noted that tranquil year-old infants became "exceedingly bashful" before someone they did not know, a state the psychoanalyst René Spitz would later call "stranger anxiety." That seemed to normally pass by around the age of two. But what caused it? Klein argued that projection was the culprit. Aggression in the very young was an overwhelming force that could only be managed by such a forceful expulsion. Little Erna awoke to a fairy tale–like world inhabited by "split" representations of all good and all evil beings. Projection created a mother-witch, and splitting preserved an angelic, all-good mother. The child shuddered before her monsters. Early childhood, Klein suggested, was a horror movie of our own making. In what Klein dubbed the "paranoid position," good and evil never mixed. Beings were one or the other. Normally, as the child matured, she developed capacities for ambivalence and guilt, and could manage her aggression so that others were allowed to take on more nuance, be whole beings.

Melanie Klein concluded that little Erna had something to teach us about sociopathic murderers. Through projection, the child/criminal must get "rid of his objects in part to silence the intolerable threats" inside. Anxiety compelled him to "destroy" the villain, which when successful only led to an increase in anxiety and the need to act again. And so, the self-pitying murderer believed "it is because he is persecuted . . . that he goes about destroying others." Meanwhile, outsiders, strangers, and foreigners need do little to fulfill the role of enemy. The Great War, Klein suggested, was a fine example of this projective dynamic in action. It had been driven by the "phantastic belief in a God who would assist in the perpetration of every sort of atrocity . . . in order to destroy the enemy and his country."

———

AS WEIMAR PSYCHOANALYSTS wrote about projections and fantasied enemies, a fragmenting Europe began to seize on its imagined ghouls. The League of Nations' Institute of Intellectual Cooperation called on Klein's colleague, the British doctor Edward Glover, to consider the psychology of war, and help them comprehend paranoid, homicidal types whose commitment to hatred was complete. In 1933, the League sponsored an exchange between Albert Einstein and Sigmund Freud. The two fabled thinkers wondered if there was a way to harness and direct human aggression elsewhere. Freud's conclusions were not encouraging. Three years later, another analyst, R. E. Money-Kyrle, described to the Oxford University Anthropological Society the newly consolidated "paranoiac" theory of war. War was a process in which projected fantastic distortions justified and moralized one's own sadism. All sides claimed they acted in self-defense. All sides used whatever means necessary. War was a communal form of mass projection that created xenophobic paranoia against vilified strangers, and when it spread, it was a collective form of suicide.

Here Money-Kryle stumbled upon a seemingly understated part of the trouble: war was the act of a collective. So too were race riots in Chicago, pogroms in Kiev, and "bear hunts" in Aigues-Mortes. These acts of terror were attributable to rioting crowds. As Europe's order collapsed before their eyes, a few analysts dared to move from their consulting rooms to group psychology to consider how projected hatreds created mobs.

By the time the psychoanalysts turned their attention to mass psychology, this field had been a focus of study, fostered in part by European colonists. The most famed effort came from the Frenchman Gustave Le Bon. Born in 1841, Le Bon began his career as a physician, who hoped to make it big with a series of thin books. Readers found them too thin. Interested in race, craniology, and collective minds, Le Bon took up colonial anthropology and Spencerian evolutionary theories. The experts who championed those theories did not take up him. Undeterred, Le Bon applied for a grant to study the inhabitants of Algeria, but was rejected. He went anyway, whipped off a book, and promptly applied for the same grant to go to India. This time, his resolve was rewarded. After penning books on the French colonies, the Arabs, and then the inhabitants of India, Le Bon began to consider a general theory of groups.

Group psychology posed grave epistemological problems; was there even such a thing as a group mind? There was, Le Bon concluded. A fierce nationalist, he had grown greatly worried about the Asian and African rabble, and the potential of a mass revolt from colonized peoples. as well as France's internal enemies, the socialists. In search of a model for such eruptions of collective madness, he turned to models of hypnotic suggestion. The French doctor Hippolyte Bernheim claimed that suggestion—in which an idea passed effortlessly from one mind to another—unconsciously occurred in normal interactions, not just among the hypnotized. Dazzling rhetoricians could play the role once reserved for a Mesmerist. When he came upon that notion, Le Bon had an "aha!" moment and dashed off the work that made his fortune, *The Psychology of Crowds.*

When individuals merge into a crowd, Le Bon proposed, they *literally* lose themselves. In so doing, they become a herd, deeply susceptible to suggestion. Crowd deliriums were due to contagious ideas traveling like lightning, not from one rational subject to another, but rather to less than fully conscious beings in the mass. Le Bon's "law of mental unity" meant that each member of the group sought to imitate the other. To manipulate a group, he wrote, "it is necessary first to take account of the sentiments by which they are animated to pretend to share them, and then try to modify them, by provoking, by means of rudimentary associations, certain very suggestive images." With the right demagogue, mass suggestion and imitation worked like charms. Almost always. An Arab or Chinese crowd was much more vulnerable than an English crowd. "Stronger" races demonstrated less susceptibility to such irrational behavior. Beware, then, the mass hysterias of inferior races, the Frenchman warned. This, he later added, included Germans.

In 1921, when Sigmund Freud began to consider mass psychology, he had to go through Le Bon, who was considered seminal despite his nationalism, racism, and reactionary politics. After a careful approach and some weak praise, Freud slowly put the knife in. Le Bon's explanatory notions, the crowd's credulity and suggestibility, were simplistic, not racial at all, but rather universally rooted in the helpless dependence of childhood. In crowds, those deferential feelings were revived through a Xenophanic projection in which the subject symbolically experienced the group leader as a parent. Therefore, the leader was imbued with love normally reserved by their followers for themselves. Rather dangerously, the leader also took command of what once derived from one's parents; the group members re-externalized their conscience and imbued their leader with this self-regulatory function. As parents once directed their children, he dictated what was right and wrong. Leaders capable of attracting such projections possessed what sociologist Max Weber called "charisma," what Le Bon called "prestige," and what Freud considered the capacity to elicit an infantile abdication of individual will.

This shared, if twisted, kind of love between supplicant and superior bound individuals into a group, created cohesive and unified teams, and even made for nations. To dissent, to fail to yield to the charismatic chief, Freud proposed, would be seen as treachery. The crowd turned on individuals who opposed them. Outsiders were a threat and an affront. "Opposition," Freud later wrote, "is not necessarily enmity; it is merely made an *occasion* for enmity." Strangers, aliens, and foreigners offered such an occasion. Before such heterogeneity, the crowd redoubled their commitment to their leader, tightened their identifications with each other, and turned their fury outward.

For Freud, there was not a little bit of irony in all this. After 1910, the doctor had become the domineering patriarch of a Freudian movement; colleagues were turned into childlike disciples or viciously attacked and excommunicated. By 1914, all the most creative followers—Eugen Bleuler, Alfred Adler, Wilhelm Stekel, and Carl Jung—had departed. The movement crumbled and then, after the Great War, Freud discovered that regrouping psychoanalysts were no longer as interested in being an infantilized group that followed his paternal lead.

By the time he sat down to write *Civilization and Its Discontents* in 1930, the Viennese thinker had watched the decay of liberalism in Europe and had grown more pessimistic. Once he had insisted that sexual libido was the sole source of unconscious human motivation. He had demolished Alfred Adler for proposing that aggression was equally a force with which to be reckoned. Of Adler, he wrote to a colleague, "he has created for himself a world without love, and I am in the process of carrying out on him the revenge of the offended goddess Libido." However, after the slaughters of World War I, Freud came to the view that Eros, the goddess of love, had a rival, an inherent aggressive drive he called Thanatos. Lately it seemed this force was winning.

Consider the stranger, Freud wrote. In Judeo-Christian society, the moral demand was to be xenophilic, to love him. Like Saint Francis of Assisi, we should spread our sublimated erotic force out over all of God's creations. "Love thy neighbor as thyself," we are urged. Love someone

Sigmund Freud with two of his sons during World War I

who has shown me no affection? Hard to do, the aged psychoanalyst conceded. To join a civilized brotherhood or sisterhood, we must repress the aggressive forces that charge our own desires and individuality. When an outsider appeared, he was a powerful magnet for such repressed aggressiveness. Strangers, Freud wrote, echoing Georg Simmel, were unwitting objects of pent-up frustration from the civilized:

The advantage which a comparatively small cultural group offers of allowing this instinct [aggression] an outlet in the form of hostility against intruders is not to be despised. It is always possible to bind together a considerable number of people in love, so long as there are other people left over to receive the manifestations of their aggressiveness.

Groups, Freud asserted, need somebody to hate. Through the offices of projection, they were therefore created. However, Freud could not but note that such aliens were, comically enough, often hardly different from the beloved insiders. Spaniards despised the Portuguese. The English and the Scottish sneered at each other. North and South Germans could not countenance their inscrutable compatriots. For anyone looking on from afar, it was absurd. Freud dubbed this quarrelsomeness "the narcissism of minor differences." As for the Soviet experiment with communism, its zeal for equality, Freud predicted, would psychically require scapegoats. For the impossible demands of fraternity, by the laws of defensive projection, would lead to a perpetual war against those who were denounced as selfish, strangers who refused immersion into the commune.

———

WITH THE 1933 ELECTION of Adolf Hitler, virulent anti-Semites massed in Germany and were on the march. Others frantically sought to make sense of this swirling hatred. Psychoanalytic efforts ranged from the Freudo-Marxist account by Wilhelm Reich's *The Mass Psychology of Fascism* to extrapolations from family pathologies by, among others, John Bowlby. Social psychologists, like Kurt Lewin, also tried to make sense of this madness. Trained in the Gestalt tradition by which the whole was greater than the sum of its parts, Lewin would coin the term "group dynamics"; he argued that groups acquired distinct emergent properties that organized them and directed their actions. After emigrating to the United States, he devoted much energy to comprehending how groups made up of quite dissimilar beings—for example, men, women, children, or an array of individuals who happen to share a religion—unite around the interdependence of shared tasks or a common fate. Lewin sought to use this model to comprehend and then intervene when groups turned on minorities, work taken up by others after his untimely death in 1947.

However, the most substantial attempt to comprehend the origins of such paranoia and xenophobia came from someone who was by training not a psychologist nor a psychoanalyst, economist, or sociologist. In fact, he and his colleagues scorned any such distinctions as "the departmentalization of the mind."

Theodor Wiesengrund-Adorno was born in 1903 to a wealthy German wine merchant who had converted from Judaism, and a Corsican mother whose passion for music was handed down to her son. His was a warm family, so that, even as an adult, "Teddy's" playful letters were animated by "Mummi, my Hippo Cow," "Archibald Hippo King," "Piggybald," "Giraffe," "Ancient Wondrous Hippo Cow Lady," and others. This display of whimsy and ease would contrast with the boy's intellectual severity. While in Frankfurt am Main, Wiesengrund-Adorno first seemed destined to be a pianist and composer. However, he began his doctoral studies in philosophy and, in 1921, fatefully introduced himself to Max Horkheimer, a much older student who also had attended a psychology seminar taught by Adhémar Gelb. Max, the student wrote home, came "from a well-to-do family" and displayed "a certain detached interest in scholarship." Two years later, Wiesengrund-Adorno met another passionate searcher named Walter Benjamin. They too became fast friends.

In 1925, after finishing his doctorate, Teddy moved to Vienna to study with the famed atonal, twelve-tone composer Alban Berg. There he immersed himself in the Viennese scene, experimented with avant-garde music, and, as a critic and journalist, honed his sensibility. However, his compositions disappointed him, and the young man—who was by his own admission "brutally serious"—deemed himself a failure. While the power, beauty, and transformative possibilities of musical experience remained a point of orientation, Wiesengrund-Adorno returned to Frankfurt to join the Institute for Social Research.

The Frankfurt Institute had become a force when Wiesengrund-Adorno's friend, Max Horkheimer, took charge in 1931. Following Horkheimer's lead, the Institute focused on, among other pursuits, an integration of social and historical analyses with in-depth, individual psychology, or, to put it simply, a synthesis of Marx and Freud. A loose affiliation with the Frankfurt Psychoanalytic Institute helped, and integrative work that sought to make for a psycho-politics commenced with the work of Erich Fromm and, later, Herbert Marcuse. Having studied Gestalt psychology as a doctoral student, intrigued by the Freudians, Wiesengrund-Adorno also threw himself into that ferment, just as the Institute launched studies that linked patriarchal authority in families with political power and economics.

As the Frankfurt community began to bear fruit, it was dispersed. With the Nazis on the rise, Wiesengrund-Adorno fled his homeland in 1934. Overnight, this atheist, born of a Christian mother and a converted Jewish father, learned that, in the Nazi symbolic order, he was simply a Jew. He made his way to the philosophy department at Oxford University. Horkheimer fled too, and reconstituted the Institute on Columbia University's campus in New York City. Relations between the two exiled friends soon began to sour. On October 25, 1934, Horkheimer wrote, "I really must vent my growing resentment toward you," and went on to list Wiesengrund-Adorno's silence, slippery activities, and unreasonable demands. The next summer, Horkheimer wrote again of the young man's haughty and unpleasant behavior, declaring that if his friend cared to repair their relations, he would need to come to New York to do so. By the fall of 1936, however, the old friends were again thick as thieves. Horkheimer became not just Wiesengrund-Adorno's confidant, but also his ally, financial savior, editor, and at times coauthor.

Through Horkheimer, this displaced exile landed a plum position at the Princeton Office of Radio Research. It was a job for which he seemed well suited. Not only was he an expert on classical and avant-garde music, but he had also thought deeply about propaganda and the way radio had been weaponized by the Führer, who regularly beamed his speeches into German living rooms. Wiesengrund-Adorno told his parents that he was moving to America to study "pop songs and monopolistic propaganda."

Now using only his mother's name, Theodor Adorno arrived in the New World, but his landing was not soft. Aloof, melancholic, and dismissive, he clashed with his boss, the patient sociologist Paul Lazarsfeld. As for American radio, Adorno argued that popular music destroyed individuality, was conformist, commodified, regressive, depoliticized, passive, masochistic, meaningless, and false. Otherwise, he loved the stuff. Adorno was even immune to the beauty of that great American idiom, jazz.

Not surprisingly, Adorno's position was terminated, and in 1941 he followed an ailing Max Horkheimer to warmer climes. In California, though, Adorno felt like a man from another planet. He had left behind Hegel and twelve-tone music for astrologers and Bugs Bunny. However, in his deep alienation, Adorno was not alone. Other brilliant German exiles had settled on the West Coast, including the novelist Thomas

Theodor Adorno

Mann, director Fritz Lang, actor Peter Lorre, and composer Arnold Schönberg. All fit Georg Simmel's description of the stranger; free of American mores, they gazed upon this new landscape with wide eyes. And one thing they peered at was the film industry, with its mix of entertainment, stereotypes, and force-fed notions. It was an anti-art that Adorno savaged as a mindless and debased product, belched up by the "Culture Industry."

Adorno acutely felt his homelessness. In *Minima Moralia: Reflections from Damaged Life*, his mix of autobiography and philosophical epigraphs, he wrote: "The past life of the emigres' is, as we know, annulled." "For a man who no longer has a homeland," he added, "writing becomes a place to live." Thus he came upon his solution. Feverishly, he wrote.

In a span of six years, Adorno completed three major works, all of which involved his interlocuter, Max Horkheimer. Written between 1944 and 1947, *Minima Moralia* was first conceived of as a birthday gift for Max. The two men then cowrote a *cri de coeur* called *Dialectic of Enlightenment*. At first glance, this work seemed perverse. Instead of following the liberal attack on fascism as a group regression from civility to tribal barbarism, Adorno and Horkheimer attacked the Enlightenment. That project of banishing premodern myth and defeating fear with science and reason had become its own antithesis, they contended. Scientific demand for certainty had resulted in a desiccated Cartesian man, whose intolerance of mystery resulted in the need to dominate not just nature but also other men. "Progress," that once liberating force, had become totalitarian. Circulated secretly for years, this influential work was published by a Dutch press in 1947. By then, the authors had added a final section on anti-Semitism that foreshadowed their next effort.

After saving many European scholars by sponsoring their emigration, the Institute for Social Research was dangerously low on funds. Adorno himself was impoverished and at times desperate. He played with the idea of training to become a psychoanalyst so as to make his way out of penury. Then, Horkheimer approached the American Jewish Committee with a proposal to edit a series of book-length studies on anti-Semitism. Anxious to make sure Nazism did not take root in the United States, the sponsors agreed to fund the most "exhaustive study of prejudice ever attempted."

The AJC research series that emerged was called *Studies in Prejudice*, but its five publications would be eclipsed by one. At just under 1000 pages, *The Authoritarian Personality* contained a mass of empirical studies conducted by a group of six psychologists. The lead author, tasked with the job of pulling all this together, was Adorno. To do so, he would argue that defenses like Freudian projection were commonplace for those who grew up under brutal patriarchs at home. Such upbringings laid the groundwork for men and women who were submissive followers of tyrants as well as angry, scapegoating anti-Semites.

In all this, Adorno leaned on research conducted in Germany by his Frankfurt colleagues. As the ranks of Nazis swelled, Horkheimer had been bewildered by the failure of the proletariat to act in its own self-interest. He had commissioned Erich Fromm, the new head of the Institute's social psychology division, to study why the working class had not risen up against the Fascists. Over 3000 questionnaires were distributed and analyzed for the presence of three character types: the Authoritarian, the Revolutionary, and the Ambivalent. This turn to character structure followed a new generation of psychoanalysts like Franz Alexander and Wilhelm Reich, who considered stable defensive patterns far more central to therapy than analyzing neuroses. In the end, however, Fromm's study was not published. By the time it was ready to go, Horkheimer was concerned that the analysis, with its valorization of the Revolutionary character, was far too Marxist for America. Instead, it was incorporated into the Institute's 1936 *Studies on Authority and the Family*, another effort to understand how harsh parental authority yielded submissive and masochistic followers, all too willing to yield to leaders, and frustrated individuals who found relief in sadistic attacks on outsiders.

While in Frankfurt, Adorno had not been centrally involved in these projects, but Horkheimer chose him for this one, knowing he needed the income badly. In March of 1943, Adorno informed his parents that the anti-Semitism research had been funded; a few months later, he announced that he would take joint leadership of it. The gathering of data and clinical cases would be done by others—especially Else Frenkel-Brunswik, Daniel Levinson, and Nevitt Sanford—but when the work was published in 1949, a great deal of the credit would go to its first author. Prior to this, Adorno had considered the vilification of Jews but had never made it central to his thought. In 1940, he suggested that Jews were the symbolic stranger, the perpetually wandering exile; later, he and Horkheimer proposed that Jews served specifically as scapegoats in capitalist economies. While the true exploiters remained mystified, the rage of the downtrodden came down on Jews, who were falsely said to be the primary beneficiaries of this rigged system. All that made sense, until the California data began to roll in.

The team went in search of anti-Semitic attitudes (A-S), as well as passions that were ethnocentric (E), pre-fascist (F), or based on political-economic ideology (PEC). The results showed strong correlations between anti-Semitism and ethnocentrism, which was defined as a general dislike of all other ethnicities. This, they found, also correlated with an uncritical admiration for one's own group. American haters of Jews, the research showed, hated a lot of non-Jewish foreigners and were blind enthusiasts for the United States. Anti-Semitism, they discovered, was part of a larger pattern of discrimination in which the choice of victim was not so determining. Anti-Semitism had "little to do with the qualities of those against whom it is directed," and therefore, if the out-group was tangible, if there was a tradition for such disdain, then the objects of hatred were exchangeable. Checking this hypothesis, the team broadened their questionnaires to test for xenophobic attitudes toward Armenians, Greeks, African Americans, and Mexicans. Jew haters tended to hate many of them, too.

Why? For Marxists like Adorno and his Institute colleagues, class conflict seemed like the answer. However, to their dismay, none of the study's scales were highly associated with any one class, income group, or profession. Dockworkers and fat cats apparently succumbed to prejudice equally. Since Marx was wrong, they shifted to Freud. The researchers delved deeper into psychology, relying on a series of projective tests and clinical interviews. Originally in search of anti-Semitism, they discovered that the nature of their prey had changed. Now the critical question seemed to be: what lay at the foundation of xenophobic prejudice? How did these pre-fascistic, antidemocratic attitudes develop?

The answer was in the book's title. To explain the "Authoritarian Personality," Adorno took off from the studies of Freud and Fromm. All children, in this model, used projection to rid themselves of shameful and guilt-ridden thoughts and feeling. Therefore, in childhood, the outer world became home to these revenants, all the denied aspects of inner life. Normally, such primitive defenses were superseded as the maturing child took up psychic defenses that did not so drastically distort reality. Not so for the child of extremely harsh, authoritarian parents. That child was forced into a superficial, overly submissive stance. He became compliant, while idealizing and adoring his terrifying figures of authority. When interviewed by Adorno's colleagues, such subjects blandly reported that their parents were perfect. They had great difficulty considering even minor flaws in their attitudes or conduct. At the same time, the subjects raged against an array of outsiders. Forced to submit to authoritarian parents, these children grew up to be authoritarians themselves; they projected their rage onto those deemed "weak" in their culture. Once they had families, the same projections molded their children. Thus authoritarians raised cowed and angry progeny who were destined to repeat the same pattern.

Products of such childhoods, Adorno argued, became hollow men, so deferential as to be unable to fully introspect. Stubbornly conventional, they filled themselves up with stereotypes and eagerly found groups to disdain. As for the particular choice of vilified object—Jew, African American, Mexican, Chinese, Turk—that was secondary. The basic need was to have *someone* to despise. For the Authoritarian Personality, hate had become their great passion. Of such a person, Adorno wrote, "he falls, as it were, negatively in love."

Strangers played an unwitting role in this drama:

> The primary hostile reaction is directed against foreigners per se, who are perceived as "uncanny." This infantile fear of the strange is only subsequently "filled up" with the imagery of a specific group, stereotyped and handy for the purpose. The Jews are a favorite stand-in for the child's "bad-man." The transference of conscious fear to the particular object, however, the latter being of a secondary nature only, always maintains an aspect of accidentalness. Thus, as soon as other factors interfere, the aggression may be deflected, at least in part, from the Jews to another group, preferably one of still greater social distance.

Brutally silenced children had grown up to be both masochistically acquiescent to conventional authority and sadistically inclined toward outsiders. Stabilized by projection and comforting stereotypes, the Authoritarian Personality found relief in hatred. Filled with rage for the lowly Jew or Negro, he stood guilt-free and superior. According to this model, the embrace of stereotypes was hardly a matter of just going to the wrong movie. There might be an accidental quality to which minority was demonized, but once discovered, these became what Adorno called a point of "orientation." If all evils were the fault of the Mexicans or the Jews, a simple ethical map emerged that made the source of many troubles clear.

Adorno emphasized something psychoanalysts knew: the rewards of hatred could be so compelling that they withstood assaults from reality. The prejudice against miserly Jews survived all the direct encounters with kind, generous Jews. Echoing Melanie Klein, Adorno noted that bigoted respondents made exceptions for the good Jew. Still, they were the exception. And so their hatred lived to define another day.

The model Adorno and his coworkers pieced together expanded on more limited notions of stereotypes or projection. This theory could not be accused of psychological or sociological reductionism, for the contributors worked hard to make room for each. And their conclusions were alarming. Education or increased contacts between groups was not enough. "Experience is determined by stereotypy," Adorno warned, and so before such an engagement could be ameliorative, the Authoritarian Personality would need to be undone.

Though sprawling and difficult to fully digest, *The Authoritarian Personality* was immediately hailed as a "landmark," unparalleled in its integration of detail and insight. Writing in the *Saturday Review*, the American sociologist C. Wright Mills called it the most influential work of the decade. Others judged it to be the most complete study of prejudice ever written. In the popular press and academic circles, it was pored over, and soon it generated a flood of new research. It was also subjected to criticism. Wasn't the "Authoritarian Personality" a crude typology, itself no more than a stereotype? Adorno replied that he was just the messenger: conformist and authoritarian culture made for identical, mass-produced man, ground down by brutal families and flattened by mass culture.

What could be done? To name a problem was hardly to solve it. The Frankfurt thinkers had long critiqued such nominalism as bankrupt. It lacked a dialectic by which it might be held up to critical examination. What personality contrasted with this type? In the Frankfurt studies done in Germany, the opposing character structure was "Revolutionary," he for whom "the freedom and independence of the individual was the prime goal." In postwar America, that would not fly. Instead, the group looked to the "Democratic Personality." Tolerant, quick to accept difference, she was raised not by a rigid patriarch but rather by an emotionally engaged, forgiving mother, who had no preoccupation with dominance and submission. The message was clear: the family, that primal community, needed to be reformed. Society, the authors concluded, did not require a political revolution, but rather a revolution in the home.

CHAPTER 12

The Enigma of the Other

IN POSTWAR FRANCE, a repulsion toward strangers would not be attributed to Pavlovian shocks, indoctrination and stereotypes, or hate-driven authoritarians. Rather, the compulsion to discriminate against outsiders would be seen as part of a universal desire to not be strange oneself. With the *xénos* recast as *l'Autre* or the Other, new theories shed light on the creation of difference and the forces that helped codify such marginalization. Over the next half century, theories of Otherness inspired penetrating ethical and sociopolitical analyses of those made into strangers, and the hidden violence to which they were subjected.

This widely influential model rather oddly emerged from a nearly unfathomable branch of philosophy. An ancient aspect of metaphysics, ontology is the study of the nature of Being. Inaugurated by German thinkers in the 1920s, a new vision of ontology emerged. It took root in France, where it was put to use exposing false racial and class divisions. It became the rallying cry for decolonization and helped frame the liberationist movements of second-wave feminists and sexual minorities. All this from ideas that in their original manifestation were almost impossible to comprehend.

The great exponent of an ontology of Otherness was a charismatic, pipe-smoking Don Juan, whose inability to edit his own mental flow made his presentation so dense and discombobulated that it seemed to dramatize one of his central claims—that no one could ever fully know another. The lion of the Left Bank, Jean-Paul Sartre, transformed German phenomenology, as derived from the apolitical Edmund Husserl and the Nazi sympathizer Martin Heidegger, in a manner that made it a basis for radical political action. Sartre's ideas spread and became fashionable; they helped spark a youth movement—the black turtleneck-wearing, jazz-loving, *zazou* attitude, which Gabriel Marcel dubbed "existentialism." And so, along with a fertile community that included Raymond Aron, Maurice Merleau-Ponty, Albert Camus, Boris Vian, Juliette Gréco, Richard Wright, Claude Lanzmann, and, most importantly, Simone de Beauvoir, Sartre stood at the head of a movement. Their credo included both an abstract philosophy of Being and a political program. So armed, they took sundry innovative positions on an array of problems, all defined in part by the idea of the Other.

Born in 1905, Sartre was a diminutive child, whose father died when he was young. Jean-Paul was happily raised by his grandparents and a doting mother, when to his disgust, his mother remarried a man the boy detested. Distressed by his own "ugly" face and a wandering eye, the often bullied youth retreated into books. Endowed with a rich fantasy life, he was gradually recognized for his talent. By the time he won acceptance to the elite École Normale Supérieure, Sartre's discomfort with himself was hidden behind an arrogant, domineering sense of his own intellect. Erudite beyond his years, he excelled in class but also harbored contempt for his professors and all their endless scholastic interpretations. Known among his classmates as a bit of a show-off, he harbored dreams of becoming a jazz singer, and at parties was prone to burst out into Al Jolson songs. However, perhaps due to a cocky attempt to argue for an original, still half-baked theory of "contingency," Sartre failed the *agrégation* exam in philosophy. Asked to stay at the ENS for an additional year to retake the test, he joined a study group, which included a Sorbonne student named Simone de Beauvoir. Over Leibniz and Spinoza, they fell in love, and for the rest of their lives—despite countless affairs and love triangles—they remained inseparable.

Both passed the test and, as was the rule in France, they were sent out to the provinces to teach. Beauvoir was assigned to Marseilles, Sartre to Le Havre in Normandy. In this port town, the young man became demoralized, fearing he would rot. He wrote Beauvoir that "this terrified contemplation of the wasteland of my future has given me a sort of nervous excitation, which is really in the end, boredom." "Consciousness diminishes," he continued, "and the body inert like a swimmer who realizes he is caught in seaweed, lets go and drifts." Le Havre was just too dull. After eating lunch and napping, he would awaken and feel "ashamed because of my noble calling as a writer—all things considered if you take the word literally, a writer should write. And that is not the case with me."

He tutored, taught classes, and struggled with a few projects, but seemed to have no message, no direction. That changed when his school chum, Raymond Aron, returned from Germany and, over aperitifs at a café, excitedly spoke of a new philosophy, one that took as its focus actual, concrete experience. Unlike the useless parsing of texts demanded by their teachers, unlike theories of God or Truth, this philosophy took up the mysteries of everyday life. To make his point, Aron pointed to the drink that sat in front of them; this new mode of thought, he added, might take up that beverage right there.

Curious, Sartre applied for and received support to study for a year at the French Institute in Berlin. In the terrible fall of 1933, just as Hitler took office, an oblivious Sartre set down his bags and dove into Edmund Husserl's "phenomenology." Phenomenology would take different turns and acquire different meanings, but it began as an attempt to focus on the experiencing consciousness. Philosophy, Husserl argued, should seek to understand consciousness as it encountered the world of things. Therefore, it should examine consciousness as it manifests itself in its *intentions*, its directed encounters with the *Lebenswelt*, the Lived-World.

Husserl undercut the problem of knowing other minds. Since individual consciousness could not be separated from the experienced world, consciousness was not individual or atomized. René Descartes with his private theater of consciousness was mistaken; minds were actually nodes in a wide web, all linked by what Husserl called the "inter-subjective" realm. Therefore, it followed that both human identity and difference should be radically rethought from this angle of approach.

Sartre soaked up Husserl then more gradually absorbed the thought of Husserl's assistant, Martin Heidegger. Enthused and inspired, the Frenchman began a philosophical work that Simone de Beauvoir advised him was actually misconceived. This, she suggested, was a novel, one that could use those hard-boiled techniques from the American crime fiction that they both loved. Sartre agreed. Initially entitled *Melancholia*, it used the diaries of a protagonist named Antoine Roquentin to tell his story. A biographer, he had traveled to a seaside town to research and write an adventurer's story, only to fall apart.

As the townspeople pass by, he watches as if from behind glass. "I live alone, entirely alone. I never speak to anyone, never; I receive nothing, I give nothing," the narrator reports. Disgusted by the "contingency," the meaninglessness of all this, a sickened feeling repeatedly sweeps through him. His senses dislocate and doorknobs turn liquid and gluey. "I dropped to my seat, I no longer knew where I was; I saw the colours spin slowly around me, I wanted to vomit. And since that time," he confesses, "the Nausea has not left me, it holds me." Convinced of man's utter solitude and the crushing weight of routine, Roquentin's despair only lifts with an epiphany. Sitting before a chestnut tree like some modern Buddha, Roquentin recognizes that he is staring not at a boring object but at a tree in bloom, bursting forth with newness and life. It is Being itself.

Prior to this book, Sartre had struggled to get his work noticed, but the publisher Gaston Gallimard showed interest in the novel and suggested a punchier title. In 1938, *Nausea* was published and Sartre's writing career began to take off, when war broke out. Called up as an army meteorologist and stationed in the Alsace, the philosopher spent as much time staring at the skies as filling notebooks with a torrent of ideas. "Anguish at Nothingness, with Heidegger?" he asked himself. Then, in a turn that would prove central: "Freedom establishes a discontinuity . . . it is the foundation of transcendence."

Freedom would soon be in short supply. Captured by the Germans on his thirty-fifth birthday, Sartre was transferred to Stalag XII-D in Trier, where he was often hungry, dirty, and lice-ridden. He passed time translating a rousted-up copy of Heidegger's *Being and Time* found in a monastery, and he began to make notes for a philosophical work of his own. During Christmastime in 1940, he convinced German authorities to let him direct a play that he wrote for his fellow prisoners. His ideas were jelling, but he had good reason to fear that they would die with him. Then in March of 1941, Sartre and another prisoner made a daring move. They used a pass that a farmer had lazily discarded to sneak away from the camp. Sartre crept back to occupied Paris, reunited with the "Beaver," as he called Beauvoir, and organized a cell of resistors. He later recalled a feeling of being at one with many, unified by a common enemy in the Lived-World. Still, Paris seemed to have "a hidden hole"; friends and neighbors suddenly fell into it and disappeared. "We looked into each other's eyes," he recalled of his time with his comrades underground, "and it was as if we saw the dead." Under the constant threat of capture, he feverishly cannibalized his army diaries and assembled an homage to consciousness and liberty, which was published in the midst of the world's worst war.

For the naive reader who picked up *Being and Nothingness*, it would be hard to imagine it causing revolutions. The 1943 tome was hardly didactic or programmatic. Much of the book was nearly unreadable. As critics pointed out, its abstractions were often messy, dizzying, or contradictory. One reviewer declared that it was a three-hundred-page work buried in a seven-hundred-page tome. However, for Sartre, writing as Nazi victory seemed imminent meant that a careful edit would take a back seat to getting this work out. For nestled inside this gargantuan text, riddled with sentences that twisted around like pretzels, Sartre presented a delineation of human relations that, though not fully original, became immensely important.

In an article written in 1937, Sartre had already challenged one of Husserl's central assumptions. Pre-reflective consciousness was not a result of Ego, but rather preceded it. Consciousness existed. What we call the Self was a product of reflection, not the other way around. "I" was an object for, created by, consciousness. In *Being and Nothingness*, Sartre used that as a starting point. Before birth and after death, there was nothingness; in between those black expanses, there was Being, that temporarily lit room. As the basis of Being, consciousness was not just another thing in the world; it was absolute, impersonal, and transcendent.

All this might have seemed esoteric to those huddled around the fireplace at the Café de Flore, watching German soldiers goose-step down the Boulevard Saint-Germain. After all, the world was burning. However, this fugitive had smuggled a critical conclusion into *Being and Nothingness*. Man was not determined by circumstances, not driven by a Freudian unconscious, Marxist economics, much less reactionary nationalist forces. Man was free. Free to choose meaning. Free to act. Free to rebel. Under

German occupation, surrounded by French collaborators, this was per-haps *the* necessary song for this underground man to sing.

Existence preceded essence, Sartre famously asserted. Existence and a pre-reflective consciousness were utterly free. Everywhere men were born imagining they were in chains, but the chains were chimeras. Actions were always, everywhere, radically unbound. Of course, such wild liberty came at a high cost, and that price was anxiety. If individuals were utterly responsible for their choices, they should be concerned. Thus, to avoid such discomfort, according to Sartre, we often deluded ourselves with "bad faith," his term for the way we betrayed our own freedom and sought to shield ourselves from the moral responsibility that accompanied it.

With this turn, Sartre's metaphysics began its descent toward earth. In the alleys and side streets of *Being and Nothingness*, the French thinker developed a set of thoughts that led him to analyze politics, ethics, and psychology. Alongside "Being-for-itself," Sartre proposed that there was also "Being-for-others," a mode built on interpersonal relations and con-flict, an encounter between you and me that led—inevitably, necessarily—to a battle. Here, Sartre relied heavily on Georg W. F. Hegel, or at least that thinker as interpreted and revived in interwar France by Alexan-der Kojève. In Kojève's popular lectures on the subject, Hegel believed the following: since humankind originated from a unified Spirit, self-consciousness sprang into existence only in relationship with an Other, who "recognized" it. However, the need by both parties for validation turned into a grim struggle. Who would be the Subject and who the Object, who would be Master and who the Slave? Each subject sought to subjugate the other.

Ontologically, then, no one was a stranger. No one was a foreigner or alien in their own Being-in-itself. Subjects had to be *made* into foreign objects. Both sides of any encounter dreaded that transformation, the loss of recognition of their inner autonomy, their enslavement. And so, in this philosophical Punch and Judy show, the duo struggled against that fate. At some point, though, the battle ended, and the Master's subjectivity demanded recognition from the Slave. The former's Being exerted control over the latter's, which became little more than an objectified tool. The Slave doled out the required acknowledgment of the Master's desires and needs. One identity reigned. Another disappeared, became a thing.

However, that was not the end. An irony soon emerged, for the Lord, as Hegel called him, was now deeply dependent on his Bondsman, who possessed extraordinary power to provide or withhold recognition. The Slave became ever more aware of the Master's inner being, understood and possessed it in a manner the unthinking Lord no longer did himself. If the Slave suffered by abdicating his own subjectivity, he secretly triumphed by possessing aspects of his Master's. The Other held the secrets of the subject.

Even when overt conflict ended, the tension between Master and Slave never ceased. After all, the Master's desire could never be totally fulfilled; there could never be adequate recognition. Since he was treated as a tool and objectified, the Slave was not fully *there*. It was as if a nervous lover asked to be told he was loved; the words never quite did the trick. The Master's power had both created and destroyed the possibility for his own recognition. Meanwhile, the Slave's consciousness, though outwardly negated, had not been annihilated. Hidden, even from the alienated Slave himself, his subjectivity still held the capacity for freedom. In Hegel, the Slave one day realized his power and, for Kojève at least, was therefore the engine for progress, the motor of history, for he was the one who imagined, hoped for, and built a better world.

Sartre employed much of this conception with one glaring exception. For Hegel, there was a way out of this endless conflict, when the two subjects strove to recognize each other and the contest of wills ceased. Kojève imagined this process of mutual recognition, but Sartre never did. His depiction of the dance between Master and Slave, between what he called the "I" and the "Other," remained driven by the desire for domination, the anxiety to maintain one's freedom, and acts of self-creation taken by objectifying the Other. Sartre delineated his theories of everyday sadism as a desire to turn the Other into a thing, and masochism as willingly becoming the Other. Love was harder. While Sartre spoke of hopes for an "us," he seemed unconvinced. To be a free subject was to pursue the captivity of the Other. "The Other is the one who excluded us by being himself, the one who I exclude by being myself." Desire itself was the impulse to capture, to steal away the Other's subjectivity. Fear came from the gaze of the Other, who threatened the "I"'s freedom. In the end, there was little relief from strife.

For Sartre, unity based on equality was a utopian quest. As one looked about, sadism was the rule. Domineering bigotry and the hatred of the Other was an everyday occurrence, common to intersubjective relations. And there seemed to be no end: domination provoked violent urges to go further, to turn the Other into stone, to destroy him, to take him ever more into the self. The flames of the farm I burn down, Sartre wrote, fuse that farm with me forever. "In annihilating it, I am changing it into myself." Or so the fantasy goes. For, in the end, the fire petered out and all that remained were ashes.

Being and Nothingness appeared under the watchful eye of Vichy censors. It would not offend them, for in all likelihood they could neither get through it nor ferret out any political message. Sartre seemed to be articulating a rather intimate battle between lovers, parents and children, bosses and workers—an eternal matter, not something dangerous. However, in fact, the Fascists were never far from Sartre's mind. In the dark days of 1941, as Nazi supremacy of Europe loomed, he vowed to make sure they lost the peace, lost a populace that now seemed—outside of Communists and Anarchists—all too willing to go along. General Pétain now castigated his people and claimed that their decadence had forced the Germans to invade. In such a world, Sartre's ontology, which insisted on absolute freedom, was an act of resistance. Anguish, fear, and bad faith might cloak this, but there was always, only choice. That was a transcendent truth, one that took shape as the Slaves rose up to remind the Masters that they had not yet been turned to ash. That, too, was Sartre's message: to refuse reification, to refuse allowing shame to paralyze oneself, was also to refuse the belief that one must collaborate with the domineering occupiers. It was never directly spelled out, but it was there.

When the war ended, that coded call to arms seemed to get lost. *Being and Nothingness* was attacked on all sides. The Catholic right denounced its atheism, its stripping away of holy consolation from a devastated population. Marxists angrily chided Sartre for his emphasis on freedom. Condemned for kicking France when it was down, Sartre fought back. Months before the war's end, he replied to attacks in a Communist weekly, *Action*, lucidly explaining how existentialism was not quietist and, despite its German roots, not Nazi. It was a call to "*action, effort, combat, and solidar-*

ity." A month after the Liberation, responding to journalists who charged that "not a single person is able to read *Being and Nothingness*," Sartre gave a lecture called "Existentialism Is a Humanism." It was delivered before throngs of cheering fans and it left no doubt about Sartre's political commitments. Instead of finding a perch in academia, he used his popular success to cofound a journal called *Les Temps Modernes*, which championed social engagement. For the next twenty years, he reigned as the undisputed leader of a new left, one that sought out all the silenced "Slaves" so as to help them speak.

Sartre and Beauvoir with Boris and Michelle Vian

———

SARTRE'S PHILOSOPHY OF existential freedom was a life raft for many survivors of Europe's midcentury. "Existentialism Is a Humanism" allowed one to consider a simplified I/Other dynamic in any relationship. Two subjects encountered each other, and the less powerful became reified, a thing, defined by the other's needs.

If Sartre's new conception had advantages, it also had obvious defects. As Simone de Beauvoir immediately realized, in this universal dynamic there was no place for history. As one Being-for-itself wrestled with another, how could one take into account how a Nazi guard and his Jewish victim were not just any Master and Slave? How was that different from a boss and an underling, a woman and her gigolo, a schoolyard bully and his prey? When everyone sought to be Master, where did ethics like equality and justice reside? Sartre's abstractions risked losing track of these critical factors, a confusion best exemplified by the most famous existential novel, a book that made Sartre and his allies swoon.

Its author was a *pied-noir*, a descendant of French colonizers in Algeria, and in the spring of 1943, marooned in occupied France, he introduced himself to Sartre at the opening of the older man's play *The Flies*. By then, Sartre knew of the younger man's work; a few months earlier, Sartre had written a long, admiring review of Albert Camus's *The Stranger*, which was "said to be 'the best book since the armistice.'" Soon, the ruggedly handsome Camus was taken into Sartre's circle; he was even asked to direct and star in Sartre's new play, initially entitled *The Others*, then later *No Exit*. It was an allegorical tale based on a miserable love triangle that ensnared Sartre, Beauvoir, and Olga Kosakiewicz. When it premiered in 1944, the play contained the famed line "L'enfer, c'est les autres," literally, "Hell, it is the others." By the time that premiere took place, Camus had bowed out, but for the next decade he remained very close to Sartre, even though his absurdist version of existentialism veered greatly away from the older man's.

As a young journalist in Algiers, Camus had discovered Sartre's *Nausea*, penned an excited review, then sat down to write his own novel of alienation. Published in 1942, *The Stranger* featured stripped-down language, a hard-boiled style that corresponded to its theme: life's traditional forms of meaning—religion, love, family—were shams. The main character, Meursault, is immune to others; he does not love or hate them, or so he tells himself. Surrounded by immorality and violence—his neighbor brutally beats the dog he loves, and a pimp abuses his unnamed Arab "whore"—Meursault does not think anything of it. Disabused of common lies, numbed, utterly without purpose, he pursues empty sex and insists that one life is the same as any other. Barren existence is all there is, and death is our only fate.

This was quite a statement to make as the Nazis strode forth. *The Stranger* features no hint of invading armies, no concentration camps, and no allegory of the lingering evil that surrounded France and French Algeria. Meursault is dislocated from any common purpose: he is a man mired in life's absurdity. After establishing this grim theme, the plot takes an odd twist, one that has long puzzled critics. Meursault tags along with Raymond the pimp, and a series of events leads our anti-hero to stalk and senselessly murder a character named the "Arab." Like the Arab "whore," this victim never receives a proper name, nor is he allowed to utter a word. Said to be the angry brother of Raymond's prostitute, Meursault tracks him, shoots him down, and then pumps four more bullets into the lifeless body.

For students of Sartre's philosophy, it would be hard not to wonder about the very title of this work. Who was the stranger? Meursault, Camus would have answered, but a persuasive case could be made for another, one so reified and made so invisible that neither Camus nor the French critics could see him. The narrative exerts great effort to explicate the subjective state of Meursault, but the "Arab" remains an utter mystery, an impassive thing. When the protagonist is arrested, his lawyer confidently informs him that the killing won't be a big deal. Meursault simply needs to tell the right colonial story: after being threatened by an armed Arab, he stood his ground. Case closed.

Then the plot takes another weird turn. As he is interrogated, Meursault's cold refusal to mourn his mother is discovered. That—not any murder—is his downfall. Damning details about the murder suddenly cannot be so easily explained away. The victim was supine, in no position to threaten anyone. The killer cannot explain why, after the first potentially "accidental" shot, he finished his victim off with four more, taken, as Meursault himself recalls, "calmly, point-blank—thoughtfully as it were."

During the trial, the court tries to fathom the ins and outs of Meursault's mind, while his unmourned victim is never given a second thought. The novel includes no testimony from the dead man's family. Who cares?

In his attempt to construct a parable of alienation, Camus fixated on *his* stranger, but it was arguably, historically, the wrong one. The silenced, dominated Other was the voiceless Algerian; he became the tool by which Meursault expressed himself and lived out his fate. Blinded by colonial verities, Camus seemed blissfully unaware of this irony. However, that invisibility would end a decade later, when the nameless Others revolted.

The Stranger unwittingly demonstrated, as Simone de Beauvoir worried, that the I/Other dynamic might easily become twisted around in history's complex crosscurrents. After the war ended, some existentialists, following Camus, sought to dramatize the absurdity of modern life. However, history continued to intrude. When the Algerian revolt exploded in 1954, Camus, who as a young journalist had advocated for Algerian rights, got tangled up in the moral dilemmas of his homeland. Upon winning the Nobel Prize for Literature in 1957, he was pressed by radicals to explicate his silence on Algeria, where the uprising had descended into a gruesome mix of French army torture, pied-noir militia assassinations, and Algerian rebel bombings. In a heated interview, Camus blurted out that his mother still lived in Algeria, and if forced to choose between justice and the safety of his mother, he would always choose his mother. It was an admission at once so utterly human and so wrong that it only made any fair-minded listener pray that their mother never placed them in such an untenable position.

WRITING UNDER CENSORSHIP, Sartre had been encouraged to use dramatic allegory and philosophical abstraction, but after the war he threw himself directly into politics. To do so, he added a contextual element to his thinking, as Simone de Beauvoir had recommended. The I/Other struggle needed to be placed in a historical context; it had a "Situation." Every subject lived in a "Situation"—defined by biological, economic, political, and cultural factors that limited and restricted their freedom. This idea made a minor appearance in *Being and Nothingness,* but it was put to work in a secret tract Sartre wrote during the war and then published afterward as *Reflections on the Jewish Question.*

Sartre turned his gaze from the defining qualities of the victims to those of their victimizers. The American ex-pat Richard Wright, now part of Sartre's Parisian circle, insisted that America did not have a Black problem; it had a white one. Sartre similarly asserted that France had no Jewish problem, but rather one generated by Christians. That was due to the "Situation" of the Frenchman and the Jew. Jews differed in numerous ways and were not linked by race so much as being lumped together as France's Other. "Thus," Sartre wrote, "the Jew remains the stranger, the intruder, the unassimilated at the very heart of our society." More centrally, anti-Semites had made hatred of the Other their passion, their faith, and the source of their sadistic pleasure. Inside the bigot's core, Sartre smelled fear: "He is a man who is afraid. Not of the Jews, to be sure, but of himself, of his own consciousness. . . ."

How could anti-Semitic zeal be curbed? Not by universal equality. Sartre derided those who denied the particularity of "Jew, Arab, Negro, Bourgeois or worker." Instead, he proposed a "concrete liberalism," in which citizens had rights not only as members of the nation but also as Jews, Negroes, and Arabs. For the Jew, he claimed, freedom and authenticity meant living out one's full condition as a Jew. This assertion proved controversial and ironical; had the champion of freedom made a concrete essence out of Jewishness? Undeterred, Sartre extended this thinking and called for the end of colonial domination in Algeria, Morocco, Tunisia, French Sudan, Ivory Coast, Niger, Senegal, French Volta, Togoland, Vietnam . . . the list went on. Inside France, he believed, rabid discrimination might be softened by education and public awareness, but it would be eradicated only when the bigot's situation, his economic reality, changed. In a classless society, anti-Semitism would wither. For the philosopher who once denied the possibility of any mutual recognition, this was his leap from never-ending turbulence toward shore.

Over the next decades, as one of the most famed public intellectuals in the West, the co-editor of *Les Temps Modernes* made constant pronouncements on world events. He believed he had found a critique that cut to the bone and was not afraid to slice and dice struggles in far-off lands. His fame made his opinion an event. His calls for liberation were heard, especially in the French colonies, which began the long, often violent process of decoupling. Sartre's critique acted like a solvent in those regions; it bulldozed ideological justifications and gave these situations new clarity. Anticolonial thinkers within the colonies embraced Sartre, for he helped them sort through the confusion that came with having their home be, like Camus's mother, an injustice that was also in part loved.

One such thinker was Albert Memmi, a Jewish Berber born in French Tunisia in 1920. The eldest of eight, Memmi and his family lived in penury. He later wrote of a childhood where, thanks to bigots of many sorts—Sicilians, Arab police, French teachers—humiliation was his daily bread. Anti-Semitism was also rife, but under French rule, a Jew was still a rung above a Muslim. After excelling in French schools, Memmi stumbled into adulthood, a stranger among European Jews as an African, a disliked minority among Arab Muslims as a Jew, and a double outcast among the French as a Tunisian Jew. He came to Paris and took up a pen to sort himself out. However, at the Sorbonne, he grew bitter due to what he recalled as "racist and xenophobic aggression."

In 1949, Memmi returned to Tunis and began to advocate for independence. His first autobiographical novel, while in manuscript, came to the attention of Camus and Sartre. *The Pillar of Salt* was serialized in *Les Temps Modernes* and made the author's name. In 1955, Memmi published another autobiographical novel, which explored a "mixed" marriage between a French Catholic woman and a North African. As conflict picked up in Tunisia, French readers took in Memmi's work; he also tried to help support North African writing as the editor of *Jeune Afrique*. In 1956, Memmi was delighted by the swift liberation of Tunisia. His joy, however, soon soured. For some of his countrymen, he was too Frenchified, for others he was an unwanted Jew. Exiled again, he returned to France and there he remained.

A native of neither here nor there, Memmi sought to reconcile his mixed identities in *Portrait of the Colonized, Preceded by a Portrait of the Colonizer*. He felt he could speak for both. He took up the ambiguous and reciprocal identities that defined the "situations of the colonized." As for Marxism and economic causation, he left that to others, a dereliction that Sartre chided him for in an otherwise enthusiastic introduction. Memmi focused on the psychic problems of identity and the social forces that, over decades of mixing, made for hybrid types. He went beyond stereotypes to examine the colonizer who guiltily rejected colonization, the colonizer who went native, and the self-hating, "I wish I were white" colonized. The I/Other paradigm helped him explain how Master and Slave got so entwined. Memmi would continue to write on these issues, struggling to expand the definition of racism to include other forms of discrimination.

After *Portrait* was published in 1957, Memmi became well known and was summoned to a meeting with Sartre. The great man received the new luminary in what seemed to be a graduate student's quarters, littered with books and a grimy armchair. Smoking nonstop, the *éminence grise* peppered the young immigrant with questions and seemed eager to hear his opinions. Memmi immediately fell for the sage but kept him at arm's length, worried that "God-the-Father-Sartre" would cannibalize his work. In this premonition, he was not all wrong, as became clear from the work of another writer of hybrid identity and no home, one who worshipped Sartre and paid a price.

In one of the last acts of his short life, the revolutionary doctor Frantz Fanon flew to Rome in 1961 for a *rendez-vous* with his hero. He did not dare fly to France, where he feared what would await him. Simone de Beauvoir and Claude Lanzmann met the physician at the airport and whisked him off to his assignation. Sartre knew of Fanon's work, for as early as 1952 he had published the psychiatrist in *Les Temps Modernes*. In Rome, the two men fell into an unremitting conversation that lasted three days. The discussions were so intense that Beauvoir rebuked the young man for straining Sartre's health. Shockingly, however, it was the thirty-six-year-old who four months later would be dead.

Frantz Fanon was born of Alsatian, Indian, and African heritage and was raised in the French department of Martinique. While training as a doctor and psychiatrist in Lyon, he absorbed the work of Sartre and the politician and poet from Fort-de-France who had been his teacher, Aimé Césaire. Fanon wrote lively absurdist plays with titles like "The Drowning Eye," in which characters proclaim: "The fire of the sky / this skyful of eyes pounding on the doors of my flesh. / The lips of the world / gashed / ripped / crushed / the sucking of my blood!"

He also wrote a medical thesis on a rare neurologic disorder, a difficulty in walking that seemed to include delusions of possession. After

Frantz Fanon, psychiatrist and revolutionary

defending his dissertation in 1951, he confessed to a friend: "A win, a rather slight one, but a win all the same." Fanon had passed, but he ranked thirteenth of twenty-three. Therefore, he was unlikely to get his preferred post either at home in Martinique or in nearby Guadeloupe. Fatefully, the new doctor was sent to work in an Algerian hospital. He spoke no Arabic and discovered that, here, his blackness was a problem. Actually, it was one in a cascading series of problems. "The Frenchman does not like the

Jew," he wrote, "who does not like the Arab, who does not like the Negro." Around and backwards, so the wheel of hate turned.

By then, Fanon had already published *Black Skin, White Masks*, a book that was part memoir, part phenomenological analysis, and part psychiatric case history. The author was twenty-seven years old. In the same way that Adorno used Frankfurt sociology to augment psychoanalysis, this young psychiatrist had mixed Sartre with self-regulatory ideas developed by Alfred Adler, one of the Freudian dissidents. Adler had championed the notion of an inferiority complex, a feeling of being less than others that then led to symptoms of "overcompensation." A French psychoanalyst, Octave Mannoni, dared to hypothesize that the colonized *intrinsically* possessed inferiority complexes, whether under the boot of colonizers or not. Fanon attacked this as absurd; their inferiority complex was formed by their situation.

While Mannoni served as an exemplar of error, Fanon lavished praise on Sartre's work on anti-Semitism—"some of the finest pages I have ever read." Immersing himself in Sartre, he would later say, made him feel understood as never before. The inauthentic Black man, he realized, like Sartre's Jew, was caught in a vise. Forced to be the white man's idea of a Black, he was simultaneously urged to be *more* white. Such contradictory demands led to an inferiority complex and a frustrated search for recognition. To overcompensate for self-hatred, Fanon wrote, Black men might lust after white women, or Black women could "solve" the riddle of their identity by attaching themselves to white men. As for those whites with "Negrophobia," they created their "inferior" as a way of stabilizing their own self-regard.

Black Skin, White Masks appeared in print before Fanon arrived in Algeria. It was there that he became further radicalized. Writing for newspapers and lecturing throughout Africa, Fanon took up the cause of the colonized Algerians. His missives were not well received by all; Albert Memmi wondered who this doctor from Martinique was speaking of when he wrote of "us" and "our nation." As the Algerian war became more gruesome, Fanon was forced to flee to Ghana, where he was given the title of Itinerant Ambassador for the provisional revolutionary government. Still, when he could, he worked on a book about the Algerian revolution and the psychic costs of racism and colonization called *The Wretched of the Earth*.

As the book was nearing completion, under the alias "F. Farés," the fugitive wrote his publisher, François Maspero, to request a favor. "Ask Sartre to preface me," he wrote. "Tell him that I think of him each time I sit down at my desk." So the men met in Rome and solidified Sartre's commitment to do exactly that. This new work appeared in print as Fanon's popularity was building, especially in the French colonies. However, the introduction Sartre provided turned out to be deeply troubling, an act of upstaging that marred interpretations of the psychiatrist's last work for years to come. According to his wife, a sickly, bedridden Fanon was not pleased, but in no shape to do anything.

In this preface, Sartre correctly restated Fanon's view that indigenous people struggled with a terror of their powerful oppressors and the fear that they would themselves give in to rage. Sartre then infamously went further with his theory of counterviolence. A way to cure the "neurotic" illness that came with colonization, Sartre suggested, was by shooting a European. Hence, the colonized killed both the oppressor and the part of themselves that had been oppressed. As Hannah Arendt would note, this was never Fanon's position, but Sartre's powerful preface meant that some never found that out. Fanon had written about the need for violence to oppose the violent rule of the colonizer, but he sought to transcend the dialectic of dominant and dominated, not just reverse roles. Sartre's was a brutal, ridiculous position, one that deeply misunderstood the nature of psychic occupation, but, delivered with the Frenchman's soaring rhetoric, it echoed throughout French colonies as freedom fighters dreamed of raising their own flags.

CHAPTER 13

Self Estrangements

FRENCH DISCOURSES ON the Other commonly turned to three exemplars: the situation of American Blacks, European Jews, and colonized Arabs or Africans. In each of these paradigmatic out-groups, the socially ostracized stranger and *l'Autre* were essentially synonymous. However, phenomenological thinking about the Other would expand so as to grasp more subtle ways in which domination worked. Many of the oppressed had been more insidiously constructed, and no longer fit any traditional definition of a stranger. In fact, they were seemingly hosts, who harbored strangers inside themselves. It was in this more intimate mental landscape that French theorists, peering into everyday bedrooms and kitchens, discovered beings so commonly oppressed that their servitude had become mostly indiscernible, even to themselves.

Once a dutiful daughter, Simone de Beauvoir had thrown off expectations of marriage and bourgeois security for an uncharted life. Raised in a moderately well-to-do Parisian home, Simone was adored by her father, a man with minor aristocratic pretensions who recognized her imaginative and literary talents. By late adolescence, however, she found herself scorned by this same man, now an impoverished drunk and a right-wing xenophobe who ranted against foreigners and derided her studiousness. "Simone has a man's brain. She thinks like a man," Georges de Beauvoir would mutter.

The girl was sent to strict Catholic schools before she attended the

Sorbonne, where in 1927 she received a degree in literature and philosophy. Then, prepping for the *agrégation*, the challenging test that secured one a teaching post, she fell in with a brainy bunch of boys from the ENS, that ultra-exclusive school that women were then not eligible to attend. One was Sartre. Exuberant, funny, and brilliant, his personality overshadowed his rubbery looks. As they studied and talked, the two fell in love. They both took the *agrégation* in philosophy; Beauvoir at twenty-one was the youngest ever to sit for the test. Considering the fact that Sartre and other ENS students had many more years of training, her results were stunning. In the end, after much deliberation, the examiners ranked Sartre and Beauvoir one and two, a harbinger of what was to come as Beauvoir—thanks to the disorder she would come to diagnose—was placed behind her male companion.

She herself was unbowed, for she had come to recognize her own intellectual power. At the age of twenty-three, she wrote in her diaries, "Strange certitude that these riches will be welcomed, that some words will be said and heard, that this life will be a fountainhead from which others would draw." And so it would be. For this "sidekick," constantly associated with her free-love relation and condescendingly referred to in French newspapers as "La Grande Sartreuse," would produce the single most influential work of the movement she and Sartre founded.

Success in the *agrégation* meant teaching jobs and, sadly for the lovers, separation. They relied on an arrangement concocted by Sartre. They would protect their relationship as the single, "essential" one, while each would be free to have "contingent" affairs. One proviso: they would tell each other everything. There would be no bourgeois deception. As they became celebrities, this relationship became a legend, often discussed and analyzed. While it surely led to much misery, in the end, the pact allowed this unique couple to remain steadfast, not so much in their sexual relationship, which petered out early. Rather, theirs was a literary love affair, consummated in endless reading, writing, editing, and philosophizing.

Beauvoir was with Sartre when Raymond Aron excitedly told them about German phenomenology. Her German was better than Sartre's, so she could more readily puzzle through some of these difficult texts. She took in Husserl and Heidegger, knew Kant and Marx, and had attended Kojève's Paris lectures on Hegel. Still, she later recalled feeling as if on an island, isolated by her aestheticism, idealism, and solipsism. In 1940, after reading Hegel, she wrote in her diary, "I found a passage that I copied and would work marvelously as the epigraph of my novel. It was 'Each consciousness seeks the death of the other.'" The novel, *She Came to Stay*, indeed offered that line as its entrée, and on June 9, when she sent the quote to Sartre with another from Hegel, his address had changed. It was now "POW Transit Camp nr. 1, 9e Co., Baccarat." The Nazis had stormed France and had taken Sartre prisoner.

Simone de Beauvoir

These events would shake Beauvoir out of her slumber. The arrival of the Germans in Paris made her frantic and desperate, fearful that she would need to go into exile and never see her lover again. She left notes for him here and there, and kept imagining him turning the corner. In her diaries, she also vented, saying she was finished waiting for him to "appear from behind Balzac's statue." How would she live without him? "I still have no idea how I'll be able to do that."

Under this terrible strain, her convictions altered. On January 9, 1941, she wrote:

> One idea that struck me so strongly in Hegel is the exigency of mutual *recognition* of consciousness—it can serve as a foundation for a social view of the world—the only absolute being this human consciousness, exigency of *freedom* of each consciousness in order for the recognition to be valid and free . . . At the same time, the existentiel [*sic*] idea that human reality *is* nothing other than what it *makes itself* to be. . . .

In 1943, as the war thundered on, she finished and published *She Came to Stay*, her *roman à clef* about an open relationship that grew unhappy as it transformed into a threesome. In her diaries, she immediately dismissed this work and announced new intentions. "History took hold of me," she later recalled of those days during the occupation of France, "and never let go thereafter." The urgent need to study historical forces led Beauvoir to focus on blind spots in Sartre's ontology. While writing her novel of the resistance movement, *The Blood of Others*, she also composed *Pyrrhus and Cinéas*, a philosophical work that argued that the relation between Self and Other was not one of endless conflict. In fact, the Self was always moving toward Others, so as to build an intersubjective bridge based on reciprocity. After the war's conclusion, Beauvoir expanded this vision, seeking to redress the errors of *Being and Nothingness*, and its failure to put forth a politically grounded ethic. During the war, Sartre's insistence on man's absolute freedom struck Beauvoir as a bit much. In a 1945 lecture, "The Ethics of Ambiguity," Beauvoir argued with her lover in public. When Sartre insisted that a torture victim had the freedom to resist, she dissented; moral freedom was often restricted for the disempowered, a group, she suggested, that included children, slaves in America, Moorish women in harems, and, well, women. That last, startling generalization seemed added as an afterthought.

American Blacks, Europe's Jews, Arab women—the usual suspects. But all women? What could she mean? Written during fourteen months of feverish work at the Bibliothèque nationale, *The Second Sex* was the answer. To produce this work on womankind, Simone de Beauvoir waded through a swamp of diatribes, moralizing claptrap, pseudoscience, legal discriminations, and religious cant. From the story of Eve onward, Judeo-Christian texts had counseled men to beware of the weaker sex. A venerable tradition existed that considered women not just dangerous and lesser, but also inscrutable. A German line of philosophical thought stemming from Arthur Schopenhauer, Friedrich Nietzsche, and Sigmund Freud concurred; women in their inner beings were so strange as to be unknowable. Tellingly, the inscrutability of gender difference, this Otherness, was not two-sided; these were not philosophers who looked to Tiresias, the mythic prophet who was born male but spent seven years as a woman. No, it was assumed that the seeker of knowledge was male, the object of mystery female.

During the first wave of Western feminism in the late nineteenth century, suffragettes and sexual moralists sought to advocate for themselves. Their successes were notable but relatively small. When Beauvoir picked up her pen, French women had only recently won the right to vote; they were still a generation away from legal birth control, much less the right to abortion, which was not legalized until 1975. As Beauvoir contemplated her situation, she recognized the power of the I/Other model to crack open a whole series of unexamined relations that had oppressed women. Encouraged by, among others, Richard Wright, she began to consider herself as Other, dominated in a manner made insidious by the fact that the struggle had been lost so long ago that defeat seemed simply natural.

How had this come about? Beauvoir methodically unfurled her reply. As with biases based on race and ethnicity, biology had falsely highlighted differences that were, evolutionarily speaking, minor. Freudian psychoanalysis had merely inscribed male domination as a matter of inevitable anatomical difference, rather than social hierarchy. That infamous line—"anatomy is destiny"—was nonsense. Marxism also failed women, for it was not possible to deduce their oppression from a historical shift to private property. Only phenomenology allowed one to understand how the female was objectified. "Just as in America there is no black problem but a white one," Beauvoir wrote, "just as 'anti-Semitism is not a Jewish problem, it's our problem,' so the problem of woman has always been a problem of men." Fearful, hostile men sought to dominate women, repress their subjectivity, and then claim that these flighty beings were impossible to comprehend.

Men have acted as masters with the power to define the female Other, Beauvoir asserted. Men created values, morals, customs, and laws that secured their own imperium. Their myths made it seem logical for women to please men, to act as their serfs. Once, very long ago, since they were disadvantaged by pregnancy, childbirth, and menstruation, women had been forced to submit. That capitulation was so far from memory that it appeared timeless. Beauvoir's notion that patriarchy was ancient and widespread had been supported by the anthropological work of her friend, Claude Lévi-Strauss. A former philosophy student at the École Normale Supérieure, Lévi-Strauss had done fieldwork with tribes in Brazil and elsewhere, and he had concluded that cultures were founded on dualities and oppositions, like Self and Other. Woman's role in these binaries was as an object, as exemplified by rules of exogamy. Incest was precluded, the anthropologist concluded, not because of some sexual delicacy but because young women were gifts, things to be offered to another clan as peace offerings.

In the second volume of *The Second Sex*, Beauvoir described the phenomenology of woman's "Lived Experience." "*One is not born, but rather becomes a woman*," the author declared from the start. She then tracked a girl's development and socialization as the Other. Beauvoir leaned on her impressive grasp of childhood development and alternative psychoanalytic theories, weaving in Alfred Adler's inferiority complex, Karen Horney's critiques of castration anxiety, and the early work of Jacques Lacan. As girls matured into young adulthood, she argued, they faced a crisis. Asked to assume an adult identity that entailed being defective, woman shared that fate with Wright's character, Bigger Thomas. "She makes her way toward the future," she wrote, "wounded, shamed, worried, and guilty."

Female sexual development was distorted by patriarchal pressure.

Women took many wrong turns in the face of being Othered; they might become mystics or narcissists or those defined by being in love. Lesbianism, however, was not an erroneous path; it could signify the emergence of an authentic self. "Homosexuality," Beauvoir wrote, "can be a way for woman to flee her condition or a way to assume it." Psychoanalysts erred by failing to envisage this.

In conclusion, Beauvoir scanned the political horizon and found little reason for hope. The Soviets promised equality to women, but had not delivered. Was misogyny anywhere in retreat? Where was it, she lamented, that being a human being was "infinitely more important than the singularities that distinguish human beings?"

Published in 1949, *The Second Sex* sold 20,000 copies in the first fifteen days. It also was met with criticism; in *Le Figaro*, François Mauriac asked if such a decadent work had a place in intellectual life. Albert Camus said it made fools of French men. But legions of readers in Europe and America made it their manifesto, and thereby unleashed a revolution. This book would become, as the young Beauvoir imagined, a "fountainhead" for second-wave feminism. It can also be seen as one of the founding documents for subsequent liberation ideologies taken up by sexual and gender minorities. All these subjects were closeted. Long quieted and estranged from themselves, they had learned to dismiss, hate, and deny their authentic experience. Having been so socialized, they alienated themselves. They had been forced to become both the xenophobes and their victims.

All this came from a woman whose father had taunted her by saying her brilliance was perversely male. Beauvoir's lucid, encyclopedic, yet eminently readable work caught on and empowered a global movement. For a long while she pushed back against feminism, preferring socialist solutions to gendered ones. Like Sartre, Beauvoir clung to the hope that a classless society would end patriarchy. By the 1970s, she displeased many of her more liberated daughters, holding out against their endeavors, insisting that the body should not be made "the center of the universe." In this irony, Beauvoir was no different than countless other radical innovators like Locke, Freud, Marx, and Sartre. Her understanding of what should be outstripped her "Being-in-the-World."

FOR TWO DECADES, postwar French political and intellectual life centered around Sartre and Beauvoir's phenomenology with its application to anti-Semitism, colonialism, and the battle between the sexes. Who else had been made Other by Western, Christian, patriarchal society? followers asked. At the same time, old problems regarding history and ethics dogged existentialists, as was made manifest by Sartre's awkward courtship with the Soviets.

After World War II, Sartre had embraced utter freedom, which made him anathema to the French Communist Party. Along with Maurice Merleau-Ponty and Beauvoir, he returned the favor and condemned Stalin and the Soviet labor camps. After Stalin's death in 1953, the Soviet Union seemed to liberalize. Sartre moved closer to Moscow, despite its oppressive politics. After all, the solution to the problems that he had diagnosed remained not some liberal notion of toleration, but rather a classless society. After the invasion of Hungary in 1956, Sartre again broke off ties. Then a few years later, he met with Fidel Castro and Che Guevara in Cuba and sang their praises, only to again denounce the Soviets when they crushed the Prague Spring in 1968.

This back-and-forth had a wearisome effect. In the last years of his life, the intellectual celebrity who did so much to create the first postwar youth culture lost a good deal of his authority. He failed to build a coherent politics that linked existential freedom with an egalitarian society. In his final years, he and Beauvoir held out hope for Chairman Mao Zedong's China and its Cultural Revolution, the path that transformed millions of Beings-for-themselves into "hooligan swine," "parasitic reactionaries," and corpses. Former allies like Raymond Aron broke with Sartre over his Marxism. The final straw between Sartre and the once beloved Camus was the latter's anti-totalitarian book, *The Rebel*.

Sartre's Olympian dicta especially wore thin on the younger generation. During the 1960s, *Les Temps Modernes* and existentialism lost ground to the circle around the journal *Tel Quel*. Lévi-Strauss's anthropology and Raymond de Saussure's linguistics helped give birth to structuralism and then—because what is a successful intellectual movement without spin-offs—post-structuralism and deconstruction. Philosophers, sociologists, literary critics, and anthropologists looked for insights into social systems as manifested by customs, rituals, common ways of thought, and language itself. From their periphery came a thinker also eager to cast off Sartre's influence. He zoomed in on Sartre's missing link, the one that made him reliant on Marxist dreams. That, Michel Foucault concluded, was a failure to more deeply comprehend power.

Born in Poitiers in 1926, Paul-Michel Foucault was the son of a surgeon, whom he later recalled as violent and domineering. Expected to follow in his father's footsteps, the awkward and reserved boy's alienation was exacerbated by being secretly gay. After attending a Jesuit secondary school, he hurried to Paris in 1946, where, during the heyday of existentialism, he won admission to the École Normale Supérieure. As a student, his menu included a large helping of phenomenology, as well as the political philosophy of Hegel and Marx as put forth by two teachers, Jean Hyppolite and Louis Althusser. Despite the lively ferment, Foucault was miserable. Isolated and obsessed with urges to self-mutilate, he cut his wrists, joked with others about hanging himself, and then in 1948 tried to commit suicide. The tormented youth entered a number of treatments; his father sent him to the inventor of Thorazine, the literate Dr. Jean Delay, who befriended the boy but did not help him. Foucault also engaged in a brief psychoanalytic treatment, which he abruptly terminated when the analyst took a vacation. Still, these experiences fostered a fascination with psychology and psychopathology, which Foucault adopted as the focus of his studies.

In 1949, a year after graduating, Foucault joined the Communist Party at the encouragement of his professor, the ardent Althusser. However, the party's demand for thought control was intolerable, and three years later he quit. During the next decade, Foucault failed and then passed the *agrégation*, taught psychology, wandered around Europe, and took a series of jobs as a French cultural representative in Uppsala, Hamburg, and Warsaw. He drove fast, indulged in drugs, and had a stormy on-again, off-again relationship with the composer Jacques Barraqué. Amid all this, he would crack up his friends by declaring that one day he would occupy a Chair of Madness at the Collège de France.

His joke turned out to be much more than that. For, in Uppsala, Foucault came upon a rich trove of books that allowed him to conduct an "existential analysis" of psychiatry. In 1960, more than ten years after graduating, this wayward student returned to Paris to defend a thesis developed from those materials. In it, he extended the focus on the Other to another group of invisible strangers. An array of previously unclassified individuals, he claimed, had been deemed "mad" during the Age of Reason. They were the Enlightenment's Other. Eccentrics, paupers, weirdos, vagrants, and sickly individuals were all reclassified and objectified, then locked up in asylums, in what Foucault called "the Great Confinement." Reason spoke through experts, and it also spoke for these silenced outcasts.

Sweeping, provocative, and powerfully written, Foucault's thesis made extraordinary claims, and despite being criticized for a great many unfounded generalizations, the prodigal student passed. His thesis, *History of Madness in the Classical Age*, was in print a year later. It would be the first in a series of stunning, critical histories in which Foucault revealed the way in which social forces led to humans who were objectified and negated in their subjectivity, redefined as deviants, criminals, or patients.

Influenced by structuralism, Foucault turned his focus to the way specific discourses and kinds of embedded logic created the authority for institutions to categorize and control these Others. They had been processed by bureaucracies, examined by doctors and assessed by judges. Such was the way power was exercised in post-Enlightenment societies. Pillars of Western rationality, these institutions had been unexamined, since they were seen as beacons of benevolence and scientific achievement. They safeguarded the normal, the reasonable, and the right. This, however, was not progress. The Age of Reason had reworked feudal codes and sought even more control, Foucault argued. They had transformed bias into the seemingly benevolent management of the irrational. Not a scream could be heard.

At first, not a review could be heard either. Foucault's book was met with bafflement and silence. Marxists and rightists agreed on one thing: it was abysmal. In *Les Temps Modernes*, the psychoanalyst Octave Mannoni called the book repetitious, confused, and obscure. Nonetheless, Foucault forged forward, examining how social structures and expert discourses defined the supposedly rational, healthy, law-abiding, nonperverse citizen by creating marginalized Others whose subjectivity was controlled by judicial, penal, medical, and psychiatric authority. Long-lost confrontations—over, for example, heterosexual norms and gender rules—had given birth to august institutions, laws, expert knowledge, and "common sense," ultimately "truths" that were—as Nietzsche once proposed—merely the truths of the victors. Disciplinary authority took in strangers and spat out "objective" categories for the psychotic, the perverse, the criminal, and the delinquent. Power smoothly exerted itself through techniques of observation, normalizing classifications and judgments, and "necessary" forms of control; it operated through measurements, statistics, psychological data, and medical science, as well as legal precedent and the rule of law. The stranger was tamed, managed, turned into an object, and thereby known without his speaking a word.

Ironically, this deeply original historian got his due only when he penned an abstract structuralist work in 1966 called *The Order of Things*. Lumped in with the fashionable *Tel Quel* crowd, Foucault suddenly became a public intellectual. He even became worthy of a series of attacks from the Sartreans, including a broadside from the master himself. The young man, Sartre thundered, was ahistorical and bourgeois; he failed to see that behind everything lay dialectical materialism. This accusation was a gift; it allowed Foucault to fire back at the old man for trying to prop up the corpse of Marxism. And he went further:

> It is around the years 1950–1955, at a time when, as a matter of fact, Sartre was renouncing, I believe, what one might call philosophical speculation, that he invested it at its interior with a behavior that was a political behavior.

The philosopher had killed his own movement, Foucault argued, to become a political oracle, who pronounced on the Middle East, Asia, Latin America, and Africa. Two years later, Foucault's position as leader of a new generation was furthered by his role in the 1968 student revolt. He was at its center, despite efforts to push him aside by the French Communist Party, whom he later concluded was spooked by his condemnation of internment and the political misuse of psychiatry, abuses of which the Soviets were prime examples.

Neither a Marxist nor a rightist, Michel Foucault occupied a rather unique place in French politics. In 1970, his allies helped him secure a

Michel Foucault

lifetime post at the Collège de France. His comical quip had come true. From that perch and visiting professorships in the United States, he continued to examine the machinery of marginalization.

Foucault gravitated toward political theory since no one, he believed, had proposed compelling answers to the twin catastrophes of the twentieth century, Fascism and Stalinism. Western liberal toleration had been underwritten by a cadre of professionals, functionaries, and judges, who divided up and managed to exclude and control the intolerable. Communists hid their dividing strategies under the pretense of classlessness, but they demonized anyone who did not echo the party line. Both dominant political systems required Others so as to unify the rest. It was the Spanish Inquisition without the drama, without the racks. And at the center of all this was one endlessly ambiguous word.

What exactly was "power"? Where was it located? How did it exert itself, and in what way could it be more meaningfully analyzed? These questions fascinated Foucault in the final years of his life. Hegel and Sartre focused on a relational model; power, they seemed to say, inhered in relationships. It stemmed from the intentional desire of the Subject. Foucault had long since moved away from such conscious intentions to show how power resided in quite rational discourses and their social structures. If Francis Bacon asserted "knowledge is power," for Foucault that statement seemed to be a tautology, since knowledge and power were so deeply intertwined as to be almost synonymous. Knowledge-power—"pouvoir-savoir" as he called it—could be hyphenated, made into one.

In his introductory volume, *The History of Sexuality*, Foucault delineated the manner in which his view of power had changed. Once following Freud, he had considered how external social and political repression took up residence in the self-regulating functions of the mind. However, studying the history of sexuality, Foucault came to realize that repression also provoked discourse, making that which was "abusively reduced to silence" also "dangerous and precious to divulge." Instead of silence, the repressed led to an incessant panoply of normalizing discourses on, for example, sexuality; they signaled and marked the manner by which social power was exercised. "What is peculiar in modern societies," he wrote, "in fact, is not that they consigned sex to a shadow existence, but that they dedicated themselves to speaking of it *ad infinitum*, while exploiting it as *the* secret."

Two years before he died, Foucault published an essay, "The Subject and Power," that can be read as his final statement on this subject. The argument is short, often more evocative than fully argued, but rich. It is built around a series of trinities, as if his Jesuit tutors still had him by the ankles. Human beings, he contended, were molded into modern subjects by three defining processes: the sciences, social dividing practices, and an individual's own self-creative efforts. The subject was then entangled in three kinds of relations: the productive, best understood by economics; the communicative, a domain for semiotics; and power relations, which still had no good method of study. A "microphysics of power" was required for such relations to be understood, for they had no center, but were widely dispersed within families, workplaces, everyday practices, customs, and institutions. One must be on the lookout for a "system of differentiations which permit one to act upon the actions of others." "Every relationship of power," he wrote, "puts into operation differentiations which are at the same time its conditions and its results." These distinctions—me and you, male and female, straight and gay, normal and strange, subject and object—were the leverage points for domination and mastery.

In 1984, while working on his multivolume history of sexuality, Foucault died of AIDS, but his work continued to grow in stature. The fear and hatred of strangers, he had shown, not only manifested itself in pogroms and race riots but also lurked in seemingly reasonable places, inside the heart of society, perhaps inside all hearts. Dividing practices that led to homophobic attacks silently inhered in institutions and practices. They created "safe" domains to be a citizen, to be normal, never the *xénos*, always the host. Institutional racism, homophobia, and anti-immigrant bias exercised their will in these closeted ways, which is why in interviews and lectures, Foucault called for the "insurrection of subjugated knowledges." Only confrontation forced such normalized bigotry out into the open.

Michel Foucault was a penetrating moralist. His focus on unjust forms of social control, embedded in Western, post-Enlightenment discourses and institutions, permeated the thought of the next two generations. At the same time, a good number of his exact historical claims were unsound, and his declarations—subjected to much critique—exposed his own biases. For example, Foucault could be accused of romanticizing premodern times. Was the fate of the mad actually better in fourteenth-century Europe? Was it true that the panopticon of the modern penitentiary was more repressive than the strategies used by the Inquisition? This proclivity for nostalgia can be tied to Foucault's worst misstep. In 1978, he threw his support behind the exiled Ayatollah Khomeini and his revolutionary mission to return Iran to a purer time. In this misalliance between Foucault and Khomeini, the Frenchman asserted his own freedom from modern Western secular attitudes, and sided with his fantasy of all the West was not. He took up the cause of his imagined Iran.

In that light, what might be seen merely as a failure of judgment can be recognized as a form of Western knowledge/power quietly at work.

Foucault would have acknowledged that he did not stand outside the web he so painstakingly described. No one was free, not even those who decoded these traps. Supported by unspoken assumptions, seemingly plausible logic, cherry-picked rules, and furtive desires, our ways of defining ourselves by exercising power over the Other were often obvious only to those on the outside. As Georg Simmel knew, this gave strangers their eerie power. Michel Foucault's extraordinary journey highlighted how we secretly yearn to objectify and control, how, unwittingly or not, we lust for the hit of elation that accompanies dominance. Caught up in this trap were not just France's anti-Semites, American racists, colonizers, patriarchal men, and homophobes but, in ways hard to acknowledge, you and me.

PART III

THE RETURN OF
THE STRANGER

. . . either I am nobody or I am a nation.

—DEREK WALCOTT, "The Schooner's Flight"

You were not killed because you lived
in a body made by God.
You were killed because you were the future.

—ADONIS, "Desert"

CHAPTER 14

Why We Hate Them

XENOPHOBIA BEGAN AS a psychiatric diagnosis for an irrational fear of others and, a bit more commonly, as a way to describe how ultranationalists saw external enemies everywhere. Afterward, it migrated and now named a full-blown crisis as Western imperialism stretched out across the globe, and rebellions were sparked in China, Morocco, Ethiopia, and elsewhere. Xenophobia then functioned as a crude map: the accuser would be from the civilized West, and the xenophobe from the wild and primitive East. Like other Orwellian abstractions—border pacification, colonizing mission, and racial science—xenophobia quickly began its somersault into irony. Soon, it seemed that this accusation would be left at the lexical dump, junked for being no more than dressed-up name-calling, its use an example of xenophobic aversion itself.

Instead, this term was rescued by those who recognized xenophobia in their own kind. This transformation from convenient accusation to unflattering mirror was part of a longer tradition of self-inquiry heralded by Las Casas, Montaigne, and other moralists who accused their own nations and people of stranger hatred. As waves of immigrants swept forth in the late nineteenth century, a call for self-reflection followed, as did newly apt descriptions such as Georg Simmel's "stranger," Robert Park's "marginal man," and all those trapped in what W. E. B. Du Bois called "double consciousness." Hyphenated beings like the Polish-Englishman Joseph Conrad, European Jews like Freud, Boas, and Adorno, and African

Americans like Ida B. Wells, Richard Wright, and Ralph Ellison reported from within and without. They were joined by once colonized rebels like Albert Memmi and Frantz Fanon, women like Simone de Beauvoir, and sexual minorities like Michel Foucault. Thanks to these and other efforts, cloaks of invisibility were torn away. During the second half of the twentieth century, cries of "Go back where you came from!" now had a clinical-sounding name, though this was no medical disorder. More disturbingly, as psychologists amply demonstrated, this darkness lurked in the most destructive corner of the everyday mind.

After the Holocaust, the idea that strangers were by definition blood enemies became widely seen as a murderous fallacy. For those who once followed Thomas Hobbes on the brute struggle between men, Herbert Spencer on the survival of the fittest, or Carl Schmitt on politics as the need for enemies, there were harsh rebukes that came from places like Treblinka. As trade and technology pulled the world's peoples closer, others pointed to cooperation as the natural state of complex societies. In 1947, the philosopher Emmanuel Levinas, a Jewish Lithuanian exile and adopted Frenchman, flipped Hegel over and proposed that the encounter between the I and the Other was not based on a struggle for supremacy. When we stand face-to-face, he proposed, I immediately recognize your common humanity and become responsible for you. Mutual responsibility was the actual state of being; dominance and objectification were the immoral rejection of that intersubjective dependence.

As widespread efforts took up the complex mix of identity, affect, and group affiliation that comprised xenophobia, this phenomenon became atomized, broken up into different professional discourses, and called by other names. Microanalyses and narrow explanations that focused on individuals and discrete groups emerged from within models of human behavior which targeted conditioned fear responses, cognitive prejudice, forms of paranoid projection, and the process of Othering. Four different root systems. No single tree.

And so it remains. No grand synthesis or novel paradigm has since emerged. However, there has been the creation of much knowledge. Biologists have furthered our understanding of anxiety, phobias, and trauma. Researchers, for example, startled the scientific world when they showed that traumatized rats passed on the effects of chronic stress, via altered modulators of gene expression. Epigenetics confirmed the possibility that a parent's anxiety might result in a child more physiologically prone to phobias. The impressive work of Joseph LeDoux demonstrated how conscious experiences of fear—based on memory, inner schemas, sensory processing, and bodily feedback—took place in the brain's prefrontal cortex. Being consciously scared was thus distinguishable from amygdala-based, nonconscious threat reactions, which drove physiological responses without the inner experience of fear. Fascinating studies like these indicate how much more we have to learn about fear, trauma, violence, and their biology.

Cognitive scientists have conducted a vast number of studies on our assumptions regarding outsiders. Timothy Levine, whose Truth-Default Theory was popularized by Malcolm Gladwell, argued that we often are duped into trusting others who seem like us. Hugo Mercier concluded that such credulousness was exaggerated; his research indicated that we routinely remain vigilant, searching other minds for evidence of frauds, phonies, and sharks. A specific nuance was added by Daniel Ames, who discovered that when the Xenophanic projection—I'm like you—broke down, stereotypes stepped in, defining—rightly or wrongly—what was ambiguous. The power of these cognitive schemes to determine behavior was furthered by the discovery of "stereotype threat," in which children of a socially maligned group tended to conform to those negative assumptions.

Social psychologists have struggled to locate the forces that sweep up crowds, for experiments that isolate a single variable in groups are extremely difficult to construct. Much work has followed an old, but still seminal study, often described as *Lord of the Flies* brought to life. In 1954, the psychologist Muzafer Sherif gathered "well-adjusted" boys of like "kind and background" at Robbers Cave, a camp in Oklahoma. Divided into teams, the children were surreptitiously observed. Sherif and his "camp counselors" reported three major findings. When placed in direct competition for a prize, the boys quickly polarized. They established friendships only in their group, and over time they devolved into little monsters who taunted their hated rivals, burned the other team's flag, and raided their cabins. Once this us-versus-them dynamic took shape, increased contact—Gordon Allport's hope—failed. Hanging out over hot dogs did not increase empathy and cooperation. However, when the "counselors" cut off the camp's sole water supply, this crisis made prior animosities melt away. Rivals joined hands to meet the moment.

The Robbers Cave experiment became a touchstone, in part because no one could quite figure out what it meant. This strife, while not based on pre-existing stereotypes, seemed to demonstrate how communal animus could be easily whipped up. But why? Sherif's Realistic Conflict Theory attributed the intergroup aggression to objective concerns over scarce resources. Others found evidence for a quite opposite view. No boy was starving. No one needed to burn the other team's flag. Social Identity Theory suggested that the boys' affiliations drove their bellicosity.

As this debate made clear, there was a need for more precise ways to distinguish why some groups embraced coexistence while others fumed and flared. At London's Tavistock Institute of Human Relations, Wilfred Bion believed that he had the answers. Assigned four hundred mentally

Boys from Sherif's camp experiments

"disabled" soldiers and low on manpower, Dr. Bion made a virtue out of necessity. He created "therapeutic groups" and required each recovering veteran to join up. Different clusters focused on set tasks like woodworking or map-reading. While some teams got on with it, others fell prey to destructive digressions and furious conflicts. Little got done. Why?

For groups to function, Bion concluded, three basic "assumptions" must be met. Dependency needs must be assuaged by a competent leader, who in essence acted as a reassuring, surrogate parent. Safety concerns—the quelling of fears like rejection—also were required so as to avoid "fight or flight" responses. Finally, the leader must not be so domineering as to hinder smaller alliances. Groups that met those three conditions avoided squabbling, schisms, and scapegoating.

Bion believed that the psychological makeup of the leader was important, an insight that other analysts have focused on, none more astutely than Otto Kernberg. This pioneer studied how grandiose, easily enraged, and secretly shame-ridden narcissists captivated their followers. For Kernberg, normal members of a dysfunctional group might regress, temporarily transformed by this figurehead's malignant coping devices. Similar theories were tested by Vamik Volkan, whose extensive field research showed how such leaders engendered a childlike regression. Never sorry, always sure, they encouraged their followers to fall into line and see the world through their eyes. A world made of the all-good-us and the all-bad-them could be thereby conjured up, and reinforced through ritualized acts of remembrance. An ethnic or religious or national group's "chosen glories" and "chosen traumas" filtered through families, schools, and houses of religion to become simply "who we are." The many now reacted as one. Otherwise insignificant differences with one's rivals became essential. Morality became absolute. Reasoning turned magical. Members would do whatever it took to safeguard their group.

Finally, in the wake of Sartre, Beauvoir, Fanon, and Foucault, the cultural and political ramifications of discourses on the Other have been explored by two generations of scholars. They have interrogated literature and art, questioning the canon and its received truths. Through genealogies that uncover hidden exercises of power, they have reconsidered pedagogy, the social sciences, law, and medicine. Exclusionary sexual and gender norms have been challenged by, among others, Judith Butler. The influential Palestinian-American critic Edward Said explored the way in which Western constructions of the nineteenth-century Oriental created phantasms that still directed thought and belief. Bustling new disciplines arose to focus on gender and postcolonial representations and their power.

This aerial map of more recent work is far from complete. And its brevity may offend those who have devoted themselves to one aspect of this work. That is not my intent. Rather, these sketches are merely meant to illuminate a matter only observed from afar, which is this: if we had hoped for a unified theory to help us name, decode, and defuse the different kinds of xenophobia described in this history, we remain disappointed. No single approach has vanquished the others. In fact, if we peer closer, we see why these varied methods of inquiry might prefer to remain siloed. For otherwise, each runs into devilish trouble.

Behaviorism fits well with animal studies, but it can't make sense of the way ideas and identities work. Neuro-behaviorists also can't explain why habituation and exposure do not eliminate entrenched bigotry in those who have never been traumatized. Cognitive scientists run into a wall when they try to account for disdain toward strangers that is more than a rigid thought. What can make these notions highly valued, even cherished aspects of the self? As for psychoanalysis, can this model really account for the way whole nations might take up hatred? Has everyone become neurotic at once? Similarly, why do a good number of such projection-ridden self-haters, by simple education and habituation, free themselves of such bias? And finally, the complex disciplines that emerged to unearth exercises of power toward the Other hold a glaring simplicity. Is their denominator, the "I," truly indivisible? Are the myriad processes of identity, intention, and recognition really accessible through the "I"'s phenomenal experience? Is there really even a superordinate, causal *thing* called the "I"? And if there isn't, if that is all a language game, what does that mean for the "Other"?

Given the complexity of fully explaining any mental phenomenon, much less one as complex as xenophobia, it is not surprising to find such incongruities. Hidden from sight, mental life is too undetermined by empirical facts to live and die by a commitment to scientific falsifiability, and it is too important to simply abandon. Mental life thus beggars any desire for certainty and simplicity. Once we enter its maze, we must make do with scattered data points that, at best, can be gathered up into imperfect explanatory models.

Nearly a century of often brilliant study has now bequeathed us a rich collection of such findings and theories on stranger hatred. Can they be tentatively pulled together? If so, what would be the shared object of so many, seemingly disparate observations and accounts? Would it be conditioned reflexes, stereotypes, prejudice, in-group bias, projection, narcissistic groups, the Other, ethnocentrism, ultranationalism, racism, misogyny, sexism, anti-Semitism, homophobia, transphobia, or Islamophobia? Is there any one term specific enough to not be meaningless, while broad enough to allow us to consider whatever common strands exist between these phenomena?

Xenophobia, I propose, is such a word. By recovering its rich past, encompassing far more than an animus against immigrants, and by examining the numerous concepts of stranger hatred to which it is linked, we may repurpose this term so that it serves to organize and promote attempts at synthesis. Multiple root systems, the same tree.

This reframing would force disparate viewpoints of stranger fear and hatred into conversation. That could lead to more nuanced models and more effective policies. While we must continue to study the historical specifics of, for example, racism or sexism, we now also could consider their common manifestations and shared causes. Hence, we might resist inadvertently slipping into Frantz Fanon's depressing cascade, his recognition that the hatred of Others flowed from the Frenchman toward the Jew, from the Jew to the Arab, from the Arab to the Black, then backwards and on.

To pursue such a synthesis, let's start with what xenophobia is *not*. It cannot be reduced to some genetic defect or neural pathology. Xenophobia is not hardwired in some subset of the human population. If only. Hannah Arendt and, more recently, Sander Gilman and James Thomas have demonstrated that while it would be comforting to think of virulent racists as insane, that would only defame the mentally ill. Normal specimens of our biologic kind commit most hate crimes; they pulled the switches at Auschwitz. While toxic leaders may be ill, xenophobia is not literally an illness. More disturbingly, it is a part of the psychic violence of everyday life.

Nor is xenophobia the direct product of economic distress. Ever since Adam Smith, economists have argued that foreigners were targeted due to justifiable concerns regarding their threat to local livelihoods. Surely rational economic actors should not be called "xenophobic" for merely defending their turf. However, research has demonstrated that throughout the twentieth century, regions swept up by xenophobia have not shown decreased wages or increased unemployment. Most xenophobes have not emerged solely, or even mostly, from a threatened labor pool. And history has amply demonstrated that the *identity* of the foreign workers, not just their economic threat, played a role in these outbreaks. Finally, what to do with the inconvenient but recurrent fact that outbursts of xenophobia often first emerge in desolate settings, where there has been little economic competition from foreigners, because there were almost no foreigners? While economic pressures like increased poverty or loss of work lead to helplessness and despair, and therefore may be contributing factors to xenophobic outbreaks, they do not always do so.

Similarly, xenophobia cannot be reduced to a straightforward desire for cultural preservation. Patriotism, traditionalism, and conservativism, that argument goes, have been unfairly labeled as an irrational rejection of foreigners. Societies that consider themselves homogenous—a stance that, as Renan pointed out, always required a great deal of amnesia—upon encountering foreigners, may reject heterogeneity. Tribes resist change and hold on to their traditions. Was the Navajo Nation "xenophobic" for seeking to preserve its language from American attempts to extirpate it? Hardly.

Like that sixteenth-century debate in Spain over whether the Aztecs were obliged to welcome "visitors" like Cortés, this challenge hinges on one factor: power. Can we fairly weigh discrepancies between the hosts and their outsiders? Can we distinguish those who come with arms, wealth, and a foreign state behind them, those who stride forth as conquerors, from those who arrive with no such desire or advantages? When is the cultural threat from the strangers supported by such facts, and when is it symbolic? For while shifts in populations may correlate with some manifestations of xenophobia, these migrations do not always result in the vilifying of the strangers. Far from it. Something else is required.

What then causes xenophobia? This history suggests tentative answers that pull from domains like philosophy, psychology, and sociology. While purists from those disciplines may protest, let us first divide this question and distinguish between *Other anxiety, overt xenophobia,* and *covert xenophobia.*

Other anxiety is known to us all. It is an ontological state of being. Humans can't read each other's minds or easily fathom each other's intentions. We must rely on analogies to our own minds, and clues from appearance, behavior, and communication. Upon meeting a stranger, we thus become embroiled in a mystery. Who is the foreigner from Elea to whom Socrates posed his queries? What's with the fellow with no valise who boarded the ship in Herman Melville's *The Confidence-Man*? "Whodunit" mysteries offer the vicarious pleasure of experiencing a touch of that *anxiety* and, in the end, resolving it. Ritualized forms of greetings and pleasantries like those attached to the Greek rules of *xenia* function to diminish some of that uncertainty. Still, as many children's tales remind us, the wolf at our door may come in peace, but he may be sporting that grin because he just spotted his next meal.

The cognitive scientist Daniel Kahneman explored ways we may have evolved to master *Other anxiety.* For survival, humans developed associative, unconscious assessments that take a stab at the truth, what he called "System 1" thought. These shortcuts, he experimentally demonstrated, sprint ahead of deliberate decision making. "Fast thinking" allows us to instantly read anger on another's face. We immediately finish sentences like: "Thieves are usually . . ." Whatever once led to such an association has long been forgotten. As with Joseph LeDoux's amygdala-based threat reactions, there may be no conscious experience of fear. Rather, this reaction is nonconscious, automatic, lifesaving, and too often wrong.

Stereotypes, for Kahneman and many cognitive scientists, are simply the stuff of fast thinking. This, unfortunately, can lead to a confusion of tongues, since categorizing a chair, for example, surely must be distinguished from motivated negative portrayals of, say, Asians or lesbians. The difference emerges when we recall that System 1 reactions, as associative links, are forged in a social world. Hence, they may be *false* associations, displacements that, like the ones drilled into the minds of Pavlov's dogs, we learn and live by. G. Stanley Hall's questionnaire featured Blacks as the most feared American stranger. How did they come to be so chosen? How did certain strangers and outsiders become swiftly seen, known, and denigrated while others did not? As any targeted minority knows, therein lies a sea of assumptions in which one might easily drown.

Other anxiety, in theory, can be managed. The behaviorists' cure of exposure and habituation can be put to work to diminish such conditioned reflexes through social mixing and integration. Unconscious biases can be reworked through relearning. Workplace sensitivity training often rests on this premise. Dialogue with the Other can restore the capacity for empathy and the possibility of mutual recognition. In one encouraging study, California canvassers found that by simple fifteen-minute discussions, they were able to significantly reduce prejudice against transgender people in ten percent of their subjects. If the hosts and strangers work, play, and love together, the psychic processes that drive conditioned threat reactions and unconscious bias can diminish. We learn to tolerate an initial discomfort, take in new information, refine our appraisals, and go beyond categorical judgments as our slower, conscious capacities for judgment kick in.

For this to occur, we must be challenged. Online tools may help us encounter our own "implicit biases," but the Black lesbian feminist Audre Lorde put the task best: "*I urge each one of us here to reach down into that deep place of knowledge inside herself and touch the terror and loathing of any difference that lives there. See whose face it wears.*"

That alone, sadly, may not be enough. Kahneman found little evidence to support an individual's capacity to rein in his or her own stereotypes, and pointed us to thought "factories," those entities that help manufacture opinion. Institutions and media play important roles in furthering or, conversely, displacing bigoted stereotypes. What credos can keep us alert to *Other anxiety* and its destructive effects? For Saint Paul and Las Casas, the Christian Church served this purpose: we are all God's children, the Bible taught. For Diderot and post-Enlightenment secularists, it was the democratic nation, based on the self-evident truth of human equality and the requirement for toleration. For those shocked into action by the Holocaust, it was a commitment to international human rights and a redoubling of efforts to dismantle racial, religious, and sexual hierarchies.

Other anxiety should be distinguished from *overt xenophobia*, in which fear and hatred of the Other has solidified into more than an errant anxiety or a cognitive error. Here, it has become a defended solution. *Overt xenophobes* need their villain; they hate the *xénos* so as to stabilize themselves.

Xenophobia, like *Other anxiety*, is marked by stereotypes, but these are more rigid. They do not easily alter, for the focus on the degraded Other as bad, defective, or immoral is desired. In this way, the world has been simplified and purified: we are good and they are bad. The reliance on defensive projection can be discerned by three tell-tale signs: a vanishing capacity to consider "the gray zones," an inability to tolerate affective ambivalence, and the loss of a capacity for guilt. The xenophobic are always justified, always the victims, even after perpetrating violence. External condemnation falls on deaf ears. In-between arguments are swept aside as weak. Shaming the offender only provokes rage.

Sadism is prominent in *overt xenophobia*. There is pleasure, as Sartre and others reminded us, in the "I"'s domination of the Other. Psychoanalysts, however, considered this to be motivated by *self-hatred*. Defensive projection makes the need to control the Other never-ending. The evil out there must be constantly reasserted, or those same attributes might find their way back to their rightful owner. Xenophobia therefore can seem, in a descriptive not a clinical sense, to be both paranoid and obsessional. Its repetitive function is to cleanse the xenophobe of his own self-loathing by constantly soiling the devalued Other.

Groups, by definition, share common notions of the not-us, those that lie outside our boundaries, but these exclusionary criteria are usually not also the collective's only core commitments, its *raison d'être*. For xenophobic groups, however, that is precisely the case. Their rigid borders, defined by diminished Others, give both definition to members and provide the main purpose for the group. To allow the *xénos* passage in, then, poses an existential threat to this community.

Xenophobic groups, over the last century, seem to have emerged as a symptom of broader social failures, in which, for example, affiliative bonds in a nation-state weaken. Joining a xenophobic group thereby may become a solution. However, a price must be paid upon entry: these communities demand ideological purity. Dissent brings with it the risk of being wrong, that is, being shamed (again) oneself. Meanwhile, leaders encourage regressive submission by offering relief of internal conflict; they take up the role of group conscience. Members are then lifted up on two fronts: they are identified with the Great One, and they are distinct from the denigrated stranger.

If the social conditions are right, xenophobic groups can grow quickly. Their divisiveness and demagoguery may encourage those who may possess run-of-the-mill *Other anxiety* to adopt harsher beliefs, as a solution to their own isolation, helplessness, and weakness. We are *not* the scared and debased; they are. Charismatic leaders masterfully play on these emotions, because they too often dance around the fires of shame themselves. As Adorno showed, authoritarian families, societies, and political parties all engender fears of humiliation and offer relief through a regressive dependence on an idealized leader. Those red faces shouting in the crowd are ecstatic for being so accepted; they are determined to never be cast out, to never be strangers themselves.

Unfortunately, the ameliorative efforts that quell *Other anxiety* will fail here. As numerous studies reveal, diversity training and sensitivity classes often do not have the hoped-for effect. Exposure and habituation with this population go nowhere. Cognitive models—what Kurt Lewin called "re-education"—don't stick either, not among those who belong to groups that reinforce an obligatory commitment to hate *them*. Bigots switch the station from television programs that humanize their demons; they don't care if the Iraqis had anything to do with 9/11. That policeman is not just jumpy; he is quick to shoot a Black motorist because he knows that's one of the "bad guys."

What to do? For those who take the long view, the path leads back to the family. The greatest ally of the hyper-intellectual Freudo-Marxists, ironically enough, was that homespun purveyor of homilies, Dr. Benjamin Spock. Schooled in psychoanalytic theory, Spock's immensely popular parenting guides called for less harsh, shame-driven forms of child-rearing. Social groups that mirror these forms of self-regulation may also be less prone to authoritarian solutions.

When *overt xenophobia* has emerged, what is to be done? How may we confront vilifying groups without vilification, not merely out of some lofty virtue but because otherwise it won't work. To shame the already shamed only heightens their defenses. And, yet, to coddle xenophobes or retreat from their accusatory polemics only makes their cause and their aggression grow stronger.

If reeducation and exposure here do nothing, if this is not strictly a matter of economics or cultural preservation as I have argued, then the guiding principle for amelioration must focus on matters of identity. In my view, as an ethical absolute and a political guiding force, radical egalitarianism poses the greatest threat to xenophobia. That rudder will help opponents steer clear of the temptation to demonize the demonizers, and transform into their doubles. Alongside that view of equality and basic human rights, I agree with Joshua Greene, who argued that toleration should not be seen as solely a liberal value, but rather a rule for all, a "meta-morality." We therefore confront bigotry while offering acceptance to all, except those who, as Karl Popper argued, would destroy toleration. Over time, such constancy may attract those who have lost their taste for submission, or have grown tired of the turbulent drama that comes with maintaining fantasies of a world so divided. Meanwhile, legal protections must be robust in their defense of the victims of these projections.

Finally, consider *covert xenophobia*. This form of discrimination operates in the shadows. It deploys the "dividing strategies" that Michel Foucault illuminated, and it does so freely. The battles, if ever fought with the Other, have been long won. The victor can be naturalized, the vanquished, too. These discriminatory rules seem just like the way "we" prefer to do things. In this way, highly socialized and accepted forms of xenophobia disappear into norms, conventions, and discourses.

Unlike cognitive notions of implicit bias, these forms of discriminations are not mere associative errors; they are quietly motivated. Those desires may be disavowed, but they make themselves known as a resistance to change. Unfair? Devaluing? When so accused, counter-forces kick up, baffling those cognitive scientists who would teach away all implicit bias. For example, my medical school was hardly alone in purportedly having a quota for Jews some seventy years ago; admitting too many Jews just wasn't a good idea, the leaders seemed to agree. However, when pressed a little, when lectured about the evils of bias, they did not amend their ways. After a cognac at the club, if asked to defend this rule, the deans might become shockingly overt about why too many Jews was not a good idea. Mostly, they did not need to explain.

TABLE 4

FORMS OF XENOPHOBIA	CAUSAL MODELS	FORMS OF AMELIORATION
"OTHER" ANXIETY	BEING WITH STRANGERS (Phenomenology)	DIALOGUE, MUTUAL RECOGNITION
	NOVEL THREATS AND MISASSOCIATION (Behaviorism)	EXPOSURE AND HABITUATION
	NEGATIVE STEREO-TYPES, SYSTEM 1 PROCESSING (Cognitive Science)	UCS. BIAS TRAINING/ EDUCATION VIA SYSTEM 2 COGNITION
OVERT XENOPHOBIA	PROJECTION (Psychoanalysis)	INTERPRETATION/ WORKING THROUGH OF SHAME / GUILT DYNAMICS
	REGRESSED GROUPS AND AUTHORITARIAN LEADERS (Group Psychologies)	SOCIAL STRUCTURES THAT INHIBIT AGGRESSION AND SUPPORT EQUALITY, TOLERANCE, RECONCILIATION
COVERT XENOPHOBIA	LEGAL/ INSTITUTIONAL FORMS OF DISCRIMINATION (Structuralism)	CRITICAL ANALYSIS, REFORM

Covert xenophobia operates then at the level of individuals as well as institutions, organizations, and social structures. However, no individual—it would seem—need take responsibility. Rule-based dictums inscribe hierarchies, logical relations, and differentials, all of which support discrimination against the degraded group. These ways of thought create, protect, and enforce power. Foucault's followers have sought to pry open how Western discourses and institutions hid these effects and redefined them as benevolence. The marginalized of a social order thus take their place in a series of legal, medical, bureaucratic, and institutional matrices that define and limit them. The machinations of *covert xenophobia* quietly purr along, then they may come to light due to an egregious crisis or scandal. Only when looking through the wreckage do these structural forms of discrimination become clear.

———

THIS OUTLINE IS but one attempt to synthesize a century of efforts from a number of disciplines. It is my hope that it will be replaced by others that employ more data and yield more explanatory power. In the end, I insist on only one thing. The Balkanization of stranger fear and hatred into many moral, political, historical, psychic, and social entities has blinded us to their possible commonalities. In *addition* to specialized working vocabularies, and the instructive histories of distinct, maligned communities, we need an overarching concept that organizes our thinking about similarities.

Others have made the same point. The psychologist Gordon Allport pulled many biases into his notion of "prejudice," but his effort, as Elisabeth Young-Bruehl deftly showed, led to overgeneralizations and obfuscations. She herself sought to rehabilitate Allport's term by dividing up kinds of prejudice between three psychoanalytic character types, an ambitious effort that was so specific, and so unsupported empirically, that it collapsed under its own weight. The closest proposal to my own came from Albert Memmi. The author of *The Colonizer and the Colonized* had experienced what it was like to be the object of anti-Arab, anti-Semitic, and anti-French vitriol. He understood the need for a broadly encompassing term that linked such hatreds together. In 1982, Memmi proposed to call it "heterophobia," a fear of the dissimilar, which led to forms of "domination based on real or imagined differences." His logic was impeccable, but Memmi's coinage never caught on. Perhaps at that historical moment, the whole matter, like xenophobia itself, seemed rather academic.

CHAPTER 15

The New Xenophobia

UNLIKE NUMBERS, words gather new meanings. They grow and mutate, so much so that poor Noah Webster and his lot must string lists of definitions to a sole entry. What happens when words transform or when they suddenly travel and pop up amid new signs and symbols? Then our verbal calculations may quietly go awry. No one may notice that things add up differently, but they do. The story of xenophobia has been of a word that has gone through a series of alterations and migrations. A late-nineteenth-century neologism that was brought forth in French and English became a tool, a map, a mirror, an atmosphere of opinion, and finally a curse.

Curses, of course, matter. In 1934, one of the Frankfurt School's exiles, Norbert Elias, published *The Civilizing Process*, in which he examined some ways in which cultural adaptations occurred. Social disruptions led to shifting standards of behavior, he argued, so that what was once acceptable—like eating with your hands or spitting under your host's dinner table—became dishonorable, disgusting, and shameful. After 1945, xenophobia came to represent such a taboo. What once was condoned or ignored now warranted a rebuke. How that prohibition related to the word's past meanings became obscured. No matter. The Holocaust and the continued mixing of the world's populations made it critical to forcefully reject the assumption that foreigners and strangers were enemies.

During the Cold War years, Western liberal democracies as well as socialist nations shared this revulsion. Soviets and Americans each took pride in their defeat of Fascism and Nazism. They each conceived of themselves as the Hitler slayers, the ones who ended the genocide of the Jews. As these Goliaths pointed their nuclear arsenals at each other, this much they shared. After millions of dead, the prayers for a new moral code, those entreaties that linked Bartolomé de Las Casas to Raphael Lemkin, seemed to have been answered. During the postwar years, xenophobia had become a curse. Its problems seemed to belong to a bygone era. It was hard to imagine that they would ever return.

———

BREXIT AND THE election of Donald Trump almost made no sense to me at first. They seemed to contradict assumptions I held for most of my adult life. During the 1980s, I came of age awash in the belief that a broad-based commitment to human rights was slowly but inexorably progressing. In college psychology class, we asked whether the James-Lange theory or misplaced associations or stereotyped ideas made for prejudice. Historians and sociologists examined how communal affiliations sequestered and distorted knowledge. Literary and semiotic studies analyzed the power of misrepresentation in everything from literary masterpieces to ads for the Marlboro Man. Many of us studied Freud, the Frankfurt School, Beauvoir and the second wave of feminists. My campus hummed with excitement thanks to illuminations and, somehow, sexy obfuscations emerging from deconstruction and the French invasion.

With the Holocaust hovering not far behind us, and American racism all around, these pursuits hardly seemed abstract; they translated into a concern with language and politically correct culture, which in my time was a rather timid call for self-restraint. Prohibitions were strong against the N-word, a few derogatory terms for Jews and women, not much more. Gay men and lesbians generally stayed in the closet, and other minorities, myself included, mostly kept quiet. When a New York society girl called my wife's Nicaraguan friend a "spic," that was supposedly good fun, though he got the better of the encounter when he replied, "and you are de*spic*able."

The long arc of history, I trusted, would bend toward justice. While passage of the Equal Rights Amendment failed, women became leaders at my medical school. We marched and South African apartheid fell. The Oslo Accords seemed to augur peace in the Middle East. The Iron Curtain came down. Closeted friends and colleagues stepped forth to claim their sexual identities.

In these struggles, xenophobia seemed of dwindling relevance. Across much of the political spectrum, commentators advertised their repulsion and rejection of racism, anti-Semitism, and sexism. Sometimes they added xenophobia, but it was only for good measure. The world had changed. Everyone had squeezed under two nuclear umbrellas, and in this bipolar conflict, dangerous political ideologies marked the enemy. In Chairman Mao's China, Stalin's Soviet Union, and Pol Pot's Cambodia, repressive violence targeted dissident belief. In the United States, how did fear of foreigners apply to lingering McCarthyism or military deployments into Southeast Asia, Central America, and the Middle East? For everyone from George Kennan to Henry Kissinger, Marxist dominoes mattered more than ethnicity. The world faced tense Cold War dilemmas. Xenophobia did not seem to be one of them.

Besides, for believers in liberal democracy, that problem already had found its solution. Toleration was the cure, xenophobia the illness; they were the necessary virtue and perilous vice of expanding, pluralistic societies. Within private life, such egalitarianism was neither demanded nor expected; after all, people liked people who were like them. Nothing wrong there. However, before the law, within institutions, and more broadly in public discourse, toleration affirmed the self-evident equality of all political, legal, and moral subjects. This ethos was codified in 1948 by the United Nations' Universal Declaration of Human Rights. While many dismissed the document as utopian, Nelson Mandela considered it a noble bulwark against hatred. After its ratification, this declaration lay dormant until it was roused to life three decades later by American president Jimmy Carter. Its human rights credos have since spread, as part of what Michael Ignatieff called "moral globalization."

In socialist and communist nations, xenophobia was also considered an anathema, and they too believed they had found a solution. Followers of Karl Marx and Vladimir Lenin argued that national, ethnic, and religious bigotry would disappear in a classless society, where equality was ensured and enforced by the state. Once the bourgeoisie were eliminated,

workers of the world would brush off minor differences and unite as comrades. For nations under the sway of the Soviet Union or for intellectuals
like Jean-Paul Sartre, capitalist exploitation was the deep structure that
led to outbreaks of xenophobia. Scapegoats would vanish when the true
source of suffering did as well.

In either case, both superpowers agreed that hatred of strangers was
a plague that must be prevented. A great lesson had been learned. Or so
it seemed. Then, in 2016, we awoke to a shock. The ground had been
moving underneath us without our knowing it. Xenophobia was again
on everyone's lips. Across Europe and in America, the attacked minorities and immigrants did not derive from one category or group. Racism did not quite cover this; neither did anti-Semitism, Islamophobia, or
anti-immigrant sentiment. Different kinds of outsiders were targeted in
Poland, Hungary, Ukraine, Austria, Russia, Sweden, France, Germany,
Great Britain, the United States, and more. What had happened?

The history of our predicament has not yet been written. And the
passing of time will no doubt expose our contemporary blind spots. Still,
having studied the forms and major theoretical elaborations for stranger
fear and hatred, what can we tentatively suggest? To consider this question, we need to flip our lens from its focus on individuals and small
groups to the perspective with which our story began, zooming out to
consider the macroscopic forces of Western history. Only then can we
hope to understand how such varied locales all were swept up in the
same xenophobic tide. What were the political forces, the "situation," that
rewarded such divisive thought and action, so much so that tribal hatred
spread to so many nations? What conjectures can we offer that might aid
some future, fuller history?

When Brexit and Trump's election took place, many pundits and
politicians argued that this was a delayed result of the 2008 stock-market
meltdown. Others pointed to the European migrant crisis from Syria and
North Africa, as well as the flow of humanity from Central America and
Mexico into the United States. These arguments relied on the economic
competition and cultural invasion models, and as we have seen, while
these factors may be important, they remain insufficient. Whether it is a
sudden global expansion, the collapse of empire, an influx of immigrants,
or the devaluation of a currency, these social pressures by themselves do

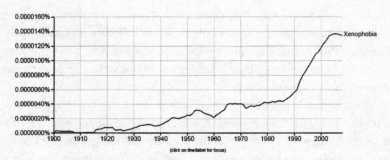

English usage of xenophobia via Google ngram

not explain how and why such troubles transform into xenophobia. Most economic suffering manifests as . . . well, economic suffering. Many communities have accommodated influxes of newcomers without turning on them. These narrow explanations obscure the essential riddle, which is how such stressors morph into our three-headed beast.

With Brexit and the election of Donald Trump, I too first followed the politicians and economists who suggested this was a delayed response to the 2008 crisis. Then I began to dig around. If the usage of "xenophobia" in English, French, Italian, Spanish, and German was an accurate indicator, I found that a sudden, intense resurgence of the word had occurred years earlier. Alarms had been going off in all those languages, but I hadn't heard them. And the inflection point from linear growth to a wild upswing came at an auspicious time, one that some historians like to call the end of the twentieth century.

———

THE CALENDAR YEAR of 1989 marked the beginning of a series of cataclysms that created a crisis of identity around the Western world. In the span of three years, the Berlin Wall fell, the Soviet Union collapsed, and the Cold War ended. In an astonishing and unprecedented turn, a global superpower peacefully gave up the ghost. Forty-five years of ideological war ended without a whimper. Almost no one was prepared for it. One of the orienting poles of a bipolar world had vanished. Disorder and confusion, personal and political, were inevitable. The collapse of the Soviet Union raised two monumental questions. What would happen when this gigantic entity dissolved? And what would happen to the United States, which had been so vigilantly poised against this Other for half a century, now that its nemesis was no more?

The Soviet Union was a massive land empire whose gobbled-up colonies contained over one hundred different ethnic groups. Their constitution defined citizens by ethnic-national identities—Armenian, Ukrainian, even the "nation" of the Jews. After Lenin, Soviet leaders understood that they had to manage a potential "nationalities" problem, especially in places like Estonia, Latvia, and Lithuania, which had already tasted autonomy. Police-state oppression secured the peace, and a forced commitment to Marxist ideology brought the many together in thought and identity.

Such collective unity was enhanced and further defined by a common ideological enemy: Western capitalism and its champion, the United States. Throughout the Soviet Union, Americans served as an example of all that the Soviets were not. *Life, liberty and the pursuit of happiness*? What about the Ku Klux Klan? *Freedom*? To engage in what, shopping? To let wealth for some destroy the pursuit of happiness for most? These were Cold War tropes, coins of the realm that could be passed out whenever needed. They are the bigots, not us. They are empty and unhappy. We march for progress and a more egalitarian society. To question such dogma was, since Stalin's show trials in 1936, potentially traitorous. And so, the same song was sung over and over again.

Meanwhile, an increasingly sclerotic Soviet leadership clung to ideological purity as the failures of their state-run economy mounted. After all, capitalism was in its "late" stages, not communism. Any movement toward a somewhat freer economy went against history and could seem tantamount to defection. Locked in by their dogma, the Soviets withered. Then a series of seemingly minor events proved to be cataclysmic. In 1979, Pope John Paul II visited Poland and with his tacit support, a year later, a trade union named Solidarity was born. Unlike revolts in Hungary and Czechoslovakia, the Soviets held their military back. After a year, Solidarity had ten million members. Meanwhile, American president Ronald Reagan had adopted a muscular foreign policy, seeking to foment nationalism in Warsaw Pact states and discard decades of prior commitments regarding nuclear weapons. The policy of mutually assured destruction (known as MAD) during the postwar years had been credited with both avoiding nuclear Armageddon and creating a massive arms race. Reagan sought to end that standoff; he dangled the prospect of denuclearization before the Soviets while openly funding a military buildup. Then rather fantastically, he announced that the United States would build a Strategic Defense System to shoot down incoming warheads. That of course meant the end of MAD and American victory. The claim itself was theater, the stuff of science fiction, and much derided in the press, but leaders in Moscow, filled with fantasies of their adversary's power, grew terrified.

During this turbulent time, Soviet leadership reeked of decay. In the span of less than three years, a long-invalid Leonid Brezhnev, the frail Yuri Andropov, and the nearly catatonic Konstantin Chernenko, all died in office. As central authority teetered, regional aspirations grew. In 1985, a youthful Mikhail Gorbachev took office and recognized the need for reform. Four years later, he decided to allow the nations of Eastern Europe to decide their futures for themselves. In a flash, Poland, Hungary, Czechoslovakia, East Germany, Romania, and Bulgaria waved goodbye. The gravitational pull that kept the Soviets' spheres in their orbit had lost power. And the implosion did not end there. On December 31, 1991, after a tumult-filled two years, the Union of Soviet Socialist Republics disbanded. The Soviet Union was no more.

What happened? Recently, the Cold War historian John Lewis Gaddis deployed a scientific metaphor—criticality—to capture this stunning change. In chemistry, for example, a "critical" temperature marks the precise reading when, say, all of a liquid simultaneously becomes a gas. The criticality here, however, was of exactly what? The answer must be the *union.*

Authoritarian regimes, due to the intense levels of submission that they demand, are inherently fragile systems. Such regimes require a great abdication of individuality in exchange for the fulfillment of security and dependency needs. Internal dissatisfaction must be constantly managed, for little cracks can spread swiftly. One time-honored strategy to maintain internal order is to remain in a constant state of conflict with an enemy. War enhances communal bonds and encourages a regressive posture toward "our" protector, the supreme leader. That figurehead, however, must be vigilant, aware of the Wizard of Oz effect, by which a photo or revelation transforms the supreme leader into a short, plump fellow behind a curtain.

During the run-up to the Soviet collapse in 1991, much of that unwieldy machinery seized up. The Soviets were once again experiencing economic deprivation from their command economy, but they had survived that before. Now it was combined with a string of leaders who were a visibly pathetic, impotent set. Meanwhile, the Pope and Lech Walesa offered the possibility of an alternative community, one with more autonomy. And Western soft power with its jeans, sexual liberation, and rock and roll had diminished some of the disdain for the American enemy. As a backpacker visiting Prague in 1981, I witnessed that firsthand when I was adopted by a group of underground Lennonists. One night we crept down to a graffiti-filled wall, where, alongside anti-regime slogans, they had created a memorial to the recently murdered Beatle. Each morning, they gleefully informed me, the authorities would whitewash the wall. Every evening, they would return, wine bottles in hand, to sing half-garbled Dylan and Lennon songs, and rebuild their shrine. Eight years later, when the Berlin Wall fell, the Lennon Wall in Prague had become a legendary symbol of revolt.

The fall of the Soviet empire made a great many like those Lennonists rejoice. They could now imagine a future free of fear, spies, and persecution. Legions of silenced and scared citizens joyously celebrated this new day. For some, however, as Svetlana Alexievich so poignantly recorded, this was a nearly insupportable disaster. Proud, older comrades who once were buoyed by stereotypes of Western materialism and exploitation suddenly discovered they were no longer proletariats, just abjectly poor. Humiliated and afraid, a segment of this populace looked to ultranationalists like the grandiose Vladimir Zhirinovsky, who called for a return to a police state and played ethnic cards, such as calling for the expulsion of all "Asians" from eastern Russia. He also indulged in gross anti-Semitism despite—psychoanalysts would say due to—his own long-denied Jewish patrimony.

Reborn as an unregulated haven, *plus capitaliste que les capitalistes*, Russia now existed alongside Ukraine, Belarus, Moldova, Azerbaijan, Uzbekistan, Georgia, Tajikistan, and Armenia. The possibility for rivalries within and between these states was great, as each sought to define and reinforce their borders while creating binding commitments that distinguished them from neighbors who, until very recently, were submerged in the same empire. Populists like the puffed-up Zhirinovsky latched on to an old, pre-Soviet enemy or a historical grievance so as to rally his bereft and frightened constituents, urging them to identify with and take comfort in him. This was a model that Vladimir Putin refined and employed as he gradually assumed dictatorial powers.

What would happen to the new nations that coalesced as the Soviet Union crumbled? The threat of war over ethnic, religious, and national differences loomed large. It became a horrific reality in Yugoslavia, which experienced the worst outbreak of xenophobic violence since 1945. In this multiethnic federation, the iron-fisted, communist rule of Josip Tito had glued together four languages, three religions, and at least five ethnic groups. With Tito's death in 1980, a glaring absence of leadership followed. After all, the very idea of the nation had been embodied in his person, and the constitution forbade anyone from succeeding him. Somehow the nation held on, but the collapse of the Soviet Union further destabilized its wobbly neighbor. In 1991, Yugoslavia splintered into five: Serbia-Montenegro, Bosnia-Herzegovina, Slovenia, Macedonia, and Croatia. Slovenia and Croatia were Catholic, while the southern regions were a mix of Orthodox Christians and Muslims.

Ethnic nationalists and religious competitors turned on once fellow countrymen. Stereotypes in the local media revived tribal identities and fears. War broke out first in Croatia, then in Bosnia and Herzegovina, and from there it continued to spread. In Serbia, the would-be successor to Tito, Slobodan Milošević, began to rail against "foreigners" like Croats. The ensuing wars lasted eight years and resulted in a genocide, directed by the likes of Bosnian Serb General Ratko Mladić. In 1993, an international war crimes tribunal was created at the Hague to finally make good on Raphael Lemkin's work: as the Cold War ended, other international bodies like the International Criminal Court would also soon take up this task. In the end, Milošević, Mladić, and 161 others were indicted at the Hague for genocide and crimes against humanity. By then, three hundred thousand former Yugoslavs were dead and three million had gone into exile.

The collapse of Yugoslavia seemed to be a harbinger of more xenophobic battles to come. For in the newly liberated Warsaw Pact states, the Soviets had yielded power to . . . well, save for Solidarity in Poland, there were few established parties to whom one might hand power. Instead, a vacuum was quickly filled by populists who called for a return to a homogenous, nationalist identity as well as homegrown democrats, identified with Europe. With an array of new countries hoisting their flags, the American political scientist John Mearsheimer predicted a return to pre–Cold War times, with more gruesome battles to come over national identity. Experts documented a resurgence of European nationalism. Around 1995, a number of scholars declared that post–Cold War Europe had become plagued by a "new xenophobia."

Miraculously, however, much of the reshuffling that occurred after the fall of the Soviets remained peaceful. Even in multiethnic Czechoslovakia, after some struggle, the Czechs and Slovaks simply decided to go separate ways. Bloodshed was likely averted in part because, just as the Soviets were cracking up, Europe was pulling itself together. The European Union, established in 1992, offered a new, supranational identity that allowed local democrats to outflank xenophobic populists. The EU also offered a common currency and the full, free circulation of goods, services, and people. Open internal borders meant immigration between member states was relatively effortless. Centered around a reunified Germany, France, and the United Kingdom, the EU set out to transform the region into an economic colossus ensured by a military alliance, NATO. For the sudden nation-states of the former Soviet Union, the desire to join this club was powerful, helping anti-populists gain traction. If their nations ascribed to democratic, tolerant norms and managed to keep their debt and deficits within a proscribed range, they could join Europe. While it is hard to prove a negative, it seems likely that the rise of the European Union undermined xenophobic forces and saved lives.

Not everyone, however, was sold on this union. Put to a plebiscite, Denmark and Switzerland rejected the proposal, and the United Kingdom and Sweden barely rounded up the majority needed to ratify their admission. Among the recalcitrant, there was an understandable unease about handing national fiscal policy to Brussels. Not so for the new nations on the periphery of Europe, who continued to seize this opportunity. By 1999, Poland, the Czech Republic, and Hungary signed up, and five years later, others came on board including Bulgaria, Croatia, and Latvia. The European Union seemed to bring to a happy end what had been a devastating century for the so-called civilized Western world. And while worries about xenophobia surged after the collapse of the Soviet empire, one could be thankful that there was one Yugoslavia, not many.

However, when the 2008 crisis hit, lingering conflicts in the European Union burst into the open. Resentment came forward from nations who had shouldered much of the cost for bailing out the highly leveraged, nearly bankrupt nations of Spain and Greece. Local producers and workers in various nations worried that their governments would not protect them, given their EU commitments.

Despite these centrifugal pressures, debates continued over whether the EU should continue to grow. If so, who should rightly be considered? What were the ethnic, religious, or geographic limits of the EU? These long-debated questions became acute with the case of Turkey. Atatürk's nation pitched itself to the EU by heralding its secular status. Geographically, it was almost entirely not part of the European continent, yet, if admitted, Turkey would become the second-largest and one of the poorest member states. Official negotiations began in 2004 but stalled, and they stayed that way. This was hardly a surprise, for Turkey had been briskly moving away from the EU's requirements. Under Recep Tayyip Erdoğan, the country had become less democratic, less secular, and less tolerant. By 2008, the Turks were nowhere near acceptance into the union, but their futile efforts to gain admission were seized upon by Nigel Farage and others in the United Kingdom, who raised grave fears about an impending invasion of Turkish immigrants. This, I discovered, was the source of the worried gossip I had overheard in that London sweater shop.

After the crash of 2008, an array of anti–European Union, anti-globalization nationalists came up from the cellar. Some, like the Le Pens in France, had been toiling away since the early 1970s, earning the father, Jean-Marie, a conviction for inciting racist hatred thanks to his Holocaust denial. After years of demonizing Arabs and Jews, it seemed he and his daughter's time had come. In the once mighty empire of Great Britain, nostalgia combined with resentment against their increasingly multicultural capital and the imperious demands coming from Brussels. In France and Great Britain, nativist slogans like "France for the French" and "Eng-

Anti-immigrant Brexit poster, 2016

land for the English" made a return from the dark corners of pre–World War II history. Anti-immigrant nationalists emerged into the mainstream. In the wake of Islamicist terrorism, politicians like Nicolas Sarkozy in France and David Cameron in Great Britain did not just denounce radical fanaticism, but declared the principle of multiculturalism to be dead. Alongside the retreat of these centrists, openly xenophobic populists— some harboring fond memories of midcentury fascism—stepped forward in Hungary, Italy, Poland, Austria, Germany, and the United Kingdom.

Long-standing xenophobic fantasies of foreign invasion were given tangible form when, three years after the economic crash, desperate immigrants began to wash up on Europe's shores. In 2011, the Syrian and North African migrant crisis erupted and built to a peak four years later. A shivering mass of Syrians, Iraqis, and Afghanis, as well as Albanians and Kosovans, desperately sought asylum. They came to Hungary, Austria, Sweden, Italy, France, and, most of all, Germany. These foreigners embodied helplessness, that same desperate state many Westerners had just experienced as their savings vaporized. If such a mutual experience of vulnerability brought forth sympathy from many, it also made others consider these refugees to be a threat and an intolerable burden. As large as this migration was, nativists in host countries dramatically overestimated their numbers and the amount of government aid they received.

Caught up in complex economic turmoil, no longer solely in control of their monetary policy or their borders, unclear if their local leaders had the power or will to protect their own interests, a growing number of Europeans found a tangible source for their discontent in an alien Other. Some nations that once embraced the idea of a unified Europe registered their distress by turning to authoritarian nationalists, who offered security and safety by focusing their rage on the half-drowned refugees on their shores. In Hungary, Viktor Orbán ratcheted up his anti-immigrant, anti-Muslim rhetoric and built a wall to repel the migrants. Soon he would move on from Muslims to grand, anti-Jewish conspiracy theories involving that advocate of open societies, George Soros. In Germany, Angela Merkel's policies welcomed one million Syrian migrants and ushered forth a far-right reaction. The extremist Alternative for Germany was founded in 2013, and four years later, it was the third-largest party in that country. Most of its early followers lived far from the urban centers that hosted many immigrants, but they nonetheless railed against these intruders. In the first six months of 2019 alone, Germany recorded over 4000 violent attacks by xenophobes from the extreme right.

IN THE UNITED STATES, the swift end of the Cold War caused a stunned, disorienting euphoria. Kremlinologists were almost universally befuddled when this so-called mighty superpower proved to be feeble. What had they missed? Primed to assess the Soviet threat, ready to leap into action and prevent a nuclear assault, had they been blind to their enemy's frailty? Years of Cold War stereotypes built up the threat of the "Evil Empire" and primed Americans to miss the big story.

President George H. W. Bush conceded that he and his advisers were utterly taken aback by the USSR's collapse. When the dust cleared, Bush proclaimed the rise of a New World Order, a unipolar world in which American military power, individualism, free-market capitalism, and democracy reigned. "Neoliberalism"—with its rejection of the welfare state—now stood triumphant. Right-wing attacks on the safety net—Social Security, Medicare, and Medicaid—were redoubled, launched from the high ground of ideological supremacy. "Trickle-down" economics, inaugurated nearly a decade earlier by Ronald Reagan, continued to magically justify cutting taxes on the wealthy. Opponents who questioned this were said, in an Orwellian turn of phrase, to be engaged in class warfare. Governments and centralized bureaucracies no longer were the solution; they needed to get out of the way of the private sector. An obscure State Department official named Francis Fukuyama wondered if humanity's final acceptance of Western capitalism and liberal democracy represented the "end of history."

History, it turned out, had a few tricks in store. The demise of the Reds was a bigger problem for the Red, White, and Blue than first imagined. When the celebrations ended, America had lost something, too. For nearly fifty years, this diverse, multicultural nation, which cherished its exceptionalism, had in part defined itself by being armed and ready to confront a clear and common enemy. Its running conflict with the totalitarian Soviets had been an ennobling battle that helped highlight America's commitment to liberty and to being the leaders of the free world. The specter of the Soviet Union unified Americans who were urban and rural, white and minority, traditional and progressive, as well as rich and poor. Victory ended that.

When the militaristic Romans defeated the long-detested Carthaginians, that grand day, Sallust determined, was followed by decades of internal rivalry and civil war. After 1991, with the Soviets gone, American political life similarly became more riven. The traditional left, those one-time champions of labor, were upended by the victory of free-market economics. Liberals turned their focus more to the expansion of individual and civil rights. Many moderate Democrats followed Bill Clinton's third way and stepped back from economic justice and statist interventions, all of which now reeked of failed Soviet models. Meanwhile, Republican Cold Warriors were even more disoriented. They had lost their *raison d'être*. What was their role in this New World Order? Many turned their sights toward reviving a more traditional, Christian America, which meant defeating their secular and cosmopolitan compatriots.

The 2001 attacks on the World Trade Center provided new enemies and old answers. Islamic terrorists like al-Qaeda were small fry by American geopolitical standards, but they now had murdered more citizens on our homeland than any before them. As for negative stereotypes, these extremists were right out of Hollywood's central casting: swarthy, fanatical, and willing to die just to kill Americans. In the years following 9/11, Muslims became, for the old Cold Warriors, a new American enemy, adding weight to the Harvard political scientist Samuel Huntington's prediction—some argued his fervent wish—that with the Soviets gone, a clash between the Western and Islamic civilizations was inevitable. Xenophobia made a comeback, as rote stereotypes of Muslims and Arabs from Hollywood and Madison Avenue flooded the American imagination. After the terrorist strikes on New York, while President George W. Bush admirably stated that our ensuing wars were not against Islam, the cynical run-up to the war in Iraq demonstrated that Saddam Hussein, Osama bin Laden, and Arabs in general could be lumped together to serve as a unifying Other.

However, it was neither Communism nor radical Islam that nearly felled the United States. If 1991 marked the final sigh of the Soviets, 2008 was the year that brought the Cold War victors to their knees. The dangers, it turned out, were internal. While the Soviets showcased how a state-controlled economy could shrivel, America demonstrated how unregulated capitalism could spin out of control. Starting in 1979, income disparities had grown so that, by 2016, the U.S. Census Bureau reported that a measure of inequality, the Gini index, was the highest ever. Under Ronald Reagan, American policy makers not only cut taxes on the wealthiest but also began to loosen restrictions on banks. Depression-era policies were repealed, and despite a nearly immediate crisis, deregulation continued. Markets, it was said, would "self-regulate," a fancier and more pretentious way of abiding by Adam Smith's faith in "sympathy" and the market's invisible hand. Obscure investment vehicles like derivatives were liberated from oversight; freedom was on the march. This ideology found its apogee in 2004, when the regulatory body, the U.S. Securities and Exchange Commission, proposed that financial institutions be allowed to oversee themselves. The fox was in the henhouse, and not just in the United States; the leader of the free world had spread the same model of unrestrained markets around the globe.

Meanwhile, the emergence of the Internet brought forth global synergies, mergers, and growth. A newly interconnected world was busy being born, when suddenly there was a terrifying sound. In 2008, Bear Stearns and Lehman Brothers exploded. This set off a chain of reactions that led to the meltdown of the equities market and the tottering of too-big-to-fail banks. Like Watson's quivering Little Albert, citizens looked on, unable to comprehend where all the pain was coming from. After inquiring, they heard about the Clinton-era repeal of the Glass-Steagall Act, complex instruments like credit default swaps, and repackaged subprime mortgages. The crash of 2008 inaugurated the worst American economic contraction since 1929. The untrammeled forces of freedom had nearly self-immolated. No one was sure the global economy would survive. The president of the sole superpower was reported to have exclaimed, "This sucker could go down."

When the United States had had their nemesis, no matter what trouble brewed at home, there was a likely cause in Boris Badenov and his Stalinist ilk. In a unipolar world, however, Americans had no one to blame for this sudden impoverishment, this helplessness and fear. The greatest military in world history was useless. Economic shock, humiliation, and resentment were now the lot of many in the richest nation on earth. Polarization increased between the wealthy and a slipping middle class, between a shrinking white majority and a rainbow of minorities, and between those positioned to benefit from expanding, global commerce and those left behind. Toleration was put to the test as twenty-four-hour cable news stations featured screaming partisans who furthered these divides. As hot-button issues were stoked, Americans spun apart as if in a centrifuge. Many seemed to be willing to vote against their own interests and close their eyes to blatant realities so as to remain secure within their own political tribe. Group ideologies solidified distrust of the other side and transformed suspicion into a rigid, unyielding hatred of the American Other. Whole states committed to the same conclusion before the facts: they were in the bag as red or blue. Swing states swayed, studies showed, due to the waxing and waning of white grievances against Blacks and immigrants.

The election of Barack Obama, who, unlike his opponent, demonstrated great poise in the midst of the Wall Street meltdown, was a watershed moment. It demonstrated the diminished force of racism for a majority of Americans, and it also fueled a furious backlash. The New York developer and television personality Donald Trump wildly decried the election of this foreigner, this illegitimate, "Nigerian-born" president. Tea Party populists, stirred up by Rupert Murdoch's Fox News, denounced the browning of America and its flood of immigrants. Migrants, it was said, were threats, economically, criminally, and culturally. Statistics did not bear this out, but no matter. Trump's nativist, anti-immigration stances and his devotion to building a wall on the southern border were portrayed as sticking up for besieged whites. His carnival show included baiting and belittling an array of minorities, stoking contempt and fear of Mexican and Muslim immigrants, and trafficking in contemptuous views of women, not to mention Hispanic and Black Americans. This would-be demagogue seemed to be searching for whatever negative stereotypes of the Other would stick, and in the fall of 2016, many of us discovered to our shock that a startling number had done just that.

———

WHAT HAD HAPPENED? By 2016, the belief in a New World Order with neoliberalism as its guiding ideology had come undone. A number of Western nations had retreated behind their borders. Some flirted with strongmen, who focused their followers' rage and helplessness on a chosen outsider. It took some doing not to realize that these attacks on different kinds of foreigners and minorities were not isolated events, but I must admit, I was one of the blind men. Perhaps I should have paid more attention to reports out of Austria. The Poles? Hungarians? What did that have to do with me? In 2016, I realized, the answer was a great deal. The postwar order, off balance since the victory of the West, now had hurtled off the tracks. Newly empowered voices, oblivious to the post-Holocaust moral order, emerged. Xenophobia had come back from the dead.

The extent of this reawakening remains to be seen. It seems inevitable that there will be a reckoning, for despite this retreat behind hardened borders, many of the most desperate challenges we face remain global. Overpopulation, competition for limited natural resources, tragic numbers of asylum seekers and refugees, public health crises that do not respect national borders: all these are pressing twenty-first-century problems that can only be solved internationally. How much does it cost to purchase a nuclear weapon on the black market in the Baltics? Not enough. What is the next virus to hop from animals and terrorize mankind? Speculation is back on Wall Street; the result could be mass unemployment in far-off lands. Artificial intelligence, powerful new forms of propaganda, and cyber-warfare are potential threats that remain hard to fully fathom. Like nuclear weapons after Hiroshima, this novel force will remain deeply destabilizing until some international armistice can be negotiated. Automation and the loss of work may also make for millions of bereft souls who refuse to stay put, as their opportunities evaporate. And, most dauntingly of all, climate change bears down upon us. If unchecked, it will make crops fail and droughts impossible to endure. Water shortages, deforestation, and desertification will make for eco-exiles, perhaps in massive numbers. If patterns of weather, that very basic foundation for sedentary civilization, become chaotic and altered, how many more will be forced to turn back to migratory existences?

At the same time, each little corner of the world has been overrun. Like the waves of change brought forth by the telegraph, telephone, mass media, and moving pictures, an expanded, virtual reality now has swept through our lives. Digital technologies have muddied the very boundaries between the strangers and their hosts. What will it mean to be virtual in one's identity and social affiliations, to be more a member of a virtual nation, than one's own? Identity theft is not just a problem with credit cards; it is a metaphor. Our online "homes" may be invaded and occupied by unseen entities. We rightly worry that invisible beings steal our data, hack our histories, and feed us fake stories. They may control our beliefs, our behaviors, even our minds. Knowledge, the very basis of open, secular societies and the backbone of democracy, now comes to many of us through the most powerful propaganda tool ever constructed. Do gadgets once meant to connect you with a high-school flame ignite riots, get presidents elected, and foment mass murder? They already have. Welcome to the twenty-first century.

These disruptions are ones no nation-state alone can manage. The answers must be global as well as local. That requires tacking back and forth, not just in our politics and policies but, as the problem of xenopho-

bia makes clear, in our identities. How can I be defined by my difference—
my personal experiences, my language, my nation, my heritage, my needs,
desires, and choices—and at the same time remain identified with all
those foreigners in my nation, in my species? How can I advocate for
my own parochial interests, while also not ending up like Albert Camus,
necessarily choosing my motherland over justice? For the poet Walt Whitman, the answer was radical empathy; I contain, he famously wrote, multitudes. One of Whitman's heirs, the postwar poet A. R. Ammons, put it
in less heroic terms. We should not strive to be "homogenous pudding,"
but rather:

> united differences, surface difference expressing the common,
> underlying hope and fate of each person and people, a gathering
> into one place of multiple dissimilarity, each culture to its
> own cloth and style and tongue and gait, each culture, like
> the earth itself with commonlode center and variable surface . . .

Integrated minds, the poet wrote, made for an integrated nation, and
the possibility of unity between nations. Conversely, unified nations help
to foster the psychic integration of their citizens. As we have seen, xenophobia is debilitating and distorting on our inner lives, our local communities, and our broader political world. All of us possess the "commonlode
center" as well as the diverse richness of surface variety. Universal human
rights and radical egalitarianism reside in the former; toleration, cultural
relativity, and local adaptations in the latter. Given our new global hori-
zons, we cannot but strive to embody these truths and be, in this manner,
two-minded.

We have no better choice. While some may yearn for simpler times,
pressing problems preclude taking care of our own and forgetting the rest.
Whether we like it or not, whether by peace or war, whether by authoritarian fiat or democratic resolve, the immediate future will be determined
by our capacity to solve global dilemmas. Some will seek a semblance of
order and safety through division and the falling in hate with some outsider. Since that path leads to head-in-the-sand self-destructiveness and
spirals of violence, the other path must be our hope. On that road we may
find mutual aid, merger, hybridization, and new possibilities.

Powerful societies succeed because they integrate the new into the old. Cooperation and assimilation have made for wonders, like the millions who peacefully coexist outside my New York City door. Thanks to these forces, in 2019, measures of literacy, extreme poverty, and life expectancy have never been better for our species. Every second, as Emmanuel Levinas reminded us, strangers take care of each other, and, more so, they see it as their responsibility. With that as our guide, might we not come together in new ways and forge greater commonality, an even wider us?

For such hopes not to be vacuous, much must be done. New norms and self-aware institutions must help us weed out the invasive species of stereotypes, fears, and assumptions that fill our minds. To lessen xenophobia, we must develop ways to diminish the need for this rigid buttress for the self. Such prescriptions, I know, might lead the hard-headed to despair. And yet, as this history has demonstrated, cultures adapt, at times rapidly. What reader in Paris would have guessed that only decades after learning of xenophobia by the Boxers in China, that this term would take on its present meanings? We now stand in a long line of those who risked a great deal to create that shift. They threw themselves on top of the explosive trouble we once again confront. Thanks to these forebearers, we come to this crisis carrying concepts, forms of analysis, collective memories, and moral commandments. It may seem laughable that we should go into this battle so poorly armed. However, words and ideas do things; they change the way we think and act. Xenophobia is one such word, and with its rise there comes the hope that we too can stop the floods of hatred before they rush forth again.

CODA: IN THE PYRENEES

THE CHURCH BELLS TOLL. What time is it? Outside my window, another dazzling, azure day has commenced. I rub my eyes and pull myself out of bed.

For the last three decades, my wife and I have spent our summer break in this remote French village, her childhood home. Perched halfway up a mountain in the Pyrénées-Orientales, we look south directly into Spain. This is a border zone, and it has changed allegiances throughout history, but to me, it seems not so much French, or Catalan, or Spanish, as Mediterranean. The ever-present sun, the fragrant air, and the aloes and palms make me feel that when I put my feet in the sea, I cross over to the eastern shore and touch up against my family's ancestral home in Lebanon, the one I have not seen since the war.

I dizzily head toward the kitchen, make coffee, and from our terrace, gaze out past the cypresses to a timeless, granite horizon. Our modest, stone house was made from these mountains. Built behind castle walls a few centuries ago, it once belonged to my mother-in-law. A painter from Argentina, she fell in love with the golden light here and bought this simple abode from a Catalan laborer named Alvarez. He and his family had fled Franco by crossing these hills. Penniless, they were rescued from a harsher fate by the mayor of our village, who allowed them to take shelter in what was a ruin. Our jasmine-scented village long since has been gentrified; it now hosts artists, Parisians on holiday, a handful of British exiles, but also more than a few children of refugees from the Spanish Civil War. They often look a bit Moorish, that is, like me.

Today my wife and I planned a hike in the hills, not serious stuff, just a day trip along an old smugglers' path. The trailhead originated in Banyuls-sur-Mer, so we jump in our little Peugeot. Sleeping late, we soon realize, was dumb. Once we park and begin to march up the AL-59 trail, the breeze falls away and the August heat grows fierce. I zigzag upward, hoping the next bend might magically make my imaginings real. There was a plateau that should have seven large pine trees. At least it did a long time ago.

On September 25, 1940, the gentle, unearthly Walter Benjamin started up this trail. Friends like Adorno had urged him to flee Paris, but he had resisted. When war broke out, he was interned as a possible Nazi enemy within. Eventually, this absurdity became clear and he was allowed to return to Paris. However, once Hitler's forces stormed France, Benjamin fled. He made his way to Lourdes, that city of miracles, where he played chess with Hannah Arendt, worked on dark epigrams about the "Angel of History," and openly contemplated suicide. Then to Marseille, where he joined throngs hoping to escape. Benjamin had secured an American visa thanks to Max Horkheimer, but he discovered that the French refused to issue an exit permit to a German Jew. He was trapped. Chance had taken up residence inside his existence, and without its mercies he would perish. Someone, however, knew someone, who told him to make his way down to Banyuls-sur-Mer, where a woman named Lucy Fittko would lead him across the border.

This brilliant chronicler of modernity could be many things, but now he was reduced to one: a stateless refugee. Weakened from likely cardiac failure, he found Fittko and managed to survive a test run halfway up the path. However, he could not conceive of returning to town and embarking on the entire hike the next night, as planned. Instead, he insisted on sleeping on a plateau marked by seven pines, telling his guide to meet him in the morning there. Before light, Fittko and a small group of *évadés* found him. He looked pale and sickly. To make matters worse, the others noticed that Benjamin was lugging a weighty briefcase. It was crazy, they told him. The manuscript inside, he solemnly replied, was more precious than his life. And so, each member of the group took turns carrying Benjamin's burden. They trudged up and up, until finally the troupe made it to the peak of the Pyrenees and peered out at a sapphire sea. Victorious, ecstatic, they stumbled down into the Spanish town of Portbou.

Their elation was short-lived. A sudden change in Spain's asylum policies—soon to be rescinded—dictated that no new refugees were to

The trail to Portbou

be accepted. Apprehended and in despair, the captives were placed in a guarded hotel and told they would be returned to the French authorities in the morning. Benjamin did not wait. That evening, he swallowed the morphine pills that he carried for this occasion. When his body was discovered, confused Francoist authorities gave a Catholic burial to a "Benjamin Walter." His briefcase was never found.

The story of Walter Benjamin's flight is famous, and it has long haunted me. Did this brilliant wanderer, this European *flâneur*, know that in the end he would become mythic as a man on the run, a *xénos* turned away, crushed by cool legalisms enforced at foreign ports and borders? In his final despair, did he know his story would be rewritten backward, so that this hike would become a tourist destination, and his spirit would forever linger in dingy Portbou?

And what of his briefcase? What was in it? Many have speculated, but I think the simplest answer is hope. That leather bag contained Walter Benjamin's last appeal. It was what remained of a trembling, failing trust that perhaps his voice might vault over the highest walls of hatred to reach far-off, perhaps quite foreign beings who might join with him over those pages. Sometimes I imagine that if one stumbled upon that dusty valise and pried it open, as in *The Thousand and One Nights*, it would release the roaring voices of history's refugees and exiles, all their lamentations, their laughter, and their stories, all their accusations and confessions, all freed from oblivion together in a waterfall of sound so grand, so sublime that for an instant, it would stop everything, even time.

History is a trip into the spirit world. It is an attempt to wake the graveyard and give our ancestors voice and form, so that we can confront them and free ourselves from their spells. History, at its best then, carries the hope not only of resurrection but of exorcism. It holds the desire that by remembering we will not repeat. *Of Fear and Strangers* has been my attempt to remember for myself, for you. Xenophobia is not some antiquated, classical term. It is our word. We have a name for what is happening to us, what has been growing in scope, flashing red, spreading. The only questions are how extreme will it become, what forms will it take, who will it target, and who will stand to oppose it? This hatred will not end of its own accord. This is our catastrophe. That poet who once grilled me about my history, himself descended from enslaved people, wrote that "nightmare begins responsibility." That responsibility, I know now, to ourselves, to each other, is not just to wake up, but to remember it all when we do.

August 2019,
New York City and Eus, France

ACKNOWLEDGMENTS

Of Fear and Strangers was inspired by stories of my Texan-Lebanese grandfather. It follows the paths cut by my intrepid father and mother, Jack and Odette Makari; my fearless mother-in-law, Olimpia Aimaretti Ogilvie; as well as my sisters, Grace and Doris, co-conspirators in the joys and challenges of becoming Americans. Thus, I have been considering these themes for much of my adult life and have thereby accrued many debts along the way. First, I would like to declare my love for the late poet Michael S. Harper. MSH gave me the courage to consider myself a writer, and instilled in me the moral obligations of that craft. Fortune favored me a second time, when I was taken under the wing of the ever-erudite and generous Sander L. Gilman, whose work on representations of difference were formative. My gratitude to him is immeasurable.

Since arriving at Weill Cornell's Department of Psychiatry, and its utterly unique DeWitt Wallace Institute of Psychiatry: History, Policy, & the Arts, I have been lifted up by that incredible community. My deep thanks go to the Institute's associate director Nathan Kravis and administrator Megan Woolf, who have been wonderful colleagues. *Of Fear and Strangers* greatly benefited from discussions of two chapters from this book in the Institute's Working Groups. My gratitude goes out to the dazzling members: Rachel Aviv, Alexandra Bacopoulos-Viau, Thomas Dodman, Lawrence Friedman, Stefanos Gerolanos, Lenny Groopman, Dagmar Herzog, Ben Kafka, Jonas Knatz, Nate Kravis, Robert Michels, Orna Ophir, Camille Robcis, Ted Shapiro, Nirav Soni, Katherine Tabb, and Milt Viederman. Thanks to Institute member Samantha Boardman for her insights into contemporary research on communal bias.

The Institute contains the world-class Oskar Diethelm Library, and

I have freely made use of its riches. My deepest gratitude goes out to the Diethelm's research librarians. Marisa Shaari proved to be a veritable Sherlock Holmes, as she helped me track down the many usages of xenophobia. Her successor, Nicole Topich, has been cheerfully capable of seemingly impossible feats.

Three decades of friendship with Anthony Walton have been a gift and an education. Our discussions on writing, race, and America would inevitably slip deep into the night; this book is far better because of him. Thanks to Sander Gilman, whose comments during the late stages of this project saved me (once again) from error. Diane McCoskey offered her expertise on the ideological role of the classics, and my long-lost relative, Jack Balagia of Houston, provided that wonderful photo of the Jacobs' Austin rug store. My writing on the Spanish empire is deeply indebted to Arabella Ogilvie, whose extensive knowledge on that subject was formative. I also relied upon her formidable linguistic proficiencies to help with texts in French, Spanish, Italian, Portuguese, and German.

My research has been constantly encouraged by colleagues at Weill Cornell Medicine. This book project commenced with the unequivocal support of the Department of Psychiatry's chairman, Dr. Jack Barchas, and concluded with the equal enthusiasm of his successor, Dr. Francis Lee. My gratitude goes out to both, and to the steadfast support of the DeWitt Wallace–Reader's Digest Fund at the New York Community Trust, without whom this work would not have been possible. My appreciation also goes out to my other academic home, Rockefeller University, the late, much missed, Mitchell Feigenbaum, as well as Eric Siggia and Melanie Lee.

The idea for this book was sparked by my respect, bordering on awe, for Sarah Chalfant. For the past fourteen years, Sarah has been everything one could ask for from a literary agent. I am blessed to work with Sarah, the astute Rebecca Nagel, Dorothy Janick, and everyone at the Wylie Agency. I have been thrilled to again benefit from the wisdom of editor Jill Bialosky at W. W Norton. Thanks Jill, for your insights and your trust. The Norton team of Drew Elizabeth Weitman, Nancy Palmquist, Don Rifkin, Louise Brockett, Kyle Radler, and Meredith McGinnis have been nothing short of superb.

This is a personal book and I wrote it with an anxious eye toward the future. Our failings may very well burden the next generation, but if so, Gabrielle and Jack, know that my confidence in you is unwavering. Finally, while writing over the past five years, a presence has been with me. She too has been defined by border crossing and foreign lands. By her openness and unending curiosity, she has carried me into many strange worlds and made them my home. I could not have written *Of Fear and Strangers* without having entwined my life with hers, and for that reason this book is for Arabella.

NOTES

Prologue: Out of Beirut

xii **"word of the year":** Jason Daley, "Why Xenophobia is Dictionary.com's Word of the Year," *Smithsonian*, November 29, 2016, retrieved from https://www.smithsonianmag.smart-news/why-xenophobia-dictionarycoms-wrd-year-180961225.

xiii **without beginning or end:** Franz Boas, "An Anthropologist's View of War," *The Advocate of Peace* 24, no. 4 (April 1912): 93–94; also his *The Mind of Primitive Man* (New York: Macmillan, 1911), 207. Boas wrote: "There are a number of primitive hordes to whom every stranger not a member of the horde is an enemy. . . ." On the linguistic equivalence of stranger and enemy, see Magnus Hirschfeld, *Racism*, trans. Eden and Cedar Paul (London: Gollancz, 1938), 257–58.

xiii **What was it with *them*?:** Josiah Royce, *Race Questions, Provincialism, and Other American Problems* (New York: Macmillan, 1908), 25.

xv **and never left again:** On the famine around Mount Lebanon, see George Antonius, *The Arab Awakening* (London: Hamish Hamilton, 1938). On the Ottomans and actions against internal populations of Greek Orthodox, Armenians, Assyrian and Maronite Christians, see Eugene Rogan, *The Fall of the Ottomans: The Great War in the Middle East* (New York: Basic Books, 2015).

Part I: The Origins of Xenophobia

1 **Plato, *The Sophist*:** Plato, *Plato II: Theaetetus, Sophist*, trans. H. N. Fowler (New York: Putnam, 1921), 267.

Chapter 1: In Search of *Xénos*

4 **about struggling for survival:** For Melvin Konner, "xenophobia," like genocide, though immoral, was adaptive; M. Konner, "Is Xenophobia Now Maladaptive?" psychologytoday.com, posted September 2, 2012.

5 **most destabilizing kind of disaster:** Stephen Jay Gould, "Kropotkin Was No Crackpot," *Natural History* 97, no. 7, retrieved from https://www.marxists.org/subject/science/essays/kropotkin.htm. Among evolutionary psychologists,

Jonathan Haidt suggests we are 90 percent chimp and 10 percent bee; see his *The Righteous Mind: Why Good People Are Divided by Politics and Religion* (New York: Vintage, 2013), xxii; Joshua Greene assumes ethnocentrism and in-group favoritism are not "hard-wired" and can be altered by experience. See his *Moral Tribes: Emotion, Reason, and the Gap between Us and Them* (New York: Penguin, 2013), 54–55, 69, 102. On the critical import of cultural adaptation related to climate and food production, see the powerful work of Jared Diamond, *Guns, Germs, and Steel: The Fates of Human Societies* (New York: W. W. Norton, 1997), 273. Also see 267–86. For a brief discussion of the nonspecific nature of "stress"in most neurobiological models, see Olean Babenko et al., "Stress-Induced Perinatal and Transgenerational Epigenetic Programming of Brain Development and Mental Health," *Neuroscience and Biobehavioral Reviews* 48 (2014): 79–80. On the reductive biologization of social phenomena, see Richard Lewontin, Stephen Rose, and Leon Kamin, *Not in Our Genes: Biology, Ideology and Human Nature* (New York: Pantheon, 1984).

5 **Stoics alert us to this danger?:** George Fredrickson, *Racism: A Short History* (Princeton: Princeton University Press, 2015), 6, 140. On page 6, Frederickson writes that xenophobia is a term "invented by ancient Greeks to describe a reflexive feeling of hostility toward the stranger or Other." Then, on page 140, he reiterates that xenophobia is "ancient" and "universal."

6 **would be praised:** On the meanings of *xénos*, see Émile Benveniste, "L'hospitalité," in *Le vocabulaire des institutions indo-européennes* (Paris: Minuit, 1969), 87–101. Also, for a short piece in English, see K. D. O'Gorman, "Modern Hospitality: Lessons from the Past," *Journal of Hospitality and Tourism Management* 12, no. 2 (2005): 141–51. *Xénos's* multiple meanings are exemplified by its transformation into the Latin *hostis*, the root of both "host" and "hostile." Benveniste explicitly noted, however, that the Greek *xénos* never held the connotation of enemy.

6 **between neighboring cities:** For an excellent discussion of the term *xénos* in antiquity and its philosophical and social implications, see Rebecca LeMoine, *Philosophy and the Foreigner in Plato's Dialogues*, PhD dissertation, University of Wisconsin–Madison, 2014. The rules of *xenia* were described in numerous places, including Herodotus; see Benveniste, *Le vocabulaire des institutions indo-européennes*, 94. The best scholarly exposition of this "guest-friendship" and its social obligations is Gabriel Herman's *Ritualized Friendship and the Greek City* (Cambridge: Cambridge University Press, 1987).

6 **"[xénos] strangers, god-fearing men?":** Homer, *The Odyssey*, trans. Robert Fagles (New York: Penguin, 1996), 217.

6 **"pity both to men and gods":** Plato, *Works of Plato: The Laws, Book V*, trans. George Burges (London: Bell and Daldy, 1870), 157.

6 **"love thy neighbor as thyself":** The Holy Bible, King James Version (New York: World Publishing, n.d.). The Epistle of Paul the Apostle to the Hebrews, 13:2, 198, Matthew 22:39, 24. See Tasos Kokkinidis, "Philoxenia: The Ancient Roots of Greek Hospitality," *Greek Reporter*, September 21, 2018, 1–2.

7 **they would die simultaneously:** In addition to the "Eleatic Stranger" in *The

Sophist, Plato uses strangers as a rhetorical device to challenge assumptions and beliefs. Plato, *Plato II: Theaetetus, Sophist*, 264. Plato, *The Republic of Plato*, trans. Allan Bloom (New York: Basic Books, 1968), 59, 450. On the role of the stranger in Plato, see Anne DuFourmantelle and Jacques Derrida, *Of Hospitality*, trans. Rachel Bowlby (Stanford, CA: Stanford University Press, 2000).

8   **"I will praise him":** Pindar, *The Nemean Odes*, 7:61–63, as cited in Roger Woodward, *The Cambridge Companion to Greek Mythology* (Cambridge: Cambridge University Press, 2007), 48.

8   **I spoke to experts. Nothing:** In H. G. Liddell and R. Scott, *Greek-English Lexicon* (Oxford: Clarendon Press, 1889), the term is not listed. Much later, I found this absence confirmed by the scholar Benjamin Isaac, who noted that the term "xenophobia" is not to be found in ancient Greek; Benjamin Isaac, *The Invention of Racism in Classical Antiquity* (Princeton: Princeton University Press, 2004), 38.

8   **"are in nature the same":** Aristotle, *Politics*, trans. C. D. C. Reeve (Indianapolis: Hackett, 1998), 2.

9   **a particularly menacing group:** Plato, *Republic of Plato*, 149–50. For a lucid discussion of the literature and distinctions between the *xénoi* of nearby city-states and religiously and linguistically different *barbaroi*, as well as the scholarly debates over the evolution of this term for barbarians, see LeMoine, *Philosophy and the Foreigner in Plato's Dialogues*, 8–33. Also John Boardman et al., *Greece and the Hellenistic World* (Oxford: Oxford University Press, 1986), 34, 42.

9   **rendered as "*xénos*":** *A Dictionary of the Bible*, ed. James Hastings, vol. 4 (New York: Scribner, 1898–1904), 622–23.

10   **"a barbarian unto me":** The Holy Bible, King James Version, Paul to the Corinthians, 1, 14:10–11 (Oxford: Oxford University Press, 1997), 218. We will later find this passage cited by Las Casas and Montaigne. Also see Matthew 25:35.

11   **very identity of Western civilization:** Rodolfo Lanciani, "The Archaeological Budget of Rome for 1908," *The Athenaeum*, March 13, 1909, 324–25.

12   **entitled to do right now:** See the groundbreaking, if controversial, work of Martin Bernal, *Black Athena: The Afroasiatic Roots of Classical Civilization*, vol. 1 (New Brunswick, NJ: Rutgers University Press, 2003). Also Eliza Butler, *The Tyranny of Greece Over Germany* (1935; Cambridge: Cambridge University Press, 2012); and Paul Michael Kurtz, "How Nineteenth-Century German Classicists Wrote the Jews Out of Ancient History," *History and Theory* 58, no. 2 (2019): 210–32.

12   **perfect choice for the dig:** See Salomon Reinach, "Paul Gauckler," *Revue archéologique* 18 (July–December, 1911): 458–60.

12   **could become Roman citizens:** See Mary Beard, *SPQR: A History of Ancient Rome* (New York: Liveright, 2015), 66–67, 77, 497, 519. Also Denise Eileen McCoskey, *Race: Antiquity and Its Legacy* (New York: Oxford University Press, 2012), 75.

13   **a German scholar, Christian Hülsen:** George H. Chase, "Archaeology in 1909. Part II," *Classical Journal* 6, no. 3 (1910): 99–107, quote on page 103. Also see his "Archaeology in 1910. Part II," *Classical Journal* 7, no. 3 (1911): 114–25.

14   **"the spade could decide":** Chase, "Archaeology in 1909. Part I," 103.

14   **"Oriental Gods," another proclaimed:** William N. Bates, "Archaeological News," *American Journal of Archaeology* 15, no. 1 (1911): 77–129. William F. Bade, "A Semitic Discovery in Rome," *American Antiquarian and Oriental Journal* 32, no. 2 (1910): 115–17; Anonymous, "Necrology—Paul Gauckler," *American Journal of Archaeology* 16 (1912): 112.

14   **"and the Italian government":** Ralph Van Deman Magoffin, "The Grove of Furrina on the Janiculum," *Classical Weekly* 2 (1909): 244.

14   **over to the other side:** The answer might be found in Suetonius, who noted that the leader may have been Nero, who "despised all religious cults except that of the Syrian Goddess." Suetonius, *The Twelve Caesars*, trans. Robert Graves (New York: Penguin, 1957), 245.

14   **coils of the serpent's tail:** Paul Gauckler, *Le sanctuaire syrien du Janicule* (Paris: Libraire Alphonse Picard, 1912). Also see Nicholas Goodhue, *The Lucus Furrinae and the Syrian Sanctuary on the Janiculum* (Amsterdam: Hakkert, 1975), and his "Janiculan Mysteries? A Consideration of CIL VI 32316 and 36804," *Pacific Coast Philology* 10 (1975): 29–34.

14   **and ended his life:** On Gauckler's death, two years after his dig was stopped, as he was suffering from poor health and depression, see George Chase, "Archaeology in 1910. Part II," *Classical Journal* 7, no. 3 (1911): 122, as well as *Journal des débats politiques et littéraires,* December 10, 1911, 341. Also see the obituary by Salomon Reinach, "Paul Gauckler," *Revue archéologique* 18 (July–December 1911): 458–60.

15   **strangers at all:** Lanciani himself referred to that shift away from toleration; he suggested that the secret Syrian shrine with Bacchus and Isis had been concealed, around 377, when Gracchus ended toleration for pagan practices. Later, this fluidity would be undercut when, in 1916, an American archaeologist acknowledged such mixing and blamed it for the fall of the empire. Tenny Frank, "Race Mixture in the Roman Empire," *American Historical Review* 21, no. 4 (1916): 689–708. Also see McCoskey. *Race: Antiquity and Its Legacy.*

15   **"history of Roman excavation":** Lanciani, "Archaeological Budget of Rome for 1908," 325.

15   **due to *"xenophoby"*:** Gauckler was a correspondent for the *Académie des inscriptions et belles lettres* as well as a member of *l'Académie de France à Rome*, and so his work was avidly covered in France, in scholarly journals but also newspapers like *Le Radical* and *Journal des débats politiques et littéraires*, where his exciting Janiculum finds were lauded. The French crowing about his success was reported by D. Anziani, "Paul Gauckler," in "Mélanges d'archéologie et d'histoire," *École française de Rome* 31 (1911): 457–58.

Chapter 2: *Avant la lettre*, or The Black Legend

19   **"without a theory of toleration":** Henry Kamen, *The Spanish Inquisition: A Historical Revision* (New Haven: Yale University Press, 2014), 10; debates about

medieval Spain and the "Black Legend" are intense, part of the culture wars of today, with strong polemics against and for; see Maria Rosa Menocal, *The Ornament of the World: How Muslims, Jews, and Christians Created a Culture of Tolerance in Medieval Spain* (New York: Little, Brown, 2002); Brian Catlos, *Kingdom of Faith: A New History of Islamic Spain* (New York: Basic Books, 2019); and the review of Robert Irwin, "The Contested Legacy of Muslim Spain," *New York Review of Books*, March 21, 2019, 49–51.

19 **sought to curry favor:** Edwin Williamson, *The Penguin History of Latin America* (London: Penguin, 2009), 58–61. Also see Robert Goodwin, *Spain: The Centre of the World, 1519–1682* (London: Bloomsbury, 2015).

19 **and eventually civil war:** On Gaius Sallustis Crispus, a.k.a. Sallust, and his theory, see Duane F. Conley, "The Stages of Rome's Decline in Sallust's Historical Theory," *Hermes* 109, no. 3 (1981): 379–82; and Neal Wood, "Sallust's Theorem: A Comment on 'Fear' in Western Political Thought," *History of Political Thought* 16, no. 2 (1995): 174–89. Of course, in itself, this was a crude, insufficient theory for the decline of Rome, as has been widely acknowledged. See John Boardman et. al., *The Roman World* (Oxford: Oxford University Press, 1990), 50, 58, 82, 232–34.

20 **what lurked in her heart?:** Miguel de Cervantes, *Don Quixote*, trans. Edith Grossman (1605/1615; New York: HarperCollins, 2005), 810–16. The framing narrative of *Don Quixote* is itself revealing; in a market in Toledo, the narrator finds Arabic manuscripts that tell of Don Quixote. These are then translated into Castilian. The episodes with Ricote occur in the second volume, which was published in 1615, six years after the Muslim expulsion.

21 **find themselves accused:** Another way to safeguard oneself was to become ultra-devout like Ricote's daughter. When the young Teresa Sánchez de Cepeda y Ahumada entered the Carmelite convent in Ávilla in 1535, her knowledge of the Bible was suspiciously good. Someone must have taught her more than the New Testament, and in fact, this future saint, revered in the Roman Catholic faith, was the granddaughter of a Jewish *converso*. Her haunting poems to the Lord would forever link her with her confessor, the soon-to-be-beatified mystic who wrote of the "dark night of the soul," Saint John of the Cross. He, too, was the descendant of *conversos*.

23 **demon-worshippers, and cannibals:** On Columbus's shifting perceptions of the "Indians," see the excellent work of Tzvetan Todorov, *The Conquest of America: The Question of the Other*, trans. Richard Howard (Norman: University of Oklahoma Press, 1999). Also Bernal Díaz del Castillo, *The Conquest of New Spain*, trans. J. M. Cohen (1568; London: Penguin, 2009), 26.

23 **to their knees and wept:** Bartolomé de Las Casas, *History of the Indies*, trans. Andrée Collard (New York: Harper & Row, 1971), 38–39. This work has never been fully translated into English.

23 **work their masters demanded:** Todorov, *Conquest of America*, 12, 50.

24 **stood as his motto:** Francisco de Vitoria, *Political Writings*, ed. A. Pagden and J. Lawrence (Cambridge: Cambridge University Press, 1991), 231, and on forced conversions, 339.

24 **his fellow "travelers":** Siep Stuurman, *The Invention of Humanity: Equality and Cultural Difference in World History* (Cambridge: Harvard University Press, 2017), 213.

24 **debates over xenophobia:** See Vitoria, *Political Writings*. In his 1538 "On the Indians, On the Laws of War," he wrote that under natural law it is "considered inhuman . . . to treat travelers badly." See G. Scott Davis, "Conscience and Conquest: Francisco de Vitoria on Justice in the New World," *Modern Theology* 13, no. 4 (1997): 475–500; and Anthony Anghie, "Francisco de Vitoria and the Colonial Origins of International Law," *Social and Legal Studies* 5, no. 3 (1996): 321–36.

24 **By what right?:** Las Casas, *History of the Indies*, 183–86.

25 **to their sinful ways:** Las Casas, *History of the Indies*, 274–75. Shortly afterward, Father Montesinos sailed back to Spain, where his testimony shocked King Ferdinand. New laws were established for the colonies, ones that explicitly rejected the claim that the natives were Aristotelean "natural" slaves or animals. The 1512 Laws of Burgos insisted that these humans should be baptized, converted, and brought into the fold.

25 **"his concerns like the others":** Bartolomé de Las Casas, *A Short Account of the Destruction of the Indies* (1552; New York: Penguin, 1992). On Las Casas, see Lewis Hanke, *Bartolomé de Las Casas: An Interpretation of His Life and Writings* (The Hague: Springer, 1951); Juan Friede and Benjamin Keene, *Bartolomé de Las Casas in History: Towards Understanding the Man and His Work* (DeKalb: Northern Illinois University Press, 2008).

26 **"I can hardly believe it":** Las Casas, *History of the Indies*, xxii.

26 **"ravage the Indians":** Las Casas, *History of the Indies*, 264–65. See page 60, letter dated June 22, 1497.

27 **a just war commenced:** According to the historian Matthew Restall, this legalistic framework organized the fabricated mis-telling of the most infamous encounter of the Conquest, Cortés's conquest of the Aztecs. As Cortés and his band marched from the Yucatan toward the lake capital of Tenochtitlan, they dutifully delivered the Requirement. Upon meeting a foe, soon after hello, they would quickly demand that the heathen swear allegiance to their mighty King Carlos and give up their devil worship for Christ. In Cortés's account of his meeting with Montezuma, he delivered the Requirement, and then the great Aztec leader gave a speech, quite stunning in its improbability. Supposedly, Montezuma welcomed Cortés and declared that his arrival had been long ago foretold. It was he, Montezuma and his people, who were strangers in this land, and the newly arrived Spaniards who were its true natives. As Montezuma fetes these Spaniards in his magical palace, Cortés has him declare, "You are in your own homeland and your own house." This bizarre myth, handed down for centuries, Restall argues, has an inner logic. Montezuma's submission to the Requirement, then his revolt, justified Cortés's actions. For this was no invasion, but rather a rebellion by people who had already submitted to the Crown. Similarly, the conqueror frequently noted the idolatry and sodomy of the natives, two matters that justified a just war.

Matthew Restall, *When Montezuma Met Cortés* (New York: HarperCollins, 2018), quote on page 17.

27   **commencing their pillage:** Las Casas, *Short Account of the Destruction of the Indies*, 33.

28   **families and their lands:** Las Casas, *History of the Indies*, 52, 128–29, 231.

28   **in the eyes of God:** Las Casas, *History of the Indies*, 257–58.

28   **fingerprints on the decree:** In 1542, a bull by the Pope explicitly declared that the Indians were rational human beings. Charles V, under the likely influence of Las Casas, signed New Laws of Burgos in November of 1542.

28   **in the official proceedings:** After 1520, Franciscan, Dominican, and Jesuit missionaries began to stream to the New World to convert these natives. Of course, the problem of fake versus authentic conversions reemerged. Many indigenous peoples simply incorporated Christian saints and rituals into their own beliefs. One guileless native told a Dominican friar, "Yes sir, I am a bit Christian because I have learned to lie a bit; another day I will lie big and I will be big Christian" (Las Casas, *History of the Indies*, 280). Less obviously across the conquered lands of New Spain, everyday Nahuatl beliefs came together with those of the virgin birth of the God-man. Glittering Baroque churches rose up as a testament to this syncretic mix, such as Santa Maria Tonantzintla. The name of the church acknowledges the merger of the Virgin Mary with the indigenous fertility goddess, and the interior similarly demonstrates a mix of Nahua beliefs with those from the Bible.

28   **annihilated "whole kingdoms":** Las Casas, *Short Account of the Destruction of the Indies*, 3.

29   **two hundred remained:** Las Casas, *Short Account of the Destruction of the Indies*, 11, 12, 15.

29   **who devoured these lambs:** Las Casas, *Short Account of the Destruction of the Indies*, 11.

29   **the king were savages:** Las Casas, *History of the Indies*, cited in Alex Nava, *Wonder and Exile in the New World* (University Park: Pennsylvania State University Press, 2013), 64–66.

29   **to snatch out your heart:** Bernal Díaz del Castillo, *The True History of the Conquest of Mexico*, trans. M. Keatinge (London: J. Wright, 1800), 79; Hernán Cortés, *Letters from Mexico*, trans. A. Pagden (New Haven: Yale University Press, 2001.

30   **extermination of whole peoples:** Todorov, *Conquest of America*. Also see Benjamin Keen, *The Aztec Image in Western Thought* (New Brunswick, NJ: Rutgers University Press, 1971), 252–59; Stuurman, *Invention of Humanity*, 224.

30   **"acquires new sensitiveness":** E. M. Forster, *Aspects of the Novel* (New York: Harcourt Brace, 1927), 20.

31   **were *not* the Spanish:** Benjamin Keen, "The Black Legend Revisited: Assumptions and Realities," *Hispanic American Historical Review* 49, no. 4 (1969): 703–19; Lewis Hanke, "A Modest Proposal; for a Moratorium on Grand Generalizations: Some Thoughts on the Black Legend," *Hispanic American Historical Review* 51,

no. 11 (1971): 112–27. On Raleigh, see Jill Lepore, *These Truths: A History of the United States* (New York: W. W. Norton, 2019), 28.

32 **"not his own practice":** Michel de Montaigne, "Of Cannibals," *Selected Essays*, trans. J. M. Cohen (New York: Penguin, 1958), 105–19.

32 **others or the state:** This devout Calvinist did have a rather generous group of exceptions. Insane beliefs—initially, Locke included the views of Catholics, Jews, and, above all, atheists as mad—did not need to be accorded such acceptance. As we shall see, Locke was neither the first nor the last who proposed egalitarian ideals that he himself could not fully accept.

33 **nothing more or less than equal:** Toleration for religious difference began to be proposed in the Republic of Letters and other enlightened circles. On this critical concept's emergence and its relationship to naturalist models of personhood and the mind, see George Makari, *Soul Machine: The Invention of the Modern Mind* (New York: W. W. Norton, 2015). Of course, prior to becoming a philosophical and theological matter, it simply had been practiced in frontier societies like Andalusia.

33 **cultures did they differ:** Voltaire, *Essai sur les moeurs et l'esprit des nations* (1756; Paris: Garnier Frères, 1990). Voltaire also relied on Spanish historians like Herrera and Garcilaro de Vega. Also Charles-Louis de Montesquieu, *Esprit des loix* (1748; Paris: Didot Frères, 1862).

33 **market and Raynal's exile:** Guillaume-Thomas Raynal, *Histoire philosophique et politique des établissements et du commerce des Européens dans les deux Indes*, 2 vols. (1780; Ferney-Voltaire: Centre international d'étude du XVIIIe siècle, 2018). On this book and its immense success, see Roger Mercier, "L'Amerique et les Américains dans 'l'Histoire des deux Indes' de l'abbé Raynal," *Outre-Mers, Revue d'histoire* 65 (197): 309–24.

34 **"to save the other":** Raynal, *Histoire philosophique et politique* 2, 275–76. For the English, I have modified the translation found in Abbé Raynal, *A Philosophical and Political History of the Settlements and Trade of the Europeans in the East and West Indies*, trans. J. Justamond, vol. 3 (Edinburgh: Mundell and Son, 1804), 189.

35 **free of one's biases:** Raynal, *A Philosophical and Political History*, 307. The crimes of the Spanish crown were a "sacred fever" that now had broken, thanks in part to Las Casas and the enlightened emphasis on reason.

35 **from what was natural:** On this shift, see Lepore's excellent *These Truths*, xv.

35 **civil emancipation of Jews:** Lepore, *These Truths*, 84–99.

36 **cruel, sensual, and warm:** Alvar Núñez Cabeza de Vaca, *Chronicle of the Narváez Expedition*, trans. F. Bandelier (1555; New York: Penguin, 2002).

37 **"of which we are ashamed":** Lepore, *These Truths*, 127.

Chapter 3: The First Xenophobes

39 **cases of "nervous hydrophobia":** For the classic definition of hydrophobia, see Antoine Furetière, *Dictionnaire universel, contenant généralement tous les françois* (Rotterdam: Arnout et Reinier Leers, 1640), 289. On nervous hydrophobia, see

Philippe Pinel, *Nosographie philosophique, ou la methode de l'analyse appliquée à la médicine* (Paris: Crapelet Maradan, 1798), 70–71. This was picked up by others; see Shirley Palmer, ed., *A Pentaglot Dictionary of the Terms Employed in Anatomy and Physiology* (London: Longman, 1845), 463, and C. M. S. Sandras, ed., *Traité pratique des maladies nerveuses*, vol. 1 (Paris: G. Baillière, 1851), 299.

40   **a terror of everything:** Carl Westphal, "Die Agorophobie," *Archiv für Psychiatrie und Nervenkrankheiten* 3 (1872): 138–61. See also Felicity Callard, " 'The Sensation of Infinite Vastness,' or the Emergence of Agoraphobia in the Late 19th Century," *Environment and Planning* 24 (2006): 873–89. On Meschede and claustrophobia, see C. W. Suckling, "Agoraphobia and Allied Morbid Fears," *American Journal of Medical Sciences* 99, no. 5 (May 1890): 476–78; Theodor Meynert, *Klinische Vorlesungen über Psychiatrie* (Vienna: Wilhelm Braumüller, 1890), 179–81.

40   **"dread of meeting strangers":** C. O. Sylvester Mawson, ed., *Roget's Thesaurus* (New York: Thomas Crowell, 1911), 297; Thomas Stedman, *A Practical Medical Dictionary*, 4th rev. ed. (New York: William Wood, 1916), 1080; for years thereafter it could still be found in a few eccentric textbooks; William Sadler, *Practice of Psychiatry* (St. Louis: Mosby, 1953), 1146; W. H. Kayy, *Dictionary of Psychiatry and Psychology* (Paterson, NJ: Colt Press, 1963), 194.

40   **list of seventy-nine phobias:** Richard Hutchings, *A Psychiatric Word Book: A Lexicon of Terms* (Utica, NY: The State's Hospital Press, 1943), 247.

40   **only by the Greek dictionary:** Philip Coombs Knapp, "The Nature of Neurasthenia and Its Relations to Morbid Fears and Imperative Ideas," *Boston Medical and Surgical Journal* 135, no. 17 (October 22, 1896): 408. See the impressive list in Charles Féré, *La pathologie des émotions* (Paris: Félix Alcan, 1892), 407–13.

42   **said to be king:** See, for example, Eric Hobsbawm and Terence Ranger, eds., *The Invention of Tradition* (Cambridge: Cambridge University Press, 1983).

42   **"Anglophobiacs" or "Anglophobists":** Jules Garsou, *L'Anglophobe* (Paris: Librairie Fischbacher, 1900).

42   **succumbed to "Francophobes":** Unsigned, "L'Anglomanie," *Argus et Vert-Vert* 18, no. 802 (February 25, 1866). "Anglophobie" entered the *Dictionnaire de l'Académie française* and thereby became an officially sanctioned word in 1866 (*see* page 499, where it is defined as a horror of the English). Eleven years later, it was included in Arsène Darmesteter, *De la création actuelle de mots nouveaux dans la langue française* (Paris: F. Vieweg, 1877), 244, where "phobie," "Anglo-phobie," and "Franco-préto-phobe" are listed. Also see Philippe Chassaigne, "L'Angleterre, énemie héréditaire?" *Revue historique des armées* 264 (2011): 3–10.

42   **an irrational "Anglophobia":** From Thomas Jefferson to James Madison, May 13, 1793, *Founders Online*, National Archives, last modified March 30, 2017.

42   **"if not Anglomania":** Unsigned, "Anglophobia," *Once a Week* 2, no. 35 (August 29, 1868): 173. "Anglophobia," *Saturday Review* 16, no. 407 (August 15, 1863): 201. Unsigned, "Pacification," *Littell's Living Age* 4, no. 40 (February 15, 1845): 409. For a brief flicker in ultranationalist circles, xenophobia was paraded as a virtue.

In 1909, a French journal published a satirical dialogue between "Xénophile" and "Xénophobe," in which the former whined about the ills of France and lauded German orderliness, while the latter valiantly defended *la Patrie* against such calumny. "Parallèle," *L'Eclipse: Revue comique illustrée* 1410 (1909): 6.

43 **"Judeophobia" or "Hebrewphobia":** See, for example, "Francophobia Rampant," *Washington Post*, July 10, 1887, 5, and "General Boulanger: The Bouncing Soldier Hero to be Voted for in Paris Sunday," *The Sun*, January 1889, 5. Russophobia and Francophobia are at work in William Lee-Warner, "Our Work in India in the Nineteenth Century," *Journal of the Society of Arts* 48, no. 2463 (1900): 215. For an excellent discussion of Leon Pinsker (1821–1891) and his assessment of Judeophobia, see Sander L. Gilman and James M. Thomas, *Are Racists Crazy? How Prejudice, Racism, and Antisemitism Became Markers of Insanity* (New York: New York University Press, 2016), 34–35.

43 **"life on a comma":** For a nuanced exposition of Renan's relationship to race, see Jan Goldstein, "Toward an Empirical History of Moral Thinking: The Case of Racial Theory in Mid-Nineteenth Century France," *American Historical Review* (February 2015): 1–27. The quotes are on pages 15 and 20.

44 **the first "anti-Semite":** Ernest Renan, *Histoire générale et système comparé des langues sémitiques* (Paris: Michel Lévy, 1863), 4. My translation. On this switch from Semitic as a language group to a race, see Goldstein, "Toward an Empirical History of Moral Thinking," 17.

45 **a zealous nationalist:** Renan was subject to many biographies after his death, but very few in the last half century. See Charles Chauvin, *Renan: 1823–1892* (Paris: Desclée de Brouwer, 2000). On Renan's philology and its influence, see Maurice Olender, *The Languages of Paradise: Race, Religion, and Philology in the Nineteenth Century* (Cambridge: Harvard University Press, 2009).

45 **"and always unintelligent":** "London, Monday, April 12," *Daily News*, Monday, April 12, 1880, 4. For his lectures, See Ernest Renan, *Lectures on the Influence of the Institutions, Thought, and Culture of Rome*, trans. Charles Beard (1880; London: William and Norgate, 1885).

45 **suffered from "xenophobia":** "The Growth of Freedom in the Balkan Peninsula," *Saturday Review*, February 12, 1887, 237–38.

45 **always "xenophobe or demophobe":** This is one of the very few later usages of xenophobia as wild ultranationalism, for as we shall see, its meaning would be supplanted. However, the commentator was the sophisticated French diplomat and globalist Baron d'Estournelles de Constant, winner of the 1909 Nobel Peace Prize. See his "America's Duty," *The Atlantic* 116 (1915): 818.

46 **"hatred of the Impures":** Gaston Richard, "Sociologie et science politique," *Revue philosophique de la France et de l'étranger* 53 (1902): 300–317.

47 **"a common effort":** Ernest Renan, "What is a Nation?" delivered before the Sorbonne, March 11, 1882, 7, www.cooper.edu/humanities. Olivier Le Cour Grandmaison, "Ernest Renan: penseur de l'imperialisme français et de la Republique colonial," *Droits* 2, no. 67 (2018): 49–62.

47 **virtue into a vice:** "Lettre de Roumaine," *Le Figaro*, June 5, 1895, 4.

Chapter 4: The Boxer Uprising

50   **the French vocabulary:** "En Chine," *Le Constitutionnel*, July 17, 1900, 1; "À l'extérieur," *La Justice*, July 20, 1900, 1; "En Chine," *L'Univers et Le Monde*, August 26, 1900, 2; "En Chine," *Le Journal*, August 31, 1900, 3; "La Chine aux Chinois," *La Presse*, September 2, 1900, 2; "Les affaires de Chine," *Le Figaro*, September 2, 1900, 1–2; "Les affaires de Chine," *Le Matin*, October 5, 1900, 2. Also see "En Chine," *Le Constitutionnel*, July 14, 1900, 2; "Les affaires de Chine," *Le Figaro*, May 7, 1901, 2.

52   **"foreign to myself":** This famous quote had been translated in a number of ways. I have used Terence, *The Hauton Timorumenos, or Self-Tormenter*, trans. T. A. Blyth and T. Shrimpton (Oxford, 1880), 9. Walther Schücking (1875–1935), a German law professor and diplomat, concluded that nationalism was defunct; see his *Das Nationalitätenproblem* (Dresden: Zahn und Jaensch, 1908), and *The International Union of the Hague Conferences*, trans. Charles Fenwick (1912; Oxford: Clarendon Press, 1918). On the demands of empire and the rule of law, see Lauren Benton and Lisa Ford, *Rage for Order: The British Empire and the Origins of International Law, 1800–1850* (Cambridge: Harvard University Press, 2016); Jennifer Pitts, *Boundaries of the International: Law and Empire* (Cambridge: Harvard University Press, 2018); and Krishan Kumar, *Visions of Empire: How Five Imperial Regimes Shaped the World* (Princeton: Princeton University Press, 2017).

52   **opportunity for land grabs:** J. M. Roberts, *The Penguin History of Europe* (London: Penguin, 1996), 419–49.

52   **"of human consciousness":** Joseph Conrad, *Heart of Darkness and Selected Short Fiction* (New York: Barnes & Noble Classics, 2008), xxxi.

53   **once impenetrable domains:** See Daniel Hendrick, "The Tools of Imperialism: Technology and the Expansion of European Colonial Empires in the Nineteenth Century," *Journal of Modern History* 51 (1979): 231–63; Thomas Misa and Johan Schot, "Inventing Europe: Technology and the Hidden Integration of Europe," *History and Technology* 21, no. 1 (2005): 1–19.

54   **into hearty applause:** Ernest Renan, *La réforme intellecuelle et morale* (Paris: Michel Lévy, 1871), 92–93. Victor Hugo, "Discours sur l'Afrique du 18 Mai, 1879," *Actes et paroles: Depuis l'exil, 1876–1880* (Paris: J. Hetzel, n.d.), 115.

54   **Upper Nile—were newsworthy:** See the excellent work of Olivier Le Cour Grandmaison, *La République impériale; Politique et racisme d'état* (Paris: Fayard, 2009), 35.

54   **unwelcoming to foreigners:** "Un Missionnaire," *Aperçu historique sur la Chine* (Rome: Imprimerie polyglotte de la S.C de la propagande, 1873), 428. The anonymous author is apparently Félix Gennevoix.

54   **"hermetically sealed" for centuries:** Roger Turpaud, *La juridiction des consuls français dans les échelles du Levant d'après les capitulations* (Paris: A. Mellottée, 1902), 7.

54   **"long-nosed goblins":** Brett L. Walker, *A Concise History of Japan* (Cambridge: Cambridge University Press, 2015), 88.

55 **its own borders:** Lai Yong et al, "The Chinese Question from a Chinese Standpoint, Address to the San Francisco City Council" (1873). Retrieved from www.americainclass.org.

55 **Portugal grabbed Macao:** For the literature on the Boxer Uprising, I am especially indebted to Paul A. Cohen, *History in Three Keys: The Boxers as Event, Experience, and Myth* (New York: Columbia University Press, 1997). For the prehistory to this event, see Stephen Platt, *Imperial Twilight: The Opium War and the End of China's Last Golden Age* (New York: Vintage, 2018).

56 **"destroy the foreigners":** Their name in Chinese is "Fu-Qing mieyang." Cohen translated this as "Fist-fighters for Justice and Unity." This is also rendered as "Boxers United in Righteousness."

57 **was not Chinese:** This term spread into provincial newspapers; see "La guerre en Chine," *L'Ouest-Éclair*, August 7, 1900, 2. It also immediately spread into policy and academic circles. See, for example, *Bulletin de la Societé de géographie de l'Est* 21 (1900): 657; Marcel Dubois, "Des meilleures méthodes et des moyens pratiques d'enseignement de la *géographie* économique," *Bulletin de la Société de géographie de Toulouse* (1900): 555; *Bulletin mensuel de la Société politique nationale* (1900/1901): 186; "Le problème des missions," *Revue pratique d'apologétique* 7 (1908): 866–75.

58 **"relationship," in China:** On the use of the term *Fremdenfeindschaft* and the Boxers in China, see Alexander Tille, *Aus Englands Fiegeljahren* (Dresden and Leipzig: Carl Reigner, 1901), 11. On China and Japan's *Fremdenfeindschaft*, see Max Brandt, *Ostasiatique Fragen: China, Japan, Korea, Altes und Neues* (1897; Sydney: Wentworth Press, 2018), 211; Karl Rathgen, *Japans Volkswirtschaft und Staatshaushalt* 10, no. 4 (1891): 132. Later on, with the ascent of xenophobia, by the 1920s some Germans offered both terms together as "*Xenophobie (Fremdenfeindschaft)*"; see both Robert Michels, *Der Patriotismus: Prolegomena zu seiner soziologischen Analyse* (Munich: Duncker and Humblot, 1929), 120, 123, and Theodor Brugsch, *Die Biologie der Person: Soziologie der Person* (Berlin: Urban and Schwarzenberg, 1929), 489.

59 **"in some dictionaries!":** Jean de Saintours, "Letter to the Editor," *The Globe*, June 4, 1915, 8. The entry of "le mouvement xénophobe" into an encyclopedia happened quickly. See *La grande encyclopédie*, ed. M. Berthelot et al., vol. 29 (Paris: Sociéte anonyme de la grande encyclopédie, 1902), 1138.

59 **consul to the United States:** M. de Saint-Allais et al., *Nobiliaire universel de France* (Paris: Librairie ancienne et moderne, 1876), 220.

59 **in 137 countries:** Jean P. A. Martin, "Nécessité d'une écriture pour les colonies francaises," *Bulletin de la Société de géographie de Lyon* (1884): 13–26. Martin is listed as "Député-Consul des Etats-Unis."

59 **secondary school teachers:** In 1846, the College of Preceptors was established in London for training and testing the qualifications of teachers. Martin de Saintours joined this teaching society as a life member in 1887. In their archives, he can be found in their calendars from 1906 to 1933. College of Preceptors in London Archives, Ref COP b/1/50.

60 **to news outlets:** Martin's interventions in the stenography debates were extensive; see, for example, J. P. A. Martin, *Le graphique de la parole* (Pontoise: Amédée Paris, 1884) and "Nouvel alphabet phonétique," *L'instituteur sténographe*, 1889, 24. He placed extensive ads for his services, which allow us to track his location. On June 15, 1892, in *Le Temps*, he advertised his capacity to use telephonic connections for reporters between France and England. *Le Matin*, for his stenographic and editing skills from August 10, 1900, places him on 32 Rue du Rocher in Paris. A review of two of Martin's books on stenography listed him as "chef du service sténographique de l'agence Reuters." *L'Impartial*, June 11, 1905, 12.

61 **British "red-tapeism":** Jean P. A. Martin, "The Telephone Between England and France; à Monsieur le Rédacteur en Chef du Times," *The Times*, August 31, 1891, 5.

61 **"yutiliti, poest and pient":** Jean P. A. Martin, "Simplified Spelling; à Monsieur le Rédacteur en Chef," *Saturday Review*, February 17, 1912, 209–10.

Chapter 5: Colonial Panic

62 **hatred for foreigners:** "Francophobia Rampant," *Washington Post*, July 10, 1887, 5.

62 **Chinese were left devastated:** In China, however, their memory lingered. For Chinese officials and reformers, the rebellion was initially a terrible embarrassment. Driven by rabble, it was a symptom of the decay that magical, religious thinking had wreaked on the nation. For years thereafter, mandarins might castigate anti-foreigner sympathies by invoking the Boxers. However, after 1919, the symbolism of this revolt transformed under the influence of the growing Chinese Communist Party; new voices lauded the Boxers as heroic nationalists who resisted the hegemony of the West; see Cohen, *History in Three Keys*. For colonial powers, the Boxer Uprising also would not be forgotten. In 1912, when a British boat was attacked near the Yang-tze River, telegrams to the House of Commons reported that, despite this act, there were no signs of "xenophobe" feeling in the populace; "Telegram from Yuan Shih-kai to Canton Tu-tu, March 30, 1912," *Parliamentary Papers, 1909–1982* (Great Britain: House of Commons), vol. 1010, 18–19. When Chao-Hsin Chu wrote an appeal to the League of Nations for a revision of unfair treaties imposed on the Chinese, he felt the need to insist that his countrymen were not by nature xenophobic; see his *Revision of Unequal Treaties: China Appeals to the League of Nations* (London: Caledonian Press, 1926).

63 **deep into the wild:** Through superior self-restraint, reason, and wit, the heroes survived to tell their astonishing tale. The scenes were gaudy, fabulous concoctions that did not at all correspond to H. Rider Haggard's dreary days in the colonies of South Africa. Nonetheless, this writer, who later would be knighted for his efforts, buoyed his reader's belief in the righteousness of the British cause, while he depicted lower forms of humanity—Jews, Arabs, and Africans—as much in need of uplifting. See, for example, H. Rider Haggard, *King Solomon's Mines* (1885; New York: Barnes & Noble Classics, 2004).

64   **"chafing against restraint":** Cited in Piers Brendon, *The Decline and Fall of the British Empire: 1781–1997* (New York: Knopf, 2008), 241.

64   **"sudden, alien, nor unexpected":** Rudyard Kipling, *Plain Tales from the Hills* (1890; New York: Penguin, 1990), 91, 162. The stories quoted from are "His Chance in Life" and "Beyond the Pale."

64   **one such Black trouble:** Kipling never ceased being the voice of jingoistic imperialism and what he infamously called the "White Man's Burden." In "How the First Letter Was Written," he also constructed a fable in which illiterate primitives rectified their hostile misperceptions of a kindly "Stranger-man," by inventing written language. Rudyard Kipling, *Just So Stories* (1902; Oxford: Oxford University Press, 1998), 91–108.

64   **"eat him and are entertained":** H. Rider Haggard, *She: A History of Adventure* (1886; London: Penguin, 2004), 111.

65   **wanted to believe:** Guy de Maupassant, *Bel-Ami*, trans. Douglas Parmée (1885; New York: Penguin, 1975).

66   **"almost necessarily hostile":** John Lubbock, *On the Origin of Civilization and the Primitive Condition of Man* (London: Longmans, 1870), 129.

67   **in their racial makeup:** Roger Turpaud, *La juridiction des consuls français dans les échelles du Levant d'après les capitulations* (Paris: A. Mellottée, 1902), 177, 185.

67   **"xenophobia of the Moors":** "Anarchy in Morocco," *London Evening Standard*, August 27, 1907, 4. This accusation of xenophobia in Morocco was repeated in the same paper on February 19, May 2, August 25, and August 27 of 1908. On the supposedly "ingrained xenophobia of Musselmen," also see "The Foreign Office Bag," *The Graphic*, February 26, 1910; "Notes of the Day," *Pall Mall Gazette*, June 17, 1913; as well as the language used in debates on the uprising in Fez within Parliament. See Louis Jacob, ed., *Archives diplomatiques*, 51 année, 3rd series (Paris: Librairie Ancienne H. Champion, 1911), 112, 127.

67   **explained away revolts:** On the Japanese, see "Après La paix," *L'intransigeant*, September 18, 1905.

67   **would colonize, the Ethiopians:** Italian newspapers explicitly and immediately picked up Chinese "xenophobia" from London telegram services. See "L'avazata su Pechino: Nuovo Scopio di Xenofobia," *La Stampa*, August 5, 1900, n.p. Following Italian usage in this newspaper, we see it repeated in reference to China: "Un accesso di xenofobia in Cina?" *La Stampa*, September 15, 1906, 4; "La xenofobia dei cinesi," *La Stampa*, August 10, 1906; and "La xenofobia dei cinesi," *La Stampa*, June 29, 1909. They then expanded usage to "la xenofobia" in Ethiopia: "Lugh e il problema etiopico," *La Stampa*, January 17, 1908; Vittorio Vettori, "Come difendere gli euopei ad Addis Abeba, nel caso di un moto di xonofobia," *La Stampa*, February 6, 1909, 1. The same term was then applied to Morocco and Muslims, with their "irreducible xenophobia"; see "L'ambasciatore italiano a Constantinopoli," *La Stampa*, September 7, 1910, 1; also "Le interpellanze sul Marocco," *La Stampa*, November 13, 1907, 2. From there the term found its way into scholarly literature and colonial discourse. See, for example, "Ció che si Deve

Fare," *Minerva*, July 7, 1907, 731; and *Rivista Coloniale*, anno II, vol. 4, December 1907, 472, on the intransigent and xenophobic Orient.

67 **Morocco with the same term:** Spanish newspapers picked up this term from telegram services with regard to the Chinese by 1901. See "Chinos y Europeos," *Heraldo de Madrid*, February 9, 1901, 1. Reports from London and elsewhere continued to report on Chinese xenophobia, which then entered academic discourse; see R. P. Graciano Martinez, "La Xenofobia en China," *España y América*, January 5, 1906, no. 9, 31–35. Spanish papers then focused on xenophobia close by in Morocco. See "La Conferencia internacional," *El Correro Español*, August 8, 1905, n.p.; "La Conferencia," *El Siglo Futuro*, August 8, 1905, 1; "Ocupation de Ujda," *El Imparcial*, March 27, 1907; "Francia en Marruecos," *El Siglo Futuro*, November 13, 1907.

67 **India, and Mexico:** London "telegram" reports" of "xenophobia" in Morocco are reported in the Rio de Janeiro paper *Jornal do Commercio*, see May 3, 1903, 1, March 26, 1907, and May 7, 1903, 1, in which the article speaks of a "xenophobic delirium." On Chinese xenophobia, see February 21, 1906, 1. In India, see *The Leader*, July 20, 1912. In Mexico, see "The Egyptian Situation," *Mexican Herald*, July 8, 1906, 1. On "Oriental xenophobia" as viewed from Argentina, see P. Groussac, ed., *Anales de la Biblioteca*, vol. 4 (Buenos Aires: Coni Hermanos, 1905), 358. From Roumania, see Constantin Almanestianu, ed., *Agricultura si Industria Română în fața modificărilor tarifare de la 1903* (Bucurescu: Minerva, 1903), 31.

67 **inhabitants of Tangiers?:** "Turkey Determined," *The Leader*, Allahabad, India, July 20, 1912.

68 **"fanaticism and xenophobia":** "The Egyptian Situation," *Mexican Herald*, July 8, 1906, 1. See also Jerry Knudson, "The Mexican Herald: Outpost of Empire, 1895–1915," *Gazette* 63, no. 5 (2001): 387–98.

68 **the spirit of hostility:** "La situation économique de la Chine," October 10, 1900, *Bulletin mensuel, Société d'économie politique nationale, Compte rendu des travaux de l'année 1900*, 1900, 185–88, 203. This group discussion was chaired by the president, M. Cauwès; a paper was given on the subject by the specialist on the Orient, René Pinon.

69 **"a Moorish territory":** "Anarchy in Morocco," *London Evening Standard*, August 27, 1907, 4.

69 **Not a chance:** Eugene Lyle, "The American Influence in Mexico," *Current Literature* 25, no. 4 (1903): 418.

69 **by Emiliano Zapata:** "The Mexican Autocrat," *The Nation*, December 3, 1910, 396. This is Britain's *The Nation*, which commenced publication in 1907 and later merged with *The Athenaeum*.

69 **"xenophobic delirium":** "Telegrammas," *Jornal do Commercio*, May 7, 1903.

69 **"to welcome or assimilate":** M. A. Berl, "Modern Greece: Her Role in Eastern Europe," *Hellenic Herald*, August-September, 1907, 149. This lecture was delivered before the French Philhellenic League.

69 **thousands of Moroccans?:** "The French in Morocco," *New York Times*, August 22, 1907, 6.

70   **be toward strangers:** S. M. Zwemer, review of "Villes et Tribus du Maroc," *Moslem World* 12 (1922): 428.

70   **with an army:** See Stuurman, *Invention of Humanity*, 213.

Chapter 6: Commence the Unraveling

71   **echoing Saint Paul:** Derk Bodde and Galia Speshneff Bodde, *Tolstoy and China* (Princeton: Princeton University Press, 1950), 16.

72   **a lunatic asylum?:** Bodde and Bodde, *Tolstoy and China*, 36, 46. Dated August 8, 1900.

72   **"as well as spiritually":** Bodde and Bodde, *Tolstoy and China*, 45–46. Also Leo Tolstoy, *A Letter to a Hindu* (Musaicum Books, 2017).

72   **in their own blood:** Mark Twain, "To the Person Sitting in Darkness," *North American Review* 172, no. 531 (1901): 161–76. For quotes, see pages 164–66.

73   **a "homo duplex":** From the vast literature on Joseph Conrad, see especially the multiple readings of Conrad by Edward Said, especially in *Culture and Imperialism* (New York: Vintage, 1991). For a historicist account of globalization and Conrad, see Maya Jasanoff, *The Dawn Watch: Joseph Conrad in a Global World* (New York: Penguin, 2017). Conrad used this expression about himself in a 1903 letter; Joseph Conrad, *Collected Letters*, vol. 3, 1903–1907, eds. F. Karl and L. Davies (Cambridge: Cambridge University Press, 1988), 89. The introduction by Laurence Davies develops the resonances of this term; see pages xxiii–xxxii.

73   **her husband to die:** Joseph Conrad, "Amy Foster," in *Heart of Darkness and Selected Short Fiction*, ed. E. Michael Matin (New York: Barnes & Noble Classics, 2003), 125–52.

74   **"bow down before":** Conrad, *Heart of Darkness and Selected Short Fiction*, 41. Initially entitled "The Heart of Darkness," the first installment of Conrad's tale appeared in 1899 in the February "Special Double Issue" of *Blackwood's Edinburgh Magazine* 145 (February 1899): 193–220. Other stories in that issue included "A Daughter of the Muhammadans," "Jamaica: An Impression," and "A Letter from Salamanca." The next two installments appeared in the issues of March, 479–502, and April, 634–57. Retitled *Heart of Darkness*, it was published in book form in 1902.

75   **"purely protective":** Conrad, *Heart of Darkness and Selected Short Fiction*, 84.

76   **" 'Mistah Kurtz—he dead' ":** Conrad, *Heart of Darkness and Selected Short Fiction*, 116. See the groundbreaking essay by Chinua Achebe, "An Image of Africa: Racism in Conrad's Heart of Darkness," *Massachusetts Review* 57, no. 1 (1975): 14–27. On the ensuing debate over whether Conrad's book was racist, a depiction of racism, or both, see C. P. Sarvan, "Racism and the *Heart of Darkness*," *International Fiction Review* 7, no. 1 (1980): 6–10, and the compilation of essays in Harold Bloom, ed., *Joseph Conrad's Heart of Darkness* (New York: Infobase Pub, 2008).

77   **"I said—'utterly lost' ":** Conrad, *Heart of Darkness and Selected Short Fiction*, 41, 111.

77   **old acquaintance's help:** For an omnibus review of works on the life of Roger
Casement, see Colm Tóibín, "The Tragedy of Roger Casement," *New York Review
of Books*, May 27, 2004. https://www.nybooks.com/articles/2004/05/27/the
-tragedy-of-roger-casement/.

78   **in Leopold's Congo Free State:** The classic biography of Roger Casement is
Brian Inglis, *Roger Casement* (London: Penguin, 2002). Also see H. S. Zins,
"Joseph Conrad and the British Critics of Colonialism," *Pula: Botswana Journal
of African Studies* 12, no. 1–2 (1998): 58–68.

78   **disturbing allegations:** On the broader history of such dissent, see Priyamvada
Gopal, *Insurgent Empire: Anti-colonial Resistance and British Dissent* (London:
Verso, 2019).

78   **"white race has made":** On Conrad, Casement, and Morel, see Jeffrey Meyers,
"Conrad and Roger Casement," *Conradiana* 5, no. 3 (1973): 65; Anthony Bradley,
"Hearts of Darkness: Conrad, Casement and the Congo," *Ariel* 34, no. 2–3
(2003): 197–214; Andrea White, "Conrad and Imperialism," in J. H. Stape, ed.,
The Cambridge Companion to Joseph Conrad (Cambridge: Cambridge University
Press, 1998), 179–92.

79   **"a wretched novelist":** Bradley, "Hearts of Darkness: Conrad, Casement, and
the Congo," 201.

80   **"his memorable story":** Cited in Zins, "Joseph Conrad and the British Critics
of Colonialism," 61.

80   **massacred our "black brothers":** Edmund D. Morel, *The Congo Slave State: A
Protest Against the New African Slavery* (Liverpool: John Richardson, 1903). Also
see W. Roger Louis and Jean Stengers, eds., *E. D. Morel's History of the Congo
Reform Movement* (Oxford: Clarendon, 1968), and J. S. Cookey, *Britain and the
Congo Question, 1885–1913* (London: Longmans, 1968).

80 · **the African Holocaust:** See Adam Hochschild, *King Leopold's Ghost: A Story of
Greed, Terror and Heroism in Colonial Africa* (Boston: Mariner Books, 1998). The
death estimate is his.

81   **"material regeneration":** This 1885 statement was widely reported later on by
Leopold's critics. See "The Congo Matter," *The Advance*, March 15, 1906.

81   **knighthood, and executed:** On his trip to the Americas, see Michael Taussig,
"Culture of Terror—Space of Death. Roger Casement's Putamayo Report and
the Explanation of Torture," *Comparative Studies in Society and History* 26, no. 3
(1984): 467–97.

82   **good, kind, and beloved:** Brendon, *Decline and Fall of the British Empire*,
211–16.

82   **to stream forth:** Brendon, *Decline and Fall of the British Empire*, see especially
xix, 100, 154. On the East India Company, see William Dalrymple, *The Anarchy:
The East India Company, Corporate Violence, and the Pillage of an Empire* (New
York: Bloomsbury, 2019).

83   **on the Boer War:** See John Allett, *New Liberalism, the Political Economy
of J. A. Hobson* (Toronto: University of Toronto Press, 1981).

83   **like Cecil Rhodes:** J. A. Hobson, *The Psychology of Jingoism* (London: Grant Richards, 1901), 33, 40.

83   **for new markets abroad:** J. A. Hobson, *Imperialism: A Study* (New York: J. Pott & Company, 1902), 19. Others disputed Hobson's analysis, giving more weight to factors like the search for cheap labor and natural resources, but his view would be adopted by Vladimir Lenin, Rosa Luxembourg, and others. See Eric Stokes, "Late Nineteenth-Century Colonial Expansion and the Attack on the Theory of Economic Imperialism: A Case of Mistaken Identity?" *Historical Journal* 12, no. 2 (1969): 285–301.

83   **other human beings:** Hobson leaned on statistics to prove how imperial domination served industrialists; see his *Imperialism: A Study*, 17, 23.

84   **roll their eyes?:** Hobson, *Imperialism: A Study*, 169.

84   **"leaves nothing to be desired":** Hobson, *Psychology of Jingoism*, 55.

84   **"gravest peril of Imperialism":** Hobson, *Imperialism: A Study*, 207–28. For the notion of "masked words," Hobson credits John Ruskin, *Sesame and Lilies* (London: George Allen, 1894).

84   **"they mean oppression":** L. T. Hobhouse, *Liberalism* (1911; New York: Oxford University Press, 1964), 27. On Hobhouse and the New Liberals, I am indebted to Jack Makari's "New Liberalism and the Organic Society: Reconciling Liberalism and Community in Turn of the Century Britain," BA thesis, Brown University, 2019.

84   **strategies of extermination:** Brendon, *Decline and Fall of the British Empire*, 227–30.

85   **divide on this issue:** While some British Liberal Unionists, the French Colonial Party, and the German Conservative Party still showed an appetite for foreign adventures, an array of liberals and socialists, as well as some religious figures, emerged to challenge these policies.

85   **morally unbearable:** Hobson, *Imperialism: A Study*, 222, 223.

85   **"the Christian invaders":** Alexandre Ular, *A Russo-Chinese Empire* (1903; Westminster: Archibald Constable, 1904), 83.

85   **"xenophobic Imperialism":** Morton Aldis, "Women's Franchise in New Zealand," *The Nation*, May 11, 1912, 214.

Chapter 7: Immigrant Boomerang

88   **to alter us?:** See Rita Chin, *The Crisis of Multiculturalism in Europe: A History* (Princeton: Princeton University Press, 2017); Eric Hobsbawn, *The Age of Empire* (New York: Vintage, 1987), 27. On the notion of colonized immigrants, see Olivier Le Cour Grandmaison, "Colonisés-Immigrés et 'Périls Migratoires': Origines et permanence du racisme et d'une xénophobie d'etat (1924–2007)," *Cultures & Conflits* (2008): 19–32.

88   **by Westerners at home:** Numerous examples can be found in *The Athenaeum*, *The New Statesman*, and other papers. In *The Nation*, see "Events of the Week," October 23, 1915, 134, and "The Challenge to the League," November 1, 1919, 138.

88   *Zion,* **encouraged vigilante violence:** On the attempts of Imperial Russia to include the "foreign nation" of Jews as one of their nationalities, see Eugene Avrutin, *Jews and the Imperial State* (Ithaca, NY: Cornell University Press, 2010).

89   **he warned, had been invaded:** William Eden Evans-Gordon, *The Alien Immigrant* (London: Heineman 1903), 10, 13. On the political usages of the "Social" or "Jewish" or "Woman" question, see Holly Case, *The Age of Questions* (Princeton: Princeton University Press, 2018).

89   **population were minuscule:** Sir Alfred Zimmern, "The Aliens Act: A Challenge," *Economic Review* 21, no. 2 (1911): 187–97. Also see M. J. Landa, "Alien Transmigrants," *Economic Review* 16, no. 63 (1906): 353–64. Also see Paul Rich, "Reinventing Peace: David Davies, Alfred Zimmern, and the Liberal Internationalism in Interwar Britain," *International Relations* 16, no. 1 (2002): 117–33.

90   **for mistreated Chinese workers:** Joseph Finn, *A Voice from the Aliens, About the Anti-Alien Resolution of the Cardiff Trade Union Congress* (London: Twentieth Century Press, 1895), 1.

90   **England came at a price:** David Glover, *Literature, Immigration, and Diaspora in Fin-de-Siècle England: A Cultural History of the 1905 Aliens Act* (Cambridge: Cambridge University Press, 2012); Bernard Gainer, *The Alien Invasion: The Origins of the Aliens Act of 1905* (London: Heinemann, 1972).

90   **in *The Secret Agent*:** While some anarchists like Prince Kropotkin advocated mutuality and cooperation, others believed the "propaganda of the deed"—violence—alone could shake off the oppressive state. In an event fictionalized in Joseph Conrad's book, anarchists tried to dynamite the Greenwich Royal Observatory in 1894, attempting to destroy, symbolically at least, Western time itself. See Joseph Conrad, *The Secret Agent* (1907; New York: Doubleday, 1953). Prince Kropotkin lived in England from 1886 until 1917, where he wrote his *Mutual Aid: A Factor of Evolution* (London: Heinemann, 1902). Here this naturalist rejected the Hobbesian and Social Darwinian notions that competition and conflict were at the core of the human communities, and proposed instead that mutuality was the rule, not the exception.

91   **being openly anti-Semitic:** Glover, *Literature, Immigration, and Diaspora in Fin-de-Siècle England*, 119.

91   **twenty were gravely injured:** On these events, see Georges Liens, "Les 'Vêpres marseillaises' (Juin 1881) ou la crise franco-italienne au lendemain du traité du Bardo," *Revue d'histoire moderne et contemporaine* 14, no. 1 (1967): 1–30; Gérard Noirel, *Immigration, antisémitisme et racism en France* (Paris: Fayard, 2007). Noirel claims immigration became a "problem" only after these events; see his "Histoire populaire de la France," *Le monde diplomatique*, August 2018, 14–15.

91   **register with the police:** L. Dornel, *La France hostile: socio-histoire de la xénophobie* (Paris: Hachette, 2004); of numerous works by this author, see Pierre-Louis Buzzi, "Affrontments xénophobes et identités: les 'chasses à l'Italien' en Lorraine," *Histoire@Politique* 32 (2017): 1–13. Also Cécile Mondonico-Torri,

"Aux origines du Code de la nationalité en France," *Le Mouvement Social* 171 (1995): 31–46.

91 **Renan's writings on Semitic peoples:** Gilman and Thomas, *Are Racists Crazy?* 31. According to these authors, this claim was made in 1860 by the Austrian Jewish scholar Moritz Steinschneider, who referred to "anti-semitic" prejudice.

92 **the "Dreyfusards" had been mobilized:** Emile Zola, "J'Accuse . . . !," *L'Aurore*, January 13, 1898, 1.

93 **over the French government:** On Georges Clemenceau, see Gregor Dallas, *At the Heart of a Tiger: Georges Clemenceau and His World, 1841–1929* (New York: Carroll & Graf, 1993).

93 **through jaundiced eyes:** Francois-Jules Harmand, *Domination et colonization* (1910; Paris: Flammarion, 1919), 155.

93 **anti-Semitic travesty of justice:** Hannah Arendt, *The Origins of Totalitarianism* (New York: Schocken, 1951), 239. This was also the view of the French-Martinique poet Aimé Césaire. "First," he wrote, "we must study how colonialism works to decivilize the colonizer, to brutalize him . . . each time a head is cut off or an eye put out . . . a gangrene sets in, a center of infection begins to spread. . . . And then one fine day, the bourgeoisie is awakened by a terrible reverse shock; the gestapos are busy, the prisons fill up, the torturers around the rack invent, refine, discuss." Aimé Césaire, *Discourse on Colonialism*, trans. Joan Pinkham (1955; New York: Monthly Review Press, 1972).

93 **Integration was suicidal:** Léopold de Saussure, *Psychologie de la colonisation française: dans ses rapports avec les sociétés indigènes* (Paris: F. Alcan, 1899).

94 **same rights as Frenchmen:** Harmand, *Domination et colonization*, 11, 18, 55. On Harmand, see Oliver Le Cour Grandmaison, *La république impériale* (Paris: Fayard, 2009), 84–115. Also see his *Coloniser, exterminer: sur la guerre et l'état colonial* (Paris: Fayard, 2005).

94 **were simply "xenophobic":** A. Jeancourt-Galignani, *L'immigration en droit international* (Paris: A. Rousseau, 1908).

94 **easily found in Paris:** Richard, "Sociologie et science politique," 300–317.

94 **of the global proletariat:** On the debates in France, see Nicolas Delalande, *La lutte et l'entraide: L'âge des solidarités ouvrières* (Paris: Seuil, 2019), and Dornel, *La France hostile*. Also see Hobsbawm, *The Age of Empire*, 116, 154.

94 **34 percent Slavic:** See Geoffrey Wawro, *Sons of Freedom: The Forgotten Soldiers Who Defeated Germany in World War I* (New York: Hachette, 2018), 20. Also see Erika Lee, *America for Americans: A History of Xenophobia in the United States* (New York: Basic Books, 2019).

95 **for six decades:** See Reverend O. Gibson, *The Chinese in America* (Cincinnati: Hitchcock and Walder, 1877). On American immigration, see Daniel Okrent, *The Guarded Gate* (New York: Scribner, 2019). Also see Richard Mayo-Smith, *Emigration and Immigration: A Study in Social Science* (New York: Scribner, 1895), 248–49, 255–58.

96 **abolished and equity prevailed:** This early discourse on phobias, some say, was inspired by a prescient if whimsical letter to an editor, written by the prominent physician Benjamin Rush, who in 1786 proposed a series of phobias; see "To

the Editor," *The Columbian Magazine*, November 1786. While not taken up in the medical literature, some suggest that abolitionists took inspiration from Rush. On "Colorphobia," "Blackphobia," and "Negrophobia," see, for example, Frederick Douglass, "The Black-phobia in Rochester," *The North Star*, October 3, 1850, 2, and his "Colorphobia in New York!," *The North Star*, May 25, 1849, 2. Also see April Gemeinhardt, "'The Most Poisonous of All Diseases of Mind or Body': Colorphobia and the Politics of Reform," MA thesis, University of Montana, 2016.

96   **to China and Italy:** On the history of lynching in America, see Christopher Waldrep, ed., *Lynching in America: A History in Documents* (New York: New York University Press, 2006). Also Manfred Berg, *Popular Justice: A History of Lynching in America* (Lanham, MD: Ivan Dee, 2011).

96   **by 10,000 people:** On the early history of the Council, see Cyrus Field Adams, ed., *The National Afro-American Council Organized 1898: A History of the Organization* (Washington, DC: Cyrus Field Adam, 1902). On the protests against lynching, see Ida B. Wells-Barnett, "Lynch Law in America," lecture dated 1900, retrieved from www.blackpast.org/1900-ida-b-wells-lynch-law-america. Also see her *On Lynchings* (Mineola, NY: Dover, 2014), which collects three pamphlets from 1892 to 1900. On the birth of the NAACP, see Charles Kellogg, *NAACP: A History of the National Association for the Advancement of Colored People, Vol. 1, 1909–1920* (Baltimore: Johns Hopkins, 1967).

97   **"and complex issues?":** Josiah Royce, *Race Questions, Provincialism, and Other American Problems* (New York: Macmillan, 1908), 25.

97   **such as his own:** A. Jeancourt-Galignani, *L'immigration en droit international* (Paris: Rousseau, 1908), 14.

97   **at the present hour:** "Xenophobia," *New York Times*, January 9, 1923, 22.

Chapter 8: The Road to Genocide

100   **the biologically cursed:** See Adam Cohen, *Imbeciles: The Supreme Court, American Eugenics, and the Sterilization of Carrie Buck* (New York: Penguin, 2017). On the history of eugenics, see the classic work of Daniel Kevles, *In the Name of Eugenics: Genetics and the Uses of Human Heredity* (Cambridge: Harvard University Press, 1998).

100   **of the fine-skulled:** See Jennifer M. Hecht, "Vacher de Lapouge and the Rise of Nazi Science," *Journal of the History of Ideas* 61, no. 2 (2000): 285–304. Vacher de Lapouge was placed at the beginnings of German racism by Magnus Hirschfeld in his 1938 book *Racism* (Port Washington, NY: Kennikat Press, 1973), 35–39.

101   **founding African outposts:** Peters ruled colonies of Chaga people with such savagery that even the half-blind could not but notice. After he murdered his African concubine and her lover, he returned home first to honors and accolades. Outed by Socialists in 1896, the doctor was ultimately dishonorably discharged; see David Olusgoa and Casper Erichsen, *The Kaiser's Holocaust* (London: Faber and Faber, 2011).

101   **its inevitable path:** Jürgen Zimmerer, "Annihilation in Africa: The 'Race War'

in German Southwest Africa (1904–1908) and Its Significance for a Global History of Genocide," *GHI Bulletin* 37 (2005): 51–57. B. Madley, "From Africa to Auschwitz: How German South West Africa Incubated Ideas and Methods Adopted and Developed by the Nazis in Eastern Europe," *European History Quarterly* 35, no. 3 (2005): 429–64.

101   **in French, "*le racisme*":** As early as 1884, a French-English dictionary translated "racisme" as "to ostracize"; see *A Practical Dictionary of the French and English Language* (London: Longmans, Green, 1884), 303. Originally, that term was a description of pride in one's exalted heritage, but by 1900, skeptics writing in French, English, and German began to proclaim it a dubious and dangerous prejudice. For a general history, see George Fredrickson, *Racism: A Short History* (Princeton: Princeton University Press, 2002). On the origins of racism, one eminent historian considers the earliest use to date to be Albert Myabon in 1902; see Jan Goldstein, "Toward an Empirical History of Moral Thinking: The Case of Racial Theory in Mid-Nineteenth-Century France," *American Historical Review* 120, no. 1 (2015): 1–27. Also see Franz Samuelson, "From 'Race Psychology' to 'Studies in Prejudice': Some Observations on the Thematic Reversal in Social Psychology," *Journal of the History of the Behavioral Sciences* 14 (1978): 265–78.

102   **"religion of duty":** Felix Adler, "Atheism: A Lecture," given on Sunday, April 6, 1879, at the Society for Ethical Culture (New York: Cooperative Printers, 1879). Felix Adler, *Creed and Deed* (New York: Putnam, 1877); Felix Adler, *The Religion of Duty* (New York: McClure Phillips, 1915).

103   **and global conflict:** On this being the brainchild of Adler, see Ulysses Weatherly, "The First Universal Races Congress," *American Journal of Sociology* 17, no. 3 (November 1911): 315.

103   **Adler's congress dwarfed that:** "Nationalities and Subject Races, Report on Conference Held in Caxton Hall," Westminster, June 28–30, 1910 (London: P.S. King, 1910). Lecturers included E. B. Morel on slavery and indentured labor in Mexico, Peru, and Africa. For the claim on the unique nature of the congress, see A. C. Haddon, "The First Universal Races Congress," *Science* 34, no. 871 (September 1911): 304.

103   **"women with short hair":** Gustav Spiller, ed., *Papers on Inter-Racial Problems, Communicated to the First Universal Races Congress, Held at the University of London, July 26–29, 1911* (London: P.S. King, 1911), v–vi. Also see Weatherly, "The First Universal Races Congress," 315–28; his comment about the long and short hairs is on page 327. On the instability of race as a category, see Haddon, "The First Universal Races Congress," 304–6.

104   **"and a heartier co-operation":** Spiller, ed., *Papers on Inter-Racial Problems*, v.

104   **questions in the negative:** On the questionnaire, see Weatherly, "The First Universal Races Congress," 316.

104   **dissolved into racism:** On this shift, see George Stocking, *Race, Color and Evolution* (Chicago: University of Chicago Press, 1982); Elazar Barkan, *The Retreat of Scientific Racism* (Cambridge: Cambridge University Press, 1996); and Nell Painter, *The History of White People* (New York: W. W. Norton, 2011).

104 **home with a new passion:** Franz Boas, *Franz Boas Among the Inuit of Baffin Island, 1883–1884, Journals and Letters*, ed. L. Muller-Wille, trans. William Barr (Toronto: University of Toronto Press, 1998), 63. Letter dated August 10, 1883. On Boas, see Rosemary Zumwalt, *Franz Boas: The Emergence of the Anthropologist* (Lincoln: University of Nebraska Press, 2019), as well as the excellent omnibus essay by Kwame Anthony Appiah, "The Defender of Differences," *New York Review of Books*, posted online May 28, 2020.

106 **answer in his presentation:** Franz Boas Papers, Correspondence with Felix Adler, American Philosophical Society Library Archives. Mss.B.B61. See letters dated March 30, 1899, April 28, 1899, March 23, 1904, and October 5, 1914. On Boas's relation to the Society for Ethical Culture, see Morris Opler, "Franz Boas: Religion and Theory," *American Anthropologist* 69, no. 6 (December 1967): 741–44.

106 **then that was all wrong:** Franz Boas, "Instability of Human Types," in Spiller, ed., *Papers on Inter-Racial Problems*, 99–103. Also see Haddon, "The First Universal Races Congress," 304–6. On Boas, see Lee Baker, *From Savage to Negro: Anthropology and the Construction of Race, 1896–1954* (Berkeley: University of California Press, 1998; also Painter, *History of White People*, 228–44.

106 **as all bias and egoism:** Royce, *Race Questions, Provincialism, and Other American Problems*, 53.

106 **their respective cultures:** Gustav Spiller, "The Problem of Race Equality," in Spiller. ed., *Papers on Inter-Racial Problems*, 104.

106 **"as fictions of our brains":** Jean Finot, *The Death-Agony of the "Science" of Race*, trans. C. A. Grande (1905; London: Stead, 1911). Finot's critique was considered by one historian to be the most "decisive" attack on the theory of race; see Théophile Simar, *Étude critique sur la formation de la doctrine des races* (Brussels: Lamertin, 1922), 3. He also credited two later works, John Oakesmith's 1919 *Race and Nationality* and F. Hertz's 1915 *Rasse und Kultur*. Also see Helen Tilley, "Racial Science, Geopolitics, and Empires: Paradoxes of Power," *Isis* 105 (2014): 773–81; Robert Holton, "Cosmopolitanism or Cosmopolitanisms? The Universal Races Congress of 1911," *Peace Research Abstracts* 40 (2003): 5; Jennifer Hecht, "The Solvency of Metaphysics: The Debate over Racial Science and Moral Philosophy in France, 1890–1919," *Isis* 90 (1999): 1–24.

107 **to reject false hierarchies:** W. E. B. Du Bois, "The Negro Race in the United States of America," in Spiller, ed., *Papers on Inter-Racial Problems*, 348–64. Also see Michael Biddiss, "The Universal Races Congress of 1911," *Race* 13, no.1 (1971): 348–64; and Anthony Appiah, "The Uncompleted Arguments: Du Bois and the Illusion of Race," *Critical Inquiry* 12, no. 1 (1985): 21–37.

107 **was nothing to dread:** Felix Luschan, "Anthropological View of Race," in Spiller, ed., *Papers on Inter-Racial Problems*, 23.

107 **race was "chimerical":** Haddon, "The First Universal Races Congress," 304–6.

108 **colonial rivalries in Africa:** W. E. B. Du Bois, "The African Roots of War," *Atlantic Monthly*, May 1915.

108 **"strangers who had immigrated":** Massimo Livi-Bacci, *A Short History of Migration*, trans. Carl Ipsen (Cambridge: Polity Press, 2012), 72.

108 **colonized and stateless peoples:** Woodrow Wilson, "Fourteen Points Speech to Congress," delivered on January 8, 1918, accessed on https://www.britannica.com/event/Fourteen-Points. On Wilson and the anti-Colonial movement, see Erez Manela, *The Wilsonian Moment: Self-Determination and the International Origins of Anticolonial Nationalism* (New York: Oxford University Press, 2007).

109 **meager resources ran out:** "League of Nations Notes," *Bulletin of International News* 5, no. 1 (July 7, 1928): 24–26; Carole Fink, "The League of Nations and the Minorities Question," *World Affairs* 157, no. 4 (1995): 197–205; On the Nansen passport, see Louise Holborn, "The League of Nations and the Refugee Problem," *Annals of the American Academy of Political and Social Science* 203 (1939): 124–35.

109 **proposition was adopted:** On the League of Nations, see Ruth Henig, *The Peace That Never Was: A History of the League of Nations* (London: Haus Publishing, 2019). On the interwar problem of immigrants, see Claudena Skran, *Refugees in Inter-War Europe: The Emergence of a Regime* (Oxford: Clarendon Press, 2011). Also see Imre Ferenczi, "International Migration Statistics," in *International Migrations, Volume 1: Statistics*, ed. Walter Willcox (Cambridge: National Bureau of Economic Research, 1929), 47–76, and his "Les étrangers dans le monde d'aujourd'hui," *Annales d'histoire économique et sociale* 8, no. 37 (1936): 29–41; and J. L. Rubinstein, "The Refugee Problem," *International Affairs* 15, no. 5 (1936): 716–34.

110 **hospitals, and prisons:** Stéphane Lauzanne, "Faites payer les étrangers mais ne les embêtez pas!" *Le Matin*, August 2, 1926, 1.

110 **"France is no exception":** "The Folly of Xenophobia," *Christian Science Monitor*, January 24, 1924, 18.

110 **"is the Xenophobia":** J. M. Kenworthy, "The Alien Question in England," *American Israelite*, September 3, 1925, 8. Also Ernest Marshall, "European Nations Cool to Strangers," *New York Times*, August 29, 1926, 57–58. Also Colin Holmes, *Anti-Semitism in British Society, 1876–1939* (New York: Holmes and Meier, 1979).

111 **"wave after wave of xenophobia":** H. M. Kallen, "Of War and Peace," *Social Research* 6, no. 3 (1930): 361.

111 **Swahili than in German:** For accusations of xenophobia, see Edwin Slosson, "The Anti-Semitic Scare," *The Independent*, December 25, 1920, 427; Herbert Adams Gibbons, *An Introduction to World Politics* (New York: The Century, 1922), 307; "Lays Our Ills to Xenophobia, Defends Foreign Press," *New York Times*, February 23, 1928, 24; Louis Adamic, "Aliens and Alien-Baiters," *Harper's* 173 (November 1936): 564; Norman Bentwich, "The League of Nations and Refugees," *British Yearbook of International Law* 16 (1935): 114–29; Walter Adams, "Refugees in Europe," *Annals of the American Academy* 203, no. 1 (May 1939): 37–44. Also see Walter Willcox, ed., *International Migrations, Volume 2: Interpretations* (Cambridge: National Bureau of Economic Research, 1931), which gives interwar statistics on migratory movements around the world.

111   **for Germans to move in:** Mark Mazower, *Hitler's Empire: How the Nazis Ruled Europe* (New York: Penguin, 2009), 19–20.

112   **purity a rallying cry:** Cited in Mazower, *Hitler's Empire*, 22.

112   **of Jews and Aryans:** See Shelley Baranowski, *Nazi Empire: German Colonialism and Imperialism from Bismarck to Hitler* (Cambridge: Cambridge University Press, 2010).

112   **stunned the populace:** The extent to which the colonial experience of Germany led to the Holocaust is a highly debated topic. Baranowski accepts some parallels but insists that Imperial Germany was not Nazi Germany, and that their campaigns were no different from other imperial powers; Baranowski, *Nazi Empire*, 49–50. Mazower argues that the war for a greater Germany helped transform that nation and pave the way for the Holocaust. See his *Hitler's Empire*, 11.

112   **possibility of redemption:** Historians have argued over the relationship between colonialism and the Holocaust, and while discontinuities clearly exist between, say, the Herero genocide and the much different war on the Jews, continuities exist as well. See the excellent review by Thomas Kühne, "Colonialism and the Holocaust: Continuities, Causations, and Complexities," *Journal of Genocide Research* 15, no. 3 (2013): 339–62; he argues that Saul Friedlander's notion of "redemptive anti-Semitism" was key to that genocide.

113   **find an eager audience:** On Schmitt's life, see Gopal Balakrishnan, *The Enemy: An Intellectual Portrait of Carl Schmitt* (London: Verso, 2000).

114   **be ready for combat:** Carl Schmitt, *The Concept of the Political*, trans. George Schwab (1928; New Brunswick, NJ: Rutgers University Press, 1976), 32. See W. E. Scheuerman, *Carl Schmitt: The End of Law* (Lanham, MD: Rowman & Littlefield, 1999). On debates about Schmitt's legacy, see Giovanni Sartori, "The Essence of the Political in Carl Schmitt," *Journal of Theoretical Politics* 1, no. 1 (1989): 63–75, and Jacopo Martire, "From Enemy to Xenos: the Evolution of a Schittian Category," in A. Matos et al., eds, *Democracy, Justice and Exception* (Initia Via Editora, 2015), http://hdl.handle.net/1893/23885.

115   **crushing of human possibilities:** Equality, after Locke, resided not in the soul but in the fallible mind. Ideas, including ones of identity and ethics, were predicated on the contingency and uncertainty of human knowledge. Hence, theoretically there was much room for variance. However, these details were lost when Napoleon's troops rode into town carrying his banner of universal truths, and pillaging and raping as they pleased. See Makari, *Soul Machine*, 103–27, 354–95.

115   **those of the Germans:** An early assessment of the Nazi apologists and Carl Schmitt can be found in Samuel Rosenberg, "Three Concepts in Nazi Political Theory," *Science and Society*, January 1, 1936, 221–30.

115   **hate Slavs and Jews?:** William Rappard, "Die Stellung der Universität in der gegenwärtigen Zeitlage," *Die Friedes-Warte*, 37, no. 1 (1937): 1–10. Quote on page 2. Rappard was an influential diplomat at the League of Nations. On German complaints regarding the *Auslandsdeutsch* to the League of Nations, see Carole Fink, "The League of Nations and the Minorities Question," *World Affairs* 157, no. 4 (1995): 197–205.

116   **the hereditarily unfit:** Mazower, *Hitler's Empire*, 584–87.

116   **moral and spiritual weight:** Simone Weil, "Á propos de la question coloniale dans ses rapports avec le destin du peuple français," in *Contre le colonialisme*, ed. V. Gérard (1943; Paris: Payot et Rivages, 2018), 85–110, and Hannah Arendt, "From Dreyfus Affair to France Today," *Jewish Social Studies* 4, no. 3 1942): 195–240. Also see Arendt's *The Origins of Totalitarianism*.

116   **"nor Christian, nor even European":** Alfred Rambaud, *Histoire de la civilisation française* (Paris: Armand Colin, 1885), 417. The quote reads: "Or, quelle est la situation des juifs? Ils sont comme une colonie asiatique établie en France. Ils sont chez nous comme en terre étrangère. Triplement étrangère. Car ils ne sont, ni des Français, ni des chrétians, ni même des Européens." On the use of this quote in occupied Paris, see Laurent Joly, "L'état contre les Juifs," *Le Monde*, October 5, 2018, 4, from his book, *L'état contre les Juifs: Vichy, les Nazis, et la persecution antisémite* (Paris: Grasset, 2018). Rambaud's enthusiastic expansionist views can be found in Alfred Rambaud, ed., *La France colonial: histoire, géographie, commerce* (Paris: Armand Colin, 1893).

117   **colony in their midst:** On the argument that colonialism in part paved the way for the Nazi genocide, see Jürgen Zimmerer, "Annihilation in Africa," *GHI Bulletin* 37 (2005): 51–57, and his "Colonialism and the Holocaust: Towards an Archaeology of Genocide," in *Genocide and Settler Society*, ed. A. Dirk Moses (New York: Berghahn Books, 2005), 46–76; A. Dirk Moses, ed., *Empire, Colony, Genocide: Conquest, Occupation, and Subaltern Resistance in World History* (New York: Berghahn Books, 2008); Benjamin Madley, "From Africa to Auschwitz," *European History Quarterly* 35, no. 3 (2005): 429–64. For a subtle discussion, see Kühne, "Colonialism and the Holocaust," 339–62.

117   **of German political life:** See David Furber and Wendy Lower, "Colonialism and Genocide in Nazi-occupied Poland and Ukraine," in Moses, ed., *Empire, Colony, Genocide*, 372–402; the authors distinguish settler and exploitation colonies in German occupation.

117   **"triple foreigners," the Jews:** Those estimates came from Walter Laqueur and Judith Baumel, eds., *The Holocaust Encyclopedia* (New Haven: Yale University Press, 2001).

117   **"something awesome":** Mazower, *Hitler's Empire*, 306.

119   **"cover next to nothing":** Alvin Johnson, "The Rising Tide of Xenophobia," *American Journal of Economics and Sociology* 4, no. 4 (1945): 498.

119   **"reverting to primitivism":** Cited in Shlomo Bergman, "Some Methodological Errors in the Study of Anti-Semitism," *Jewish Social Studies* 5, no. 1 (1943): 49.

119   **"crime without a name":** Quoted in Samantha Power, *A Problem from Hell: America and the Age of Genocide* (New York: Basic Books, 2013), 29. According to Power, the term "Holocaust" would not be broadly adopted until around 1970. The Hebrew "Shoah" also shouldered some of the weight of this tragedy, as did the spine-chilling Nazi term, the "Final Solution."

119   **in response in 1944:** Raphael Lemkin, *Axis Rule in Occupied Europe: Laws of Occupation: Analysis of Government, Proposals for Redress* (Washington, DC:

Carnegie Endowment, 1944), 79–98. Also Raphael Lemkin, "Genocide: A Modern Crime," *Free World* 9 (1945): 39–43.

119 **him as "Beilus":** On Lemkin, see Raphael Lemkin, *Totally Unofficial, The Autobiography of Raphael Lemkin,* ed. Donna-Lee Frieze (New Haven: Yale University Press, 2013). Lemkin's story and impact are well told in Power, *A Problem from Hell,* 1–78. Also see Douglas Irvin-Erickson, *The Life and Works of Raphael Lemkin,* PhD dissertation, Rutgers University, 2014, and his *Raphael Lemkin and the Concept of Genocide* (Philadelphia: University of Pennsylvania Press, 2017).

121 **got away with it:** The literature on the Ottomans and their Christian minorities is large. See, for example, Eugene Rogan, *The Fall of the Ottomans: The Great War and the Middle East* (New York: Basic Books, 2015). Rogan estimates that a minimum of 600,000 and a maximum of 1.5 million Armenians died, as did 250,000 Assyrians. He also discusses the forced exiles of Greek Orthodox Christians.

121 **this time his own:** For a translation of Lemkin's 1933 proposal, see http://www .preventgenocide.org/lemkin/madrid1933-english.htm.

122 **got him out of Europe:** Lemkin, *Totally Unofficial,* 1, 18–19, 25, 33, 54.

122 **"of humanitarian feelings":** Lemkin, *Axis Rule in Occupied Europe,* 74, 79–80. On the impact of Lemkin and this concept, see the excellent Power, *A Problem from Hell*; also Mark Levene, *The Meaning of Genocide* (London: Bloomsbury, 2005), 187–88.

123 **worst atrocities in history:** United Nations Department of Public Information, *Universal Declaration of Human Rights* (New York: King Typographic Service, 1949). See John Cooper, *Raphael Lemkin and the Struggle for the Genocide Convention* (London: Palgrave and Macmillan, 2008); and Irvin-Erickson, *The Life and Works of Raphael Lemkin,* 197.

123 **kill off an entire people:** The United Nations also had put forward its Universal Declaration of Human Rights, spearheaded by Eleanor Roosevelt. This insisted on the equality and common rights of all humans; Article 14 stated that all of mankind had the right to "seek and enjoy asylum" from persecution. Raphael Lemkin bitterly complained that unequal treatment and prejudice were hardly the same as the annihilation of a whole group and would provide cover for those embarrassed by their own reluctance to accept international rules for genocide. On the criticism and reception of the Genocide Convention, see Power, *A Problem from Hell,* 54–72.

124 **"strain and stress?":** Nathan Reich, "Anti-Semitism," *Journal of Educational Sociology* 18, no. 5 (1945): 294–302.

Part II: Inside the Xenophobic Mind

127 **William Carlos Williams, *In the American Grain*:** William Carlos Williams, *In the American Grain* (Norfolk, CT: New Directions, 1925), 112.

127 **Ralph Ellison, *Invisible Man*:** Ralph Ellison, *Invisible Man* (New York: Random House, 1952), 3.

Chapter 9: Little Albert and the Wages of Fear

129   **"in reality essentially psychologic"**: Imre Ferenczi, "Les étrangers dans le monde d'aujourd'hui," *Annales d'histoire économique et sociale* 8, no. 37 (1936): 29–41.

130   **lay in his audience's hands:** On this declaration, see Anne Harrington, *Mind-Fixers: Psychiatry's Troubled Search for the Biology of Mental Illness* (New York: W. W. Norton, 2019), 86–87.

131   **Why Worry?:** George Beard, *American Nervousness: Its Causes and Consequences* (New York: Putnam, 1881), 11–85; C. W. Saleeby, *Don't Worry (Worry: The Disease of the Age)* (New York: F. Stokes, 1907); George Walton, *Why Worry?* (Philadelphia: Lippincott, 1908).

132   **leapt irrationally into battle:** On G. Stanley Hall, see Dorothy Ross, *G. Stanley Hall: The Psychologist as Prophet* (Chicago: University of Chicago Press, 1972). Long anticipated, the connection between fear and aggression was codified as the "fight or flight" response by Walter B. Cannon. See his *Bodily Changes in Pain, Hunger, Fear and Rage* (New York: Appleton, 1915).

133   **a fear of strangers:** G. Stanley Hall, "A Study of Fears," *American Journal of Psychology* 8, no. 2 (1897): 147–249. See page 152.

133   **"to almost all strangers":** Hall, "A Study of Fears," 218.

133   **maturity tempered such reactions:** Hall, "A Study of Fears," 218, 247. G. Stanley Hall, *Adolescence: Its Psychology and Its Relations to Physiology, Anthropology, Sociology, Sex, Crime, Religion and Education* (1904; New York: Appleton, 1914), 370.

134   **Jews as recalcitrant children:** Hall, *Adolescence*, 648–748. See especially pages 724, 737.

135   **the result of learned connections:** On Pavlov, see Daniel Todes, *Ivan Pavlov: A Russian Life in Science* (Oxford: Oxford University Press, 2014).

135   **there it would remain:** On these mistranslations, see Todes, *Ivan Pavlov*, 1, 248–50, 287, 767. Also see Ivan Pavlov, *Conditioned Reflexes*, trans. G. V. Ansesep (1927; Mineola, NY: Dover, 2003). For a contrary claim on Pavlov and his bell, see Rand Evans, "Correcting Some Pavloviana regarding 'Pavlov's Bell' and Pavlov's 'Mugging,'" *American Journal of Psychology* 110, no. 1 (1997): 115–25.

136   **"selfish, conceited cad":** Kerry Buckley, *Mechanical Man: John Broadus Watson and the Beginnings of Behaviorism* (New York: Guilford, 1989), 50.

136   **an infantile phobia:** J. B. Watson and R. Raynor, "Conditioned Emotional Reactions," *Journal of Experimental Psychology* 3 (1920): 1–14.

137   **"or black from yellow":** John Watson, *Behaviorism* (1924/1925; New Brunswick, NJ: Transaction Publishers, 2009), 76.

138   **for individuals and societies:** Watson and Raynor, "Conditioned Emotional Reactions," 12. On this case, see Ben Harris, "Whatever Happened to Little Albert?" *American Psychologist* 34, no. 1 (1979): 151–60, and his "Letting Go of Little Albert," *Journal of the History of Behavioral Sciences* 47, no. 1 (2011): 1–17; also H. P. Beck et al., "Finding Little Albert," *American Psychologist* 64, no. 7 (October 2009): 605–14. On the case of Peter, see Mary Cover Jones, "A

Laboratory Study of Fear: The Case of Peter," *Pedagogical Seminary* 31 (1924): 308–15.

138 **of endless social improvement:** For reviews of Watson's *Behaviorism*, see Stuart Chase, "Eat the Apple," *New York Herald Tribune*, June 21, 1925, D5. Also see Louis Kalonyme, "Man at Birth Has No Fear, Tests Reveal," *New York Times*, January 4, 1925, 6, and the skeptical Evans Clark, in the *New York Times*, August 2, 1925, 3:14, who found the author too "cock-sure." The book went through three revised editions, in 1914, 1919, and then in 1924/1925, and became progressively more radical. In 1919, Watson first pronounced his psychology to be the only scientific one.

139 **due to conditioned reflexes:** M. V. O'Shea, ed., *The Child: His Nature and His Needs* (New York: The Children's Foundation, 1924), 42.

140 **frightening, from loved to hated:** Aldous Huxley, *Brave New World* (New York: Harper and Brothers, 1932).

140 **kingdom of human behavior:** Arthur Koestler, *Darkness at Noon* (1941; New York: Scribner, 2019); Edward Hunter, *Brain-Washing in Red China: The Calculated Destruction of Men's Minds* (New York: Vanguard), 1951.

140 **indoctrinate the unwitting:** Joost Meerloo, *The Rape of the Mind* (New York: World Publishing, 1956), 37–48. Also see Anonymous, *Are the American People Being Brain-Washed into Slavery?* (Valley Center, CA: Freedom Builders of America, n.d.). This fascinating pamphlet, published by a secretive right-wing group, the Freedom Builders of America, associated with Reverend Kenneth Goff, is said to be written by L. Ron Hubbard, founder of Scientology, and was supposed to be the confession of a former Communist agent in Wisconsin, who saw the route to total domination of the American populace through using Comrade Pavlov as a mole who penetrated American psychiatry and education.

140 **segregation and racism:** Richard Wright, "Plans for Work on *Native Son* Submitted to the John Simon Guggenheim Memorial Foundation," n.d., JWJ MSS3, series 1, Richard Wright Papers, Beinecke Library, Yale University.

141 **Bigger kills it:** Richard Wright, *Native Son*, in Richard Wright, *Early Works*, ed. Arnold Rampersad (1940; New York: Library of America, 1991).

142 **"tension in his muscles":** Wright, *Native Son*, 550.

142 **"into someone's face":** Wright, *Native Son*, 650.

142 **"handling the problem":** Wright, *Native Son*, 707.

142 **"set-up that conditioned it":** Peter Monro Jack, "A Tragic Novel of Negro Life in America," *New York Times*, March 3, 1940, 2; Milton Rugoff, "A Feverish Dramatic Intensity," *New York Herald Tribune*, March 3, 1940, 5. Also see J. R. Johnson, "On *Native Son* by Richard Wright," *Labor Action* 4, no. 7 (May 1940): 1–3.

143 **these reactions are impossible:** Dorothy Canfield Fisher, "Introduction," in Richard Wright, *Native Son* (New York: Harper & Brothers, 1940), ix. This was later excised and does not appear in later editions.

144 **maligned around the world:** Richard Wright, "How Bigger Was Born," in Wright, *Early Works*, 851–82. Also see his "The Ethic of Living Jim Crow," a

1937 essay written for the Federal Writers' Project, which in 1940 was added to *Uncle Tom's Children* and is in Wright, *Early Works*, 225–38.

144   **future author of *Invisible Man*:** Ralph Ellison, "Richard Wright's Blues," *Antioch Review* 5, no. 2 (1945): 198–211. Ralph Ellison, *The Selected Letters of Ralph Ellison*, ed. John Callahan (New York: Random House, 2019), 144–45. Letter dated November 3, 1941. In this letter, Ellison is also reacting to Wright's 1941 essay with photographs called *12 Million Black Voices* (New York: Viking, 1941).

145   **"each other is thinking":** Wright, *Early Works*, 773. Wright portrays institutional racism as it seeps into relationships. The Daltons are well-intentioned liberals, but they refuse to consider how they deeply profit from their real estate business in the Black Belt of Chicago.

145   **"loved and had hurt him":** Wright, *Early Works*, 715.

145   **these conclusions themselves?:** See Louis Menand, "The Hammer and the Nail: Richard Wright's Modern Condition," *The New Yorker*, July 13, 1992; https://www.newyorker.com/magazine/1992/07/20/the-hammer-and-the-nail.

145   **"blind play of social forces":** Wright, *Early Works*, 811. In 1946, Wright tried to do something about the destructive effect of racism by supporting the first free psychiatric clinic in Harlem. See Gabriel Mendes, *Under the Strain of Color: Harlem's Lafargue Clinic and the Promise of an Antiracist Psychiatry* (Ithaca: Cornell University Press, 2015).

146   **"shaped his personality":** Ellison, *Selected Letters*, 129, 132. The letters are dated April 14, 1940, and April 22, 1940.

146   **racist fear and hatred:** Richard Wright, *Uncle Tom's Children*, in Wright, *Early Works*, 239–75.

147   **result of racial prejudice:** Martin Bulmer, *The Chicago School of Sociology: Institutionalization, Diversity, and the Rise of Sociological Research* (Chicago: University of Chicago Press, 1984), 46-47. See 1909 Class notes by Emory Bogardus, in "W. I. Thomas and Social Origins," *Sociology and Social Research* 43 (1959): 365–69.

147   **to 8000 Americans:** Emory Bogardus, "Social Distance and its Origins," *Journal of Applied Sociology* 9 (1925): 216–26. Also see Robert Park, "The Concept of Social Distance as Applied to the Study of Racial Attitudes and Racial Relations," *Journal of Applied Sociology* 8 (1924): 339–44. On this scale, see Colin Wark and John F. Galliher. "Emory Bogardus and the Origins of the Social Distance Scale," *American Sociologist* 38, no. 4 (2007): 383–95.

148   **this animosity ran deep:** Emory Bogardus, *Immigration and Race Attitudes* (Boston: D. C. Heath, 1928).

148   **on the Armenian genocide:** Cited in Power, *A Problem from Hell*, 505.

149   **"his own personal experiences":** Bogardus, *Immigration and Race Attitudes*, 43.

149   **his ilk dismissed:** Nella Larson, *Passing* (1929; New York: Penguin, 2003), 40–41.

149   **any alteration at all:** Bogardus, *Immigration and Race Attitudes*, 148.

Chapter 10: The Invention of the Stereotype

151 **impossible to imagine:** On the role of ideas in the mind, see Makari, *Soul Machine.*

151 **called "natural kinds":** J. S. Mill, *An Examination of Sir William Hamilton's Philosophy* (1865; London: Longmans, 1867), 234ff. Also see the excellent essay by Ian Hacking, "A Tradition of Natural Kinds," *Philosophical Studies* 71, no. 1/2 (1991): 109–26.

152 **"the heaviest guns":** Walter Lippmann, *Public Philosopher: Selected Letters of Walter Lippmann*, ed. J. M. Blum (New York: Ticknor and Fields, 1985), 37. On Lippmann, see Ronald Steele, *Walter Lippmann and the American Century* (London: Routledge, 2017).

154 **"how public opinion is made":** Lippmann, *Public Philosopher,* 132. Letter dated November 18, 1919.

154 **then easily reproduced:** Walter Lippmann, *Public Opinion* (1922; Greenbook Publications, 2010).

155 **theater of its own making:** Lippmann, *Public Opinion*, 80–81, 96.

155 **"rushed out of the hall":** Lippmann, *Public Opinion*, 82.

156 **fill in the blanks:** On this experiment, see F. van Langenhove, *The Growth of a Legend*, trans. E. B. Sherlock (New York: Putnam, 1916), 120–22.

156 **Stereotypes ruled:** Lippmann, *Public Opinion*, 99.

156 **"and abstracts falsely":** Lippmann, *Public Philosopher*, 173. Letter dated January 13, 1925.

156 **lodged in their heads:** Lippmann, *Public Opinion*, 79–82, 90, 101.

157 **His name was Josef Goebbels:** For a corrective to the often ignored influence of Lippmann's *Public Opinion*, see Lepore, *These Truths*, 414–57.

158 **the public as never before:** *The Birth of a Nation*, director: D. W. Griffith, D. W. Griffith Corp., 1915; *Intolerance*, director: D. W. Griffith, D. W. Griffith Corp., 1916.

159 **"nothing strange not made familiar":** On these films and cartoons, see Christopher Lehman, "Black Representation in American Short Films, 1928–1954," PhD dissertation, University of Massachusetts, 2002; and also C. Richard King et al., "Animated Representations of Blackness," *Journal of African American Studies* 14 (2010): 395–97.

160 **they took in the action:** Abel Gance, as cited in Walter Benjamin, "Art in the Age of Mechanical Reproduction," *Illuminations*, trans. Harry Zohn (New York: Schocken, 1968), 227.

160 ***Son of the Sheik:*** *The Sheik,* director: George Melford, Paramount Pictures, 1921; and *The Son of the Sheik*, director: George Fitzmaurice, United Artists, 1926.

160 **were created or reinforced:** Kenneth Gould, "Cinepatriotism," *Social Forces* 7, no. 1 (1928): 121.

161 **"character of all opposition":** Lippmann, *Public Opinion*, 120.

161 **called them "dynamic stereotypes":** On Lippmann and Locke, see Clyde King, " 'Public Opinion' by Walter Lippmann," *Annals of the American Academy*

of Political and Social Science 103 (1922): 153–54. On Pavlov's shift, see Todes, *Ivan Pavlov*, 652–59.

162   **led to gross errors:** Stuart Rice, " 'Stereotypes': A Source of Error in Judging Human Character," *Journal of Personnel Research* 5 (1926): 267–76.

162   **the subjugation of the Negro:** Abram Harris, "Race, Cultural Group, Social Differentiation: Economic Foundation of American Race Division," *Social Forces* 5 (1926): 474.

162   **prejudice based on stereotypes:** D. Katz and K. Braly, "Racial Prejudice and Racial Stereotype," *Journal of Abnormal and Social Psychology* 30, no. 2 (1933): 175–93.

162   **"the Oriental or the immigrant":** Kimball Young, "Primitive Social Norms in Present Day Education," *Social Forces* 5 (1927): 572.

162   **did it all the time:** John Grier Hibben, *A Defence of Prejudice and Other Essays* (New York: Scribner, 1911, 1–16). A professor of logic, Hibben was made president of Princeton University in 1912. He defended prejudice as opinion, guesswork, "sub-conscious" reactions, and fast thinking in situations that require this. He made no reference to troubles surrounding racial or religious prejudice.

163   **stranger's work and revived it:** On Georg Simmel, see Donald N. Levine, ed., *Georg Simmel on Individuality and Social Forms* (Chicago: University of Chicago, 1971).

164   **"a pariah and an outlaw":** Robert Park, "The Bases of Race Prejudice," *Annals of the American Academy of Political and Social Science* 140, no. 1 (1928): 12.

165   **they divided up communities:** Park, "Bases of Race Prejudice," 20.

165   **the European Jew:** Georg Simmel, "The Stranger," in *Georg Simmel on Individuality and Social Forms: Selected Writings*, ed. Donald N. Levine (1908; Chicago: University of Chicago Press, 1971), 143–49. Also see Georg Simmel, "The Sociology of Secrecy and of Secret Societies," *American Journal of Sociology* 11, no. 4 (1906): 441–98. Also E. M. Rogers, "Georg Simmel's Concept of the Stranger and Intercultural Communication Research," *Communication Theory* 9, no. 1 (1999): 58–74.

165   **"the marginal man":** Robert Park, "Human Migration and the Marginal Man," *American Journal of Sociology* 33, no. 6 (1928): 881–93. Also Everett Stonequist, "The Problem of the Marginal Man," *American Journal of Sociology* 41, no. 1 (1935): 9. Park with Bogardus formulated "social distance" as a concept by which the grade and degrees of social intimacy and interaction could be used as a variable when considering prejudice. See Park, "The Concept of Social Distance," 339–44; Bogardus, "Social Distance and its Origins," 216–26.

166   **European Jews and American Blacks:** Margaret Mary Wood, *The Stranger: A Study in Social Relationships* (1934; New York: Columbia University Press, 1971). In her dissertation on strangers and their reception, Wood recognized that Eskimos welcomed the stranger with a feast; others welcomed him with a fist. In the welcoming cultures, rites of passage and rituals managed the competing need of increased power—which came through the assimilation of new members—and fear that the original group might be overrun. While Australian aborigines

exclusively attacked strangers and therefore remained perpetually few in number and weak, gift exchange in the Trobriand Islands safeguarded and routinized the foreigner's passage and, as a result, made for a larger, more robust clan.

166 **"two educations, and two environments":** W. E. B. Du Bois, *The Souls of Black Folk* (1903; New York: W. W. Norton, 1999), 11; and T. E. Lawrence, *Seven Pillars of Wisdom: A Triumph* (1935; Hertfordshire: Wordsworth Editions, 1997), 14.

166 **unreliability of court witnesses:** On the evolution of the stereotype in the United States from its origin as a printing process to rote forms to negative symbols and imagery, see the *New York Times*'s theater reviewer, Mordaunt Hall, who frequently used the term in the 1920s and 1930s as a critique of stock characters, as in "Stereotyped Villainy and Cumbersome Comedy," *New York Times*, September 12, 1926, X5. The transition to Lippmann's sense can be found in academic work, such as Joseph Cohen, "Report on Crime and the Foreign Born: Comment," *Michigan Law Review* 30, no. 1 (1931): 99–104; and Ralph Lutz, "Studies of World War Propaganda, 1914–1933," *Journal of Modern History* 5, no. 4 (1933): 496–516. Later, this usage made its way into newspapers; see "Aid to Propaganda in Films Charged," *New York Times*, February 27, 1938, 36.

167 **drowned out by wild applause:** *Gone With the Wind*, director: Victor Fleming, Metro-Goldwyn-Mayer, 1939. On the *Saturday Evening Post* and other racist media, see Painter, *History of White People*, 291–300, 361.

167 **by these crude forms:** The so-called Father of the Harlem Renaissance, Alain Locke wrote this in "The Negro's Contribution to American Art and Literature," *Annals of the American Academy of Political and Social Science* 140, no. 1 (1928): 239. On the rise of the "New Negro" and its unfortunate reinforcement of notions of an "Old Negro," see Henry Louis Gates, *Stony the Road: Reconstruction, White Supremacy, and the Rise of Jim Crow* (New York: Penguin, 2019), especially pages 186–203. George Schuyler's review appears in "Two 'New Negroes' Discuss Negro Art in the 'Nation,'" *New York Amsterdam News*, June 23, 1926. When Wright's shattering *Native Son* was published, an editorial in Harlem's *Amsterdam News* asked why Wright's depiction of a murdering, raping Black man had not been denounced as stereotypical, the way critics had savaged Eugene O'Neill's *Emperor Jones*. The answer, he supposed, was that African Americans had grown "more self-assured" because they were no longer so boxed in by such stereotypes; Hodge Kirnon, "Why No Criticism of 'Native Son'?" *New York Amsterdam News*, May 11, 1940, 16.

167 **about these aliens:** For examples of early American immigrant literature, see Abraham Cahan, *The Rise of David Levinsky* (1917; New York: Penguin, 1993); James T. Farrell, *Studs Lonigan* (1932–34; New York: Penguin, 2001); Ameen Rihani, *The Book of Khalid* (1911; Brooklyn: Melville House, 2012); Ole E. Rolvaag, *Giants in the Earth: A Saga of the Prairie*, trans. L. Colcord (1927; New York: HarperCollins, 1999); and Sui Sin Far, *Mrs. Spring Fragrance* (1912; Mineola, NY: Dover, 2013).

167 **actions and visual effects:** Cited in Benjamin, "Art in the Age of Mechanical Reproduction," 246.

168 **war effort against Hitler:** John McManus and Louis Kronenberger, "Motion Pictures, the Theater, and Race Relations," *Annals of the American Academy of Political and Social Science* 244, no. 1 (1946): 152–58. Also Lepore, *These Truths*, 494–99. Frank Murphy quote is on page 496.

168 **foundations of American equality:** *Why We Fight*, directors: Frank Capra, Anatole Litvak, and Anthony Veiller, U.S. Army Pictorial Service, 1942–45. The first of these seven documentary films was *Prelude to War*, director: Frank Capra, 20th Century Fox, 1942.

169 **the Declaration of Independence:** *The Negro Soldier*, director: Stuart Heisler, War Activities Committee, 1944. *The House I Live In*, director: Mervyn LeRoy, RKO Radio Pictures, 1945. The evils of anti-Semitism also were taken up in movies like *This Land Is Mine*, director: Jean Renoir, RKO Radio Pictures, 1943, and *The Hitler Gang*, director: John Farrow, Paramount Pictures, 1944.

169 **primitive, barbaric, and civilized:** Edward B. Tylor, *Primitive Culture*, 2 vols. (London: John Murray, 1871).

169 **"reached at the present time":** Franz Boas, "The Mind of Primitive Man," *Science* 13, no. 321 (1901): 288.

170 **their bonds grew closer:** Boas, "The Mind of Primitive Man," 289.

170 **Edward Sapir, and Ruth Benedict:** See Baker, *From Savage to Negro*, 99–126, 148–50.

170 **"ultimately abolish warfare":** Boas, "An Anthropologist's View of War," 95.

170 **just myths—that is, stereotypes:** Ruth Benedict and Gene Weltfish, *The Races of Mankind*, Public Affairs Pamphlet No. 85, New York, 1943.

172 **groups as *between* them:** *The Brotherhood of Man*, director: Robert Cannon, United Productions of America, 1946.

172 **use stereotypes to divide us:** *Don't Be a Sucker*, director: not listed, U.S. War Department, 1943. The effect of this film was analyzed by Eunice Cooper and Helen Schneider, " 'Don't Be a Sucker': A Study in Communication," *Public Opinion Quarterly* 15, no. 2 (1951): 243–64.

173 **"dignity are in this fact":** James Agee and Walker Evans, *Let Us Now Praise Famous Men* (1941; Boston: Houghton Mifflin, 1979), 12–13.

174 **"gone dead in you":** James Agee, *Agee on Film, Volume 1* (New York: Perigee, 1983), 35, 80, 125.

174 **Mexicans as lazy:** See Edgar R. Clark, "Negro Stereotypes," *Journal of Negro Education* 17, no. 4 (1948): 545–49; N. D. Humphrey, "The Stereotype and the Social Types of Mexican-American Youths," *Journal of Social Psychology* 22, no. 1 (1945): 69–78; Rose Zeligs, "Children's Concepts and Stereotypes of Dutch, French, Italian, Mexican, Russian and Negro," *Journal of Education Research* 43, no. 5 (1950): 367–75.

174 **the walking dead:** On his estimate of prejudice, see Gordon W. Allport and Bernard Kramer, "Some Roots of Prejudice," *Journal of Psychology* 22, no. 1 (1946): 9. For his use of the stereotype, see Gordon Allport, *The Nature of Prejudice* (Cambridge: Addison-Wesley, 1954), 191ff. Also see Daniel Katz and

Kenneth Braly, "Racial Prejudice and Racial Stereotypes," *Journal of Abnormal and Social Psychology* 30 (1935): 175–93.

Chapter 11: Projection and the Negative of Love

176   **in fact, was through projection:** This philosophical problem took two forms. The spooky ontological version was: how do I know anybody else other than me possesses a mind? Am I deluded? Perhaps everyone else is a zombie or a robot? I can't see their minds, I can't check for its tangible reality, so what does such a conclusion rest on? The more quotidian, psychological version of the problem was: how could one subject know the silent contents and goings on of another mind? See J. S. Mill, *An Examination of Sir William Hamilton's Philosophy* (1865; London: Longmans, Green, Reader and Dyer, 1867), 234ff.

176   **mind was all a projection:** See Ludwig Wittgenstein, *Philosophical Investigations*, trans. G. E. M. Anscombe et al. (1953; Oxford: Wiley-Blackwell, 2009). Also see Gilbert Ryle, *The Concept of Mind* (1949; Chicago: University of Chicago Press, 2000); A. J. Ayer, *The Concept of a Person and Other Essays* (New York: St. Martin's Press, 1963); Donald Davidson, "First Person Authority," *Dialectica* 38, no. 2–3 (1984): 101–11; Søren Overgaard, "The Problem of Other Minds: Wittgenstein's Phenomenological Perspective," *Phenomonology and the Cognitive Sciences* 5 (2006): 53–73; and Thomas Nagel, *The View from Nowhere* (New York: Oxford University Press, 1986).

177   **"for purposes of defense":** Sigmund Freud and Wilhelm Fliess, *The Complete Letters of Sigmund Freud to Wilhelm Fliess, 1887–1904*, trans. J. Masson (Cambridge: Harvard University Press, 1985), 110.

178   **Sameness ruled:** Freud also uses "projection" in the Xenophanic sense in his discussion of transference, where he refers to "stereotypes" in the pre-Lippmann sense of the term; see Sigmund Freud, "The Dynamics of Transference," *The Standard Edition of the Complete Psychological Works of Sigmund Freud* [Hereafter: *S.E.*], vol. 12, trans. James Strachey et al. (1912; London: Hogarth Press, 1958), 99.

178   **some unwitting Not-Me:** Freud, "Psychoanalytic Notes on an Autobiographical Account of a Case of Paranoia," *S.E.*, vol. 12 (1911/1958), 3–83. In the case of the psychotic Dr. Schreber, projection meant a transformation, from "I hate him" to "he hates me." See the excellent discussion of these varied meanings in Jean Laplanche and J. B. Pontalis, *The Language of Psychoanalysis*, trans. D. Nicholson-Smith (New York: W. W. Norton, 1974), 349–56.

179   ***Civilization and Its Discontents:*** Freud's thinking on anxiety and the phobias emerged in conflict and dialogue with Wilhelm Stekel; see George Makari, *Revolution in Mind: The Creation of Psychoanalysis* (New York: HarperCollins, 2008), 156–61; Freud, *Civilization and Its Discontents*, *S.E.*, vol. 21 (1939/1958), 22.

179   **in all of us:** On the case of Erna, see Melanie Klein, *Love, Guilt and Reparation, and Other Works 1921–1945* (1929; New York: Free Press, 1984), 136, 160, 199.

180   **later call "stranger anxiety":** On this abashed state, see William Preyer, *The Mind of the Child*, trans. H. W. Brown (New York: Appleton, 1888), 55; and J. M. Baldwin, *Mental Development in the Child and the Race* (New York: Macmillan, 1897), 149–50. On "stranger anxiety," in 1926, Freud suggested that the howl from tiny Gustav came from the recognition that this stranger was not mother, who was lost forever. One his followers, René Spitz, made it central to research on what he called "stranger anxiety." A Viennese Jew, Spitz fled to Paris and taught psychoanalysis at the École Normale Supérieure; he began to observe anxious children and presented his ideas in papers on December 27, 1945, and February 21, 1946, both entitled "Separation from Mother": Rene Spitz Papers, University of Akron, then later published as "Anxiety in Infancy," *International Journal of Psychoanalysis* 31 (1950): 138–43. Infants, he found, naively smiled at anyone who smiled at them; they recognized a face, and any face was good enough. At around eight months, however, if a stranger approached, the child burst into tears and tried to flee. This "8 month anxiety" or "stranger anxiety" could be quelled only by the presence of mother. Such fears, it was said, normally subsided by the age of two. The ubiquity of this stage in childhood has now been disproven; see Rebecca Brooker et al., "The Development of Stranger Fear in Infancy and Toddlerhood: Normative Development, Individual Differences, Antecedents, and Outcomes," *Developmental Science* 16 (2013): 864–78.

180   **movie of our own making:** Klein, *Love, Guilt and Reparation, and Other Works*, 220.

180   **"destroy the enemy and his country":** Klein, *Love, Guilt and Reparation, and Other Works*, 59–60.

181   **collective form of suicide:** On these attempts to use psychoanalysis to confront the advent of illiberal regimes, see Makari, *Revolution in Mind*, 405–66.

181   **theory of groups:** See Robert A. Nye, *The Origins of Crowd Psychology: Gustave Le Bon and the Crisis of Mass Democracy in the Third Republic* (London: Sage Publications, 1975), 50; Le Bon's authority would be heavily relied on by others who shared this view, like Jules Harmand and Leopold de Saussure.

182   ***The Psychology of Crowds:*** Gustav Le Bon, *Psychologie des foules* (Paris: F. Alcan, 1895), 101. Also see Nye, *Origins of Crowd Psychology*, 69–71; and Jaap van Ginneken, *Crowds, Psychology, and Politics, 1871–1899* (Cambridge: Cambridge University Press, 2006).

182   **he later added, included Germans:** Nye, *Origins of Crowd Psychology*, 77.

183   **individual will:** Freud, *Group Psychology and the Analysis of the Ego*, S.E., vol. 18 (1921/1958), 65–143.

183   **"an *occasion* for enmity":** Freud, *Civilization and Its Discontents*, 59.

185   **"of their aggressiveness":** Freud, *Civilization and Its Discontents*, 61.

185   **into the commune:** Freud, *Civilization and Its Discontents*, 22, 58–63, 193. As anti-Semitism in Vienna grew rampant, Freud devoted himself to this subject. *Moses and Monotheism* was intended to penetrate into the role of the religious stranger in Christian, Muslim, and pagan societies. While written in 1934, the normally brave Freud held the work back for fear of political reprisals. It would

be published in 1938 after Freud had been driven from his home to spend his last days in London, witnessing how modernity and "progress had allied itself with barbarism." Freud, *Moses and Monotheism*, *S.E.*, vol. 23 (1938/1958), 54.

185 **among others, John Bowlby:** Wilhelm Reich, *The Mass Psychology of Fascism*, trans. T. Wolfe (1933; New York: Orgone Institute Press, 1946). This is the third, revised English translation. Also E. F. M. Durbin and John Bowlby, *Personal Aggressiveness and War* (London: Kegan, Paul, 1939). On the psycho-politics that developed in psychoanalysis prior to World War II, see Makari, *Revolution in Mind*, 405–67.

186 **untimely death in 1947:** Kurt Lewin, *The Complete Social Scientist: A Kurt Lewin Reader* (Washington, DC: American Psychological Association, 1997). See especially Lewin's "Action Research and Minority Problems," *Journal of Social Issues* 2, no. 4 (1946): 34–46. Lewin's MIT Research Center for Group Dynamics inspired numerous researchers, including the influential Leon Festinger.

186 **"departmentalization of the mind":** Theodor Adorno, *Minima Moralia: Reflections on a Damaged Life*, trans. E. F. N. Jephcott (1951; London: Verso, 2005), 21.

186 **became fast friends:** Theodor W. Adorno, *Letters to His Parents, 1939–1951*, ed. C. Gödde and H. Lonitz, trans. W. Hoban (Cambridge: Polity, 2006). See, for example, pages 128, 297, 325. Also see Detley Claussen, *Theodor W. Adorno: One Last Genius*, trans. Rodney Livingstone (Cambridge: Harvard University Press, 2008), 79–81.

187 **political power and economics:** Martin Jay, *The Dialectical Imagination: A History of the Frankfurt School and the Institute of Social Research* (Berkeley: University of California Press, 1996), 23–24, 98–99.

187 **and at times coauthor:** Max Horkheimer, *A Life in Letters: Selected Correspondence*, ed. and trans. M. Jacobson and E. Jacobson (Lincoln: University of Nebraska Press, 2007), 52, 55, 67, 167.

187 **"monopolistic propaganda":** Adorno, *Letters to His Parents*, 5. Letter dated July 8, 1939.

188 **American idiom, jazz:** Theodor Adorno, "On Popular Music," *Studies in Philosophy and Social Science* 9 (1941): 17–48. See Jay, *Dialectical Imagination*, 189–93; and Claussen, *Theodor W. Adorno: One Last Genius*, 140.

189 **the "Culture Industry":** Theodor Adorno, *The Culture Industry: Selected Essays on Mass Culture* (New York: Routledge, 1991).

189 **Feverishly, he wrote:** Adorno, *Minima Moralia*, 46, 87.

189 **but also other men:** Max Horkheimer and Theodor W. Adorno, *Dialectic of Enlightenment*, trans. John Cumming (1944/47; New York: Continuum, 1994). The text was written in 1941. On its development and publication history, see Claussen, *Theodor W. Adorno: One Last Genius*, 221.

189 **"of prejudice ever attempted":** Jay, *Dialectical Imagination*, 221.

190 **scapegoating anti-Semites:** Theodor Adorno et al., *The Authoritarian Personality* (1950; New York: W. W. Norton, 1969).

190 **attacks on outsiders:** Max Horkheimer, ed., *Studien uber Authorität und Familie*

(Paris: Felix Alcan, 1936). This work received mixed reviews; see Hans Speier's review in *Social Research* 3, no. 4 (1936): 501–4, who called the empirical results "meagre." On Fromm's crucial role, see José Brunner, "Looking into the Hearts of the Workers, or How Erich Fromm Turned Critical Theory into Empirical Research," *Political Psychology* 15, no. 4 (1994): 631–54. See page 635. Also see Jay, *Dialectical Imagination*, 116–17, 131.

191   **of this rigged system:** See Jay, *Dialectical Imagination*, 230–32.

191   **for one's own group:** See Donald Campbell and Boyd McCandless, "Ethnocentrism, Xenophobia, and Personality," *Human Relations* 4, no. 2 (1951): 185–92. They developed an "X" or xenophobia scale.

191   **hate many of them, too:** Adorno et al., *Authoritarian Personality*, 607.

192   **"negatively in love":** Adorno et al., *Authoritarian Personality*, 611. On the qualities of the scapegoat, see page 608.

193   **many troubles clear:** Adorno et al., *Authoritarian Personality*, 618, 622–27. Also see Jay, *Dialectical Imagination*, 240.

193   **need to be undone:** Adorno et al., *Authoritarian Personality*, 617.

193   **flattened by mass culture:** On the reception of this work, see, for example, Nathan Glazer, "The Authoritarian Personality in Profile," *Commentary*, January 1, 1950, 573–83; M. Brewster Smith, "Review of 'The Authoritarian Personality,'" *Journal of Abnormal and Social Psychology* 45, no. 4 (1950): 775–79; R. A. Schermerhorn, "Review of 'The Authoritarian Personality,'" *Social Forces* 29 (1951): 334–35; Betty Dowling, "Some Personality Factors Involved in Tolerance and Intolerance," *Journal of Social Psychology* 41 (1955): 325–27. On whether this typology was a new stereotype, see Bernard Stotsky, "The Authoritarian Personality as a Stereotype," *Journal of Psychology* 39 (1955): 325–28. For a comprehensive account of its impact, see William Stone et al., eds., *Strength and Weakness: The Authoritarian Personality Today* (New York: Springer-Verlag, 1993).

194   **"was the prime goal":** The third category, the "compromise oriented," was not seen as possessing the virtue of toleration, but rather of being neutral, even confused about class conflict, not a great attribute; see José Brunner, "Looking into the Hearts of the Workers, or: How Erich Fromm Turned Critical Theory into Empirical Research," *Political Psychology* 15, no. 4 (December 1994): 639, 645.

194   **dominance and submission:** See T. Adorno, "Freudian Theory and the Pattern of Fascist Propaganda," in *The Essential Frankfurt School Reader*, ed. A. Arato and E. Gebhardt (1951; New York: Urizen, 1978), 118–37.

194   **revolution in the home:** Brunner, "Looking into the Hearts of the Workers," 641. The "Democratic" personality also proved to be a more stable antimony, for authoritarian characteristics were soon discovered in an array of "Revolutionary" individuals. For example, when an MIT team proposed to study the "Xenophilic Personality," perhaps a different antithesis to the authoritarian, they discovered that these were actually rigid authoritarians in reverse. Their unconscious hostility was simply projected onto their own in-group. See Howard Perlmutter, "Some Characteristics of the Xenophilic Personality," *Journal of Psychology* 38 (1954): 291–300.

Chapter 12: The Enigma of the Other

197 **"the case with me":** J. P. Sartre, *Witness to My Life: The Letters of Jean-Paul Sartre to Simone de Beauvoir, 1926–1939*, trans L. Falnestock and N. MacAfee (New York: Scribner, 1992), 33, 36. These letters are dated 1930, then October 9, 1931.

198 **It is Being itself:** Jean-Paul Sartre, *Nausea*, trans. Lloyd Alexander (1938; New York: New Directions, 1964), 6, 18–19.

198 **"foundation of transcendence":** Jean-Paul Sartre, *War Diaries: Notebooks from a Phony War, November 1939–March 1940*, trans. Q. Hoare (New York: Verso, 1999), 132.

199 **"if we saw the dead":** Jean-Paul Sartre, "Paris Under the Occupation," *Sartre Studies International* 4, no. 2 (1945; 1998): 1–15. Quote on page 8.

199 **became immensely important:** Jean-Paul Sartre, *Being and Nothingness, A Phenomenological Essay on Ontology*, trans. Hazel Barnes (1943; New York: Washington Square Press, 1992).

200 **by Alexander Kojève:** Alexandre Kojève's lectures on Hegel in Paris during the 1930s were very influential and were credited with revitalizing Hegel studies in France. On the Master and Slave dialectic, see G. W. F. Hegel, *The Phenomenology of Mind*, trans. J. B Baille (1807; New York: Harper and Row, 1967), 228–40.

201 **secrets of the subject:** Sartre, *Being and Nothingness*, 321–32.

201 **objectifying the Other:** Sartre also put an idiosyncratic spin on the encounter with the Other. Sartre emphasized the process of seeing and being seen, the gaze or *le regard*, and the way such a look could freeze and define another. I discover that I exist, he reasoned, when seen by an Other. I then realize that for her, I have become an object. Thus her gaze engenders shame, the passing of judgment by me on myself. It also accompanied an understanding that I am now as the Other sees me, a perspective that though I may try, I never can truly comprehend. She knows something about me as an object in the world and through that knowledge possesses the power to control and constrict my freedom. I am mortified. And so, the contest begins: I stare back at her, intent on making her my object. See Sartre, *Being and Nothingness*, 303–40.

201 **little relief from strife:** Sartre, *Being and Nothingness*, 319, 358.

202 **that remained were ashes:** Sartre, *Being and Nothingness*, 477, 532–33, 756.

202 **"effort, combat, and solidarity":** Jean-Paul Sartre, "Existentialism: A Clarification," in *We Have Only This Life to Live: The Selected Essays of Jean-Paul Sartre, 1939–1975* (New York: New York Review of Books, 2013), 91.

203 **"Existentialism Is a Humanism":** Jean-Paul Sartre, *L'existentialisme est un humanisme* (1945; Paris: Gallimard, 1996). The book includes attacks by Pierre Emmanuel and others cited, who had stated that no one could possibly read *Being and Nothingness*.

204 **" 'since the armistice' ":** Sartre, "The Stranger Explained," in *We Have Only This Life to Live*, 26–43, quote on page 26.

204 **from the older man's:** In a closed space later revealed to be Hell, a man and two women struggle to achieve something like recognition, but the objectifying gaze makes this impossible, hence, the famous line.

205   **and death is our only fate:** Albert Camus, *The Stranger*, trans. Matthew Ward
      (1942; New York: Vintage International, 2013), 41.

206   **Who cares?:** Camus, *The Stranger*, 67–68, 99.

206   **the nameless Others revolted:** On the absence of Arab subjectivity in this novel,
      see George Makari, "The Last Four Shots: Problems of Intention and Camus' The
      Stranger," *American Imago* 45, no. 4 (1988): 359–74; and Kamel Daoud's brilliant
      The Meursault Investigation: A Novel, trans. John Cullen (New York: Other Press,
      2015).

206   **an untenable position:** See Albert Camus, *Algerian Chronicles*, trans. A.
      Goldhammer (1958; Cambridge: Harvard University Press, 2013). What
      Camus said exactly in a debate with a supporter of the Algerian revolt became
      a matter of controversy. His actual quote was: "People are now planting bombs
      in the tramways of Algiers. My mother might be on one of those tramways.
      If this is justice, I prefer my mother." It was reported, however, as: "Between
      justice and my mother, I choose my mother." See Alice Kaplan, "New
      Perspectives on Camus' Algerian Chronicles," in Camus, *Algerian Chronicles*,
      1–22, note 19.

207   **"of his own consciousness":** Jean-Paul Sartre, *Anti-Semite and Jew*, trans.
      George Joseph Becker (New York: Schocken, 1948), 53, 67, 83, 91.

207   **turbulence toward shore:** Sartre, *Anti-Semite and Jew*, 55, 117, 148, 149.

208   **his daily bread:** Albert Memmi, *La terre intérieure; Entretiens avec Victor Malka*
      (Paris: Gallimard, 1976), 101–3.

208   **"xenophobic aggression":** Memmi, *La terre intérieure*, 114. On Albert Memmi's
      early life, see these revealing interviews as well as his autobiographical novel *The
      Pillar of Salt*, trans. E. Roditi (1953; Boston: Beacon, 1955).

208   **there he remained:** Memmi, *La terre intérieure*, 116. Also see Guy Dugas, "Albert
      Memmi: Portrait du colonisé précédé d'un portrait du colonisateur: Note sur une
      postface autographe inédite," *Afrique-Caribe*, 33 (2011): 119–26.

209   **other forms of discrimination:** Albert Memmi, *Portrait du colonisé, précédé du
      portrait du colonisateur* (Paris: Correa, 1957). The book appeared in English in
      1965 as *The Colonizer and the Colonized*. Also Albert Memmi, *Racism*, trans.
      Steve Martinot (Minneapolis: University of Minnesota Press, 1982), 200. This
      volume includes an excellent foreword by Kwame Anthony Appiah.

209   **would cannibalize his work:** Memmi, *La terre intérieure*, 168–71.

209   **"the sucking of my blood!":** Frantz Fanon, *Alienation and Freedom*, eds. Jean
      Khalfa and Robert Young, trans. Steven Corcoran (London: Bloomsbury, 2018),
      100. From the large literature on Fanon, see David, Macey, *Frantz Fanon: A
      Biography* (London: Verso, 2000), Lewis Gordon et al., eds., *Fanon: A Critical
      Reader* (Oxford: Blackwell, 1996), and recently Camille Robcis, "Frantz Fanon,
      Institutional Psychotherapy, and the Decolonization of Psychiatry," *Journal of the
      History of Ideas* 81, no. 2 (2020): 303–25.

211   **"does not like the Negro":** Frantz Fanon, *Black Skin, White Masks*, trans.
      Charles Lam Markmann (1952; New York: Grove Press, 1967), 103.

211   **formed by their situation:** Fanon, *Black Skin, White Masks*, 98.

211   **their own self-regard:** Fanon, *Black Skin, White Masks*, 93, 181. Also see Irene
       Gendzier, *Frantz Fanon: A Critical Study* (New York: Pantheon, 1973), 29–31.

212   ***The Wretched of the Earth:*** Frantz Fanon, *L'an V de la revolution algérienne*
       (1959; Paris: La Découverte, 2011), and Frantz Fanon, *The Wretched of the Earth*,
       trans. Constance Farrington (New York: Grove Press, 1963).

212   **"sit down at my desk":** Fanon, *Alienation and Freedom.* Dated April 7, 1961,
       689.

212   **that had been oppressed:** Fanon, *The Wretched of the Earth*, 22. See also pages
       384–85.

212   **not just reverse roles:** Fanon, "Pourquoi nous employons la violence," in *L'an
       V de la revolution algérienne.* Also see Elizabeth Frazer and Kimberly Hutching,
       "On Politics and Violence: Arendt contra Fanon," *Contemporary Political Theory*
       7 (2008): 90–108.

Chapter 13: Self Estrangements

214   **"others would draw":** Simone de Beauvoir, *Diary of a Philosophy Student, Volume
       1, 1926–27*, ed. Barbara Klaw, Sylvie Le Bon de Beauvoir, and Margaret Simons,
       trans. B. Klaw (Urbana: University of Illinois Press, 2006), viii. Also see Michèle
       Le Doeuff, "Simone De Beauvoir and Existentialism," *Feminist Studies* 6, no. 2
       (Summer 1980): 277–89.

215   **had taken Sartre prisoner:** Simone de Beauvoir, *Wartime Diary*, ed. S. Le Bon
       de Beauvoir and Margaret Simons, trans. Anne Cordero (Urbana: University of
       Illinois Press, 2009), 270.

216   **"able to do that":** Margaret Simons, "Introduction," in Beauvoir, *Wartime Diary*,
       14. For quotes, see pages 270, 315.

216   ***makes itself* to be":** Beauvoir, *Wartime Diary*, 319. Dated January 9, 1941.

216   **announced new intentions:** Beauvoir, *Wartime Diary*, 320.

216   **"never let go thereafter":** Simone de Beauvoir, *The Prime of Life: The
       Autobiography of Simone de Beauvoir, 1929–1944*, trans. Peter Green (New
       York: De Capo, 1965), 359. Also see Ursula Tidd, "The Self-Other Relation in
       Beauvoir's Ethics and Autobiography," *Hypatia* 14, no. 4 (1999): 163–74.

217   **harems, and, well, women:** Simone de Beauvoir, *The Ethics of Ambiguity*, trans.
       Bernard Frechtman (1947; Secaucus, NJ: Citadel Press, 1975). The initial lecture
       was delivered in 1945.

218   **impossible to comprehend:** Simone de Beauvoir, *The Second Sex*, trans.
       Constance Borde and Sheila Malovany-Chevallier (1949; New York: Vintage,
       2011), 148. Also see 12, 58.

218   **another clan as peace offerings:** Beauvoir, *Second Sex*, 6–8, 83, 156.

218   **"worried, and guilty":** Beauvoir, *Second Sex*, 283–84, 311, 340.

219   **failing to envisage this:** Beauvoir, *Second Sex*, 419. Beauvoir's book gradually
       attracted readers and critics, who took her to task for a number of shortcomings,
       including having a masculinist bias and a model of liberation that applied only
       to the educated and unimpoverished. Beauvoir believed that one of the hobbling

effects of patriarchy was for women to live like children, outside work and the exercise of power. Some of the blame, she believed, accrued to the oppressed, who too often were happy to annihilate their own subjectivity, conceal their own dependence from themselves, and serve a tyrannical male; see Beauvoir, *Second Sex*, 746.

219   **anywhere in retreat?:** Beauvoir, *Second Sex*, 763.

219   **"that distinguish human beings?":** Beauvoir, *Second Sex*, 763.

219   **fools of French men:** On the immediate condemnation of the book, see Mari-Jo Bonnet, *Simone de Beauvoir et les femmes* (Paris: Albin Michel, 2015), 222.

219   **"Being-in-the-World":** On this debate, see Bonnet, *Simone de Beauvoir et les femmes*, as well as the more condemning portrait drawn in Deirdre Bair, *Simone de Beauvoir: A Biography* (New York: Summit, 1990), 550–59. Other views include Toril Moi, "Simone de Beauvoir: The Making of an Intellectual Woman," *Yale Journal of Criticism* 4, no. 1 (1990): 1–23, and her book of the same name published by Blackwell, Oxford, 1994; and Lisa Appignanesi, *Simone de Beauvoir* (London: Haus Publishing, 2005).

220   **book, *The Rebel*:** In 1950, Merleau-Ponty had already asked in wonderment, "how has October 1917 been able to end up in the cruelly hierarchical society whose features are gradually becoming clear before our eyes?" Maurice Merleau-Ponty, *Signs*, trans. Richard McCleary (Evanston, IL: Northwestern University Press, 1964), 265. He wrote this piece in 1950.

221   **focus of his studies:** For a biography of Foucault, see James Miller, *The Passion of Michel Foucault* (New York: Simon & Schuster, 1993), 54–55, 63. For his university recollections, see Maurice Pinguet, *Le text Japon introuvables et inédits* (Paris: Seuil, 2009); also see David Macey, *The Lives of Michel Foucault* (New York: Verso, 1993), and Sylvère Lotringer, ed., *Foucault Live: Collected Interviews, 1961–1984*, trans. L. Hochroth and J. Johnston (New York: Semiotexte, 1996).

221   **at the Collège de France:** Didier Eribon, *Michel Foucault et ses contemporains* (Paris: Fayard, 1994), 105.

222   **deviants, criminals, or patients:** Michel Foucault, *History of Madness*, trans. Jonathan Murphy (1961; London: Routledge, 2006).

222   **repetitious, confused, and obscure:** Eribon, *Michel Foucault et ses contemporains*, 183.

223   **his speaking a word:** Michel Foucault, *The Birth of the Clinic: An Archaeology of Medical Perception*, trans. Alan Sheridan (1963; New York: Vintage, 1973).

223   ***The Order of Things*:** Michel Foucault, *The Order of Things: An Archaeology of the Human Sciences*, trans. not given (1966; New York: Vintage, 1994). The French title was *Les mots et les choses*.

223   **dialectical materialism:** Eribon, *Michel Foucault et ses contemporains*, 168–69. Also "Jean-Paul Sartre répond," *L'Arc* 30 (1966): 87.

223   **"was a political behavior":** My translation of "C'est à peu près vers les années 1950–1955, à une époque d'ailleurs òu, precisément, Sartre lui-même, renonçait, je crois, à ce qu'on pourrait appeler la spéculation philosophique, il l'investissait

à l'interieur d'un comportement qui était un comportement politique." Michel Foucault, *Dits et Ecrits, 1: 1954–1969* (Paris: Gallimard, 1994), 662–68.

223 **Soviets were prime examples:** See Michel Foucault, "Truth and Power," in *Power/Knowledge: Selected Interviews and Other Writings 1972–1977* (1977; New York: Pantheon, 1980), 109–33. Also Miller, *Passion of Michel Foucault*, 150.

225 **one endlessly ambiguous word:** Foucault noted that the problem of creating Others through confined marginalization followed "every socialist country, insofar as none of these since 1917 has managed to function without a more-or-less developed Gulag system." Foucault, *Power/Knowledge*, 137.

225 **"as *the* secret":** Michel Foucault, *The History of Sexuality, Volume I: An Introduction*, trans. R. Hurley (1976; New York: Vintage, 1980), 35.

226 **domination and mastery:** Michel Foucault, "The Subject and Power," *Critical Inquiry* 8, no. 4 (Summer 1982): 777–95.

226 **out into the open:** Foucault, "Two Lectures," *Power/Knowledge*, 81.

226 **return Iran to a purer time:** Foucault defended Khomeini, arguing that minorities would be protected and spirituality would again infuse politics. When the Iranian revolution occurred in 1979, it became evident that it brought catastrophe down on all those who valued freedom: citizens, women, non-Muslims, gay men and lesbians, and political dissidents. See Janet Afary and Kevin Anderson, *Foucault and the Iranian Revolution: Gender and the Seductions of Islamism* (Chicago: University of Chicago Press, 2005).

Part III: The Return of the Stranger

229 **Derek Walcott, "The Schooner's Flight":** Derek Walcott, "The Schooner Flight," in *The Star-Apple Kingdom* (New York, Farrar, Straus, 1979), 4.

229 **Adonis, "Desert":** Adonis, "Desert," in *The Pages of Day and Night*, trans. Samuel Hazo (Evanston, IL: Marlboro Press, 1994), 94.

Chapter 14: Why We Hate Them

232 **of that intersubjective dependence:** Emmanuel Levinas, *Totality and Infinity: An Essay on Exteriority*, trans. Alphonso Lingis (1947; Pittsburgh: Duquesne University Press, 1969).

233 **and their biology:** For a broad review of the literature on epigenetics, see Rachel Yehuda and Amy Lehmer, "Intergenerational transmission of trauma effects: putative role of epigenetic mechanisms," *World Psychiatry* 17, no. 3 (2018): 243–57. For a summary of his work, see Joseph LeDoux, *Anxious: Using the Brain to Understand and Treat Fear and Anxiety* (New York, Viking, 2015). LeDoux is one of the most synthetic researchers, and unlike most has bridged behavioral and cognitive models.

233 **frauds, phonies, and sharks:** Timothy Levine, *Duped: Truth-Default Theory and the Social Science of Lying and Deception* (Tuscaloosa: University of Alabama Press, 2020); Malcolm Gladwell, *Talking to Strangers* (New York: Little, Brown,

2019); Hugo Mercier, *Not Born Yesterday: The Science of Who We Trust and What We Believe* (Princeton: Princeton University Press, 2020). These discrepant studies make one wonder, as Elisabeth Young-Bruehl argued regarding studies of prejudice, whether both are in part right (and in part worng) for different populations, distinguished by character types.

233 **conform to those negative assumptions::** See, for example, Mark Snyder et al., "Social Perception and Interpersonal Behavior: On the Self-Fulfilling Nature of Social Stereotypes," *Journal of Personality and Social Psychology* 35, no. 9 (1977): 656–66; Charles Stangor, "Content and Application Inaccuracy in Social Stereotyping," in *Stereotype Accuracy*, ed. Y. T. Lee et al. (Washington, DC: American Psychological Association, 1995), 275–92; Daniel Ames, "Strategies for Social Inference: A Similarity Contingency Model of Projection and Stereotyping in Attribute Prevalence Estimates," *Journal of Personality and Social Psychology* 87, no. 5 (2004): 573–85; Daniel Ames, "Inside the Mind Reader's Tool Kit: Projection and Stereotyping in Mental State Inference," *Journal of Personality and Social Psychology* 87, no. 3 (2004): 340–53; Patricia Devine, "Stereotypes and Prejudice: Their Automatic and Controlled Components," *Journal of Personality and Social Psychology* 56, no. 1 (1989): 5–18, and C. Neil Macrae et al., "On Resisting the Temptation for Simplification: Counter-Intentional Effects of Stereotype Suppression on Social Memory," *Social Cognition* 14, no. 1 (1996): 1–20; Adam Galinsky and Gordon Moskowitz, "Perspective-Taking: Decreasing Stereotype Expression, Stereotype Accessibility, and In-Group Favoritism," *Journal of Personality and Social Psychology* 78, no. 4 (2000): 708–24. Claude Steele and Joshua Aronson, "Stereotype Threat and the Intellectual Test Performance of African Americans," *Journal of Personality and Social Psychology* 69, no. 5 (1995): 797–811. This landmark study launched hundreds of follow-ups.

234 **to meet the moment:** The émigré German psychologist Kurt Lewin established a group dynamics center at MIT in 1944 before his untimely death. His field theory considers these two forms of group formation; see Kurt Lewin, *Field Theory in Social Science: Selected Theoretical Papers* (New York: Harper & Brothers, 1951). The idea that socially unifying targets were required to prevent tribal warfare was put forth in William James, *The Moral Equivalent of War* (1910; London: Read Books, 2013).

234 **out what it meant:** In this endless debate, there is a message. Scientific experimentation in social psychology has been very difficult, for the "social" is so vast that to control for variables becomes impossible. See Kurt Danziger, "Making Social Psychology Experimental: A Conceptual History, 1920–1970," *Journal of the History of the Behavioral Sciences* 36, no. 4 (2000): 329–47. For a recent study of knowledge and social affiliations, see Mikael Klintman, *Knowledge Resistance: How We Avoid Insight from Others* (Manchester: Manchester University Press, 2019).

234 **drove their bellicosity:** In the past decades, rivers of ink have flowed in favor of each of these models and some in between. See Muzafer Sherif, "Experiment in Group Conflict," *Scientific American* 195, no. 5 (1956): 54–58. Also Muzafer

Sherif, *Group Conflict and Co-operation: Their Social Psychology* (London: Routledge, 1967). On Sherif, see Gina Perry, *The Lost Boys: Inside Muzafer Sherif's Robbers Cave Experiment* (Melbourne: Scribe, 2018), as well as the review by Alex Haslam, "War and Peace and Summer Camp," *Nature* 556 (April 17, 2018): 306–7. Subjective impressions of such competition are factored into "relative deprivation theory," see T. F. Pettigrew et al., "Relative Deprivation and Intergroup Prejudice," *Journal of Social Issues* 64, no. 2 (2008): 385–401. For the Social Identity theory, see the work of Michael Platow, John Hunter, and M. Hewstone, who have created a body of research on such affiliative processes and causal misattribution.

235   **schisms, and scapegoating:** Wilfred Bion, *Experiences in Groups* (London: Tavistock, 1961). Bion's study of group dynamics ceased long before 1961 when he published *Experiences in Groups*, but in the decades since, an array of sociologists and clinicians have sought to apply them. For a collection of more recent work, see Malcolm Pines, ed., *Bion and Group Psychotherapy* (London: Jessica Kingsley, 2000).

235   **to safeguard their group:** See Vamik Volkan, *Blind Trust: Large Groups and Their Leaders in Times of Crisis and Terror* (Charlottesville, VA: Pitchstone, 2004). Also Vamik Volkan, *Bloodlines: From Ethnic Pride to Ethnic Terrorism* (New York: Farrar, Straus, 1997), and his *Immigrants and Refugees: Trauma, Perennial Mourning and Border Psychology* (London: Karnac, 2017). In addition, see Salman Akhtar, *Immigration and Identity* (Lanham, MD: Rowman & Littlefield, 1999), and his *Immigration and Acculturation* (Lanham, MD: Rowman & Littlefield, 2010); also see Otto Kernberg, *Ideology, Conflict and Leadership in Groups and Organizations* (New Haven: Yale University Press, 1998). I am especially indebted to the brilliant, synthetic work of Sander Gilman, who developed a model that linked visual stereotypes with psychoanalytic theories of splitting; see his *Difference and Pathology: Stereotypes of Sexuality, Race, and Madness* (Ithaca, NY: Cornell University Press, 1985).

236   **representations and their power:** See Edward Said, *Orientalism* (New York: Vintage, 1979); Benedict Anderson, *Imagined Communities: Reflections on the Origin and Spread of Nationalism* (London: Verso, 1983); Gayatri Spivak, *A Critique of Post-Colonial Reason* (Cambridge: Harvard University Press, 1999); Homi Bhabha, *The Location of Culture* (London: Routledge, 1994); Judith Butler, *Gender Trouble* (London: Routledge, 1990).

237   **psychic violence of everyday life:** On the medicalization of bias, see Gilman and Thomas, *Are Racists Crazy?*

238   **almost no foreigners?:** For a contemporary assessment of the data on rational economic competition, see Andreas Wimmer, "Explaining Xenophobia and Racism: A Critical Review of Current Research Approaches," *Ethnic and Racial Studies* 20, no. 1 (1997): 17–41.

239   **and *covert xenophobia*:** Wimmer, "Explaining Xenophobia and Racism." This same distinction is made in W. G. Stephan and C. W. Stephan, "An integrated threat theory of prejudice," in S. Oskamp, ed., *Claremont Symposium on Applied*

Social Psychology (Hillsdale, NJ: Lawrence Erlbaum, 2000), 23–46. They combine realistic threats, symbolic threats, negative stereotypes, and intergroup anxiety so as to understand prejudice.

239 **too often wrong:** Daniel Kahneman, *Thinking, Fast and Slow* (New York: Farrar, Straus, 2011). This is also central to "Social Identity Theory," as formulated by H. Tajifel and J. C. Turner, "The Social Identity Theory of Intergroup Behavior," in S. Worchel and W. G. Austin, eds., *The Psychology of Intergroup Relations* (Chicago: Nelson-Hall, 1986), 7–24. In this model, social identity is predicated on symbolic markers, and therefore might make for support for a xenophobic political party, while personal relations with members of that group might be relatively unbiased. See V. M. Esses et al., "Attitudes Towards Immigrants and Immigration: The Role of National and International Identity," in D. Abrams et al., eds., *The Social Psychology of Inclusion and Exclusion* (New York: Psychology Press, 2005), 317–37. On his view of stereotypes, see Kahneman, *Thinking, Fast and Slow*, 168–69. Kahneman discusses how, when concerned about safety, we may assess how dominant or trustworthy the other is. See page 90.

240 **of their subjects:** David Brockman and Joshua Kalla, "Durably Reducing Transphobia: A Field Experiment on Door-to-Door Canvassing," *Science* 10 (2016): 1126. Also see "Canvassing Conversations Reduce Transphobia," *Science Daily*, April 7, 2016.

240 *"whose face it wears"*: On the psychology of stereotypes and implicit bias, see Anthony Greenwald and Mahzarin Banaji, "Implicit social cognition: attitudes, self-esteem and stereotypes," *Psychological Review* 102, no. 1 (1995): 4. On their Implicit Association Test, see Anthony Greenwald, Debbie E. McGhee, and Jordan Schwartz, "Measuring Individual Differences in Implicit Cognition: The Implicit Association Test," *Journal of Personality and Social Psychology* 74, no. 6 (1998): 1464. The quote is from Audre Lorde, "The Master's Tools Will Never Dismantle the Master's House," in *The Glorious American Essay: One Hundred Essays from Colonial Times to the Present*, ed. Phillip Lopate (New York: Pantheon, 2020), 778.

240 **help manufacture opinion:** Kahneman, *Thinking, Fast and Slow*, 418.

241 **to stabilize themselves:** In this distinction between the more passive and cognitive forms of prejudice and the more active desirous ones, I am in agreement with Elisabeth Young-Bruehl. On the transformation of strangers into the Other, see M. Mazas-Sanchez, *Racisme et xénophobie* (Paris: Presses Universaires de France, 2004).

241 **paranoid and obsessional:** Like many psychiatrists, I distinguish common patterns of thought and behavior that can be described as obsessional or paranoid from those that fulfill the criteria for disorders such as Obsessive Compulsive Disorder or Delusional Disorders.

242 **forms of child-rearing:** A bestseller that went through many editions and racked up over fifty million books sold, Spock was psychoanalytically influenced. See Benjamin Spock, *The Common Sense Book of Baby and Child Care* (New York:

Duell, Sloan, and Pearce, 1946). More recently, some psychoanalysts have focused on "insecure" early attachments. See Roger Kennedy, *Tolerating Strangers in Intolerant Times* (London: Routledge, 2018).

243   **a "meta-morality":** Joshua Greene, *Moral Tribes: Emotion, Reason, and the Gap Between Us and Them* (New York: Penguin, 2013).

243   **the victims of these projections:** While toleration should be the rule, Karl Popper discerned one exception. The refugee philosopher argued that those who embraced intolerance could not be tolerated. "In order to maintain a tolerant society," Popper famously concluded, "the tolerant must be intolerant of intolerance." Karl Popper, *The Open Society and Its Enemies*, vol. 1 (London: Routledge, 1945), note 4 to chapter 7. The scant empirical research on possible remedies for xenophobia is reviewed in Margarita Sanchez-Mazas and Laurent Licata, "Xenophobia: Social Psychological Aspects," in James D. Wright, ed., *International Encyclopedia of the Social and Behavioral Sciences* (Oxford: Elsevier, 2015), 802–7. For one of the few attempts to synthesize critical theory, political science, and empirical studies in social psychology, see Osksana Yukushko, *Modern Day Xenophobia: Critical, Historical and Theoretical Perspectives* (Cham, Switzerland: Palgrave Macmillan, 2018).

245   **"real or imagined differences":** For her critique, see Elisabeth Young-Bruehl, *The Anatomy of Prejudice* (Cambridge: Harvard University Press, 1996), 57–70. Her proposal of a spectrum of "prejudices" based on three character structures follows. On heterophobia, see Memmi, *Racism*, 118–19.

Chapter 15: The New Xenophobia

246   **disgusting, and shameful:** Norbert Elias, *The Civilizing Process: Sociogenetic and Psychogenetic Investigations*, trans. Edmund Jephcott (1939; Malden, MA: Blackwell, 2000).

247   **made for prejudice:** The James-Lange theory was established in the late nineteenth century by William James and Carl Lange. It dictated that emotional arousal precedes and creates the cognitive experience of that emotion.

248   **who were like them:** See Kwame Anthony Appiah, *The Ethics of Identity* (Princeton: Princeton University Press, 2005).

248   **called "moral globalization":** On the Declaration of Human Rights, see Geraldine Van Bueren, "I am because you are," *Times Literary Supplement*, December 21 and 28, 2018, 5. On the spread of moral norms, see Michael Ignatieff, *The Ordinary Virtues: Moral Order in a Divided World* (Cambridge: Harvard University Press, 2017). Also his *Human Rights as Politics and Idolatry* (Princeton: Princeton University Press, 2000); and Samuel Moyn, *The Last Utopia: Human Rights in History* (Cambridge: Harvard University Press, 2012). This liberal value became critical as trade and technology tied the world into a tighter knot. This was especially so in "super-diverse" cities like New York, Los Angeles, London, and Tokyo, where millions of strangers were forced to cooperate so as to meet the day. If the idea of a single setting with over a hundred

ethnic groups and religions interacting might once have been fodder for a fantasist like H. G. Wells, by 1990 such international cities were booming. Denizens of such megalopolises not surprisingly embraced this Lockean ideal, more so than their rural brethren, for whom its necessity was less apparent. Also see Joseph Stiglitz, *Globalization and Its Discontents* (New York: W. W. Norton, 2002).

250 *via Google ngram:* Google ngrams, while interesting tools, are not definitive data. They are most accurate from 1800 to 2000 in English, and drop off in other languages and outside of those dates. On the data set and methodological issues, see Jean-Baptiste Michel et al., "Quantitative Analysis of Culture Using Millions of Digitized Books," *Science*, online, December 16, 2010. For the usage of xenophobia in English, see https://books .google.com/ngrams/graph?content=xenophobia&year_start=1900&year_ end=2000&corpus=26&smoothing=3.

    For *xénophobie* and *xénophobe* in French, see https://books.google.com/ ngrams/graph?content=x%C3%A9nophobie&year_start=1900&year_end=200 0&corpus=19&smoothing=4&share=&direct_url=t1%3B%2Cx%C3%A9noph obie%3B%2Cc0. https://books.google.com/ngrams/graph?content=x%C3%A9n ophobe&year_start=1900&year_end=2000&corpus=19&smoothing=4&share= &direct_url=t1%3B%2Cx%C3%A9nophobe%3B%2Cc0.

250 **well, economic suffering:** I am not arguing that the reform and restraint of free-market economics is not necessary to healing our divide, only that it is not sufficient. For two economic proposals, see Martin Sandbu, *The Economics of Belonging* (Princeton: Princeton University Press, 2020), and Gene Sperling, *Economic Dignity* (New York: Penguin, 2020).

250 **of the twentieth century:** See Eric Hobsbawm, *The Age of Extremes: The Short Twentieth Century, 1914–1991* (New York: Vintage, 1994).

251 **happiness for most?:** The Soviet focus on the Ku Klux Klan started early; see "Xenophobia," *New York Times*, January 9, 1923, 22. In fact, one of the factors that undermined Jim Crow laws was not their injustice but concern from the State Department that racism was a hobbling detriment in the Cold War against the Soviets. Dean Acheson, Truman's secretary of state, referred to it as a "source of constant embarrassment." Cited in Lepore, *These Truths*, 578.

252 **power, grew terrified:** For a summary of Cold War scholarship, see John Lewis Gaddis, *The Cold War: A New History* (New York: Penguin, 2005).

252 **Soviet Union was no more:** For a general history, see Richard Sakwa, *The Rise and Fall of the Soviet Union, 1917–1991* (New York: Routledge, 1999). On the problem of nationalities, see Mark Beissinger, *Nationalist Mobilization and the Collapse of the Soviet State* (Cambridge: Cambridge University Press, 2002). For an elegant mix of history and reportage, see David Remnick, *Lenin's Tomb: The Last Days of the Soviet Empire* (New York: Random House, 1993).

253 **just abjectly poor:** See Svetlena Alexievich, *Secondhand Time: The Last of the Soviets*, trans. Bela Shayevich (New York: Random House, 2017).

254 **had gone into exile:** See Michael Ignatieff, *Blood and Belonging: Journeys into the New Nationalism* (New York: Farrar, Straus, 1993), 19–56. For a critical

review of the different explanatory paradigms of this war, see Dejan Jovic, "The Disintegration of Yugoslavia: A Critical Review of Explanatory Approaches," *European Journal of Social Theory* 4, no. 1 (2001): 101–20.

255 **of European nationalism:** John Mearsheimer, "Back to the Future: Instability in Europe after the Cold War," *International Security* 15, no. 1 (1990): 5–56. Also see Ignatieff, *Blood and Belonging*.

255 **a "new xenophobia":** See, for example, B. Baumgartl and A. Favell, eds., *New Xenophobia in Europe* (London: Kluwer Law International, 1995); Dietrich Thränhardt, "The Political Uses of Xenophobia in England, France, and Germany," *Party Politics* 1, no. 3 (1995): 323–45; R. Oakley, *Tackling Racist and Xenophobic Violence in Europe: Review and Practical Guidelines* (Strasbourg: Council of Europe, 1996); M. W. Watts, "Political Xenophobia in the Transition from Socialism: Threat, Racism, and Ideology Among East German Youth," *Political Psychology* 17 (1996): 97–126.

256 **demands coming from Brussels:** On Brexit, see Fintan O'Toole, *The Politics of Pain: Postwar England and the Rise of Nationalism* (New York: Liveright, 2019).

257 **multiculturalism to be dead:** See Rita Chin, *The Crisis of Multiculturalism in Europe: A History* (Princeton: Princeton University Press, 2017).

258 **aid they received:** Studies have shown that, at present, natives of Western countries overestimate the number of immigrants in their nations, and radically overestimate the level of government aid that they get in Western countries. See Eduardo Porter and Karl Russell, "Migrants Are on the Rise Around the World and Myths About Them Are Shaping Attitudes," *New York Times*, June 23, 2018, B1, 7. For a comprehensive history, see Peter Gatrell, *The Unsettling of Europe: How Migration Reshaped a Continent* (New York: Basic Books, 2019).

258 **from the extreme right:** Extreme right-wing anti-immigrant sentiment in Germany sprang up in eastern regions where very few immigrants resided. See Thomas Wieder, "Allemagne: Le séisme politique de l'extrême droite," *Le Monde diplomatique*, October 8, 2018, 14–16. This is not uncommon in xenophobic outbreaks from the initial Boxer outbreak to fear of al-Qaeda and Muslims in rural American states after 9/11.

259 **the "end of history":** Francis Fukuyama, "The End of History?" *National Interest* (Summer 1989): 1–18. The author's intent has been debated, but despite the question mark in his title, his conviction is clear. "The triumph of the West, of the Western idea," he wrote, "is evident first of all in the total exhaustion of viable systematic alternatives to Western liberalism" (page 2). "But surely," he writes elsewhere of the United States, "the class issue has actually been successfully resolved in the West" (page 18).

259 **individual and civil rights:** For quite different views, see Kwame Anthony Appiah, *The Lies That Bind: Rethinking Identity* (New York: Liveright, 2018), and Francis Fukuyama, *Identity: The Demand for Dignity and the Politics of Resentment* (New York: Farrar, Straus, 2018).

259 **cosmopolitan compatriots:** See, for example, Mark Lilla, *The Once and Future Liberal: After Identity Politics* (New York: HarperCollins, 2017).

261   **"sucker could go down":** Henry Blodget, "Bush on Economy: 'This Sucker Could Go Down,'" *Business Insider*, September 26, 2008.

261   **their own political tribe:** See, for example, Thomas Frank, *What's the Matter with Kansas?* (New York: Picador, 2005), argues that the red-blue divide has emerged as cultural solidarity eclipsed economic self-interest.

261   **Blacks and immigrants:** In so-called American swing states, the populace alters its commitments. The pollster Stanley Greenberg studied Michigan voters who in 1985 turned into "Reagan Democrats" and found they were aggrieved, struggling, and had changed sides to vote against a nonwhite "them." In 2016, white voters who once voted for Obama in the same Michigan county switched sides due to a similar animus, this time against immigrants. These voters were swayed to take up xenophobic positions but did not hold only such beliefs. See Eduardo Porter, "'Us' vs. 'Them,' Driving Votes by Whites," *New York Times*, May 23, 2018, B1, 6.

262   **but no matter:** If America was growing less "white," it was doing so very gradually. The Census Bureau noted that this category dropped from 80.2 percent to 72.3 percent in the quarter century that ended in 2017. The percentage of foreigners—naturalized and noncitizen—crept up from 12.5 percent in 2006 to 13.6 percent in 2017, hardly very dramatic. U.S. Census Bureau data can be found on www .factfinder.census.gov/faces/tableservices.

263   **and terrorize mankind?:** This was written before COVID-19 was loosed on the world. I decided to not alter the text. However, just before publication, I became aware of Sander Gilman and Zhou Xun, *"I Know Who Caused COVID-19": Pandemics and Xenophobia* (London: Reaktion Books, 2021).

263   **Welcome to the twenty-first century:** Social media has been implicated in numerous popular revolts and, for example, the genocide of the Rohingya in Myanmar.

264   **"center and variable surface":** A. R. Ammons, *Sphere: The Form of Motion* (1974; New York: W. W. Norton, 1995), 78–79.

265   **better for our species:** Nicholas Kristof, "This Has Been the Best Year Ever," *New York Times*, December 28, 2019.

Coda: In the Pyrenees

268   **town of Portbou:** Lisa Fittko, *Escape Through the Pyrenees*, trans. David Koblick (Evanston, IL: Northwestern University Press, 1991), 103–17. There is some debate about the exact date of Benjamin's departure. See Howard Eiland and Michael W. Jennings, *Walter Benjamin: A Critical Life* (Cambridge: Harvard University Press, 2014), 647–79.

270   **"nightmare begins responsibility":** Michael S. Harper, "Nightmare Begins Responsibility," in *Images of Kin: New and Selected Poems* (Urbana: University of Illinois Press, 1977), 57. In this poem, Harper transformed the famed line from Yeats, in which "dreams" begin responsibility, so as to speak both to his own personal tragedy and to the tragedies suffered by so many in the last century.

ILLUSTRATION CREDITS

INDEX